THE GREAT WAR AND THE BRITISH EMPIRE

In 1914 almost one quarter of the earth's surface was British. When the empire and its allies went to war in 1914 against the Central Powers, history's first global conflict was inevitable.

It is the social and cultural reactions to that war and within those distant, often overlooked, societies which is the focus of this volume. From Singapore to Australia, Cyprus to Ireland, India to Iraq and around the rest of the British imperial world, further complexities and interlocking themes are addressed, offering new perspectives on imperial and colonial history and theory, as well as art, music, photography, propaganda, education, pacifism, gender, class, race and diplomacy at the end of the *pax Britannica*.

Michael J.K. Walsh is Associate Professor in Art History, at Nanyang Technological University, Singapore. He has primarily published on English painting in the first two decades of the 20th century and the art and conservation of Famagusta, Cyprus.

Andrekos Varnava is Associate Professor in Imperial and Military History, Flinders University, Australia. He is author of *British Imperialism in Cyprus, 1878–1915: The Inconsequential Possession* (2009; paperback 2012).

Routledge Studies in First World War History

Series Editor

John Bourne

The University of Birmingham, UK

The First World War is a subject of perennial interest to historians and is often regarded as a watershed event, marking the end of the nineteenth century and the beginning of the 'modern' industrial world. The sheer scale of the conflict and massive loss of life means that it is constantly being assessed and reassessed to examine its lasting military, political, sociological, industrial, cultural and economic impact. Reflecting the latest international scholarly research, the Routledge Studies in First World War History series provides a unique platform for the publication of monographs on all aspects of the Great War. Whilst the main thrust of the series is on the military aspects of the conflict, other related areas (including cultural, visual, literary, political and social) are also addressed. Books published are aimed primarily at a post-graduate academic audience, furthering exciting recent interpretations of the war, whilst still being accessible enough to appeal to a wider audience of educated lay readers.

Also in this series

The Men Who Planned the War
A Study of the Staff of the British Army on the Western Front, 1914–1918
Paul Harris

The Gallipoli Campaign
The Turkish Perspective
Edited by Metin Gürcan and Robert Johnson

Arming the Western Front
War, Business and the State in Britain 1900–1920
Roger Lloyd-Jones and M.J. Lewis

Aerial Propaganda and the Wartime Occupation of France, 1914–18
Bernard Wilkin

The Great War and the British Empire
Culture and society
Edited by Michael J.K. Walsh and Andrekos Varnava

The Great War and the British Empire
Culture and society

Edited by

MICHAEL J.K. WALSH AND ANDREKOS VARNAVA

LONDON AND NEW YORK

First published 2017
by Routledge
2 Park Square, Milton Park, Abingdon, Oxon OX14 4RN

and by Routledge
711 Third Avenue, New York, NY 10017

First issued in paperback 2018

Routledge is an imprint of the Taylor & Francis Group, an informa business

© 2017 selection and editorial matter, Michael J.K. Walsh and Andrekos Varnava; individual chapters, the contributors

The right of Michael J.K. Walsh and Andrekos Varnava to be identified as the authors of the editorial material, and of the authors for their individual chapters, has been asserted in accordance with sections 77 and 78 of the Copyright, Designs and Patents Act 1988.

All rights reserved. No part of this book may be reprinted or reproduced or utilised in any form or by any electronic, mechanical, or other means, now known or hereafter invented, including photocopying and recording, or in any information storage or retrieval system, without permission in writing from the publishers.

Trademark notice: Product or corporate names may be trademarks or registered trademarks, and are used only for identification and explanation without intent to infringe.

British Library Cataloguing in Publication Data
A catalogue record for this book is available from the British Library

Library of Congress Cataloging in Publication Data
A catalog record for this book has been requested

ISBN 13: 978-1-138-33012-2 (pbk)
ISBN 13: 978-1-4724-6227-5 (hbk)

Typeset in Times New Roman
by Apex CoVantage, LLC

Contents

List of figures vii
Acknowledgements xi
Contributors xiii
Foreword xv

PART I   THE GREAT WAR AND THE BRITISH EMPIRE 1

1   The Great War and the British Empire: conflict, culture and memory 3
    Michael J.K. Walsh and Andrekos Varnava

2   The First World War and the cultural, political and environmental
    transformation of the British Empire 23
    John M. MacKenzie

PART II   IMPERIAL RESPONSES, IDENTITIES AND CULTURE 39

3   The 'Kaiser Cartoon', 1914–1918: a transnational comic art genre 41
    Richard Scully

4   Musical entertainment and the British Empire, 1914–1918 63
    Emma Hanna

5   "We New Zealanders pride ourselves most of all upon loyalty to our
    Empire, our country, our flag": internalised Britishness and national
    character in New Zealand's First World War propaganda 81
    Gregory Hynes

6   Heligoland: between the lion and the eagle 103
    Jan Asmussen

7   Imperial Austerlitz: the Singapore Strategy and the culture of victory,
    1917–1924 117
    Wm. Matthew Kennedy

PART III   ART, MEMORY AND FORGETTING 127

8   'Our warrior Brown Brethran': identity and difference in images of
    non-white soldiers serving with the British army in British art of
    the First World War 129
    Jonathan Black

9	The imagining of Mesopotamia/Iraq in British art in the aftermath of the Great War *Tim Buck*	151
10	Spaces of conflict and ambivalent attachments: Irish artists visualise the Great War *Nuala C. Johnson*	163
11	Empire and nation in Canadian and Australian First World War exhibitions, 1917–1922 *Jennifer Wellington*	185
12	A tribute to the British Empire: Lowell Thomas's *With Allenby in Palestine and Lawrence in Arabia* *Justin Fantauzzo*	199
13	An architecture of imperial ambivalence: the Patcham Chattri *Tim Barringer*	215
14	The Great War's impact on imperial Delhi: commemorating wartime sacrifice in the colonial built environment *David A. Johnson*	249
15	Sounds from the trenches: Australian composers and the Great War *Andrew Harrison*	265
16	'Brutalised' veterans and tragic anti-heroes: masculinity, crime and post-war trauma in *Boardwalk Empire* and *Peaky Blinders* *Evan Smith*	279
17	The politics of forgetting the Cypriot Mule Corps *Andrekos Varnava*	291

Index 305

Figures

0.1	Adrian Jones, *The Peace Quadriga*, bronze, Wellington Arch, Hyde Park Corner, London, 1911	xv
0.2	*The Illustrated London News* (3 October 1846), depicting Matthew Coates Wyatt's *Equestrian Statue of the Duke of Wellington*	xvi
0.3	Francis Derwent Wood, *The Machine Gun Corps Memorial (The Boy David)*, Hyde Park Corner, London, 1925	xviii
0.4	Adrian Jones, *Cavalry Memorial*, bronze, 1924	xx
0.5	Charles Sargeant Jagger and Lionel Pearson, *Royal Artillery Memorial*, Hyde Park Corner, 1925	xxi
0.6	Charles Sargeant Jagger and Lionel Pearson, *Royal Artillery Memorial*, Detail *Fallen Artilleryman*, bronze, Hyde Park Corner, 1925	xxiii
1.1	Walter Henry 'Harry' Walsh, third row, second from left. Ballykinlar, 1915	19
3.1	Eugenio Colmo, *L'Ingordo* (The Glutton)	44
3.2	Bernard Partridge, 'The World's Enemy', 19 August 1914	47
3.3	Jules-Abel Faivre, 'The Hussar William II', 1916	49
3.4	Bogdan Nowakowski, 'Inseparable Friends', 1914	51
3.5	Louis Raemaekers, 'To the End', 1916	53
3.6	Louis Raemaekers, 'Thrown to the Swine – The Martyred Nurse', 1916	54
3.7	James Montgomery Flagg, 'The Cartoonist Makes People See Things!', 1918	57
3.8	Will Dyson, 'Dysonised Kaiser', 1915	59
5.1	'Military Service Act, 1916', August 1916	83
5.2	Arthur Wardle, 'The Empire Needs Men!', 1915	85
5.3	'Why Britain Is at War', 1915	86
5.4	William Blomfield, 'The Spirit of His Fathers', 25 December 1915	99
5.5	'The Māoris at Gallipoli', 15 November 1915	100
8.1	Paul Nash, *Chinese Labourers Working in a Quarry*, November 1917	130
8.2	Eric Kennington, *The Indian Doctor*, 1917	133
8.3	James McBey, *Egyptian Labour Corps Landing Stores at Jaffa Harbour*, 19 November 1917	139
8.4	James McBey, *Men of the Egyptian Camel Transport Corps*, November 1917	140
8.5	James McBey, *Arsuf, A Punjabi Sentry*, September 1918	142
8.6	James McBey, *Punjabis by a Camp Fire, Tripoli, The Lebanon*, 4 November 1918	144
8.7	James McBey, *The Egyptian Cook at No. 10 Mess, GHQ*, December 1918	145
10.1	William Orpen, *The Mad Woman of Douai*, 1918	172
10.2	William Orpen, *To the Unknown British Soldier in France*, 1921–1928	173
10.3	John Lavery, *Daylight Raid From My Studio Window*, 1917	177
10.4	John Lavery, *The Forth Bridge 1917, Bluejackets Landing*, 1917	178
10.5	William Conor, *Off, the Ulster Division*, 1915	181
11.1	An image cropped from *Ça Ne Fait Rien*, 6 Bn AIF newspaper, 4 September 1918	187

viii   *Figures*

11.2	Ivor Castle, 'Over the Top'	194
13.1	The Chattri, Patcham, Sussex	215
13.2	William Bernard Cooke after J.M.W. Turner, *Battle Abbey: The Spot Where Harold Fell*, 1819	216
13.3	Studio Portrait of Lance Corporal Venkatasami	218
13.4	Ariel Lowe Varges, *On the Salonika Front*, photograph, Ministry of Information First World War Official Collection	220
13.5	Charles Hilton DeWitt Girdwood, *Indian Dogras and Highlanders in a Trench With Dugouts* [Fauquissart, France], 1915	221
13.6	C.H.D. Girdwood, 'The Four Worst Cases in the Brighton Hospital', April 1915	224
13.7	'Indian Military Hospital, Royal Pavilion, Brighton', from *A Short History in English, Gurmukhi & Urdu of the Royal Pavilion and Description of it as a Hospital for Indian Soldiers*, 1915	225
13.8	C.H.D. Girdwood, 'The Sikh Kitchens'	226
13.9	Charles Phelp, 'Brighton Gives of her best for our Wounded Indian Soldiers – Bravo Otter', *Brighton and Hove Society*, 3 December 1914	227
13.10	Douglas Fox-Pitt, *Indian Army Wounded in Hospital in the Dome, Brighton*. c.1919, oil on canvas	228
13.11	Monochrome photograph showing King George V meeting a wounded Indian soldier in the grounds of the Royal Pavilion during its use as a Military Hospital, 1915	229
13.12	'From East to West for the Motherland', Postcard, 1915	230
13.13	Sir Thomas Brock, 'Empire', bronze relief from pedestal of Queen Victoria Statue, Hove, Sussex, 1897–1901	231
13.14	'At Brighton: Children Paddling With Wounded Indian Soldiers'	232
13.15	Muslim Burial Ground, Horsell Common, Woking, Surrey, 1917	234
13.16	Swinton Jacob, Tujumul Hoosein, Ram Baksh, Shankar Lal and Chote Lal (architects), Albert Hall Museum, Jaipur, India, completed 1887	236
13.17	Red Fort, Delhi, begun by Shah Jahan, 1638	237
13.18	William H. Burke, *King George V and Queen Mary at the Red Fort presenting themselves before the crowd*, 1911	238
13.19	Humayun's Tomb, Delhi, begun 1569	239
13.20	British tomb in Nicholson Cemetery, Delhi, n.d., c. 1860	240
13.21	Delhi Durbar, with King George V and Queen Mary seated upon the dais, 1911	241
13.22	Edwin Lutyens, architect, India Gate and Canopy, New Delhi	242
13.23	C.A. Wiles, Brighton (photographer), *Dedication of the new Indian Chattri by H.R.H. the Prince of Wales on the Downs, Feb.1st 1921*	243
13.24	HRH The Prince of Wales unveiling the Indian Chattri on the Downs, Patcham, Feb 1921. Postcard.	244
13.25	The 2008 memorial service in June at the Chattri, near Brighton, for Indian soldiers who died in World War I	246
13.26	The Chattri in 2013 with newly erected tablet bearing the names of those cremated at the site	247
13.27	Anish Kapoor, *C-Curve*, 2007	248

14.1	The All-India War Memorial and the George V Memorial Statue	251
14.2	George V Memorial Statue (in its new home at Coronation Memorial Park)	260
15.1	F. S. Kelly, *Elegy for String Orchestra*, bars 1–5	267
15.2	F. S. Kelly, *Elegy for String Orchestra*, bars 30–35	267
15.3	F. S. Kelly, *Elegy for String Orchestra*, bars 31–33	268
15.4	F. S. Kelly, *Elegy for String Orchestra*, bars 39–42	268
15.5	Helen Gifford, *Choral Scenes – the Western Front, World War 1*, bars 340–345, 1999	275
15.6	Helen Gifford, *Choral Scenes*, bars 362–367, 1999	276
15.7	Andrew Harrison, *The Drumfire Was Incessant, and Continued All Night With Unabated Fury, Counterattack 1:* sections 2 and 3, 2012	277

Acknowledgements

We are conscious that in producing such a volume we have many people to thank. First and foremost, since the book emanates from the conference *The British Empire and the Great War: Colonial Societies/Cultural Responses* held in Singapore in February 2014, the organizers would like to acknowledge the generous support of the Centre for Liberal Arts and Social Sciences at Nanyang Technological University which funded the event. We would like to thank Professor Alan Chan and Professor Vibeke Sorensen at NTU and also Sir Hew Strachan, Professor Jay Winter, Professor John MacKenzie and Professor Tim Barringer for their contributions as keynotes. Eric Bogle should also be thanked for his participation and for his memorable performance. Melissa Lovell did a wonderful job copyediting the manuscript and bringing it into line before the handover to the team at Routledge who brought it to completion seamlessly. Finally, but by no means least, we thank our families for their support.

Michael J.K. Walsh & Andrekos Varnava

Contributors

Jan Asmussen is Professor at the Faculty of Command and Naval Operations at the Polish Naval Academy in Gdynia. His publications include works on diplomatic history, ethnic conflict and security.

Tim Barringer is Paul Mellon Professor and Chair of the History of Art Department at Yale University. He has published extensively on British Art, especially the Pre-Raphaelites, Art and the British Empire and American Art from the eighteenth century to the present.

Jonathan Black is Senior Research Fellow in History of Art at Kingston University. He has worked extensively on early twentieth century British art and the First World War and is currently completing a study of Winston Churchill in British Art *c*. 1900 to the present day.

Tim Buck is a former post-doctoral fellow at the Paul Mellon Centre for Studies in British Art. He has published on the imagining of empire in British art in the 1920s.

Richard Cork is an award-winning art critic, historian, curator and broadcaster. His books include *Vorticism, Art Beyond the Gallery, David Bomberg, A Bitter Truth, Wild Thing, The Healing Presence of Art, Face to Face* and four volumes of his art reviews (Yale, 2003).

Justin Fantauzzo is Assistant Professor of War and Society at Memorial University of Newfoundland, St. John's, Canada. His research focusses on the experience and memory of imperial soldiers in the Eastern Mediterranean and Middle East during the First World War.

Emma Hanna is Senior Research Fellow in the School of History at the University of Kent. She has published widely on music and film 1914–1918 and on the cultural memory of the First World War in contemporary Britain.

Andrew Harrison is a composer and pianist. He is currently completing a PhD in Music at the ANU, Australia. His research focusses on the composition of a number of works that reflect upon the narrative of the Great War as a point of creative departure.

Gregory Hynes is a DPhil candidate in History at Pembroke College, University of Oxford, working on imperial identities in British and New Zealand official First World War propaganda. He has also published on First World War visual culture and photography and on imperial racial depictions in propaganda.

David A. Johnson is Associate Professor of History at the University of North Carolina, Charlotte, with research and teaching interests in colonial and transnational history.

Nuala C. Johnson is Reader in Human Geography at Queen's University Belfast, Northern Ireland. She is author of *Ireland, the Great War and the Geography of Remembrance*

(2003; paperback 2007); *Nature Displaced, Nature Displayed: Order and Beauty in Botanical Gardens* (2011) and co-editor of *The Wiley-Blackwell Companion to Cultural Geography* (2013).

Wm. Matthew Kennedy is a PhD Candidate at the University of Sydney. His thesis examines Australian colonial political thought about the nature and destiny of Empire, and he is now working on a new project about the British Empire's global military internment camp system built to house Boer POWs during 1899–1907.

John M. MacKenzie is Emeritus Professor at Lancaster University. He has published on many aspects of British imperial history for forty years and was general editor of the 'Studies in Imperialism' series 1984–2014. He was Editor-in-Chief of the *Encyclopaedia of Empire* (2016).

Richard Scully is Senior Lecturer in Modern European History at the University of New England, Armidale, Australia. He is the author of *British Images of Germany: Admiration, Antagonism & Ambivalence, 1860–1914* (2012), and is primarily a historian of visual satire and comic and cartoon art.

Evan Smith is a Visiting Adjunct Fellow with the School of History and International Relations at Flinders University in South Australia. He has published widely on contemporary British political and social history.

Jennifer Wellington is Lecturer in Modern History, University College Dublin. Her book, *Exhibiting the Great War: Museums and Memory in Britain, Canada, and Australia 1914–1943* will be published in 2017.

Foreword
Hyde Park Corner: imperial triumph and tragedy

Early in 1912, only two years before the First World War erupted, everyone walking across Hyde Park Corner was suddenly confronted by a spectacular manifestation of imperial magnificence. The colossal Wellington Arch, first erected there in the late 1820s to celebrate Britain's victories over the French, now found itself surmounted by Adrian Jones's monumental bronze showing a tall, winged figure of Peace gesturing heroically above a boy driving a quadriga – four spirited horses rearing up in the air with wild energy (see Figure 0.1). Funded by the banker Herbert Stern,[1] this immense sculpture was erected on the Wellington Arch in January 1912. The bravura depiction of the horses must have benefited enormously from Jones's experience as a veterinary captain for twenty-three years after joining the Royal Horse Artillery at Ahmednagar in India.

Figure 0.1 Adrian Jones, *The Peace Quadriga*, bronze, Wellington Arch, Hyde Park Corner, London, 1911

Source: M. Walsh

---

1 Stern became the donor in 1907, and he had recently been created Lord Michelham of Hellingly.

Figure 0.2 *The Illustrated London News* (3 October 1846), depicting Matthew Coates Wyatt's *Equestrian Statue of the Duke of Wellington*

For a while, at least, his sculpture's full-blown dynamism probably seemed like a joyful and effervescent tribute to the spirit of the British Empire. It was, after all, a larger version of a plaster sculpture called Triumph, which Jones had exhibited at the Royal Academy. Here, in 1891, the future Edward VII admired its buoyancy so much that he asked Jones to create the far grander bronze monument for the Wellington Arch. But only two years after it was eventually installed there, the disastrous advent of the Great War transformed the national mood. Hopes of ecstatic triumph soon gave way to fears that catastrophe was imminent. And the overwhelming human losses sustained in the battlefields prompted another sculptor, Charles Sargeant Jagger, to convey a radically different order of feeling in another monument erected on Hyde Park Corner after the conflict was terminated.

In order fully to understand how far Jagger challenged traditional ideas about military memorials, we need only look at the turbulent history of sculpture created for the Wellington Arch. During the Victorian era, it had initially been topped by an enormous, unwieldy statue of the Duke of Wellington, Britain's most celebrated victor. The largest equestrian figure ever made, its overweening size caused controversy at once (see Figure 0.2). The sculptor, Matthew Coates Wyatt, had produced a predictably pompous image of Wellington pointing with god-like authority towards the invisible enemy, and this stiffly composed statue was completely disproportionate to the arch beneath.

No wonder that the Wellington sculpture was denounced with vituperative scorn by so many onlookers. In their recent history of the Arch, Steven Brindle and David Robinson describe how,

> on 27 September 1846, the giant statue was taken on a special car drawn by twenty-nine horses, accompanied by a grand military parade, to Hyde Park Corner. When lifted into

place, the statue was greeted with gales of derisive and hostile criticism. Lord Morpeth told the Memorial Committee that the government "were not enabled to think the effect favourable either to the statue or the arch", and asked for it to come down again. However, it was the Duke of Wellington himself who finally ended the debate. He had maintained a dignified silence throughout these rather undignified proceedings. Now he privately indicated to the new Prime Minister, Lord John Russell, that he would regard the removal of the statue as a humiliating mark of royal displeasure, and would feel obliged to resign all of his official commissions (which included Commander-in-Chief of the army). Faced with this ultimatum, the government caved in.[2]

Even so, hostility regarding the statue would not go away. In the early 1880s its overweening and unpopular presence finally persuaded the new Liberal government to take the statue down. After all, the original architect of the Arch, Decimus Burton, had been appalled by the arrival of the Wellington sculpture, and even the conservative Royal Academy dismissed it as 'a blot which has long been a source of annoyance to Englishmen and of derision to foreigners'.[3] So in 1885 the statue was moved away to a new location near the garrison church at Aldershot, and a committee chaired by the Prince of Wales commissioned Sir Joseph Boehm to produce an alternative image of the Duke for a different site on Hyde Park Corner. It was unveiled there in 1888. Although still revered as the British Empire's greatest commander, Wellington was now portrayed on a more modest-sized horse. He is seen looking towards Apsley House, which had been bought as his London home with funds voted by Parliament. Clutching a binocular in one hand, the Duke sits on his steed with sword sheathed, and he gazes forward in a very focussed way. Four bronze figures of elaborately uniformed military men stand guard on the corners of the monument, belonging to regiments like the 23rd Royal Welch Fusiliers and the 6th Inniskilling Dragoons. Their names are proudly inscribed alongside the statues, and the tradition of resplendent military attire continues even today, for members of the Household Cavalry wearing red cloaks and glittering golden helmets still ride through Hyde Park Corner every morning on their way to and from Buckingham Palace.

By 1914, however, the conservatism of the style developed with such professional success by Sir Joseph Boehm was dismissed in avant-garde circles. When the first issue of *BLAST* magazine appeared in the summer, announcing the arrival of the experimental Vorticist movement, its feisty editor Wyndham Lewis ensured that his belligerent manifesto attacked this once-beloved Victorian sculptor:

BLAST
    years 1837 to 1900
    Curse abysmal inexcusable middle-class
                                (Also Aristocracy and Proletariat).

BLAST
    pasty shadow cast by gigantic Boehm
               (Imagined at Introduction of BOURGEOIS VICTORIAN VISTAS).[4]

---

2 Steven Brindle and David Robinson, *The Wellington Arch and The Marble Arch* (London: English Heritage, 2001), pp. 15–16.
3 Quoted, ibid., p. 17.
4 Wyndham Lewis, ed., 'Review of the Great English Vortex,' *BLAST* (London), 1914, p. 18.

The Vorticists would have been equally withering about a Great War memorial erected on Hyde Park Corner after the Armistice. In 1925, Boehm's statue of Wellington was given a bizarre and controversial neighbour: the Machine Gun Corps Memorial by Francis Derwent Wood (see Figure 0.3). Viewed from a distance, this major monument does not appear to contain any visual references to machine guns at all. The weapons are virtually hidden by the bronze wreaths displayed on each side of the memorial along with discarded helmets and tunics. Above them, dominating our attention, stands a large and muscular figure of the youthful David. Naked apart from a modest fig-leaf which only just covers his genitals, David rests one hand on a hip while clasping Goliath's colossal sword with his other hand. He has just killed the giant with a sling shot, and for some unaccountable reason David was regarded by the memorial's commissioners as an appropriate figure to place above the monument's main inscription: 'Erected To Commemorate The Glorious Heroes Of The Machine Gun Corps Who Fell In The Great War'. Even more strange is the biblical quotation beneath these words, from 1 Samuel 18.7: 'Saul hath slain his thousands, but David his tens of thousands.' This was the ecstatic song voiced 'when David was returned from the slaughter of the Philistine', for Samuel describes how 'the women came out of all cities of Israel, singing and dancing . . . with joy, and with instruments of musick.'

Figure 0.3   Francis Derwent Wood, *The Machine Gun Corps Memorial (The Boy David)*, Hyde Park Corner, London, 1925

Source: Jonathan Black

But the biblical quotation provoked a flurry of protest after the Memorial was unveiled in 1925. By then, few wanted to rejoice in the appalling loss of life caused by machine guns during the First World War. They typified the devastating prowess of the new mechanical weapons unleashed during that conflict, and C.R.W. Nevinson had already defined the grimness of this invention in a painting called *La Mitrailleuse*, which entered the Tate's collection as an enlightened gift from the Contemporary Art Society in 1917. His vision of the war was controversial, but plenty of visitors to the gallery would have seen it on display there and understood why Nevinson showed a hunched gunner crouched over his machine while a fellow-soldier yells for assistance. He is probably hoping that someone will help him deal with the gravely injured young man lying in the darkness nearby.

Nevinson, who had served as an ambulance driver in the Great War before being invalided out, was one of the first artists to convey what Paul Nash called the 'bitter truth' of its battlefields.[5] Yet the pioneering example set by *La Mitrailleuse* was completely ignored by Adrian Jones. A decade after his triumphant four horses were installed on top of the Wellington Arch, Jones's Cavalry Memorial was unveiled at the Stanhope Gate entrance to Hyde Park (see Figure 0.4).[6] Planned in 1920 to commemorate the cavalry from Britain and the empire who had perished during the First World War, it demonstrated once again Jones's undoubted prowess as a horse sculptor. The animal's energy is prodigious, and yet the fact remains that this Cavalry Memorial has been wholly removed from the reality of modern combat. Rather than conveying the fundamental vulnerability of cavalry warfare in the early twentieth century, Jones opted instead for an armoured figure of St George. This mythical hero thrusts his weapon high in the air, exulting in the slaughter of the dragon lying beneath his horse. Although the beast has been given Kaiser Wilhelm II's upturned moustaches, it shows no visible connection with the enemy forces confronting the British Empire's cavalry during the Great War. On the plinth Jones added some scenes from the conflict of 1914–1918, but they are entirely overshadowed by the ebullience of St George, whose symbolic significance was spelled out during a speech by the Duke of York hailing this legendary dragon-slayer as 'the inspiration of those ideals of chivalry, self-sacrifice, and patriotism which are essential to the highest conduct and character'.[7]

No wonder Charles Sargeant Jagger was determined to escape from all this worn-out rhetoric. Unlike so many of the sculptors who executed memorials after the Great War, he had actually fought on the front lines and been wounded twice – first during the disastrous Gallipoli expedition and then, even more severely, at the battle of Neuve Eglise in April 1918. Jagger coped bravely with these injuries, and he was awarded the Military Cross for his courage. Nothing, however, could prevent him from attempting as a sculptor to challenge Establishment views and express, in forthright terms, his true vision of the conflict. Less than a year after the war ended, he embarked on a large bronze relief for the British School at Rome while still recovering from his second wound. Now in the Tate collection, *No Man's Land* lives up to its bleak title in a thoroughly uncompromising and powerful way. Even though several soldiers are shown here, scattered across this battered

---

5 Paul Nash, 'Paul Nash to Margaret Nash, Mid-November 1917,' in *Outline. An Autobiography and Other Writings* (London: Faber & Faber, 1949), p. 211.

6 When Park Lane was widened in 1960 the memorial was moved to its present location north-west of Apsley House, but without the architectural backdrop which Sir John Burnet had originally designed for Jones' equestrian figure.

7 Quotation from notes in the files, Department of Photographs, War Memorials Collection, Imperial War Museum.

Figure 0.4   Adrian Jones, *Cavalry Memorial*, bronze, 1924

Source: M. Walsh

landscape, only one of them is still alive. Struggling to stay vigilant, he leans over the edge of a trench. But all we can see around him are his comrades' corpses, some belonging to a stretcher-party slaughtered while they were attempting to help an injured mate. On the far right, another wretched figure hangs impaled on a barbed-wire fence, while at the other side of this remorselessly harsh relief a man's naked legs project from the mud where the rest of his body must lie buried.

At one stage, when Jagger was working on the plaster version of *No Man's Land*, he inscribed some words in the empty sky above these stricken combatants. They come from a poem called *To the Vanguard* by Beatrix Brice-Miller:

> O little mighty band that stood for England
> That with your bodies for a living shield
> Guarded her slow awaking.

By the time he cast the bronze version, however, Jagger had decided to remove these lines altogether. He doubtless realised, quite rightly, that their blandness had nothing to do with his own adamant insistence on conveying the absolute tragedy of so much human annihilation. Jagger was haunted by his appalling experiences in the Great War, and at one point during the 1920s he even confessed that his mind 'had been troubled by doubts about whether it was possible to have faith in a God who allows wars to happen'.[8]

He must therefore have felt relieved that the members of the Royal Artillery War Commemoration Fund Committee did not emphasise the importance of religion when they invited him to make their mighty memorial for a prime site on Hyde Park Corner. Jagger proved lucky: at this early point in his career, he was not very well known. And the Royal Artillery Committee had also approached senior practitioners as renowned as Derwent Wood and Lutyens. But they both refused to make a realistic image of a gun for the top of the monument. Although Derwent Wood would doubtless have preferred to place a handsome, naked man in this location, Jagger insisted that the memorial should be 'distinctive of Artillery and of its period'.[9] So he threw himself into creating an enormous stone carving of a 9.2 Howitzer, and each of the four reliefs in Figure 0.5 included his depiction of a different type of gun as well.

Figure 0.5   **Charles Sargeant Jagger and Lionel Pearson, *Royal Artillery Memorial*, Hyde Park Corner, 1925**

Source: Jonathan Black

---

8   See Ann Compton, 'A Sculptural Biography,' in *Charles Sargeant Jagger, War and Peace Sculpture*, ed. Ann Compton (London: Imperial War Museum, 1985), p. 47.

9   Quoted by James Stevens Curl, 'The Royal Artillery Memorial at Hyde Park Corner,' Compton, *Charles Sargeant Jagger, War and Peace Sculpture*, p. 84.

Even so, the most important aspect of the Royal Artillery Memorial lay in its portrayal of the soldiers themselves. Jagger felt passionately about the importance of representing these men as they were, and he would have baulked at the whole notion of allowing St George to symbolise their contribution to the Great War. The Memorial itself is inscribed with these moving words: 'In Proud Remembrance of the 49,000 & 76 of all ranks of the Royal Regiment of Artillery who gave their lives.' Jagger could remember, all too well, just how hellish the suffering of men at war really was. So he told the *Daily News* that he had no patience when, in 1921,

> some elderly members of a memorial committee came to my studio to look at a figure of a soldier. It did not please them. They thought the putties were done up too untidily, that the tin hat was too much on one side, and that altogether the Tommy wasn't respectable or smart enough for their memorial. In the end they decided not to have the soldier but a pretty symbolical figure of Victory instead.

In the same interview with the *Daily News*, he insisted that his 'experience in the trenches persuaded him of the necessity for frankness and truth . . . "I got to love the Tommy in the trenches and I've tried to show him as I knew him – not as he looked on parade at home" '.[10]

Hence Jagger's crucial emphasis, in the white stone relief occupying the east side of the Royal Artillery Memorial, on soldiers in extremis. One man struggles to carry a dead or dying man on his back, and even the gunner looks trapped as he tries to gaze through his view-finder inside a claustrophobic tent. On the right side of this relief, a warning sign in capital letters announces 'WIND DANGEROUS'. So the weather could be as potentially lethal as the ever-present threat from enemy forces, and the remarkable pallor of the white stone itself – revealed once again by a much-needed restoration in 2011 – makes everyone look ghostly. Rather than personifying the army of victory, these figures all appear unlikely to survive. Despite the forcefulness of the Howitzer thrusting up from the Memorial's topmost point, the soldiers in all the stone reliefs below seem desperately vulnerable. On the west side, another fierce and exhausting struggle is enacted where men strive to push and haul a heavy gun forward, while one young combatant is hit as he strains to control the horses who respond with panic to an enemy attack.

Jagger introduced a greater amount of solidity by placing a substantial bronze man on the east, south and west sides of the Memorial. Representing a shell-carrier, an officer and a driver, these three figures look sturdy yet haggard as they bear the weight of their uniforms and equipment. No hint of ostentation can be detected in any of these grim-faced individuals. They have nothing to do with the sword-brandishing smugness displayed by St George in Adrian Jones's Cavalry Memorial. Instead, all three men brace themselves for the tasks ahead, and they are under no illusions about the daunting immensity of the dangers confronting them. The driver stretches out his arms and rests them on the monument behind, as if acknowledging his role in transporting fellow-soldiers and heavy weapons. He embodies a willingness to assist and protect. But even drivers were at grave risk when combat flared. Hence the resigned and stoical expression on his war-weathered face – a mood he shares with the other two bronze figures standing around the Memorial.

The overall architectural design was provided by Lionel Pearson, who would later work equally well with Stanley Spencer on the Burghclere Chapel. Nothing is permitted to

---

10 Charles Sargeant Jagger, interview, *Daily News*, 14 July 1921.

interfere with the impact of Spencer's paintings inside the Chapel, and the same admirable priority can be found in Pearson's handling of the Artillery Memorial's podium. The architecture allows Jagger's carvings and bronze figures to assert their presence as we walk round the monument. Even on the north side, where the upright bronze men give way to a disturbing horizontal alternative, Pearson gives this unexpected sculpture the prominence it deserves. When the initial plans for the Memorial were drawn up and submitted, Jagger simply stated that the north end would display 'a feature in bronze'.[11] With hindsight, we can view those words as the hallmark of a clever tactician, for he wanted to place, on this prominent platform, a soldier's recumbent corpse (see Figure 0.6).

Jagger must have suspected that such an idea ran the risk of being rejected at the outset. Only at a later stage in the creation of the monument did he reveal that this 'feature in bronze' would in fact represent a dead Tommy. And even then, the angry Colonel Lewin attempted to censor it. He argued that Jagger should not be allowed to use the Royal Artillery Memorial 'as a means of forcing home on the minds of the public the horror and terror of war'.[12] A few other committee members voiced their doubts about the 'gruesomeness' of Jagger's proposal as well, but he eventually persuaded a majority of them that including a dead soldier in bronze would give the monument a more profound and moving resonance.

The committee was absolutely right to override objections and agree with Jagger. Although nothing could be further removed from the muscular heroism of Derwent Wood and Jones, this recumbent corpse sums up the overwhelming sense of loss engendered by the Great War. The dead artilleryman is almost covered by a greatcoat, which partially

Figure 0.6 Charles Sargeant Jagger and Lionel Pearson, *Royal Artillery Memorial*, Detail *Fallen Artilleryman*, **bronze, Hyde Park Corner, 1925**

Source: Jonathan Black

---

11 Curl, 'The Royal Artillery Memorial at Hyde Park Corner,' p. 86.
12 Quoted, ibid., p. 94.

overhangs the inscription running round the stone beneath: 'Here Was A Royal Fellowship Of Death.' The man's helmet is perched on top of his greatcoat, and from a distance we cannot see his corpse at all. But the nearer we approach, the more we can glimpse the young man himself. Both his hands protrude from the greatcoat, and one side of his face becomes visible as well. The intact ear, jaw, hair and thrusting chin belong to a once-vigorous figure, now motionless and waiting to be buried. It is a distressing sight, as Alan Borg emphasised in his book on *War Memorials From Antiquity to the Present*: 'Here the dead man lies directly on the plinth, at the same height as the viewer, and the impact of the figure is immediate and shocking.'[13]

Some viewers recoiled when the memorial was unveiled in 1925, and an apoplectic Lord Curzon declared that it resembled 'a toad squatting, which is about to spit fire out of its mouth ... nothing more hideous could ever be conceived'.[14] But plenty of other onlookers responded in a far more positive spirit, like the young gunner who gazed at the corpse and insisted: 'He is real. All the [bronze] men are real.'[15] Jagger had succeeded in breaking through all the formulaic barriers and redefining what a Great War memorial could achieve. He invested an enormous amount of gruelling personal experience and emotion in this heartfelt masterpiece, even to the point of making sure that his signature was inscribed directly beneath the tousled hair of the dead soldier. And the far larger words incised on the stone below emphasised that 'those whose memory is perpetuated by this memorial' would 'return never more'. Since its unveiling in 1925, the essential honesty, directness and poignancy of this monument have become ever more widely appreciated.

Richard Cork

---

13 Alan Borg, *War Memorials From Antiquity to the Present* (London: Leo Cooper, 1991), p. 122.
14 Lord Curzon, quoted by a leader, *The Times*, 29 October 1925.
15 *Manchester Guardian*, 9 October 1925.

PART I
The Great War and the British Empire

Chapter 1
The Great War and the British Empire
Conflict, culture and memory

Michael J.K. Walsh and Andrekos Varnava

The foundation of empire is art and science. Remove them or degrade them, and the empire is no more. Empire follows art and not vice versa as Englishmen suppose.[1]

William Blake

This collection is derived from the conference *The British Empire and the Great War: Colonial Societies/Cultural Responses*, which took place in Singapore in February 2014 to mark the centennial of the outbreak of the Great War.[2] The meeting placed emphasis on a decentralisation of socio-cultural analysis away from the more predictable metropolitan perspectives, to enable an analysis of the contrasts and complexities of the various responses throughout the geographical and ethnic extremes of both the 'formal' and 'informal' empire. From around the British imperial world, complex and interlocking themes were addressed examining how different strata and subsets of colonial society shaped and were shaped by the experience of total war and how disparate societies and cultures – in all their manifestations – shaped and were shaped by it.

The essays presented in this volume deal specifically with historiography, propaganda, literature, theatre, film and television, photography, fine and applied art, architecture, music and memorialisation. They traverse the globe from Cyprus, Singapore and New Zealand to Canada, Mesopotamia and the vast expanses of Australia and India, prising open fields of enquiry that are yet to be fully investigated in that 'heyday of new imperialism with its attendant controversies, vicarious exhilarations, and anxieties of decline'.[3] Holger Hoock concludes his admirable study on the art of the British Empire in the eighteenth and nineteenth centuries with the basic assertion that '[a]esthetically performed politics and politically inflected art and culture interacted in multifarious ways.'[4] By combining this fundamental assumption with Jeffrey Grey's insistence that '[i]f war defined the British nation, it also fundamentally defined the relationship between the British world and Britain in the course of the twentieth century,'[5] the *raison d'etre* for this particular collection of essays becomes clear.

---

1 William Blake, *The Complete Poetry and Prose of William Blake*, ed. David Erdman (Berkeley: University of California Press, 2008), p. 636.

2 The organisers would like to acknowledge the generous support of the Centre for Liberal Arts and Social Sciences at Nanyang Technological University, Singapore.

3 Aaron Worth, *Imperial Media: Colonial Networks and Information Technologies in the British Literary Imagination, 1857–1918* (Columbus, OH: Ohio State University Press, 2014), p. 4.

4 Holger Hoock, *Empires of the Imagination: Politics, War, and the Arts in the British World, 1750–1850* (London: Profile Books, 2010), p. 384.

5 See Jeffrey Grey, 'War and the British World in the Twentieth Century,' in *Rediscovering the British World*, ed. Phillip Buckner and R. Douglas Francis (Calgary: Calgary University Press, 2005), p. 234.

Part 1: a distant, uneasy, gaze

A measure of the unease with which commentators approach the cultural history, and indeed the memory of the British Empire, can be felt when perusing the reviews of the exhibition *Artist and Empire: Facing Britain's Imperial Past*, which was shown at Tate Britain (itself a site/family with a significant imperial history) in London from November 2015 to April 2016. Far from a celebration of a distant, resolved, and possibly even rich seam of cultural history, the critics lined up to take aim at the show itself and the rationale behind it, or to staunchly defend it (and, by default, the empire). The initial tone was set cautiously with Jonathan Jones in *The Guardian*, who stated:

> The British Empire has become invisible. It is an abstraction that people argue about. Right and left lay claim to its pride or shame, but the historical entity – whose rights and wrongs patriots and radicals now debate – lies cold in its grave, its banners, medals, statues and pith helmets neglected and ignored.[6]

This eulogy was followed by Mark Hudson in *The Telegraph* who asked '[w]here do you stand on the British Empire? Was it our nation's greatest glory or its greatest shame? Or has it become simply a self-evident historical fact, too distant to excite strong feelings either way?'[7] Matthew Collings mocked the catalogue for preparing audiences for an 'art that faces Britain's imperial past as if it were a strenuous bout of psychotherapy that the reader is about to embark on',[8] while William Dalrymple, less flippantly, insisted that the time had come to confront a less than glorious, traumatic historical reality through the lens of art (ranging from John Thomas' *The Siege of Enniskillen Castle* in 1593 to Andrew Gilbert's *All Roads Lead to Ulundi* in 2015):

> It is difficult to think of a subject that is surrounded by a more formidable minefield of potential awkwardness than the art of imperialism ... the British need to know about their empire, to face up to what the country did, and the reasons why so many people, in so many different parts of the world, actively resent, dislike and distrust them. While there are things the imperial British did that can be celebrated, these have to be weighed against a long succession of what today would be regarded as war crimes, stretching from Virginia to New Zealand.[9]

From across the Atlantic, came the mildly more sympathetic observations of the *Wall Street Journal* (accompanied perhaps by a wry smile on the part of the writer):

> 'Artist and Empire' is the result of three years of planning and hand-wringing by the 19th-century curatorial team at the Tate Britain. The first year consisted almost entirely of talks

---

6 Jonathan Jones, 'Artists and Empire Review – A Captivating Look at the Colonial Times We Still Live in,' *The Guardian*, 23 November 2015.
7 Mark Hudson, 'Artist and Empire, Tate Britain Review: "Just Not Good Enough",' *The Telegraph*, 23 November 2015.
8 Matthew Collings, 'Artist and Empire, Tate Britain, Exhibition Review: Face the Past,' *Evening Standard*, 24 November 2015.
9 William Dalrymple, 'Violence, Victors and Victims: How to Look at the Art of the British Empire,' *The Guardian*, 20 November 2015.

about how to sensitively approach the topic: How could the museum display the items without either celebrating or condemning them?[10]

In Jonathan Jones' closing comments a final, but extremely important, point was made when he noted: 'But we are different people. We do not have those square jaws and chilling looks. General Gordon stands frozen in his imperial mission, while we wonder at his utter strangeness.'[11]

The empire has gone. So has the British Empire and Commonwealth Museum in Bristol (as of 2008). Millions of former imperial subjects and generations of their children are now British citizens 'at home' in a post-EU United Kingdom which in itself has devolved governments.[12] Questions of culture, identity, nation and empire therefore have come to sit side by side while history and histories are debated with renewed vigour. Neo-colonialism jostles with post-colonialism while past lives and imperial recollections breathe influentially in modern national politics and policies. There now exist dichotomies of globalisation and migration, supranational states and the rights of small nations, ethnic conflict and racial belonging, making Timothy Parson's remarks germane when he concluded that 'the empires of the last century were short-lived engines of globalisation that left behind new and vital networks of migration, commerce, and cultural exchange.'[13] It may also be worthy of note that the British Council published a report as recently as 2014 titled *Remember the World as Well as the War: Why the Global Reach and Enduring Legacy of the First World War Still Matter Today*,[14] suggesting that the long-term reverberations of Parson's 'engines of globalisation' were and are practical as well as academic. It is because of this kind of relationship that the essays presented here focus attention on how the Great War and the British Empire affected each other and why investigating both synchronously is important.

---

10   Anna Russell, '"In Artist and Empire," Britons Face Up to the Past,' *The Wall Street Journal*, 25 November 2015.

11   Jones, 'Artists and Empire Review.'

12   See Stuart Ward, ed., *British Culture and the End of Empire* (Manchester: Manchester University Press, 2001); Although the foreign-born population in Britain has changed and continues to do so (for example, the census numbers from 2006 to 2014 suggest a sharp rise in the number of Polish nationals moving to the United Kingdom) people born in former colonies continue to dominate statistically. Population by Country of Birth and Nationality Report, August 2006, Office for National Statistics, United Kingdom; Population by Country of Birth and Nationality Report, August 2014, Office for National Statistics, United Kingdom. http://www.ons.gov.uk/ons/rel/migration1/population-by-country-of-birth-and-nationality/2013/rpt-population-of-the-uk.html In order these are India, Pakistan, Republic of Ireland, South Africa, Bangladesh, United States, China (including Hong Kong), Nigeria, Jamaica, Kenya, Sri Lanka, Australia, Zimbabwe, Somalia, Ghana, Canada, Iraq, Cyprus, Nepal, New Zealand, Malaysia, and Uganda.

13   Timothy H. Parsons, *The Second British Empire: In the Crucible of the Twentieth Century* (Lanham, MD: Rowman and Littlefield, 2014), p. 26; see also Gary B. Magee and Andrew S. Thompson, *Empire and Globalisation: Networks of People, Goods and Capital in the British World, c.1850–1914* (Cambridge: Cambridge University Press, 2010).

14   British Council, 'Remember the World as Well as the War,' p. 8, accessed 12 May 2015, http://www.britishcouncil.org/sites/britishcouncil.uk2/files/remember-the-world-report-v4.pdf.

Part 2: empire, culture, conflict

To be sure '[t]he arts did not just stimulate the pleasures of the imagination in the cultural market place. They also served the aesthetic performance of politics and helped shape political culture,' and so 'Arms and Arts!', as Holger Hoock suggested, was a successful *cri de guerre*.[15] For him 'building empires in the[ir] cultural imagination'[16] was not random, nor mere propaganda. Instead it was a device to legitimate expansion, explain the magnitude of the imperial project, and when necessary to mask defeat. Art in its widest sense could, he argued, anticipate the future and prepare for it through the creation and reinforcement of notions of masculinity, heroism and imperialism combined with political certainty and aesthetic refinement.[17] Later it would take its part in creating both memory and history. David Dimbleby, in his popular series the *Seven Ages of Britain*, made a similar case when he stated that '[a]rt implanted the British Empire in the national consciousness,'[18] claiming that through the medium the British and their imperial servants were simultaneously flattered and reassured of their mission to govern and civilise. He went on to claim that '[e]very image of empire reminded the public that Britain was engaged in a great enterprise which was enriching the nation, raising its international prestige and bringing peace and regeneration to the rest of the world.' Like the empire it represented, the art was commercial, competitive, didactic, ideological and 'the servant of education'.[19] Nicholas Dirks was therefore quick to acknowledge:

> In certain important ways culture was what colonialism was all about. Cultural forms in newly classified 'traditional' societies were reconstructed and transformed by and through colonial technologies of conquest and rule, which created new categories and oppositions between colonizers and colonized, European and Asian, modern and traditional, West and East, even male and female.[20]

And so when studying the cultural hybridity and intellectual complexity of the arts, critical ordering and understanding of its components must be borne in mind, as must the professionalisation and institutionalisation of its practitioners in order to create meaning in a relatively unfettered public forum. Hoock warned that '[c]ulture is not merely a reflection or expression of social experience or political reality; nor is it an autonomous entity.'[21] So imperialism, in its entirety, clearly 'involved not only territorial acquisition,

---

15 Hoock, *Empires of the Imagination*, p. 13.
16 Ibid., p. xvi.
17 See Andrew Stephenson, '"Wonderful Pieces of Stage Management": Reviewing Masculine Fashioning, Race and Imperialism in John Singer Sargent's British Portraits, *c*. 1897–1914,' in *Transculturation in British Art, 1770–1930*, ed. Julie F. Codell (London: Ashgate Publishing, 2012), pp. 221–42.
18 David Dimbleby, *Seven Ages of Britain* (London: Hodder & Stoughton, 2009), p. 187.
19 Ibid., p. 187–8.
20 Nicholas B. Dirks, ed., *Colonialism and Culture* (Ann Arbor, MI: University of Michigan Press, 1992), pp. 2–3; quoted in Catherine Hall, *Cultures of Empire: A Reader: Colonizer in Britain and the Empire in the Nineteenth and Twentieth Centuries* (Manchester: Manchester University Press, 2000), pp. 15–16.
21 Hoock, *Empires of the Imagination*, p. 12.

political ambition and economic interests but also cultural formations, attitudes, beliefs and practices'.[22] Tim Barringer and Geoff Quilley invite us to think further and to acknowledge that imperial flows were not unidirectional, emanating solely from the British Isles. Indeed, the empire in all its cultural diversity was also transported into the heart of Britain and the reverberations widely felt:

> London's ports, and its markets for trading stocks and commodities, made it the empire's indispensable nexus, a status protected by harshly enforced legislation as well as by economic logic. Less fully acknowledged, until recently, has been London's status as a cultural centre, a place for meetings of ideas and representations, a space for the making, selling and viewing of art.[23]

Writing in 2014 Timothy Parsons took issue with this and, building on the arguments of Bernard Porter,[24] claimed that '[a]t the imperial centre, metropolitan Britons knew very little about what actually went on in the untidy empire.'[25] Far from benefitting from a subtle and nuanced blend of ideas and aesthetics filtering into the United Kingdom from around the globe, Britons would have known little and cared less about what was going on beyond the Channel.

This 'untidy empire' was presented by Catherine Hall in her impressive *Cultures of Empire: A Reader*[26] as being made up of colonies of settlement (Australia, New Zealand and Canada), protectorates and dependencies (from the Ionian Islands to India), despots, advisors, commercial companies, governors, hereditary rajahs, commissioners, consul generals and so on. To this heady administrative mix and vast geographical horizon can be added the impact of what Patrick Deer calls 'war culture', which in the early twentieth century 'capture[d] and colonize[d] the national imagination'.[27] Now the various and diverse populations of the empire were moving and converging on an unprecedented scale (and motivated by a common, potent stimulus): India contributed around 1,400,000 recruits up to December 1919, and the dominions – including Canada, South Africa, Australia, New Zealand and Newfoundland – contributed a further 1,300,000 men.[28] Even places

---

22 James R. Ryan, *Picturing Empire: Photography and the Visualization of the British Empire* (London: Reaktion Books, Ltd., 1997), p. 12.
23 Tim Barringer, Geoff Quilley and Douglas Fordham, eds, *Art and the British Empire* (Manchester and New York: Manchester University Press, 2007), p. 13.
24 See Bernard Porter, '"Empire, What Empire?" Or, Why 80% of Early-and Mid-Victorians Were Deliberately Kept in Ignorance of It,' *Victorian Studies* 46, no. 2 (2004): pp. 256–63; Bernard Porter, *The Absent-Minded Imperialists: Empire, Society, and Culture in Britain* (Oxford: Oxford University Press, 2006).
25 Parsons, *The Second British Empire*, p. 15.
26 Hall, *Cultures of Empire: A Reader*.
27 Patrick Deer, *Culture in Camouflage: War, Empire and Modern British Literature* (Oxford: Oxford University Press, 2009), p. 14.
28 *Statistics of the Military Effort of the British Empire during the Great War, 1914–1918* (London: His Majesty's Stationery Office, 1920); which lists the contributions of the British empire in terms of manpower between 4 August 1914 and 11 November 1918 as follows: 'British Isles 5,704,416, Canada 628,964, Australia 412,953, New Zealand 128,525, South Africa 136,070, India 1,440,437, Other Colonies ('Coloured troops from South Africa, West Indies & c') 134,837.

considered small and militarily insignificant by comparison were major contributors: Cyprus contributed a quarter of its male population between 1916 to 1920 mainly as mule drivers in the Balkan theatres of conflict.[29] What is much less certain though is whether these vast movements of people led to meaningful cross-cultural encounters. Perhaps it is an act of historical *naïveté* to believe that physical proximity of different people and races to one another necessarily results in some sort of sophisticated cultural transfer. Indeed, the opposite might be the case, leading to tensions and reinforcing previously held negative views of 'the Other'.

In any case, the further we get away from the living memory of the empire (like the Great War itself) the closer we can get to drawing our conclusions about it and the more comfortable we feel about discussing and debating it, even if many matters remain unresolved.[30] Although siding with John M. MacKenzie in his debate with Porter, we agree with the latter when he claimed in an earlier study that his aim was 'to *sophisticate* people's understanding of an important historical and current phenomenon that is too often viewed simplistically and crudely'.[31] We can no longer accept simplistic assertions like those of Boris Ford who summed up the intricate multifaceted relationship between empire and culture by saying:

> The basic cultural importance of the Empire was, of course, quite simply that it kept Great Britain afloat in considerable affluence – paying, as it were, for Henry James's butler and valet, Elgar's racing, and Sargent's commissions, not to mention creating the wealth that enabled fine houses to be built and furnished for the rich.[32]

Part 3: a view from the imperial centre a century ago

How the British Empire, settler and non-settler, was perceived and represented, and how it perceived and represented itself before, during and after the Great War is the *raison d'etre* of this collection. Uncovering histories and creating understanding is not only about identifying events (or cultural manifestations) frozen into a particular geography or chronology in the past, but dependent on understanding the subsequent processes of creation and interpretation in the interim. While much is undoubtedly learned from traditional retrospective analysis (contextualised by the knowledge of 'what happened next'), so too much can be gleaned from an understanding of what contemporary observers anticipated and predicted. How did

---

29 Andrekos Varnava, 'Recruitment and Volunteerism for the Cypriot Mule Corps, 1916–1919,' *Itinerario* 38, no. 3 (2014): pp. 79–101.

30 Bernard Porter, 'Further Thoughts on Imperial Absent-Mindedness,' *The Journal of Imperial and Commonwealth History* 36, no. 1 (2008): pp. 101–17; John M. MacKenzie, '"Comfort" and Conviction: A Response to Bernard Porter,' *The Journal of Imperial and Commonwealth History* 36, no. 4 (2008): pp. 659–88; Bernard Porter, 'Popular Imperialism: Broadening the Context,' *The Journal of Imperial and Commonwealth History* 39, no. 5 (December 2011): pp. 833–45; John M. MacKenzie, 'The British Empire: Ramshackle or Rampaging? A Historiographical Reflection,' *The Journal of Imperial and Commonwealth History* 43, no. 1 (January 2015): pp. 99–124.

31 Bernard Porter, *The Lion's Share: A History of British Imperialism 1850 to the Present*, 5th ed. (New York: Pearson, 2012), p. xx.

32 Boris Ford, ed., *The Cambridge Guide to the Arts in Britain: The Edwardian Age and the Inter-War Years*, vol. 8 (London: Cambridge University Press, 1989), p. 9.

they see the months and years ahead playing out?[33] Let us turn, for example, to 1914 and to ideas of Selwyn Image, Slade Professor of Art at Oxford University and one-time student of John Ruskin's, and a lecture he delivered to undergraduates in the weeks that followed the declaration of war. In this he talked, as Ruskin had done in 1865, about how art, after such a prolonged period of peace, had become 'a sheltered sensitive-plant fearful of the passing touch'.[34] War would now, as it always had done, toughen art, regenerate it, bring back its meaning and its relevance.[35] He looked to the future in some way relieved that the threat of 'peace' had now abated:

> We have to remind ourselves with what stoicism we can muster that the effect of war upon art has never been wholly bad, nay, has on occasion been quite the reverse of bad.... For Art has her dangers – dangers coming to her from men's frivolity, their absorption in sumptuousness and luxury, their over-attention to trivialities and mere curiosities, their morbid excitement after titillating novelties, their resultant shallowness of judgement and sane appreciation. Dangers from these things and the like of them assail Art and are fatal to her fineness.[36]

Through the arrival of war, the empire and its global cultures were set for a renaissance, a prediction also seen in Charles H. Luke's *The War and the Parting of the Ways: A Short Study of the Future of the British Empire in Relation to the Great War* in 1915. For Luke the empire around him was a positive global phenomenon founded

> mainly on liberty, justice, the right of peaceful expansion, the fullest possible liberty to the individual, and the fullest possible scope for the individual temperament; the recognition of international contracts, even when made with and for small nations; and in the main, in spite of many weaknesses, a belief in a certain righteousness in its national policy.[37]

In the pages that followed he anticipated how Britain itself had needed this 'great awakening' and conjectured how it would benefit enormously from the upheavals of the recent past, of the present, and of those that as yet lay ahead. John Ruskin himself had also acknowledged, half a century earlier, that social and cultural change of this sort usually happened in time of war, when artists, writers and thinkers flourished. He had stated unambiguously that 'war is the foundation of all the arts . . . the foundation of all the high virtues and faculties of men.'[38] Art would benefit from a national spirit, swept along in an intensity of experience that was

---

33 Michael J.K. Walsh, *London, Modernism and 1914* (Cambridge: Cambridge University Press, 2010); was based entirely on the predictive nature of cultural responses to the Great War in London. The central theme was not what impact the Great War had on the arts in retrospect; it was what impact the Great War was expected to have on the arts at its outset by those who were there.
34 Selwyn Image, "Art, Morals and the War": A Lecture Delivered at the Ashmolean Museum Oxford on Thursday, 12 November 1914 (London: Oxford University Press, 1914), p. 19.
35 C.S.H. 'After the War,' *New Age* 15, 29 October 1914, p. 635.
36 Image, 'Art, Morals, and the War,' pp. 18–19.
37 Charles H. Luke A.M.S.E., *The War and the Parting of the Ways: A Short Study of the Future of the British Empire in Relation to the Great War* (London: Sampson Low, Marston & Co., 1915), p. 5.
38 John Ruskin, 'War,' in *The Crown of Wild Olive: Three Lectures on Work, Traffic, and War* (New York: John Wiley and Sons, 1881), p. 89.

catalysed by the intangible, but very real, 'release of energy' induced by war. He removed any ambiguity in the relationship by stating boldly:

> I found, in brief, that all great nations learned their truth of word, and strength of thought, in war; that they were nourished in war, and wasted by peace; taught by war and deceived by peace; – in a word, that they were born in war, and expired in peace.[39]

Where Ruskin and Luke differed was in the belief in the civility of the empire itself. Ruskin was not certain of its intrinsic 'good', neither was he convinced of its moral rectitude. So while he had stated 'there is no great art possible to a nation but that which is based on battle,'[40] he simultaneously advocated the distinction between conflicts of conquest and 'formative' ones. Essentially, noble war and great art could advance hand in hand so long as there was already an inherent genius in the people. Money, greed and lust for power and possession, which had driven England's recent efforts (he was writing with the memories of Peking, Crimea, the Fenian Rising and the Indian Mutiny still fresh) would never lead to great art.[41] Ruskin concluded 'good and noble as this state may be, it is a state of slavery.'[42] He also spoke of 'peace' ('and the *vices* of civil life' [my italics]) and went on to emphasise that it was 'wholly untenable' for 'peace and the virtues of civil life [to] flourish together', warning that peace between 'tranquil nations' could lead only to the situation where the arts 'wither utterly away'.[43]

Beyond art, Luke felt this 'great awakening' would also sort out the destinies of certain imperial nations whose loyalties were currently being brought into question and identify those around which no such doubt should exist:

> If Ireland starts on its path as a self-governing unit of the Empire by refusing to defend whole-heartedly Imperial interests, for which even the Red Indians of Canada are fighting, they will justly deserve the stigma which is attached to all traitors; and the Hierarchy, in not stirring up the people to fight, if only to revenge the crime committed against Catholic Belgium, will incur the reprobation of the whole Roman Catholic world.[44]

So while the warning was crystal clear to both the people and the church in Ireland, the Canadians, who had already sent more troops to assist the empire than the total number of troops available to the Duke of Wellington at Waterloo, were held up as model imperial subjects.

A second essay of interest is Sir Harry Johnston's *The Black Man's Part in the War* published in 1917, which brought the reader's attention to some powerful statistics and progressive ideas:

> The United Kingdom of Great Britain and Ireland rules more or less directly some 44,700,000 Africans, about 1,700,000 Aframericans in the West Indies, Honduras

---

39 Ibid., p. 90.
40 Ibid., p. 83.
41 Michael J.K. Walsh, 'Homeric Cheeses and the Breast of a Decrepit Nurse: Ruskin and Marinetti on Art and War,' in *Great War Modernism*, ed. Nanette Norris (Fairleigh: Dickinson University Press, 2016), pp. 15–33.
42 Ruskin, 'War,' p. 112.
43 Ibid., p. 88.
44 Luke A.M.S.E., *The War and the Parting of the Ways*, p. 97.

and Guiana, and about 338,000 Oceanic Negroes, Melanesians and Polynesians in the Pacific archipelagoes. And in addition the Daughter Nation of the South African Union governs another 4,000,000 of Bantu Negroes, Hottentots and half-breeds; lastly, the Commonwealth of Australia and the Dominion of New Zealand are responsible for the safe-keeping and welfare of about 400,000 Papuans, 150,000 Australoids, and 100,000 Polynesians, Melanesians and Micronesians.[45]

Having introduced a large part of the *dramatis personae* to the reader, he resumed, talking now not only about the recent past and present, but indeed the future of the empire, when the war had passed (and been won):

> British Asia will have as much as Africa (or more) to do in closing the great conflict and in helping to set the world right again. It may be advisable for some writer who knows his India, his Malaysia and Ceylon to tell the White peoples of the Empire what has been the fighting worth of the Indian troops in France, in Palestine, Mesopotamia and East Africa; and what sacrifices for the common cause have been made by coloured British subjects in Ceylon, in the Malay Peninsula and even in distant Borneo; besides the handsome financial contributions to war funds or war charities from the Chinese in Hong-Kong.[46]

In his intriguing essay Sir Harry went on to appeal for the study of ethnology (which he described as '[t]he Science of Races') within the imperial education system, not only to atone for past wrongs, but to pool talent, and to build an empire which would remain fundamentally fair, inclusive and tolerant. He went on:

> Every British boy and girl, every white, brown, and black child and student, above all those who are likely to rise to play a part, small or great in the affairs of State, should before all things be versed in a knowledge of the different races of man living at the present day. If this education were imparted in its simplest form to school-children as a subject of elementary tuition, if it were the incentive to scholarships, the cause of degrees at universities, the winner of many marks in Government examinations, we should not repeat the grievous mistakes recorded in our past colonial history and our foreign policy, our trade precepts and our warfare.[47]

Subsequent studies, in particular by Michelle J. Smith, document what happened next (contrary to Sir Harry's wishes) in the 'Golden Age' of children's literature and within a rapid post-war imperial expansion.[48]

If and when Sir Harry's recommendations could be achieved, then would come 'the distant day when the British Empire is fully organised, when the interests of all races are

---

45 Sir Harry H. Johnston G.C.M.G., *The Black Man's Part in the War: An Account of the Dark-Skinned Population of the British Empire, How It Is and Will be Affected by the Great War, and the Share It Has Taken in Waging That War* (London: Simpkin, Marshall, Hamilton and Kent, 1917), p. 7.
46 Ibid., p. 9.
47 Ibid., pp. 10–11.
48 Michelle J. Smith, *Empire in British Girls' Literature and Culture: Imperial Girls 1880–1915* (Houndsmills: Palgrave Macmillan, 2011).

fully represented in all administrations; when the Black Man, having played his part in the Great War, is secure of reaping the benefits of the resultant Peace'.[49]

Soon after the war, a number of 'official' histories also emerged, prepared largely with a view to glorifying settler and, occasionally, indigenous contributions.[50] More recently, historians have produced accounts on the Australian,[51] New Zealander[52] (including the Māori),[53] Canadian[54] and South African experiences,[55] as well as comparative accounts.[56] Research on the recruitment and experience of the non-settler colonies varies in both quality and quantity. There were, of course, several official and personal accounts published during and immediately after the war, mostly celebrating the Indian contribution.[57] There is much secondary literature on Indians,[58] yet not as much on east Africans,[59] Jamaicans in the

---

49 Ibid., p. 128.

50 James Cowan, *The Maoris in the Great War: A History of the New Zealand Native Contingent and Pioneer Battalion: Gallipoli 1915, France and Flanders 1916–1918* (Auckland: Maori Regimental Committee, Whitcombe & Tombs, 1926); Charles E.W. Bean, *Official History of Australia in the War of 1914–1918*, 12 vols (Sydney: Angus & Robertson, 1921–1942); Charles E.W. Bean, *Anzac to Amiens: A Shorter History of the Australian Fighting Services in the First World War* (Canberra: Australian War Memorial, 1946).

51 L.L. Robson, *The First A.I.F.: A Study of Its Recruitment* (Carlton: Melbourne University Press, 1970); Bill Gammage, *The Broken Years: Australian Soldiers in the Great War* (Canberra: Australian National University Press, 1974).

52 Paul Baker, *King and Country Call: New Zealanders, Conscription and the Great War* (Auckland: Auckland University Press, 1988).

53 P.S. O'Connor, 'The Recruitment of Maori Soldiers, 1914–1918,' *Political Science* 19, no. 2 (1967): pp. 48–83; Rikihana Carkeek, *Home Little Maori Home: A Memoir of the Māori Contingent, 1914–1916* (Wellington: Tōtika Publications, 2003); Christopher Pugsley, *Te hokowhitu a tu: The Maori Pioneer Battalion in the First World War* (Auckland: Reed, 1995); Alison Fletcher, 'Recruitment and Service of Maori Soldiers in World War One,' *Itinerario* 38, no. 3 (2014): pp. 59–78.

54 Tim Cook, *At the Sharp End: Canadians Fighting the Great War, 1914–1916* (Toronto: Viking, 2007).

55 Bill Nasson, *Springboks on the Somme: South Africa in the Great War, 1914–1918* (Johannesburg: Penguin, 2007).

56 For example Timothy Winegard, *Indigenous Peoples of the British Dominions and the First World War* (Cambridge: Cambridge University Press, 2012).

57 Lt-Col J.W.B. Merewether and the Rt Hon. Sir Frederick Smith, *The Indian Corps in France*, J. Murray under the authority of His Majesty's Secretary of State for India in Council (London, J. Murray, 1917); H.M. Alexander, *On Two Fronts: Being the Adventures of an Indian Mule Corps in France and Gallipoli* (London: William Heinemann, 1917); John Murray, 'Egyptian Labour Corps, January 1916–June 1917'; Government of India, *India's Contribution to the Great War* (Calcutta, 1923); Frank Cundall, *Jamaica's Part in the Great War, 1915–1918*.

58 Jeffrey Greenhut, 'The Imperial Reserve: The Indian Corps on the Western Front, 1914–15,' *Journal of Imperial and Commonwealth History* 12, no. 1 (1983): pp. 54–73; Shyam Narain Saxena, *Role of Indian Army in the First World War* (Delhi: Bhavna Prakashnan, 1987); David Omissi, *Indian Voices of the Great War* (London: Macmillan, 1999); Omar Khalidi, 'Ethnic Group Recruitment in the Indian Army: The Contrasting Cases of Sikhs, Muslims, Gurkhas and Others,' *Pacific Affairs* 74, no. 4 (2001–2002): pp. 529–52; Gordon Corrigan, *Sepoys in the Trenches* (Gloucestershire: Stroud, 2006); George Morton-Jack, 'The Indian Army on the Western Front, 1914–1915: A Portrait of Collaboration,' *War in History* 13, no. 3 (2006): pp. 329–62; Radhika Singha, 'Finding Labor from India for the War in Iraq: The Jail Porter and Labor Corps, 1916–1920,' *Comparative Studies in Society and History* 39, no. 2 (2007): pp. 412–45.

59 Donald C. Savage and J. Forbes Munro, 'Carrier Corps Recruitment in the British East Africa Protectorate 1914–1918,' *The Journal of African History* 7, no. 2 (1966): pp. 313–42.

British West Indies Regiment,[60] Chinese,[61] Fijians[62] and (only recently) on the Cypriots,[63] but nothing for example on the Maltese. As for the informal empire, there has been very little outside the Middle East[64] and Latin America.[65]

Part 4: synopsis

Almost every author and editor working on the British Empire pleads at the start of their work that there is yet more research to do and that their individual offering cannot claim to be exhaustive. Perhaps the most eloquent of these and a model for our own caveat, is that of Aviel Roshwald and Richard Stites:

> The convergence of our interests has led us to this project, which is conceived of as an occasion to spur the development of interdisciplinary approaches to history and to highlight the complex web of relations between cultural and political history. We strongly believe that a synchronic approach – which to some minds would imply comparing the incomparable in terms of levels of cultural development – is precisely the one that will allow students and scholars to look at the face of Europe in the 1910s and beyond in a novel way. To be sure, the geographical scope of this volume comes at a price, and we are well aware of the many lacunae in this study. The chapters in this collection focus, of necessity, on a small selection out of the vast array of possible topics for each nation.[66]

---

60 W.F. Elkins, 'A Source of Black Nationalism in the Caribbean: The Revolt of the British West Indies Regiment at Taranto, Italy,' *Science and Society* 33, no. 2 (1970): pp. 99–103; C.L. Joseph, 'The British West Indies Regiment, 1914–18,' *Journal of Caribbean History* 2 (1971): pp. 94–124; Richard Smith, *Jamaican Volunteers in the First World War* (Manchester: Manchester University Press, 2004).

61 Nicholas J. Griffin, 'Britain's Chinese Labor Corps in World War I,' *Military Affairs* 40, no. 3 (1976): pp. 102–8; Michael Summerskill, *China on the Western Front: Britain's Chinese Work Force in the First World War* (printed by the author, 1982); Brian C. Fawcett, 'The Chinese Labour Corps in France, 1917–1921,' *Journal of the Hong Kong Branch of the Royal Asiatic Society* 60 (2000): pp. 33–111; Paul J. Bailey, 'From Shandong to Somme: Chinese Indentured Labour in France during World War I,' in *Language, Labour, and Migration*, ed. A.J. Kershen (Farnham: Ashgate, 2000), pp. 179–96; Gwynnie Hagen, 'The Chinese Labour Corps,' in *World War I*, ed. Dominiek Dendooven and Piet Chielens (Tielt: Lanoo, 2008), pp. 136–44; Paul J. Bailey, 'Semi-Colonialism and Cultural Interaction: Chinese Indentured Labor in World War One France and the Sino-French Connection,' in *From Early Tang Court Debates to China's Peaceful Rise*, ed. Friederike Assandri and Dora Martins (Amsterdam: Amsterdam University Press, 2009), pp. 111–20; Paul J. Bailey, '"An Army of Workers": Chinese Indentured Labour in First World War France,' in *Race, Empire and First World War Writing*, ed. Santanu Das (Cambridge: Cambridge University Press, 2011), pp. 35–52.

62 Margaret Pointer, *Tagi tote e loto haaku* [My Heart Is Crying a Little] (Suva: University of the South Pacific, 2000); Christine Liava'a, *Qaravi na'i tavi* [They Did Their Duty] (Auckland: Polygraphia, 2009).

63 Varnava, 'Recruitment and Volunteerism for the Cypriot Mule Corps'.

64 See also Ashley Jackson, *Distant Drums: The Role of the Colonies in British Imperial Warfare* (Sussex: Academic Press, 2010).

65 Trevor Harris, 'British Informal Empire during the Great War: Welsh Identity and Loyalty in Argentina,' *Itinerario* 38, no. 3 (2014): pp. 103–17.

66 Aviel Roshwald and Richard Stites, eds, *European Culture in the Great War* (Cambridge: Cambridge University Press, 2002), p. 6.

Santanu Das's *Race, Empire and First World War Writing* is perhaps structurally and stylistically closest to the collection of essays presented here, as it concerns itself with recovering the war experience of different racial, ethnic and national groups from around the globe to enable a comparative and cross-disciplinary framework for understanding cultural production.[67] In some cases the work is recuperative, in others analytical, but all are bound by the *leitmotif* of war, writing and empire. Wisely, he too warns his reader from the outset that his collection is not, and cannot pretend to be, exhaustive. Instead, the essays encourage the reader to think about exploring, imagining, moralising, politicising, visualising and memorialising cultural responses to travel, encounter and conflict. Mediating between visual, textual and historical discourse, the fluidity and intrinsically contested nature of cultural production comes under the spotlight.[68]

In this present collection John MacKenzie offers an authoritative start by re-writing many long-held 'truths' about the beginning of the end of the empire. Scanning the imperial globe he cites examples that directly refute, as opposed to merely challenge, previous historical assumptions (offered for instance by Ronald Hyam)[69] that the Great War was the beginning of the end for the empire. Instead he suggests a new dawn, and the birth of what might yet have been a golden age. MacKenzie confidently presents a broad analysis (ranging from the movement of people to the rise of multinational companies, and from the boom in shipbuilding and railways to the development of 'Tudorbethan' tropical architecture in Singapore), which suggests an era of re-colonisation at least up to the onset of the Great Depression. The concept of decolonisation itself is also drawn into question, suggesting that this might merely be a misnomer more suitably replaced with 'sub-imperialism', whereby white rule was cemented, perhaps intensified, from regional hubs and centres, as opposed to from London. Setting up much in the way for discussion in the chapters which follow, MacKenzie also takes us through the cinemas and theatres to look for traces of decline, through the Wembley Exhibition in 1924, and finally into the grand scale architectural and urban projects from New Delhi to Lusaka (and echoed in Canberra). Whether looking at the rise of anthropology, forestry, linguistics, animal husbandry, soil science, geology, health, education and more, he presents an upward trajectory in the years that followed peace. Decentralisation of empire may have been a reality, but he refutes that this was the irreversible onset of decolonisation. There was nothing inevitable about the demise that came, just as there had been nothing inevitable about the great imperial powers going to war in the first place. Phillip Buckner and Douglas Francis have suggested a similar thesis elsewhere, advocating that the modern historian tread with care, as there was no real demonstrable belief that the empire was threatened, immoral or on borrowed time, at the time of the Great War.[70] Timothy Parsons also notes how, statistically at least, the war made the United Kingdom the world's only real superpower as isolationism took hold in the

---

67 Santanu Das, ed., *Race, Empire and First World War Writing* (Cambridge: Cambridge University Press, 2014); see also Joanna de Groot, *Empire and History Writing in Britain c. 1750–2012* (Manchester: Manchester University Press, 2013).

68 These are similar observations to those suggested in: Geoff Quilley, *Empire to Nation: Art, History and the Visualization of Maritime Britain c. 1768–1829* (New Haven, CT: Yale University Press, 2011).

69 Ronald Hyam, *Britain's Declining Empire: The Road to Decolonisation, 1918–1968* (Cambridge: Cambridge University Press, 2006).

70 See Phillip Buckner and R. Douglas Francis, *Rediscovering the British World* (Calgary: Calgary University Press, 2005).

United States, so much so that by 1919 the empire had 450 million subjects, over 33 million square kilometres, on six continents.[71] Bernard Porter mused at the end of his oft-reprinted study *The Lion's Share* that the war actually had the potential to bind the empire together, with a common cause, forcing it to act as one, and giving a glimpse of what it might yet be like. He observed '[t]he flavour was exciting, even intoxicating. If they could build on it after the war, there was no saying what the empire could yet become.'[72]

Part two, 'Imperial Responses, Identities and Culture', begins with a study on the war and propaganda in the empire in which Richard Scully examines 'the world's first globally-recognised cartoon character' (the Kaiser), and analyses how it, and he, was treated throughout the British imperial world. His essay demands that we take a serious and analytical look at comic art as a global phenomenon offering vital insights into networks of communication and mechanisms of information exchange brought about by empire, then catalysed by war. It is telling how cartoonists who wished 'to dip their pens in vitriol' behaved differently in Britain, France, Russia, Australia, South Africa and the United States, evoking different artistic, moral, ethical and political stances through, amongst other things, sexuality and religion. For example, Louis Raemaekers, a Dutchman in London, was an artist with a price on his head in Germany yet belonged to a 'profession' that Theodore Roosevelt said had made 'the most powerful of the honourable contributions made by neutrals to the cause of civilization'.[73] But there were others who history has forgotten and one cannot help but wonder what might *their* impact have been? John Towlinson claimed that '[t]he "lived reality" of national identity is a reality lived in representations – not in direct communal solidarity' using such devices.[74] Such, it seems, was the case and more research, as advocated by the author, is required. It is certainly a relevant and timely lesson in the power of the popular image, as a precursor to the age of ubiquitous media in which we live today. In music too, both the enthusiasm of those men and women who volunteered to entertain the troops and support services, and the impact this had, forms the focus of the next chapter by Emma Hanna. Almost immediately musical icons such as 'Pack up your troubles in your old kit bag' (a song worth six divisions to the British Army) appeared and remain, a century later, deeply embedded in our own cultural 'memory' of that fateful summer of 1914. British composers, musicians and entertainers worked to mobilise music of all kinds to boost the morale of those serving the British Empire, while at home the debate raged about performing 'enemy' composers (Richard Strauss, Richard Wagner, and so on), and all the time a steady flow of allied *émigré* composers and performers gravitated towards the nexus of London. It was clear that music mattered whether at the opera house, the music hall or charitable concerts organised by the Young Men's Christian Association – the latter promoting its own brand of philanthropic education and 'noble influence' as far away as India. Properly harnessed, and led by great names such as Gustav Holst and Edward Elgar, Hanna concludes, music proved a powerful weapon in the armoury of the British Empire during the First World War.

---

71 Timothy H. Parsons, *The Second British Empire: In the Crucible of the Twentieth Century* (Lanham, MD: Rowman and Littlefield, 2014), p. 55.

72 Porter, *The Lion's Share*, p. 198.

73 Thomas Fleming, *The Illusion of Victory: American in World War I* (New York: Basic, 2003), p. 57; Theodore Roosevelt, 'The Genius of Raemaekers,' *Land & Water*, 7 June 1917, p. 19.

74 Kathleen Wilson, 'Citizenship, Empire, and Modernity in the English Provinces, *c.* 1720–90,' in *Cultures of Empire: A Reader: Colonizer in Britain and the Empire in the Nineteenth and Twentieth Centuries*, ed. Catherine Hall (Manchester: Manchester University, 2000), p. 160.

Throughout the years a great deal has been written on loyalty and identity in the settler colonies towards the British Empire during the Great War[75] and the essay by Gregory Hynes adds yet another, somewhat unexpected, dimension to the complicated relationship. In 1907 the colony of New Zealand became a dominion, a shift that raised issues of sovereignty and national identity that would be catalysed at Gallipoli and in other theatres of the war. It is ingrained in the nation's history how the small country with a population of just over 1 million people, sent over 100,000 men to serve overseas, close to 17,000 of which were killed and over 40,000 wounded.[76] Yet Hynes demonstrates, despite cultural nationalist histories and popular myths to the contrary, that London was in fact reluctant to dictate to the dominions, and became involved by request only. It seems unusual to learn that the Colonial Office even blocked propaganda destined for New Zealand. We learn too of the intrinsic Britishness of the population of New Zealand, sharing as they did common moral, ethical and religious traits, and of how they might even have seen themselves as superior to their British ancestors and compatriots, as now they could add the 'pioneering spirit' and experience to the national characteristics inherently bequeathed to them. As one of the most distant countries on earth from the war itself, New Zealand too could claim the moral high-ground in responding to a call to quell a threat that was of no immediate concern to the islands or their inhabitants (though the indigenous population may have seen some double standards in New Zealand going to war to help the United Kingdom fight for the rights of small nations such as Belgium and Serbia). Jan Asmussen takes the focus further away from the norm by exploring a *former* part of the British Empire. His essay demonstrates clearly how the very small community of Heligoland, ceded by the British to its imperial rival Germany in 1890 after eighty-three years of control, with a people resident on apparently insignificant outcrops of land, could get caught in the ebb and flow of imperial rivalry. They, and their populations, could be bartered for and traded in geographically wide ranging deals, while the sea surrounding them, normally the source of sustainability through fishing, would become the site of the Great War's only major naval engagement at Jutland. It is a sobering tale of the ideologies and mentalities of small communities, forced to choose and change between mighty empires; of mixed loyalties and disloyalties and confused identities; of communities that in time are destroyed from the air by their one-time governors and benefactors; of the helplessness, vulnerability and perhaps culpability of a small community caught in a global conflict, and the tragic consequences that follow. It is a vivid insight into the pawns, rather than the principal pieces, in a complex imperial game of what Blyth and Jeffery referred to as 'contested entities.'[77] Matthew Kennedy then turns his attention to Singapore, to the dying days of the Great War, to the anticipation of another one to come, and to the romantic notion of 'great men' – in this case Lord Jellicoe of Scapa. In this essay he explores the proposed creation of a Far Eastern Seagoing Fleet, based in the port in Singapore (which was to act as the 'naval key to the Far East'), and created in anticipation of the expiry of the Anglo-Japanese alliance in 1921. As a modern day Horatio Nelson, the plan was submitted on Trafalgar Day (also mentioned in Greg Hynes' essay), and was designed to dwarf all previous levels of military spending. Was

---

75   Especially as regards Australia, see Michael J.K. Walsh and Andrekos Varnava, eds, *Australia and the Great War: Identity, Memory and Mythology* (Melbourne: Melbourne University Press, 2016).
76   Michael King, *History of New Zealand* (ReadHowYouWant, 2012), p. 303.
77   Robert J. Blyth and Keith Jeffery, *The British Empire and Its Contested Pasts* (Dublin; Portland, OR: Irish Academic Press, 2009).

this the proposal of a visionary, a 'great man' who crystallised the sentiment of the nation now burdened with maintaining global security, or instead, the embodiment of what Leo Tolstoy saw as poseurs, self-aggrandisers and charlatans, blinded in a culture of victory and now entrusted with imperial might?[78] And how too might the plan be received by other 'great men' globally who were far from united in their support for the authority of imperial heroes?

In Part Three of the book, titled 'Art, Memory and Forgetting', Jonathan Black takes the reader into the world of fine art, to the depiction of Indian and Caribbean servicemen, Chinese labourers, and to the power of the portrait which Benjamin Haydon called 'one of the staple manufactures of the empire'.[79] The importance of such subjects has often been downplayed in history and until recently, in some cases, almost forgotten. Santanu Das noted:

> Colonial troops were depicted, at best, as gallant, courageous, loyal, ferocious, but they were said to lack the qualities of European master: qualities of leadership, stoicism, decision making: moreover, their sexual appetites were said to be voracious, their battlefield practices savage.[80]

Whether the artist was recording the global and imperial nature of war, or codifying a respect for the civilisation and culture of the sitter in an artistic homage, the resultant canvases, often censored, speak volumes. Through the diverse works of William Rothenstein (of German-Jewish ancestry), Eric Kennington (who depicted Inuit and West Indians in the ranks of the Canadian-Highland Scots), Percy Wyndham Lewis (who drew parallels between the Western Front and *Alice in Wonderland*) and the respectful James McBey (in the 'sideshow' of Egypt, Sinai and Syria) we have an insight into not only the theatres of war in which conflict took place, but the attitudes and priorities of the artists and those who commissioned them. We see too the presence of superstitions, the appeal of notoriety and the creation of the perception of 'sober dignity' in these faraway places. New names emerge too, such as Thomas Cantrell Dugdale and Stuart Reid, with their depictions of Salonica and Palestine. We must keep in mind that when McBey returned to the Middle East in February 1919 the British Empire still had over one million men in Palestine, Lebanon, Syria and Mesopotamia. Remaining with the Middle East, specifically Iraq, Tim Buck offers a fascinating study of the various imaginative post-war configurations of painters and how these were perceived in the immediate years after the Armistice and well into the 1920s. Depicting a virtually forgotten, visually distant campaign was always going to be a challenge for artists in a geography that had produced the meandering imaginations of 'Orientalism' before succumbing to the inevitable realities of post-war westernisation. In addition, as a subject for painting this was not only war, and imperial war, it was in and from the air. Frustratingly the *avant-garde* in painting was not encouraged as a 'genre' even if the subject matter involved the excitement and dynamism of flight, aerial combat and

---

78 See Andrekos Varnava, ed., *Imperial Expectations and Realities: El Dorados, Utopias and Dystopias* (Manchester: Manchester University Press, 2015).

79 Benjamin Robert Haydon, *Life of Benjamin Robert Haydon: Historical Painter, from His Autobiography and Journals* (London: Longman, 1853), p. 377.

80 Santanu Das, *Race, Empire and First World War Writing* (Cambridge: Cambridge University Press, 2011), pp. 18–19.

the creation of the 'airscape'.[81] The job of artists, in this case Richard and Sydney Carline (and the female painter Edith Cheeseman), in this post-war theatre was to create a record of events, memorialise them, depict them, immortalise them and perhaps even historicise painful defeats like the surrender at Kut al-Amara. The British undoubtedly had had an interesting relationship with pre-war Mesopotamia, but this was now a mandate and a costly British administrative and military apparatus that came under intense scrutiny in parliament and the newspapers, and with a rapidly polarising public opinion.[82] Iraq continues to do that to this day. On some levels polarisation is also evident in Nuala C. Johnson's study of how three Irish artists, two from Belfast (in the 'Imperial Province') and one from Dublin ('Rebel Ireland'), visualised the Great War at this turbulent time. William Orpen (a Dublin Protestant) and John Lavery (a Belfast Catholic) were society artists of the British 'establishment' working through the official war artists' scheme, while William Conor (a Belfast Presbyterian) was not; Orpen and Lavery produced portfolios of the human and physical costs of war (and the emotional and moral landscapes of it) and were rewarded with knighthoods, while Conor produced depictions of the intimate spaces of community associated with soldiers in training at Ballykinlar in 1915 and munitions workers in Belfast. Yet ultimately all three painters had much in common. Their works interrogated the significance of the space of conflict and the interconnectedness between soldiers fighting and the infrastructural, economic and political support of the home front. They also touch upon the deeper complexities of ideological commitment to Ireland, described by Johnson as 'geographies of allegiance', before, during and after the Great War. On a personal note, this insight into Protestant Belfast, and the training of the 36th Ulster Division in 1915 at Ballykinlar before departure for France was an unexpected surprise as I hope Figure 1.1 illustrates. There, in the third row, second from left, is my great uncle (Walter Henry 'Harry' Walsh) training in Ballykinlar in 1915 as part of the 36th Ulster division and destined for the Somme where he received his fatal wound during the charge at Thiepval on 1 July 1916. I wonder does he appear in any of Conor's lesser known paintings or sketchbooks? The chapter is doubly poignant as it was John Lavery who painted the ghastly spectacle of the military cemetery at Etaples in 1919 where Harry was buried alongside other young Irishmen captured in this image.

Jennifer Wellington's essay follows very nicely from here as it observes the attitudes and strategies of other young nations, namely Australia and Canada, then accounts for the importance their officials placed on the collection of 'artefacts' and 'war trophies', and exhibiting photographs at the imperial centre during the war itself. This, it was believed, would not only remobilise, or rather reinvigorate, their weary populations but also offer 'authenticity', verity, realism and proximity to a public hungry for it. This was the 'reality' of fighting dominion troops, engaged in consolidating their imperial loyalty and establishing their distinctive national character that would give rise to the post-war narrative that claimed that war itself had been the crucible of the nation. The collections would, in time, form the basis for the national narrative to be retold in perpetuity while photographers such as Frank Hurley in Australia and Ivor Castle in Canada would demonstrate convincingly that,

---

81 The term was coined by Frank Rutter in the *Arts Gazette* (28 June 1917); see Michael J.K. Walsh, 'This Tumult in the Clouds,' *British Art Journal* V, no. 1, (2004): pp. 81–7.

82 See Ann Matters, 'The British Mesopotamian El Dorado: The Restoration of the Garden of Eden,' in *Imperial Expectations and Realities: El Dorados, Utopias and Dystopias*, ed. Andrekos Varnava (Manchester: Manchester University Press, 2015), pp. 210–27.

Figure 1.1   Walter Henry 'Harry' Walsh, third row, second from left. Ballykinlar, 1915

Source: Private Collection

through their medium, spectacle and empire could advance hand in hand. Staying with the power of things seen, Justin Fantauzzo's essay turns to the stage – a performative moment of immersive entertainment with significant global repercussions from a collective audience of some 4 million (in prime locations such as Madison Square Garden, the Royal Opera House, the Royal Albert Hall and so on). Jeffrey Richards confidently stated that '[t]he birth of cinema coincided with the high noon of the British Empire,'[83] while James Chapman and Nicholas Cull have reinforced this by claiming that '[f]rom its outset cinema has been a vehicle for disseminating images and ideologies of empire.'[84] Now a version/adaptation of it was being used in a complex visual presentation that was destined to bring the war in Sinai, Palestine and the Holy Land, to audiences in Australia, India and Ireland, each of

---

83 Series editor introduction in James Chapman and Nicholas J. Cull, *Projecting Empire: Imperialism and Popular Cinema* (London: I.B. Tauris, 2009), p. ix.
84 Ibid., p. 1.

whom in their own ways were experiencing shifting allegiances and ties to the empire. It mapped emergent nationalisms and new mandates at the beginning of a century that would end in chaos in the Middle East. This essay is a most telling insight into the power of the still and moving image, the projection, the stage set, music and emotive narrative not only to enable the telling of history but to its creation.

Tim Barringer turns our attention to architecture and to the important role it played and continues to play in imperial relations. The modest chattri designed by a young Indian architect, essentially modelled on Mughal India, and set in a landscape of quintessential Englishness, draws from the reader exacting questions not only about the Hindu and Sikh servicemen cremated there, but about the vast network that linked India to the empire via the war. In addition to its genesis, the study also charts an intriguing and perhaps telling course through its short history of decline, decay, re-use and pilgrimage, up to an including the present day. Within, there is the history of not only Indians in Britain, but of Britain in India and of all the itinerant debates that result on race, ethnicity, attitude, ideology, intention and honour. It is an essay too that explores the global significance of the treatment of Indian wounded in Brighton's Regency period Royal Pavilion and Dome modelled loosely by John Nash on the Taj Mahal. Reported meticulously, down to details on caste sensitivities, religious requirements in the preparation of food and bathing, the creation of separate water supplies for Hindus and Muslims and so on, the notion of a sensitive, caring and sophisticated imperialism grounded in etiquette and cultural sensitivity could migrate from Sussex to the four corners of the earth (this resonates with the 'responsible imperialism' suggested by Greg Hynes in his chapter on New Zealand and the 'enlightened despotism' suggested by David A. Johnson in New Delhi). In obvious ways David Johnson's essay flows perfectly from that by Tim Barringer, while simultaneously setting up an intriguing contrast with the 'Foreword' by Richard Cork, taking us from a war memorial in England to another in India itself. The stories of the George V Memorial Statue and the All-India War Memorial (now India Gate) in Delhi, brainchild of Edwin Lutyens and Herbert Baker (and sculptor Charles Sargeant Jagger), are fascinating examples of how the shifting sands of sovereignty changed the meaning and significance of these public spaces. Symbols and interactions of imperialism, physically linking power to sacrifice and an overall 'spirit', were unmistakable in an ever-evolving Delhi at the time of the all-important Government of India Act. Created to mark Indian sacrifices in the British armed forces, and encapsulate the narrative of human progress under British rule, its meaning and significance were soon re-crafted to honour sacrifices made in the name of the independent state post 1947. By adapting, controlling and manipulating the colonial past, a new nationalist present and future could be created on the bedrock of the experience of the Great War.

In Australia emotional adherence to empire, and indeed attitudes to studying it, is often accompanied by a 'cultural cringe'. A century ago this was not the case and the creation of 'Better Britons' or 'Neo-Britons' was quite distinct from the creation of 'anti-Britons'.[85] Through his study of Australian music of or about the Great War, composer Andrew Harrison exposes a cultural *lacunae* that is difficult to comprehend and certainly in urgent need of further scholarly examination. He claims convincingly that however familiar people may be with the great poets and playwrights (such as Henry Lawson and Alan Seymour), or with the key painted and sculpted masterpieces (by artists Arthur Streeton and Sidney Nolan)

---

85 Phillip Buckner and R. Douglas Francis, *Rediscovering the British World* (Calgary: Calgary University Press, 2005).

and other popular media (Peter Weir – film, Frank Hurley – photography, Eric Bogle – folk music), there is little familiarity with Australian 'art music' and composers in relation to the war, nor a particularly clear understanding of its relationship with the nation-building process. Harrison's essay therefore inserts into the debate names of composers hitherto almost entirely forgotten such as Frederick Septimus Kelly (a contemporary and friend of Rupert Brooke who was later killed at the Somme), Henry Tate, Roy Agnew, Martin Mather, Vincent Plush, Graham Koehne, Helen Gifford and a musical composition by the author himself. It is an original conclusion, I feel, to a lineage yet to be fully understood.

Turning to contemporary popular history in the form of television Evan Smith then explores the fictional world of the 'returned soldier', the anti-hero and the 'brutalised veteran' in an inter-war vacuum on both sides of the Atlantic where organised crime flourished. Political activism was rife too through the Irish question, the Red Scare, and the activities of the Ku Klux Klan. All in all it is a glimpse, albeit a fictional one, at a dream or rather nightmare reality, fuelled by trauma, memory and for some the unsuccessful quest for recovery. It is perhaps sobering for the historian to realise that this is how history can be created, how memories are invented and how reality can be obscured in a performative moment of forgetting. Here perhaps, a century after the event, is the personification of what Philip Gibbs had referred to when he wrote, 'Many were easily moved to passion where they lost control of themselves, many were bitter in their speech, violent in opinion, frightening.'[86] The final chapter presents a fascinating case study of forgetting: specifically of how the experience of a significant cohort of men, about 25 per cent of the Cypriot male population ages 18–35, served in the Cypriot Mule Corps between 1916 and 1920, yet did not enter Cypriot 'national consciousness' in the years that followed. Andrekos Varnava, building on his own family history, takes a multilayered approach to re-telling the story, touching upon the personal, as well as the socio-economic and socio-political conditions that contributed to this forgetting or induced amnesia. The complex 'Cyprus problem', polarised between *enosis* and *taksim*, looms large, as do the priorities and activities of Cypriot political elites, during the rise of both right and left wing movements in the island. United by an anti-imperialist agenda the political climate ensured that the Cypriot Mule Corps was reduced to a footnote of history (comparisons with Malta and Jamaica are tempting). As with so many of the other essays in this collection, we observe again how post-imperial discourses demand a reconfiguration of events in the past to suit new and desired trajectories. Where they cannot be re-crafted, they are often erased.

Part 5: concluding comments

The ideals and aesthetics of imperialism, we insist, go hand in hand with geographies of imperial imagination and creativity and thus necessitate the examination of both the culture of power and the power of culture, as well as the politics of culture and the culture of politics, in relation to the British Empire and the Great War. Cultural histories of warfare are therefore bound up in the complex responses and experiences of communities involved and affected, as well as in the representation, remembering and forgetting of these responses and experiences. Roshwald and Stites concur:

---

86 Phillip Gibbs, 'Now It Can Be Told,' cited in: Eric J. Leed, *No Man's Land: Combat and Identity in World War I* (Cambridge: Cambridge University Press, 1979), pp. 547–8.

World War I is an ideal framework for a comparative analysis of such relationships, given that the attempted total mobilization of society, the co-opting of artists into the propaganda effort, the recent emergence of film and other media technologies, the immersion of many writers and artists in the trench experience all served to make it a turning point in the development of new cultural syntheses.[87]

Whether that happened or not is still being debated. In the meantime, Kalypso Nicolaïdis, Berny Sèbe and Gabrielle Maas suggest that our options, when watching the descent of the imperial 'mission civilisatrice' into the unparalleled barbarism of the Great War, are amnesia, rejection or atonement.[88] That said, cultural production in relation to both the Great War and the British Empire is not yet confined to the past tense. The opening of the Memorial Gates at Hyde Park Corner in London to commemorate the services of the Indian sub-continent, Africa and the Caribbean; the increased space devoted to the South African Native Labour Corps in the museum for South African troops in Delville Wood in France; or the exhibition 'Man-Culture-War: Multicultural Aspects of the First World War' at 'In Flanders Fields Museum', Ypres are indicators that a re-thinking is fully under way. Simultaneously, as this manuscript goes to press, a very different kind of centenary of empire and war gets under way – that of the Easter Rising in Ireland. By contrast, 11,000 kilometres away in Southeast Asia, it will be interesting to observe the reaction that the *Artist and Empire* exhibition (with which this chapter began) garners when it closes in London and travels to the newly opened National Gallery of Singapore in late 2016 – two years after our conference, over half a century after Singapore's independence from the British Empire and more than a century after the outbreak of the Great War.

---

87 Aviel Roshwald and Richard Stites, *European Culture in the Great War* (Cambridge: Cambridge University Press, 1999), p. 5.

88 Kalypso Nicolaïdis, Berny Sèbe and Gabrielle Maas, *Echoes of Empire: Memory, Identity and Colonial Legacies* (London: I.B. Taurus, 2015).

Chapter 2
The First World War and the cultural, political and environmental transformation of the British Empire

John M. MacKenzie

Historians are professionally inclined to look over their shoulders. It is not just that they have to be wary about the daggers out to stab them in the back, it is also the fact that their trade deals in *a posteriori* explanations. Looking backward is in the nature of the practice of their profession. The search for origins and causes is hard-wired into the very systems of their methodologies. Thus they take great epoch-making turning points, such as the First World War of the twentieth century, and seek to establish the roots of such transformatory events. They not only set out to develop theories based on deductions from past facts, they are constantly thinking in terms of origins, of sources – sources as in rivers rather than documents – that lead to the great flows of history. This often leads them to deal in what become myths of origin that colour the writing of their histories.

Studies of the First World War offer a notable example. It is apparent that the Great War was one of the most destructive conflicts of modern history. The observable fact that Europe blew up into unconscionable violence in 1914 has led some historians to imagine that the preceding quarter or half-century must have led inexorably to this point. Pending conflict offered meaning to imperial scrambles, Nile confrontations, Central Asian anxieties, dangerous alliance systems, Moroccan crises and the like. Imperialism as both a set of historical facts and as a concept seemed to have competition and tension built into its very fabric. But it may well be that the reality was very different, that European powers actually spent a great deal of time cooperating in the whole business of the establishment of imperial power in the wider world. There is no need to tread on that hoary old controversy of whether the First World War had its origins in imperial activity or not. The point is a different one. This is that if you take the Great War out of the equation and avoid seeing the era of high imperialism through the lens of the war, you get a wholly different viewpoint, one that reveals a series of carefully organised conferences dealing with imperial ground rules, with (albeit spurious) concepts like 'effective occupation', with the slave trade, with firearms and indigenous peoples, with the conservation of wildlife, with scientific and medical endeavours, with missionary activity, with systems of administration and so on.[1] We are only just becoming aware of the fact that in European imperialism, cooperation

---

1 These treaties include the General Act of the Conference of Berlin of 1885, the Brussels treaty or Convention relative to the Slave Trade and the importation into Africa of firearms, ammunition and spirituous liquors of 1890, the Heligoland Treaty also of 1890 and the Convention for the Preservation of Wild Animals, Birds and Fish in Africa of 1900 (sometimes known as the London Convention).

and communication may have been more significant than competition and conflict.[2] But we should always remember this is not necessarily a benign phenomenon: these were invariably forms of cooperation that militated against the interests of indigenous peoples.

There are three examples – which are all connected in a chain – in the pursuit of the interests of imperial rule. First, European powers were eager to eradicate the African and Indian Ocean slave traders.[3] As recently converted sinners, they knew well that here was a convenient means of legitimating their approach to Africa – and this offered a form of legitimation that seemed to create a civilised club, one in which Europeans could indeed cooperate. Another locus of cooperation was ensuring that firearms were kept out of the hands of Africans.[4] This was billed as a means of creating peace, as a route to the suppression of that very slave trade and to various forms of internal disorder. It was also, of course, a means of ensuring that opposition to European rule was rendered more difficult. Another convenient connection to firearm suppression and confiscation related to the environment. Europeans sought to ensure that the right to hunt wild animals should be regulated by legislation, by permits, by the restriction in the use of firearms and by the (later) establishment of wildlife reserves and national parks in many African colonies.[5] The Germans and the British, for example, cooperated closely in these objectives and they can be seen in every case as militating against the interests of Africans; not just in denying them access to the protein products of the hunt, but also in removing land, sometimes very large tracts of land, from areas that might otherwise be inhabited by indigenous peoples. All of this led to the notorious claim that Europeans were bringing forms of, what they ironically called, 'pacification' to their colonies, colonies which were often about to be subjected to unprecedented acts of European violence.

We can add to all of this the fact that balm had been spread on the real pressure points of imperialism in the years before the First World War. Anglo-French tensions in Africa had been resolved, particularly after the 1904 concord. Even that great running sore, the Great Game on the north-west frontier of India, seemed to have been healed by the Anglo-Russian agreement of 1907. Meanwhile, the Germans and the British were in such a mood for cooperation that in the aftermath of the fall of the Portuguese crown in 1910, they cheerfully and secretly collaborated on a design to carve up the Portuguese empire in Africa between

---

[2] John M. MacKenzie, 'European Imperialism: A Zone of Co-Operation Rather Than Competition,' in *Imperial Co-Operation and Transfer, 1870–1930*, ed. Volker Barth and Roland Cvetkowski (London: Bloomsbury, 2015), pp. 35–53; and other contributions to the same volume.

[3] The propaganda surrounding the death of David Livingstone was very much devoted to this end. See also Sir Frederick Lugard, *The Rise of Our East African Empire*, vols. 1–2 (London: Blackwood, 1893). The classic imperial historian Sir Reginald Coupland was in the same business in his books *East Africa and Its Invaders* (Oxford: Clarendon, 1938); and Coupland, *The Exploitation of East Africa, 1856–1890* (London: Faber & Faber, 1939).

[4] All British colonies, as well as those of France, Belgium, Germany and Portugal legislated to this effect by the end of the nineteenth century or early in the twentieth century.

[5] John M. MacKenzie, *The Empire of Nature: Hunting, Conservation and British Imperialism* (Manchester: Manchester University Press, 1988); Bernhard Gissibl, *The Nature of German Imperialism: Conservation and the Politics of Wild Life in Colonial Tanzania* (Oxford: Berghahn, 2016); Bernhard Gissibl, Sabine Höhler and Patrick Kupper, eds, *Civilising Nature: National Parks in Global Perspective* (Oxford: Berghahn, 2012).

them.[6] This was on the assumption that the Portuguese republic would have no stomach for empire. In fact, of course, the opposite was eventually the case and that extraordinary agreement never came into play.

The same mistaken backward-looking search for origins applies to decolonisation. We now know that the post–Second World War period led to an extraordinarily rapid sequence of acts of decolonisation, starting with the supposed liberation of Asian colonies, India, Pakistan, Ceylon, Burma, by the British, together with Indonesia in the case of the Dutch, in the late 1940s, as well as the scuttle out of Palestine as the British handed over an intractable problem to the United Nations. These acts of decolonisation accelerated with striking speed into withdrawals from Indochina, West Africa and elsewhere in the 1950s, then, perhaps even more surprisingly, a further wave of African decolonisation by the British, the Belgians and the French in the 1960s, and then the Portuguese in the 1970s, and we have to add to that the rapid departure from the West Indies. The great imperial behemoths of the nineteenth century were thrown off in the space of twenty to thirty years. All this was totally unexpected, but the fact of rapid decolonisation has led historians into all sorts of myths of origin. The fabric of empire must have been already threadbare for this to happen. The seeds of decolonisation must have been sown in preceding historical events. The First World War, with its apparent fillip to the nationalisms of the British white dominions, leading to the Balfour Report and Definition of Dominion Status of 1926 and the Statute of Westminster of 1931, must offer just such a source.[7] Likewise the serious unrest the Great War uncovered in the Indian sub-continent leading both to violent resistance and acts of repression in 1919 and later to reluctant acts of constitutional advance in the 1930s. The conditions leading to the events of the 1940s to 1970s were laid down then.

Thus the First World War becomes a sort-of catch-all explanation. On the one hand it leads to a search for its origins in conflict amongst the European empires. This is the backward-looking gaze. Then, the great constitutional turning point of decolonisation stimulates a search for origins in the weakening of European empires in the First World War, the re-balancing of international power systems, weakening and re-balancing which is more than amply confirmed by the events of the Second World War. The First World War becomes a sort of hinge or lever that articulates the events of the decades that went before and also those that came afterwards. Decolonisation is thus seen as almost a deterministic event, one that is inseparably related to shifts in the tectonic plates of power relationships and strategic realities. The point I am making here is not that historians are necessarily wrong to establish these connections, but that they are wrong to highlight them to the exclusion of all others.

We should also, perhaps, feel uncomfortable with historical explanations that concentrate solely on high politics, grand power relationships, the apparently geological scale of historical events and great explanatory designs. We may perhaps call this the 'space station' approach. The world is looked at from outside the realities on the ground. Real people, with the exception of a few power brokers, presidents and prime ministers, are scarcely seen at all, indigenous people and women of all ethnicities are totally invisible.

---

6 P.H.S. Hatton, 'Harcourt and Solf: The Search for an Anglo-German Understanding Through Africa, 1912–1914,' *European History Quarterly* 1, no. 2 (1971): pp. 123–45.

7 Ronald Hyam, *Britain's Declining Empire: The Road to Decolonisation, 1918–1968* (Cambridge: Cambridge University Press, 2006); this constitutes a classic statement of this view, among several others.

And, above all, cultural and environmental phenomena are almost entirely left out of the equation. If we look at those real people, if we examine cultural and environmental concerns, we come up with rather different viewpoints.

The fact of the matter is that what we know as the inter-war years, 'the long weekend' in the words of Robert Graves, only became a brief Saturday, Sunday and Monday of respite between two massive conflicts in retrospect.[8] For people of the colonising powers who were around in the years after the First World War, it was, hopefully, business as usual. When it comes to the British Empire, far from these years seeming like a final struggle on the edge of the precipice of decolonisation, the era felt like a hoped-for new dawn.[9] Obviously the major problem here is the sheer diversity of the British Empire in its five main categories – first the white dominions, second India, third the so-called dependent empire in Africa and South-East Asia, fourth the new mandates created in the aftermath of war and fifth the island colonies of the Caribbean, the Indian Ocean and the Pacific plus of course surviving oddments in the Mediterranean. Conditions in each of these were very different. Economies and societies can be categorised in a variety of ways, but perhaps most clearly as between those with dominant settler groups, those with mining or agricultural sectors and between those where the war had stimulated some industrialisation and import substitution and those where such a development was impossible. We should perhaps add in, as a wholly separate category, Ireland, where developments during and after the First World War constituted a form of decolonisation within the British state itself. Here, the war was certainly crucial, at least in speeding up the rate of political change, although all the conditions for Irish revolution were there in the years leading up to the conflict.

But despite the diversity of the extra-European colonial systems of the British, we can detect some empire-wide trends, and we can test this sense of new beginnings, rather than a declining fall in a variety of ways. First, the post-war economic boom, however brief, certainly served to mask realities in all sorts of ways. In the case of Britain itself, the shipbuilding industry, for example, seemed to flourish again re-building the losses of the war years. This was also true of some other industries, even if some degree of import substitution in the Dominions, as well as evidence of the decline of such industries (as that of jute) in Dundee seemed now fairly apparent, in the latter case, as a result of effective Indian competition in Bengal.[10] But the great imperial cities of Britain, notably Glasgow, Liverpool and Manchester seemed to make some return to the conditions of the pre-war years. Infrastructural developments across the empire had similar effects, for example in the building of new ports or the continuation of railway and locomotive building. Moreover, some of the raw materials of empire emerged as truly important in this period. These would include copper in Northern Rhodesia (Zambia) and tin or rubber in Malaya (Malaysia), both stimulated by the new industrial developments of the age. In the case of rubber, the considerable growth in the manufacture of cars and trucks, as well as the continuing popularity of the bicycle, were the key stimulants. Although overproduction,

---

8 Robert Graves and Alan Hodge, *The Long Weekend* (London: Faber & Faber, 1941).

9 Krishan Kumar, 'Empire, Nation, and National Identities,' in *Britain's Experience of Empire in the Twentieth Century*, ed. Andrew Thompson (Oxford: Oxford University Press, 2012), p. 312. Krishan Kumar has supported the notion that there was 'increased confidence' in the empire after the First World War.

10 For jute, see Gordon T. Stewart, *Jute and Empire* (Manchester: Manchester University Press, 1998); and Jim Tomlinson, *Dundee and the Empire: "Juteopolis", 1850–1939* (Edinburgh: Edinburgh University Press, 2014).

both in rubber and tin, produced dramatic price fluctuations, to some extent this was truly the heyday of the Malayan plantation culture and that, of course, had a considerable effect upon the trade of Singapore.[11] Continuing with this local focus, peak prices were obtained for rubber up to the slump of 1920 and for tin in 1926. Yet despite the economic instability of these years, underlying growth continued. New exports like palm oil and pineapples developed in this era. Imperial and multinational companies moved in and required housing for their staffs. The civil service similarly grew. Singapore exported a very high proportion of the trade of Malaya, and the Colonial Secretary Leopold Amery boasted at the imperial conference of 1926 that it had grown from £78 million in 1923 to £150 million in 1925. And the architectural fabric of this island colony is full of evidence of the boom years. For example, the distinctive black and white 'Tudorbethan tropical' architecture of the time produced multiple examples, not only in elite private residences, but also in public buildings.[12] Developments like this can be replicated in many other colonies, even if the whole period culminated in major labour problems in, for example, the Caribbean and Northern Rhodesia.

If we turn to the question of the mobility of Europeans, this is a period of renewed migration. Indeed, migration to the territories of settlement of the British Empire, as a proportion of total migration, increased rapidly on the eve of the war. Eric Richards has calculated that between 1891–1900, a mere 28 per cent of British emigrants went to the Dominions; between 1901–1912, it was 63 per cent while in 1913 it was 78 per cent. In the 1920s, it was roughly 66 per cent on a rather lower total figure of well over 600,000.[13] Despite intensive renewed propaganda, migration was in decline. But continuing migration was helped by new technologies and relatively comfortable ocean passages. Migrants also headed for the regions of informal empire in South America, as well as in smaller trickles to settler territories like Kenya or Southern and Northern Rhodesia, although it must be said that they seemed more like larger streams than trickles to the local peoples. There were post-war soldier settlement schemes[14] and continuing plans to 'export' supposedly disadvantaged children, arrangements that have produced a sense of scandals and shocked disbelief in more modern times.[15] As well as renewed migration, admittedly pent up by the conditions of the war, the rhetoric that migration constituted social reform writ large and even a means of overcoming the problems of unemployment, made a re-appearance. In addition, there were economic and cultural indicators that led James Belich to suggest

---

11   Standard histories chart these economic shifts: D.G.E. Hall, *A History of South-East Asia* (London: Macmillan, 1961); J. Kennedy, *A History of Malaya* (London: Macmillan, 1961); C.M. Turnbull, *A History of Modern Singapore, 1819–2005* (Singapore: National University of Singapore Press, 1977).

12   Julian Davison, *Black and White: The Singapore House, 1898–1941* (Singapore: Talisman, 2009); Norman Edwards, *The Singapore House and Residential Life, 1819–1939* (Oxford: Oxford University Press, 1991).

13   Eric Richards, *Britannia's Children: Emigration from England, Scotland, Wales and Ireland since 1600* (London: Hambledon, 2004), p. 236. See also Marjory Harper and Stephen Constantine, *Migration and Empire* (Oxford: Oxford University Press, 2010).

14   Kent Fedorewich, *Unfit for Heroes: Reconstruction and Soldier Settlement* (Manchester: Manchester University Press, 1995).

15   Harper and Constantine, 'Children of the Poor: Child and Juvenile Migration,' chap. 9, *Migration and Empire*, pp. 247–76.

that this was an era of what he called 'Recolonisation'.[16] It is certainly the case that many industries as well as shipping companies and financial institutions saw this as a renewed period of opportunity. Even such publishing ventures as travel guides – which at that time contained a great deal more business information than they would today – expanded their editions, their scope and indeed their number of pages in these years.[17]

It is true that all of this encountered an economic Armageddon in the Great Depression. This led to the considerable expansion of the phenomenon of return migration back to the United Kingdom and other European countries. By 1931, there was net immigration to the United Kingdom, for the first time in the era of migration, but no one could foresee that in 1918–1919 when the empire was billed as a whole series of lands 'fit for heroes'.[18] To all the migration and economic indices of Belich's concept of Recolonisation (see following) we can add the fact that we do of course encounter the re-distribution of imperial possessions at Versailles, albeit through the mandates system of the League of Nations. This ensured that the British and the French empires reached their maximum extent in this period. Moreover, Australia, New Zealand and South Africa further developed their own forms of sub-imperialism in the Pacific and in South-West Africa. But even putting such geographical facts to one side, we find many cultural expressions of an apparently healthy return to imperial normality.

In Britain, the most obvious of these was the great Wembley Exhibition of 1924–1925, by far the grandest imperial exhibition in the exhibition tradition leading back to 1851, although it is certainly the case that empire only came to be foregrounded in such exhibitions from the Colonial and Indian in South Kensington in 1886.[19] But by any standard Wembley was an extraordinary expression of imperial confidence and power. It was attended by over 17 million visitors in 1924 and 9 million when it re-opened in 1925; its pavilions covered virtually the whole empire, and its projection of economic might seemed formidable. Migration propaganda was issued with statistics purporting to show that between 1893 and 1913 the proportions going to the United States and to the empire had been reversed, with more than 600,000 heading for the United States and over 1.2 million for the empire. Clearly the message – if not the reality – was that such flows, in the post-war world, were now accelerating, thus encouraging intending migrants to ensure than an even higher proportion would head for the empire. The whole thing was also a major commercial event, a showcase for all sorts of imperial products and companies associated with them. Moreover, the newly opened Wembley stadium featured the massive pageant of

---

16 James Belich, *Replenishing the Earth: The Settler Revolution and the Rise of the Anglo-World, 1783–1939* (Oxford: Oxford University Press, 2009), part 3.

17 John M. MacKenzie, 'Empires of Travel, British Guide Books and Cultural Imperialism in the 19th and 20th Centuries,' in *Histories of Tourism: Representation, Identity and Conflict*, ed. John K. Walton (Clivedon: Channel View, 2005), pp. 19–38; MacKenzie, 'Empire Travel Guides and the Imperial Mind-Set from the Mid-Nineteenth to the Mid-Twentieth Centuries,' in *The British Abroad Since the Eighteenth Century, Volume 2: Experiencing Imperialism*, ed. Martin Farr and Xavier Guégan (Basingstoke: Palgrave Macmillan, 2013), pp. 116–36.

18 Marjory Harper, ed., *Emigrant Homecomings: The Return Movement of Migrants, 1600–2000* (Manchester: Manchester University Press, 2005).

19 John M. MacKenzie, 'The Imperial Exhibitions,' chap. 4, *Propaganda and Empire: The Manipulation of British Public Opinion, 1880–1960* (Manchester: Manchester University Press, 1983), pp. 96–120. See also the Official Guide to the Exhibition (1924) and the entry on Wembley in John E. Findling, ed., *Encyclopedia of World's Fairs and Expositions* (Jefferson, NC, 2008), pp. 230–6.

empire, involving no fewer than 12,000 performers in repeat performances right through the summer, which projected British history as bound up with a confident imperial past. The Wembley Torchlight Tattoo, with 1,000 musicians performing, together with the Imperial Scout and Guide jamboree all similarly set about depicting a worldwide empire community. Of course some historians have pointed to the pleasures of the funfair, to the Won't Go to Wembley society, and the very real objections of the West African Students' Union to the demeaning displays of indigenous peoples, but many other organs of the media – including Billy Bunter and his friends as depicted to the readers of the comic *The Magnet* – accepted it for what it was, a major and popular expression of imperial might. And it would have been *The Magnet* and other similar comics which would have been the standard reading material of many of us had we been young around that time. Nevertheless, it has to be said that it all made a loss, partly because the capital cost of over £12 million had been so enormous.

Some historians have seen this as the last of the great imperial exhibitions, but such a London-centric view simply does not hold water. Some may argue that the Empire Marketing Board, imperial preference and all the propaganda produced by such organisations may now be seen as a symptom of weakness and decline, but at the time they marshalled print culture, poster arts and film-making activities to their ends.[20] And as we have seen Belich has used this period to confirm his theory of recolonisation, that as the political ties of empire, in the case of the Dominions, weakened, the economic ties strengthened, with trade flows that indicated the extent to which the British economy, so dependent on the Dominion contribution in the First World War, continued to be closely linked with Dominion production. Belich has also set out to show that, at least in the rhetorical flourishes of politicians, imperial sentiment continued to be strong in the Dominions until as late as the 1960s. On the other hand, John Griffiths seems to be arguing that imperial sentiment in the public culture of Australasian cities was relatively weak in this period.[21] It is nevertheless the case that exhibitions held within the empire tended to promote the imperial economic and cultural message. These would include the exhibition in Singapore in 1922, the New Zealand and the South Seas exhibition held in Dunedin in 1925–1926 and the Johannesburg exhibition of 1936–1937, despite the obvious problems presented by Afrikaner nationalism to the survival of imperial sentiment. Then there was the major New Zealand centennial exhibition in Wellington in 1939–1940, which pulled over 2.5 million people through its turnstiles. This celebrated not only a century of New Zealand nationhood, but also 100 years of the imperial connection.[22]

Returning to Britain, there were minor exhibitions like 'Peeps at the Colonial Empire' in London in 1936, but there was another mighty expression of empire in the British Empire Exhibition in Glasgow of 1938, again a massive display of imperial prospects and potential, here exhibited as a means for the regeneration of the Scottish and by extension British economies as trade and industry apparently began to lift itself out of the great slough of economic despond of the Depression. This one cost £10 million, was built in wholly

---

20 Stephen Constantine, '"Bringing the Empire Alive": The Empire Marketing Board and Imperial Propaganda, 1926–1933,' in *Imperialism and Popular Culture*, ed. John M. MacKenzie (Manchester: Manchester University Press, 1986), pp. 192–231.

21 John Griffiths, *Imperial Culture in Antipodean Cities, 1880–1939* (Basingstoke: Palgrave Macmillan, 2014).

22 These exhibitions have entries in Findling, ed., *Encyclopedia of World's Fairs and Exhibitions*.

modern art deco styles and was visited by 12.5 million visitors, many of whom must of course have indulged in multiple visits.[23] Wholly new economic developments such as the oil industry in Burma were highlighted. This exhibition made only a minor loss. Thus the supposedly self-confident exhibitionary complex certainly covered the entire period of the inter-war years.[24] The key point here is that all of this looked to an imperial future, to an integrated economy, a sterling zone that still had the capacity to renew itself. In passing, this was also true in France where the Vincennes Exhibition of 1931, with 8 million visitors, was a truly major expression of these same forces. In the best French manner it was also a considerable publication event.

But exhibitions were not alone. Thirty years ago, I argued that the central role of empire in the British theatre of the pre-war years was passed on to the new medium of the cinema. The pervasive theatrical presentation of empire has now been more than confirmed by the work of the American theatre historian Marty Gould, as well as by Jeffrey Richards in his studies of the cinema and of pantomime.[25] It can be found in straight plays, in musical comedy, in such popular forms as melodrama and pantomime. As such it was a phenomenon that went far beyond the vibrant London stage, but could be found all over Britain. Bernard Porter's extraordinarily bold suggestion that the British theatre was uninterested in empire simply does not hold water.[26] His research technique in arriving at this firm conclusion appears to have consisted of examining the titles of plays presented in the theatre in Victorian and Edwardian times. But titles never represented content. Who, for example, would have imagined that the play *Cheer Boys Cheer* of 1895, which was immensely popular, would actually be about the Anglo-Ndebele war of 1893 in Rhodesia (now Zimbabwe) and satirised the whole business of golden El Dorados and the dubious 'kaffir boom' (as it was known) in what may be called share shenanigans?[27] But the inter-war years theatre was joined by the immensely popular film medium, and the building of dedicated cinemas became a major architectural development throughout Europe and the European empires. By the 1930s, some of the most popular films in the cinemas of Britain, the Dominions and also the United States were about the glories of empire. The box office does not lie, and it seems unlikely that people would have flocked to see cinematic depictions of events and ideologies of which they disapproved or to which they were indifferent. These films were matched by the propagandist and uncritical interest of the newsreels, by such propagandist

---

23 See the official guide to this exhibition in MacKenzie, *Propaganda*, pp. 112–13.

24 MacKenzie, *Propaganda*, chap. 4. Paul Greenhalgh, *Ephemeral Vistas: Exhibitions and Expositions Universelles* (Manchester: Manchester University Press, 1988).

25 Marty Gould, *Nineteenth-Century Theatre and the Imperial Encounter* (New York: Routledge, 2011); Jeffrey Richards, 'Drury Lane Imperialism,' in *Politics Performance and Popular Culture: Theatre and Society in Nineteenth-Century Britain*, ed. Peter Yeandle, Kate Newey and Jeffrey Richards (Manchester: Manchester University Press, forthcoming, 2016); for films, see Jeffrey Richards, *Visions of Yesterday* (London: Routledge, 1973); James Chapman and Nicholas J. Cull, *Projecting Empire: Imperialism and Popular Cinema* (London: I.B. Tauris, 2009); for music, Jeffrey Richards, *Imperialism and Music: Britain, 1876–1953* (Manchester: Manchester University Press, 2001), pp. 174–198; Nalini Ghuman, *Resonances of the Raj: India in the English Musical Imagination, 1897–1947* (Oxford: Oxford University Press, 2014).

26 Bernard Porter, *The Absent-Minded Imperialists* (Oxford: Oxford University Press, 2004), p. 140 and passim.

27 For a discussion of this play, which Porter ignored, see MacKenzie, *Propaganda*, pp. 53–4.

bodies as the Empire Marketing Board and the GPO Film Unit.[28] James Burns has recently demonstrated just how potent these cinematic representations of empire were throughout the colonies.[29] Empire was certainly alive and well in British cultural forms in these years and that was surely also true of the Dominions.[30]

Thus, films had the capacity to travel around the empire. And it is in the empire that you can find other expressions of an apparent imperial confidence. It has long seemed to be a curious fact that the height of the expression of imperial self-confidence comes towards the end of empire, rather like pride coming before the fall. How can we interpret this? Does it reflect the fact that those who projected such self-confidence simply had no conception of what was about to happen? Is it about a continuing and blind faith in a great imperial future? Or does it come from the shaky realisation that perhaps the end is indeed near and that consolatory building programmes stave off the evil day? Either way, the fact is that these are the years of the construction of New Delhi, where the buildings of Lutyens and Baker seem to project continuing imperial power on a strikingly grand scale.[31] But it was not just New Delhi. The British were busy building Lusaka in Northern Rhodesia, their new capital which was going to take over from the somewhat unhealthy Livingstone located on the Zambezi.[32] And the urban planning and designs for Lusaka are also redolent of faith in an imperial African future. Meanwhile, the Italians were building the great Italianate Art Deco capital of Asmara in Eritrea.[33] Canberra was of course still being built too, but that might be considered an expression of Australian political nationalism rather than of imperialism, perhaps symbolically designed – and dedicated to the motor-car – by an American. And that leads us to recognise in passing the increasing cultural influence of the United States in this period.

When it came to travelling around the empire, no one did this more assiduously than the playboy Prince of Wales, the future Edward VIII. Bored though he might have been – his boredom somewhat alleviated by his often adulterous womanising – his presence produced extraordinary public reactions. Consider the scope of these travels. August to November of 1919 found him in Canada, where he bought himself a ranch in Alberta. March to October 1920, it was Australia and New Zealand. From October 1921 to June 1922 it was India, Burma, Borneo, Sri Lanka and Egypt, as well as other non-imperial places in the Far East. From March to October 1925 he was in West and South Africa, then South America. In 1927 back to Canada for the celebrations of the Diamond Jubilee of Confederation, and in 1928 he was in East Africa. It has been said that he was the most photographed celebrity of his time. And he carried with him the aura of his involvement in the First World War. He

---

28 Ibid., chap. 3.

29 James Burns, *Cinema and Society in the British Empire, 1895–1940* (Basingstoke: Palgrave Macmillan, 2013).

30 The role of the monarchy continued to be significant throughout the empire, not least through royal visits. See Philip Murphy, *Monarchy and the End of Empire* (Oxford: Oxford University Press, 2013).

31 Robert Grant Irving, *Indian Summer: Lutyens, Baker and Imperial Delhi* (New Haven: Yale University Press, 1981); Thomas R. Metcalf, *An Imperial Vision: Indian Architecture and Britain's Raj* (London: Faber & Faber, 1989).

32 *Lusaka: The New Capital of Northern Rhodesia, Opened Jubilee Week 1935* (London: Jonathan Cape, 1935), no author, private circulation.

33 Jochen Visscher, ed., and Stefan Boness (photographs), *Asmara: The Frozen City* (Berlin: Jovis, 2006).

joined the Grenadier Guards in 1914 and made frequent visits to France, at least witnessing some of the realities of trench warfare. He was even awarded the Military Cross.

All these empire travels were accompanied by quite staggering public acclaim, at least in the territories of white settlement. Each one was followed by the publication of a book of the travels, and of course they were endlessly featured in the press and in newsreels. Amongst the books, there was Charles Turley's *With the Prince Around the Empire* of 1926 that contains ecstatic descriptions of the crowds and his reception in Canada and Australasia, although we do know that his reception in India was somewhat more strained. G. Ward Price produced *With the Prince in West Africa* and *To South Africa with the Prince*. Edward's photo opportunities with indigenous peoples, sometimes dressed in their alleged native costume – as with Canadian First Nations people – were legendary, although his private views of some people are so racist as to be barely printable.[34] His brothers also travelled, and at the very least all this gave the appearance of the continuation of loyal imperial sentiment. The various publications (which include *Prince George's African Tour* of 1934) reveal the continuation of the traditions of late Victorian and Edwardian times.[35] The Royal Navy's Empire Cruise of the Special Service Squadron of six major vessels, including the *Hood* and the *Repulse*, in 1923 was also clearly designed to promote imperial sentiment. This visited West, South and East Africa, Ceylon, Malaya and Singapore, Australia and New Zealand, the Pacific islands and Canada. Again the voyage was celebrated in a book.[36]

But there are still more significant reasons for seeing these years as in some respects the golden age of imperialism, certainly in Africa and to some extent in South-East Asia and the island colonies. That prime imperial discipline, anthropology, only truly emerged in this period under the influence of such figures as A. R. Radcliffe-Brown (1881–1955), Bronislaw Malinowski (1884–1942) and E. E. Evans-Pritchard (1902–1973). Professional and highly trained anthropologists began to fan out into the empire conducting studies of indigenous people, studies that would be of considerable value both to colonial administrations and to later scholars. Here was a profession that also attracted highly talented women. Audrey Richards (1899–1984) in Northern Rhodesia (Zambia) from 1930, Hilda Kuper (1911–1992) in Swaziland in the 1930s and many others such as the American Margaret Mead (1901–1978) in Samoa, and elsewhere in the Pacific and South-East Asia from 1925 began to conduct studies that continue to be of value today even if their theoretical foundations

---

34   These journeys are detailed in: Sir Percival Phillips, *The Prince of Wales' Eastern Book: A Pictorial Record of the Voyages of H.M.S. "Renown", 1921–1922* (London: Hodder & Stoughton, 1922); St. John Adcock, *The Prince of Wales' African Book: A Pictorial Record of the Journey to West Africa, South Africa and South America* (London: Hodder and Stoughton, n.d.); G. Ward Price, *With the Prince to West Africa* (London: Gill, 1925); Price, *Through South Africa with the Prince* (London: Gill, 1926); Charles Turley, *With the Prince Round the Empire* (London: Methuen, 1926). All these books contained prefaces by the prince extolling the wonders of the empire and the ways in which the public, not least boys and girls, should be aware of its importance and unity.

35   A.A. Frew, *Prince George's African Tour* (London: Blackie, 1934). This book contained a preface by Jan Smuts, extolling the immense popularity of the prince and the enthusiastic reception by the public, and a foreword by G. Martin Huggins, prime minister of Southern Rhodesia, which more darkly wrote of dangerous times and the need for imperial leadership.

36   V.C. Scott O'Connor, *The Empire Cruise* (London: Riddle, Smith and Duffus, 1925). This was privately printed. A future study will have to attempt to establish the circulation of some of these works.

may have been seriously challenged.[37] This was a European phenomenon, as Helen Tilley and her collaborators in the book *Ordering Africa* have pointed out.[38] It was one of many respects in which academic cooperation within empires continued to take place.

Moreover, it is only in this period that technical services of various sorts are properly established with fully professional cadres to man them – and unlike anthropology, they were generally male preserves. This is true, for example, of forestry.[39] Here was a service that had been set up in the nineteenth century with a strange mix of personnel: maverick figures of the frontier, botanists and non-British officers, particularly Germans. British forestry training had begun to produce graduates at the end of the century and university chairs had been founded, but all of this only came properly to fruition in these years. If this was the case with forestry it was equally true of other services, like agronomy or public health.[40] It was in these years that the Colonial Service itself was placed on a much more professional footing in terms of its recruitment and training. The Oxford courses to train colonial officials started with summer schools in 1926 and were later developed, in the 1930s, by another remarkable woman, Margery Perham (1895–1982). She had embarked on her career of surveying colonial administrative and native systems and was soon immersed in evolving a curriculum for future officials, which included elements of anthropology, linguistic training and some attempt at imparting administrative techniques in colonies with major indigenous populations.[41] The vast survey of the British Empire by the former Indian Governor Lord (Malcolm) Hailey (1872–1969) was also developed in this period. It was first published in 1938 under the auspices of the Royal Institute of International Affairs, with a second edition in 1956. It was partly influenced by Perham, and if you survey it carefully, you get very little impression that Hailey was aware of the imminent end of empire. Instead, it seems to look to a longer future and a distant decolonisation. The general thrust is developmental, administrative and intellectual with sections on, for example: the study of African languages, anthropology, traditional law, demography, technical and environmental issues such as agronomy, animal husbandry, irrigation, soil science, forestry, health, geological survey, health and education.[42] The imperialism of Frederick Lugard's (1858–1945) dual mandate appears here to be getting its act together for

---

37 See, for example, Audrey Richards, *Land, Labour and Diet in Northern Rhodesia: An Economic Study of the Bemba Tribe* (Oxford: Oxford University Press, 1939).

38 Helen Tilley, ed., and Robert J. Gordon, *Ordering Africa: Anthropology, European Imperialism, and the Politics of Knowledge* (Manchester: Manchester University Press, 2007); Michael W. Young, *Malinowski: Odyssey of an Anthropologist* (New Haven: Yale University Press, 2004).

39 Gregory A. Barton, *Empire Forestry and the Origins of Environmentalism* (Cambridge: Cambridge University Press, 2002).

40 Terry Barringer, ed., *How Green Was Our Empire? Environment, Development and the Colonial Service* (London: ICS, 2005). See, for example, the articles by MacKenzie, Kirk-Greene, Mares and Wilmot. There is now an extensive literature on tropical medicine, much of which emphasises the significance of the inter-war years. See, for example, John Farley, *Bilharzia: A History of Imperial Tropical Medicine* (Cambridge: Cambridge University Press, 1991); and Maryinez Lyons, *The Colonial Disease* (Cambridge: Cambridge University Press, 1992).

41 C. Brad Faught, *Into Africa: The Imperial Life of Margery Perham* (London: I.B. Tauris, 2012).

42 Lord Hailey, *An African Survey: A Study of the Problems Arising in Africa South of the Sahara* (Oxford: Oxford University Press, 1938). The second edition appeared as late as 1956, still clearly offering material of value to colonial officials. Hailey also produced a series of supplements on *The Native Administration of the British African Territories*, in five volumes, all published in the early 1950s.

the long haul.[43] Moreover, the economic difficulties of the inter-war years, which produced social and labour unrest in Africa and the West Indies in particular, led to the framing of new colonial developmental policies at the time of the Second World War and its aftermath. These have the appearance of attempting to reform and shore up empire, offering little hint of pending decolonisation.[44]

There are other indicators of the apparent health of the imperial ideology and its manifestations on the ground. This was not a revisionist period in terms of the writing of biographies or of imperial histories. The heroic tradition and the hagiographical approach continued unabated. True revisionism in this respect was not to arrive until the 1960s and 1970s. Imperial historians, for example the Beit Professor of Colonial History at Oxford, Sir Reginald Coupland (1884–1952), continued to write in a tradition that linked back to earlier years. Amidst his prolific output, his biographies of Wilberforce and Raffles in the early 1920s and his books on the British takeover of East Africa of the late 1930s, as well as his many constitutional writings up to the early 1950s, convey his conviction in the moral rectitude of imperialism and of its modern manifestations. While Indian nationalists had begun the process of 'writing back' at the British from the end of the nineteenth century, the same transition in the writing of Caribbean and African history was only in its infancy at the time of the Second World War and truly effective responses came later. Indeed, it seems extraordinary when we consider the extent to which new forms of the writing of colonial history only fully emerge at the time of decolonisation itself. There are relatively few advance hints of the revolutions to come in this period.[45] The critical voices, like that of Norman Leys in Kenya in the early 1920s, tend not only to be isolated, but also to be writing within existing traditions.[46] Perhaps this is also true of Jomo Kenyatta's anthropological work *Facing Mount Kenya*.[47]

In any case, we should surely feel a twinge of anxiety when historians write of the loosening of the bonds of empire through the development of Dominions' nationalisms. What this alleged loosening actually represents is the tightening of white strength and influence. If we see imperialism as being essentially about the exercise of authority by one ethnicity over others given imbalances in technological and military power, then further nationalist development in the Dominions simply concealed a continuing and growing authority over indigenous peoples, which surely constitutes the very essence of imperialism.[48] This was true in Canada and Australasia, and obviously in South Africa.

---

43 Frederick Lugard, *The Dual Mandate in British Tropical Africa* (London: Blackwood, 1922). This went through at least four subsequent editions. It constituted a fundamental ideology – combined with that of indirect rule, also largely formulated by Lugard – which continued to be central to imperial governance until the 1940s and 1950s.

44 Stephen Constantine, *The Making of British Colonial Development Policy, 1914–1940* (London: Cass, 1984); Ian Drummond, *British Economic Policy and the Empire, 1919–1939* (London: Allen and Unwin, 1972).

45 Bill Schwarz, ed., *West Indian Intellectuals in Britain* (Manchester: Manchester University Press, 2003).

46 Norman Leys, *Kenya* (London: Hogarth Press, 1924); Leys, *The Last Chance in Kenya* (London: Hogarth Press, 1931).

47 Jomo Kenyatta, *Facing Mount Kenya: The Tribal Life of the Gikuyu* (London: Secker and Warburg, 1938). Kenyatta was heavily influenced by Malinowski, who wrote an introduction to his book.

48 This constitutes the fundamental element of the definition of empires in John M. MacKenzie, ed., *Encyclopedia of Empire* (4 vols., Malden, MA; Oxford, UK: Wiley Blackwell, 2016), Vol. 1, p. lxxxiii.

In every case, white power in these Dominions led to the tightening of controls, social, political and economic, over indigenous peoples (New Zealand is a rather different case). These continued to ensure that it was exceptionally difficult for indigenous people to enter immigrant areas on anything other than the sufferance of the dominant whites. Losses of land continued, entry into the white economy except as menial paid labour was difficult or impossible and indigenous people invariably lacked citizenship rights and the vote. In the case of Canada, citizenship was not granted until 1961.[49] Australia was equally slow in respect of Aborigines, and of course the South African situation led to full-blown apartheid, which only began to be shaken off after the elections of 1994.

In all these we have a distinct parallel with the settler regimes in Southern Rhodesia and Kenya, where the white minority was tiny, but all forms of discrimination, not just by colour as identified by Lake and Reynolds,[50] but more particularly on the land, in marketing, in labour relations, in social contacts, were ratcheted up during this period. In Southern Rhodesia, the efforts to exclude Africans from the cash economy by any means other than paid labour for whites were heightened. And the severe segregation on the land, in wholly unbalanced ways, was confirmed in the Land Apportionment Act of 1931. Similar tendencies occurred even where white minorities were particularly tiny as in Northern Rhodesia (Zambia) and Nyasaland (Malawi). Meanwhile, through the mandates South Africa developed its hold on the former German South-West Africa (Namibia) in ways that were going to be important in keeping the Afrikaans nationalists in power after 1948. Australia with its class C mandate in New Guinea and New Zealand with its mandate in the former German Samoa, both saw their new mandate responsibilities as more about the extension of an Anglophone imperial authority rather than an idealistic trust. And this was to be borne out by their subsequent administrations in these territories. It was certainly the case in South-West Africa. Given the relatively loose oversight of the mandates by the League of Nations, which of course became increasingly weakened as the 1930s wore on, the mandates did seem to offer new imperial opportunities, as was certainly the case in the new British administrations in East and West Africa. All that can be said is that Lugard's theory of the Dual Mandate in British Tropical Africa introduced some elements of trust for the future into the imperial relationship. But it was trust within the context of indirect rule, a ruling methodology that tended to divide rather than unite peoples, serving to preserve the authority of indigenous elites with the effect – and possibly the intention – of frustrating the newly educated bourgeois and évolué groups. Thus, when we take the perspective of indigenous peoples, as we must, the notion that the shackles of imperialism were loosened by the First World War, as is the contention of traditional imperial historians, is clearly erroneous. All that happened was that in the British Empire, imperial power was relocated from London to Ottawa, Pretoria, Canberra, Wellington (to a certain extent), as well as Salisbury (Harare) and Nairobi. Imperial power took the course of the multiple moving metropolises, but despite such continuing devolution, the fundamental characteristics of imperial rule, not least in respect of indigenous people, continued and were often strengthened.

---

49   I am indebted to my friend and former post-graduate student, Professor David McNab, for discussions on these points.

50   Marilyn Lake and Henry Reynolds, *Drawing the Global Colour Line: White Men's Countries and the International Challenge of Racial Equality* (Cambridge: Cambridge University Press, 2008).

If the power of colonialists over the indigenous populace was confirmed in these ways, it is also the case that all the economic activities of the inter-war years in mining, agricultural production and urban growth had major effects upon colonial environments that have not been studied as much as they might have been. Indeed, moving back once more, there has been in my view a paucity of research on the environmental impact of the First World War itself. This takes us back to Africa and the necessity of establishing an African perspective. The main colonial theatre of the Great War was indeed Africa, with campaigns against the Germans in West, South-West and, above all, East Africa.[51] These wars were largely fought by African troops or askaris as well as by porters who were feeding the supply lines. It has been estimated that some one hundred thousand askaris were involved and perhaps up to a million porters. Thus large numbers of males were recruited, often forcibly, from agricultural environments with inevitable effects upon indigenous agricultural production. It is certainly the case that there were instances of famine in some areas. But consider the impact on women. We know from areas of high labour migration, for example in southern Africa, that the role of women in agricultural production and in social life was transformed. The wartime removal of large numbers of young males, some of them permanently through their deaths in combat or from disease, must have had similar effects, and such effects must have been felt in forms of environmental change as well as family and social organisation. In his impressive *History of Malawi*, John McCracken characterised the effects of the First World War as bringing about death, dearth and disease.[52] The war introduced the spread of motorised vehicles, which reduced the need for porterage in its aftermath. And of course few if any Africans had access to such vehicles. The coercive colonial state was reinvigorated through increased tax demands and forced labour, while one of the major environmental results was the spread of the tsetse fly and its baleful effects upon animal husbandry and on humans. Thus the effects of the war on Africans were largely malign. And the colonial state ended up stronger.

In the aftermath of the war, raw material prices – as elsewhere – experienced a sudden boom followed by collapse. When that was taken together with currency crises and the continuing high prices of manufactured imports, it is apparent that the terms of trade yet again moved against the peoples of tropical Africa. Moreover, this is an era when large tracts of land were gazetted as game reserves and national parks, often with attempts to exclude African populations from within them. This was an international movement, reflecting the ways in which certain forms of conservation had become a new environmental mantra.[53] Perhaps we need more comparative research on the effects upon indigenous peoples everywhere, in North America, South-East Asia and Australasia. Meanwhile, sticking with Africa, these developments in the tropical regions of the continent contrasted powerfully with the ways in which industrialisation proceeded in South Africa, such that continuing mining wealth, import substitution, protective tariffs and further infrastructural development led to a combination of a massive reduction in national debt together with further confirmation of white political and economic power, in respect of the majority black

---

51   Hew Strachan, *The First World War in Africa* (Oxford: Oxford University Press, 2004).
52   John McCracken, 'Malawi & the First World War,' chap. 6, *A History of Malawi, 1859–1966* (Woodbridge: James Currey, 2012), pp. 147–61.
53   See MacKenzie, *The Empire of Nature: Hunting, Conservation and British Imperialism*; Gissibl, *The Nature of German Imperialism*; Gissibl, Höhler and Kupper, eds, *Civilising Nature: National Parks in Global Perspective*.

population. At least one major politician, Jan Smuts, the convert from Boer resistance to loyal fascination with the British Empire, had his prestige heightened by military rank and by his aura as a successful general in the First World War; even if that did not particularly protect him from fellow Afrikaners who saw him as an imperial traitor to their nationalist cause.[54]

Elsewhere, it is generally accepted that the experience of indigenous troops in the war inevitably had a dramatic influence upon the ways in which they viewed the world and in particular the dominant imperial masters. Military organisation is celebrated for having an effect on the dance societies of East Africa, which fed into the later nationalist movement. West Africans who had served in the West African Frontier Force also contributed to a growing sense of dissatisfaction. Large numbers of Indian troops famously served on the Western Front and no fewer than ninety thousand Chinese labourers were recruited in WeiHeiWei for work in France.[55] But we often know more about the horses than we do of the lives and deaths of those Indians and Chinese. However, the letters written by Indian troops hospitalised in Britain are invariably remarkable for their imperial loyalties as for their sense of incipient nationalism, though they were of course censored.[56] The Indian princes also frequently treated the Great War in the same way. Sums of money were raised in India for causes associated with it and even Gandhi was concerned with an ambulance corps. In ways that were very different from the Second World War, the reactions to the Great War cut two ways. When it comes to sentiment, if not to more practical concerns, there can be little doubt that the First World War produced a certain degree of ambivalence. And, although there were some 'reds under the beds' scares, it took some time for the influence of the Russian Revolution to be felt.

Finally I return to settlers. Scholarly interest in them has grown greatly of late. Settlers, both permanent and temporary sojourners, secured a tremendous infusion of power in this period. They commanded the environment more effectively, as well as the levers of colonial economies. The new disciplines I mentioned earlier also tended towards this enhancement of power, despite the aura of liberalism that surrounds some of them. The First World War served their interests in all sorts of ways, technologically, economically, environmentally, culturally and politically. Settlers were the microbes of empire, spreading and multiplying as they did so. It seems to me that instead of concentrating on their incipient nationalism, we should be looking at all the areas in which they developed their power in this period. They also help us to develop a synoptic approach covering many territories of empire. Of course, it is the case that in empires, there is always a major tension between the power objectives of the centre and the restlessness of the imperial and colonial territories that used to be slightly disparagingly known as the periphery. But the notion that the First World War stoked up nationalism everywhere, from the white Dominions to India and even to colonies in the dependent empire, is surely simplistic. Truly the 1920s felt like business as usual. It may be the job of historians to take a long view and discern the origins of decolonisation, but contemporaries can never foresee the future and the idea that the end of empire was

---

54 W.K. Hancock, *Smuts, Vol.!: The Sanguine Years, 1870–1919* and *Smuts: Vol 2: The Fields of Force, 1919–1950* (Cambridge: Cambridge University Press, 1962 and 1968).

55 The material in this paragraph is derived from entries in the Wiley-Blackwell *Encyclopedia of Empire*. See footnote 48.

56 David Omissi, *Indian Voices of the Great War: Soldiers' Letters, 1914–1918* (Basingstoke: Palgrave Macmillan, 1999).

going to occur within half a century would never have occurred to most people. Even elite intellectuals and administrators such as Margery Perham and Lord Hailey, however liberal they may have seemed, had no conception of such an outcome from the standpoint of the late 1930s. The major fragmentations of power that were about to occur still seemed a long way off. Imperialism was alive and well.

Acknowledgements

This chapter was originally delivered as a keynote at the conference 'The British Empire and the Great War: Colonial Societies/Cultural Responses' in Singapore in February 2014. I am particularly grateful to Michael J.K. Walsh, Andrekos Varnava and Bee Kuen Hong, as well as all the participants, for making this conference such a stimulating and enjoyable experience.

PART II
Imperial responses, identities and culture

Chapter 3
The 'Kaiser Cartoon', 1914–1918
A transnational comic art genre

Richard Scully

It would not be controversial to claim that the German Kaiser, Wilhelm II (r.1888–1918) was the most visible and well-known public figure in the world between 1914 and 1918.[1] Already by the outbreak of war, the Kaiser had established an unparalleled public role as speech-maker, publicist for Germany's national destiny and representative figurehead of the German Empire.[2] Paradoxically – both at home and abroad – this role was frustrated, as well as enhanced, by the negative publicity he attracted, and particularly via the satirical version of the Kaiser promulgated by cartoonists.[3] To friend and foe alike, Wilhelm II seemed 'the very incarnation of the "waxing vigour" of his nation'.[4] His upturned moustache and enthusiasm for 'stormy declarations, spectacular voyages and military display' ensured that he was a gift to cartoonists of all kinds.[5] With several significant modifications – and based very much on a new, far more critical appreciation of his pre-war image – this was a comic role that continued into wartime caricature.[6] Imagined as a mad dog, the Beast of the Apocalypse or simply the owner and originator of 'the Kaiser's War', 'no personality

---

1 Richard Scully, 'Kaiser Cartoons,' *Wartime – Official Magazine of the Australian War Memorial* 65 (2014): pp. 35–9; this chapter has its origins in this earlier, popular history piece.

2 Martin Kohlrausch, 'The Workings of Royal Celebrity: Wilhelm II as Media Emperor,' in *Constructing Charisma: Celebrity, Fame, and Power in Nineteenth-Century Europe*, ed. Edward Berenson and Eva Giloi (Oxford: Berghahn Books, 2013), pp. 52–66; Michael A. Obst, *'Einer nur ist Herr im Reiche': Kaiser Wilhelm II als politischer Redner* (Paderborn: Ferdinand Schöningh, 2010); Christopher Clark, *Wilhelm II:' A Life in Power* (London: Penguin, 2009), pp. 218 ff.; Martin Kohlrausch, *Der Monarch im Skandal: Die Logik der Massenmedien und die Transformation der wilhelminischen Monarchie* (Berlin: Akademie Verlag, 2005).

3 Richard Scully, *British Images of Germany: Admiration, Antagonism & Ambivalence, 1860–1914* (Basingstoke: Palgrave Macmillan, 2012), pp. 213 ff.; Jost Rebentisch, *Die vielen Gesichter des Kaisers: Wilhelm II. In der deutschen und britischen Karikatur, 1888–1918* (Berlin: Duncker & Humblot, 2000). Also see A.T. Allen, *Satire and Society in Wilhelmine Germany: Kladderadatsch and* Simplicissimus, *1890–1914* (Lexington: The University Press of Kentucky, 1984); W.A. Coupe, 'Kaiser Wilhelm II and the Cartoonists,' *History Today* 30, no. 11 (1980): pp. 16–23.

4 Scully, *British Images of Germany*, p. 213; Hew Strachan, *The First World War – Volume I: To Arms* (Oxford: Oxford University Press, 2001), p. 6.

5 Jean-Jacques Becker, 'Heads of State and Government,' *The Cambridge History of the First World War, Volume II – The State*, ed. Jay Winter (Cambridge: Cambridge University Press, 2014), p. 11; Rebentisch, *Die vielen Gesichter des Kaisers*, pp. 160, 193.

6 Lothar Reinermann, 'Fleet Street and the Kaiser: British Public Opinion and Wilhelm II,' *German History* 26, no. 4 (2008): pp. 469–85. See for an overview. Also: Lothar Reinermann, *Der Kaiser in England: Wilhelm II. und sein Bild in der britischen Öffentlichkeit* (Paderborn: Ferdinand Schöningh, 2001).

drew more abuse' from the Entente side than did Wilhelm II between 1914 and 1918 (and beyond).[7] After all, as Barbara Tuchman noted in 1962, who better to represent all that Germany stood for than 'the Supreme War Lord, whose name was signed to every order of OHL (*Oberste Heersleitung* – the High Command), so that he seemed the author of all German acts'.[8] Despite the real Wilhelm swiftly becoming a *Schattenkaiser* ('shadow-emperor') after 1914, and even shunning the public gaze that had sustained him for so long, the cartoon Kaiser became even more prominent, and those chronicling his misadventures saw no indignity in descending to 'the basest and blood-thirstiest character assassination'.[9]

Although such images are already very familiar to the historian of the Great War, they have tended to be lumped together with other forms of press reportage, or – aside from the notable comparative contribution by Jost Rebentisch – analysed only in the individual national contexts in which they appeared.[10] A more in-depth analysis of these cartoons in their own right reveals that the cartoon Kaiser was a far more complex character than is generally appreciated, and moreover was one that transcended British, French or other cartooning traditions to become the world's first globally-recognised cartoon character.[11] Indeed, when viewed from the perspective of that still-new, and rather nebulous, cross-disciplinary field known as 'comics studies', the 'Kaiser Cartoon' stands out as one of the most intriguing genres of political cartoon art, with important implications for how one can interpret the broader corpus of wartime hate cartoons. As a genre, it has its origins in critical cartoons of political enemies from well before Wilhelm's time; indeed elements of wartime Kaiser Cartoons owe much to British and other imaginings of the Kaiser's own grandfather, Wilhelm I (r.1861–1888).[12] And while wartime cartoonists continued to aim their barbs at two distinct 'types' of German (the 'corseted, monocled, spike-helmeted Prussians' and 'the Bavarians arrayed in fat beer bellies, sausages, clay pipes, and Lederhosen'), or allegorical apes and monsters, as Richard Stites has noted in the context of Russia, 'Kaiser Wilhelm remained the primary object of scorn and hate.'[13] The Kaiser Cartoon was thus the basis upon which wartime hate cartoons were built, and Wilhelm II as a 'representative individual' was a catch-all character when other, narrower characterisations seemed less effective.

---

7   Harold D. Lasswell, *Propaganda Technique in World War I* (Cambridge, MA and London: The MIT Press, 1971), pp. 89–90.

8   Barbara Tuchman, *The Guns of August* (London: The Folio Society, 1997), p. 294.

9   Lamar Cecil, *Wilhelm II: Emperor and Exile, 1900–1941* (Chapel Hill: University of North Carolina Press, 1996), p. 212; John C.G. Röhl, *Wilhelm II: Into the Abyss of War and Exile, 1900–1941* (Cambridge: Cambridge University Press, 2014), p. 1108; Reinermann, 'Fleet Street and the Kaiser,' p. 469.

10   See Wolfgang K. Hünig, *British and German Cartoons as Weapons in World War I: Invectives and Ideology of Political Cartoons, a Cognitive Linguistics Approach* (Frankfurt am Main: Peter Lang, 2002), pp. 34, 43. In one key work, the author freely admitted to having 'ignored the cartoons which deal with the German Kaiser and his political role', although this was justified in quantitative as well as qualitative terms.

11   H. Pearl Adams, ed., *International Cartoons of the War* (New York: E.P. Dutton, 1916). A sense of this was apparent in this early work.

12   Richard Scully, 'The Other Kaiser: Wilhelm I and British Cartoonists, 1861–1914,' *Victorian Periodicals Review* 44, no. 1 (2011): pp. 69–98.

13   Richard Stites, 'Days and Nights in Wartime Russia: Cultural Life, 1914–1917,' in *European Culture in the Great War: The Arts, Entertainment and Propaganda, 1914–1918*, ed. Aviel Roshwald and Richard Stites (Cambridge: Cambridge University Press, 2002), p.16.

While it is certainly encouraging that the 'visual turn' seems definitively to have occurred in relation the scholarship of the First World War, it remains true that far more attention has been given to other kinds of visual source material (such as poster art or cinema) than to the political cartoon.[14] This is partly a problem of disciplinary boundaries: because cartoons were aspects not only of mass print journalism but also artistic expressions, they have tended to be caught between analyses of journalism and analyses of a more art-historical nature in terms of the Great War.[15] It is also true that Great War cartoons tend to be scattered across a variety of archives, making their easy location and analysis more difficult.[16] Yet it is odd that many of the keynotes of First World War press and propaganda analysis fail to make more than passing mention of these dynamic and important sources.[17] The call by Jay Winter to 'do full justice to the visual propaganda of private enterprise' (of which cartoons were undoubtedly an essential component) has yet to be fully heard, more than two decades later.[18] In part, it seems that while historians are now finally taking visual culture seriously as a source-base and as a subject for study in its own right, there is still an inability to take *comic* image-making seriously.[19] There have been some notable studies of political cartoons in the Great War context, but by-and-large the literature has been dominated by heavily-illustrated compendiums of cartoon images, with relatively little in the way of detailed analysis.[20] Historians have also been far more likely to plunder the cartoon archive for useful representative illustrations – or to treat them as adjuncts to other source material – rather than to focus their analysis on the cartoons themselves.[21]

---

14   James Aulich, *War Posters: Weapons of Mass Communication* (London: Thames & Hudson, 2011); Pearl James, ed., *Picture This: World War I Posters and Visual Culture* (Lincoln, Nebraska and London: University of Nebraska Press, 2009); Jim Aulich and John Hewitt, *Seduction or Instruction? First World War Posters in Britain and Europe* (Manchester: Manchester University Press, 2007); Michael Paris, *The First World War and Popular Cinema: 1914 to the Present* (Edinburgh: Edinburgh University Press, 1999); Andrew Kelly, *Cinema and the Great War* (London: Routledge, 1997); Leslie Midkiff DeBauche, *Reel Patriotism: The Movies and World War I* (Madison, WI: University of Wisconsin Press, 1997).

15   Dietrich Grünewald, ed., *Politische Karikatur: zwischen Journalismus und Kunst* (Kromsdorf/Weimar: Verlag und Datenbank für Geisteswissenschaften, 2002).

16   Aulich and Hewitt, *Seduction or Instruction?*, p. 19; Kate O'Brien, 'British Newspaper Cartoons from 1914,' 12 March 2014. Kings College London, Lindell Hart Centre for Military Archives, accessed 24 March 2014, http://kingsarchives.tumblr.com/post/79351010028/british-newspaper-cartoons-from-1914-selected-by.

17   David Welch and Jo Fox, eds, *Justifying War: Propaganda, Politics and the Modern Age* (Basingstoke: Palgrave Macmillan, 2012), pp. 55, 78, 166–7; Alan Axelrod, *Selling the Great War: The Making of American Propaganda* (New York: Palgrave Macmillan, 2009), pp. 94, 142; J. Lee Thompson, *Politicians, the Press, & Propaganda: Lord Northcliffe & the Great War, 1914–1919* (Kent, OH: The Kent State University Press, 1999), p. 147.

18   J. M. Winter, 'Nationalism, the Visual Arts, and the Myth of War Enthusiasm in 1914,' *History of European Ideas* 15, no. 1–3 (1992): p. 359.

19   Brian Maidment, *Comedy, Caricature and the Social Order, 1820–1850* (Manchester: Manchester University Press, 2013), p. 16.

20   Lucinda Gosling, *Brushes and Bayonets: Cartoons, Sketches and Paintings of World War I* (London: Osprey, 2008); Mark Bryant, *World War I in Cartoons* (London: Grub Street, 2006); Roy Douglas, *The Great War, 1914–1918: The Cartoonists' Vision* (London: Routledge, 1995).

21   Richard Scully and Marian Quartly, eds, *Drawing the Line: Using Cartoons as Historical Evidence* (Clayton, VIC: Monash University ePress, 2009), p. 01.1.

Figure 3.1   Eugenio Colmo, *L'Ingordo* (The Glutton)

Source: French postcards, 1915

The broader context of wartime print culture and journalism is, of course, impossible to escape. Kaiser Cartoons in various forms were part of that formidable 'paper barrage' that the Entente launched against the Central Powers from the outset of the war, and which was sustained well beyond the Armistice.[22] The extent of this print campaign was enabled by 'the unprecedented development of networks of communication and information that the war brought into play and that the industrialisation of printed media made possible'.[23] That these networks were global and transnational – and mechanisms of formal as well as informal imperialism – ensured that cartoon depictions of Wilhelm II were shared amongst the Entente and other nations: *L'Ingordo* (the Glutton) (see Figure 3.1) a famous image

---

22   Christophe Didier, ed., *Orages de papier, 1914–1918: les collections de guerre des bibliotèques* (Paris: Somogy, 2008), p. 12.

23   Anne Rasmussen, 'Mobilising Minds,' in *The Cambridge History of the First World War, Volume III – Civil Society*, ed. Jay Winter (Cambridge: Cambridge University Press, 2014), p. 391.

of the Kaiser attempting to devour the world, was created by the Italian Eugenio Colmo (1885–1967) but arguably found its widest audience via mass-produced French postcards.[24]

Similarly, the Dutchman Louis Raemaekers (1869–1956) was 'the most significant cartoonist in the American press during the war' and the London *Punch*'s September 1914 supplement 'The New Rake's Progress' – which reproduced many of their most critical images spanning Wilhelm's entire reign – was available on the newsstands of Sydney within a few months.[25] As well as tapping into existing global networks and mechanisms of information exchange (of which the formal and informal British Empire must be counted the most significant), the conflict itself 'created a global mass market for visual representations of the war that could explain or at least help convey a sense of what was going on'.[26]

In his useful survey of cartoons within the broader context of total war, Eberhard Demm sees 1914 as something of a watershed for cartoonists, who had spent the previous decades revelling in their role as 'social critics who sharply attacked the authoritarian structures of the government'.[27] This tends to conflate all cartoonists with a kind of heroic, subversive image so dear to those inhabiting the left and doesn't take into account the patriotic and conservative bent of perhaps the majority of pre-war cartoonists. In truth, when war was declared in early August 1914, the Entente governments hardly needed to consider an organised propaganda campaign against the Kaiser; cartoonists as well as journalists, publishers and academics competed with one another 'to dip their pens in vitriol'.[28] There also was often a commercial imperative behind this gadarene rush – including in the case of French satirical magazines like *Le Rire* (and *Le Rire Rouge*) – the need to appeal to new readerships, as competitor papers folded under the pressures of war, or regular readerships departed en-masse to become 'regulars' of another kind, in the army.[29] Once at the front, and away from the normal periodical or newspaper-reading culture of home, soldiers also lampooned the Kaiser in the various publications that were created in and around the trenches.[30] In addition to published political cartoons, spontaneous caricatures of Wilhelm II appeared in all manner of other contexts, with cartoons and effigies being used as targets in funfair attractions, and newspapers holding competitions for the best amateur 'Kaiser Cartoon'.[31] Cartoonists of all kinds – whether conservatives or radicals, professionals or

---

24 'Golia' [Eugenio Colmo], *L'Ingordo Trop Dur* ['Too Hard for the Glutton'], 1915.

25 Stephen Hess and Sandy Northropp, *American Political Cartoons: The Evolution of a National Identity, 1754–2010* (New Brunswick and London: Transaction Publishers, 2013), pp. 82–83; Hess and Northropp, 'Kaiser in Cartoon,' *The World's News* (Sydney), 7 November 1914, p. 21.

26 Richard Scully, 'A Comic Empire: The Global Expansion of *Punch* as a Model Publication, 1841–1936,' *International Journal of Comic Art* 15, no. 2 (2013): pp. 6–35; Arndt Weinrich, 'Visual Essay: War and the State,' in *The Cambridge History of the First World War, Volume II – The State*, ed. Jay Winter (Cambridge: Cambridge University Press, 2014), p. 663.

27 Eberhard Demm, 'Propaganda and Caricature in the First World War,' *Journal of Contemporary History* 28, no. 1 (1993): pp. 163–92, esp. 166–7; Eberhard Demm, *Der Erste Weltkrieg in der internationalen Karikatur* (Hannover: Fackelträger, 1988).

28 Reinermann, 'Fleet Street and the Kaiser,' p. 480.

29 Laurent Bihl, '*Le Rire* (1894-vers 1979, Paris),' *Ridiculosa – Les revues satiriques françaises* 18 (2011): p. 180.

30 Australian War Memorial and C.E.W. Bean, *The ANZAC Book*, 3rd ed. (Sydney: University of New South Wales Press, 2010), front endpaper and pp. xiv, 115, 135, 138.

31 'Celebrating a Century of Luna Park,' *Divercity: The Official Newsletter of the City of Port Phillip* 65, December 2011, January 2012, p. 5; 'Luna Park,' *The Argus* (Melbourne), 31 October 1914, p. 20; 'The Kaiser Competition,' *Sunday Times* (Perth), 6 September 1914, p. 14.

amateurs – therefore mobilised themselves in keeping with established publishing practices; the key difference being the intensity of their responses and the remarkable similarity of the imagery they adopted across national contexts.

Undoubtedly, 'the dominant mood' conveyed by Kaiser Cartoons was straightforward 'hatred of the enemy'.[32] But this was not a simple, one-dimensional phenomenon. Rather, it was one that underwent a number of changes and developments during the period of the conflict. Some Kaiser Cartoons might draw a grimace of hate and determination, but in others, they might draw a derisory laugh, as cartoonists set out to ridicule the fool whose hubris would bring about inevitable destruction.

'The World's Enemy', by Bernard Partridge (1861–1945), published in the London *Punch* is a good example that encapsulates much of the genre that developed over the course of the war (see Figure 3.2).[33] Partridge was the senior cartoonist at *Punch* and the bearer of a cartooning tradition that stretched back to John Leech (1817–1864) and Sir John Tenniel (1820–1914) that depended upon the qualities of woodblock engraving for much of its power. In what was his first 'large cut' cartoon of the war, Partridge employed his well-established, heavy, cross-hatched texture to give the scene its darkness and the form of the Kaiser and the allegorical 'Spirit of Carnage' their respective shapes.[34] Surrounded by death and destruction, and in company with the forces of darkness, Wilhelm II is portrayed not only as an agent of evil, but also a fool for unwittingly unleashing the satanic hordes upon mankind. In taking the world to war, the Kaiser has lost all his friends and doomed himself (and probably his subjects) to certain damnation. When republished – only a month after this first appearance, as part of *Punch*'s 'New Rake's Progress' supplement – Partridge's debt to the pre-war style of depicting the Kaiser was made clear. Similar in style to Partridge's own 1905 offering 'The Sower of Tares' (referring to the first Moroccan crisis), 'The World's Enemy' was re-imagined as the culmination of a decades-long tradition of criticising Wilhelm II and Wilhelm's Germany (that, incidentally, completely ignored *Punch*'s equally long history of admiration for the Kaiser).[35] However, as well as representing aspects of continuity with past critiques, 'The World's Enemy' was also a departure – literally far darker and more condemnatory than anything that had come before.

In terms of cartoon print media, as a serio-comic weekly magazine, *Punch* – and its more populist counterpart *John Bull*, with cartoons by Frank Holland (fl. 1895–1925) – were actually in a minority by 1914, with an increasing majority of British political cartoons appearing in daily newspapers. This transition had begun in the United States in the 1880s, with the circulation battles between Joseph Pulitzer (1847–1911) and William Randolph Hearst (1863–1951), before prompting similar change in Britain during the 1890s, with the advent of the 'new journalism' of entrepreneurs such as W. T. Stead (1849–1912) and press barons like Alfred Harmsworth (1865–1922; known from 1906 as Lord Northcliffe).[36] The shift was partly technological and linked to the move away from woodblock engraving to

---

32 Annette Becker, 'Arts,' in *The Cambridge History of the First World War, Volume III – Civil Society*, trans. Helen McPhail, ed. Jay Winter (Cambridge: Cambridge University Press, 2014), p. 504.
33 Bernard Partridge, 'The World's Enemy,' *Punch*, 19 August 1914, p. 167.
34 Scully, *British Images of Germany*, pp. 306, 309–10.
35 Ibid., p. 309.
36 Hess and Northrop, *American Political Cartoons*, pp. 68–70; Joseph W. Campbell, *Yellow Journalism: Puncturing the Myths, Defining the Legacies* (Westport, CT: Praeger, 2001), pp. 32–3; Richard Scully, 'Accounting for Transformative Moments in the History of the Political Cartoon,' *International Journal of Comic Art* 16, no. 2 (2014): pp. 349–51.

Figure 3.2   Bernard Partridge, 'The World's Enemy', 19 August 1914

Source: Punch (London)

the use of 'process' etching. This involved the photographic transfer of an original drawing onto a metal plate, which was treated and etched so that the lines were in relief, thus enabling a relatively rapid turnaround from artist, to printer, to published product.[37] This was ideal

---

37   Nicholas Hiley, 'Showing Politics to the People: Cartoons, Comics and Satirical Prints,' in *Using Visual Evidence*, ed. Richard Howells and Robert W. Matson (Maidenhead: Open University Press, 2009), p. 30.

for the schedule of a daily paper, and men like Sir Francis Carruthers Gould (1844–1925) at the *Westminster Gazette* and William K. Haselden (1872–1953) at Northcliffe's *Daily Mirror* could thus have their work swiftly transferred to process plates, moulded and set with text, to be printed on enormous, industrial printing presses that utilised drum-shaped rollers and huge reels of cheap, thin, wood-pulp paper.[38] Haselden's regular comic strip (another innovation of the nineteenth century that affected the political cartoon) dealt with the 'Sad Experiences of Big and Little Willie' (little Willie being the Crown Prince) and became extremely popular and was released as a separate book in 1915.[39] A great many other British newspaper cartoonists also released compendiums of this sort, including Jack Walker (fl. 1911–1924) from the *Daily Graphic* and, perhaps most famously, E. J. Sullivan (1869–1933) in his book *The Kaiser's Garland*.[40]

Cartoonists the world over imagined Wilhelm II in similar terms to Partridge and Haselden: 'In apocalyptic visions, he is surrounded by death and the devil' or sometimes, actually is the Devil himself; 'exile in St Helena or the gallows await him'.[41] *Punch* and daily newspapers were published in black and white, and this was also the case for the majority of French publications, but in some magazines, the Kaiser's features were demonised in full, blazing colour. The first edition of the French weekly *La Baïonnette* devoted its cover to 'Le Kaiser rouge'; Charles-Lucien Léandre (1862–1934) depicting a wild-eyed, slavering monster armed with a broken sword and fiery cat-o-nine-tails descending on the ruins of a French village.[42] Also, unlike the cartoons of *Punch*, French cartoons tended to be chromolithographs or zinc chromotypographs, and therefore better able to convey 'crayon-like effects', unique textures and reproduce photographs in a manner peculiar to those media: a useful comparison is between Partridge's 'World Enemy' and 'The Hussar William II' (see Figure 3.3) by Jules-Abel Faivre (1867–1945).[43]

The French had been pioneers of 'process' from as early as the 1850s and were less wedded to traditional cartoon printing methods than their British counterparts.[44] In this, French caricature was heavily influenced by (and contributed to the development of) the 'golden age' of French poster art, which was still very much at its peak during the Great War, and which incorporated much imagery and style established by previous generations of cartoonists, as well as employing many of the same contemporary artists.[45] There was also significant overlap in terms of the fine arts as well; for instance, in one huge canvas (little different from the kinds of cartoon images then in mass-circulation) the French artist Otto Friez 'showed the

---

38   Ibid., pp. 30, 33.
39   W.K. Haselden, *The Sad Experiences of Big and Little Willie, during the First Six Months of the Great War: August, 1914–January 1915* (London: Chatto & Windus, 1915).
40   Jack Walker, *The Daily Graphic Special War Cartoons, Nos. 1–7* (London: The Daily Graphic, 1914–1915); E.J. Sullivan, *The Kaiser's Garland* (London: William Heinemann, 1915).
41   Demm, 'Propaganda and Caricature,' p. 179.
42   Charles-Lucien Léandre, 'Le Kaiser Rouge,' *La Baïonnette* 1, 8 July 1915, cover.
43   B.E. Maidment, *Reading Popular Prints, 1790–1870* (Manchester: Manchester University Press, 1996), p. 16; Jules-Abel Faivre, 'A Guillaume II, Le Hussard Reconnaissant,' in *L'Esprit Français – Les Caricaturistes* (Paris-Nancy: Berger-Levrault, 1916), p. 6.
44   Frankie Morris, *Artist of Wonderland: The Life, Political Cartoons, and Illustrations of Tenniel* (Charlottesville, VA: University of Virginia Press, 2005), p. 116; Hiley, 'Showing Politics to the People,' p. 30.
45   Pearl James, 'Introduction: Reading World War I Posters,' in *Picture This*, ed. James, p. 4; Aulich and Hewitt, *Seduction or Instruction?*, pp. 66, 107, 135.

Figure 3.3   Jules-Abel Faivre, 'The Hussar William II', 1916

Source: L'Esprit Français – Les Caricaturistes

triumph of German death with torture orchestrated by the Devil/Kaiser in which the world of God, justice and truth struggles with the world of the Devil, death and lies'.[46]

The cartoonists of France had always been more forthright in their criticism of the Kaiser than the British. Quite apart from the strand of admiration that characterised British attitudes towards Wilhelm – that for obvious reasons had no counterpart across the Channel – French caricature was far freer in its use of the grotesque, sexualised and scatological imagery that had fallen from favour in Britain since the 1830s. As such, there was greater continuity in French Kaiser Cartoons from the pre-war to wartime, with even the real Wilhelm's carefully-concealed withered arm being mercilessly depicted both prior

---

46   Becker, 'Arts,' p. 513.

to and long after 1914 (sometimes gripping a bloodied dagger in a parody of Wilhelm's own tendency to disguise his arm by affixing it to the hilt of his ceremonial sabre).[47]

Russian cartoonists likened the Kaiser to Napoleon, ridiculed his imagined home life and generally characterised him as 'a figure of fun and infamy'.[48] Some liberal cartoonists took particular joy in caricaturing what could not be openly ridiculed in Russia, even though political caricature had been permitted in some form since the Revolution of 1905: a monarch with pretensions to absolutism.[49] Generally, though, cartoonists toed the official line and – like their French and British counterparts – needed little encouragement from the Tsarist authorities to imagine for their readers the 'insane eyes and twisted moustaches' of the Kaiser.[50] In Warsaw, in the Russian-ruled section of Poland, Bogdan Nowakowski (1887–1945) drew a ghostly Death whispering sweet nothings in the ear of a bored-looking Kaiser – skulls and blood-stains lie beneath his jackbooted feet (see Figure 3.4).[51]

His compatriot Henryk Nowodworski (1875–1930) adopted a similar style, though it was far more attached to the grotesque than Nowakowski. It was not until the beginning of 1915 – after a boom in patriotic caricatures and anti-German cartoons at the outbreak of war – that depictions of Wilhelm II began to decline rapidly in number, as cartoonists instead turned their attention to internal strife and away from what could be achieved through 'yet another funny picture of Wilhelm or the sultan'.[52]

Before the decline of Russian images of the Kaiser, it was particularly conventional to see the conflict as a war of religion, 'a crusade against the barbarity of enemies without conscience, the incarnation of morality and civilisation denied'.[53] Although the decidedly secular French and British cartoonists employed religious imagery to lend their productions greater weight, Russian cartoons and prints were imbued with a greater formalised religiosity, for example in 'The Great European War', a poster of 1915 in which Russia's patron Saint George battles the many-headed dragon (one of which bears the Kaiser's face), or 'The German Anti-Christ'.[54]

Cartoonists of all the Entente nations 'took extreme pleasure' in comparing the Kaiser's pretensions regarding *Kultur* with the real (or invented) war crimes committed by German soldiers in the occupied territories.[55] No cartoonist excelled more greatly at this than Louis Raemaekers. Raemaekers owed his 'extraordinary celebrity' to a number of factors, not the least was his status as a neutral observer (of German descent, no less).[56] It may seem obvious to a twenty-first century audience, well-suited to scepticism of images and

---

47 Leonetto Cappiello, 'La Paix Allemande,' *La Baïonnette* 84, 8 February 1917, cover.

48 Lesley Milne, '"Novyi Satirikon," 1914–1918: The Patriotic Laughter of the Russian Liberal Intelligentsia during the First World War and the Revolution,' *Slavonic and East European Review* 84, no. 4 (2006): p. 644–5; Hubertus F. Jahn, *Patriotic Culture in Russia during World War I* (Ithaca, NY: Cornell University Press, 1995), pp. 48–9.

49 Milne, '"Novyi Satirikon," 1914–1918,' p. 645. There is something of this double-meaning in a 'Kazan Cat' print of Wilhelm II, based upon a centuries-old satire of Tsar Peter the Great (see: Bryant, *World War I in Cartoons*, p. 47).

50 Stites, 'Wartime Russia,' p. 16.

51 Bogdan Nowakowski, 'Inseparable Friends,' *Mucha*, 1914, in Mark Bryant, *The World's Greatest War Cartoonists and Caricaturists, 1792–1945* (London: Grub Street, 2011), p. 128.

52 Jahn, *Patriotic Culture*, p. 39.

53 Becker, 'Arts,' p. 513.

54 Bryant, *World War I in Cartoons*, pp. 27, 67.

55 Demm, 'Propaganda and Caricature,' p. 176.

56 John Horne and Alan Kramer, *German Atrocities, 1914: A History of Denial* (New Haven: Yale University Press, 2001), p. 297.

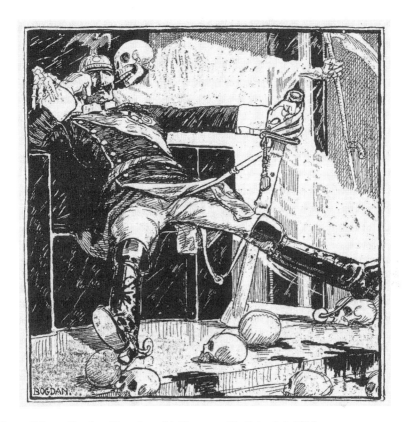

Figure 3.4   Bogdan Nowakowski, 'Inseparable Friends', 1914

Source: Mucha

messages pedalled by corporations and governments, but it was also true at the time of the Great War that in order 'to be more credible, propaganda needed to be removed from its true official origin'.[57] Hailing from the Netherlands and published in Amsterdam's *De Telegraaf*, Raemaekers provided just the right sort of critical distance required to make his cartoons seem more impartial (despite not being 'neutral in [their] sympathies') and therefore less likely to be affected by the private passions stirred and manipulated by propagandists.[58]

Wartime legends about Raemaekers abound, and so it is difficult to ascertain precisely why he departed Amsterdam for London in November 1915.[59] Some claimed that the German

---

57   Rasmussen, 'Mobilising Minds,' pp. 402–3.
58   'The Cartoonist of the War – A Dutchman's Genius,' *The Times*, 18 November 1915, p. 11.
59   Ariane de Ranitz, *"Met een Pen en een Potlood als Wapen!" Louis Raemaekers (1869–1956) Schets van een Politick Tekenaar* (Amsterdam: University of Amsterdam, 1989). An intriguing mix of myth and mundanity, Ranitz's study is still the definitive biography of Raemaekers. A new edition of this thesis was launched at Kaiser Wilhelm's place of post-war exile (Huis Doorn) in October 2014: Ariane de Ranitz, *Louis Raemaekers – 'Armed with Pen and Pencil': How a Dutch Cartoonist Became World Famous during the First World War* (Roermond: Fondation Raemaekers, 2014). Raemaekers

government had placed a 12,000-guilder price on his head (alternatively said to have been 12,000 German marks), following a failed attempt to pressure the Dutch authorities to have him silenced for breaches of neutrality.[60] The Municipal Council of The Hague certainly banned his cartoons from public display in September 1915, and there was some pressure brought to bear on the Dutch government from within the Netherlands, but whether Wilhelm II himself really did take personal offence at Raemaekers's cartoons – and demand revenge – is open to question.[61] Certainly, it was no accident that Raemaekers's arrival in London coincided with a major exhibition of his works at the Fine Arts Society. He was already being sponsored from afar by Lord Northcliffe, who saw in Raemaekers's cartoons the ideal form of propaganda for use at home and abroad.[62] Raemaekers may therefore have been moved by the prospect of fame and fortune in accepting the invitation to decamp to the United Kingdom, rather than compelled by the imagined threat of a German assassin.

Fame and fortune is certainly what Raemaekers found in London. Thousands flocked to see his exhibition every day (subtitled *A Neutral's Indictment*, and again emphasising the credibility of an outside observer).[63] Adored by the populace and 'lionized by London society', he was received at Downing Street by Asquith, the Prime Minister, who also attended the exhibition, and wrote an appreciation that was included in the *Land and Water* edition of Raemaekers's cartoons.[64] This famous edition was published in twenty-six fortnightly parts, each priced at a shilling, and attracted an enormous popular response.[65] Original Raemaekers drawings were must-have items and sold well at auctions in support of the war effort.[66] When he and his exhibition crossed the Channel in early 1916, Raemaekers found similar success. Feted by his fellow cartoonists – including a complete special edition of *La Baïonnette* devoted to his work – the crowds at the Galerie Georges-Petit were of comparable size to those in London.[67] Raemaekers was finally able to receive in person the *Légion d'honneur*, which had been awarded some time before *in absentia*, and he was also received at the Sorbonne.[68] In perhaps the ultimate tribute, not only did Raemaekers readily find publishers in Paris, but enterprising Frenchmen also ensured that his cartoons

---

was in London and staying at the Savoy by late November 1915, see Louis Raemaekers, 'Public Opinion in Holland,' *The Times*, 22 November 1915, p. 9.

60 'The Man Who Pursues the Kaiser – His Mission,' *The Register* (Adelaide), 4 December 1917, p. 9.

61 Maartje M. Abbenhuis, *The Art of Staying Neutral: The Netherlands in the First World War, 1914–1918* (Amsterdam: Amsterdam University Press, 2006), pp. 170–1; 'Greatest War Cartoonist – Louis Raemaekers, Bane of the Assassins – Kaiser Puts Price on Head,' *The Globe and Sunday Times War Pictorial* (Sydney), 18 March 1916, p. 5.

62 Louis Raemaekers 'American Newspaper,' *Editor & Publisher* 49, 1917, p. 22; Russell Stannard, *With the Dictators of Fleet Street: The Autobiography of an Ignorant Journalist* (London: Hutchinson & Company, 1934), pp. 115–16.

63 Louis Raemaekers, *The Great War: A Neutral's Indictment – One Hundred Cartoons by Louis Raemaekers* (London: The Fine Art Society, 1916).

64 Horne and Kramer, *German Atrocities*, p. 297; H.H. Asquith, 'An Appreciation from the Prime Minister,' in *The "Land and Water" Edition of Raemaekers' Cartoons* (London: 'Land and Water', n.d., [*c*. 1916]).

65 Steve Baker, 'Describing Images of the National Self: Popular Accounts of the Construction of Pictorial Identity in the First World War Poster,' *The Oxford Art Journal* 13, no. 2 (1990): p. 24.

66 'Buy Raemaekers' Prints,' *Cartoons Magazine*, 10, 1916, p. 634.

67 *La Baïonnette – Numero spécial Entièrement Consacré a Raemaekers* 32, 10 February 1916; Horne and Kramer, *German Atrocities*, p. 529.

68 Francis Stopford, Introduction to *Raemaekers' Cartoons* (Garden City, NY: Doubleday, Page & Company, 1916).

were smuggled into occupied Belgium, and published in the underground newspapers *La Cravache* and *Patrie!*.[69]

Raemaekers eventually produced well in excess of 500 cartoons in the course of his wartime career (possibly over 1,000), and although only a fraction of these depicted Wilhelm II, the Kaiser was – by a considerable margin – the real-world figure most commonly depicted.[70] As a reviewer in the *Times* noted, Raemaekers's Kaiser was 'not only the Kaiser himself to the life', but was 'also an idea of the Kaiser and what he represents'.[71] Aside from deliberate depictions of Wilhelm II, for example, in the company of the Horsemen of the Apocalypse (Figure 3.5), Raemaekers also incorporated the Kaiser into his more allegorical, generic

Figure 3.5   Louis Raemaekers, 'To the End', 1916

Source: Raemaekers' Cartoons

---

69 Sophie de Schaepdrijver, 'Occupation, Propaganda, and the Idea of Belgium,' in *European Culture in the Great War: the Arts, Entertainment, and Propaganda, 1914-1918*, ed. Aviel Roshwald and Richard Stites (Cambridge: Cambridge University Press, 1999), no. 21, p. 406; Horne and Kramer, *German Atrocities*, p. 315.

70 Horne and Kramer, *German Atrocities*, p. 298; Bertrand M. Patenaude, *A Wealth of Ideas: Revelations from the Hoover Institution Archives* (Stanford, CA: Stanford University Press, 2006), p. 31.

71 'The Cartoonist of the War – A Dutchman's Genius,' *The Times*, 18 November 1915, p. 11.

Figure 3.6 Louis Raemaekers, 'Thrown to the Swine – The Martyred Nurse', 1916

Source: Raemaekers' Cartoons

cartoons of German atrocity.[72] 'Thrown to the Swine – the Martyred Nurse' (Figure 3.6), for instance, shows a gory scene in which the pure white corpse of an idealised female is about to be devoured by a group of slavering pigs in *pickelhaube*s.[73] It cannot be coincidental that the tusks of the dominant boar in the sty curl upward in the manner of the Kaiser's moustache.

---

72 Louis Raemaekers, 'To the End,' in *The 'Land and Water' Edition of Raemaekers' Cartoons* (London: 'Land and Water', n.d. [*c*. 1916]), p. 83.

73 Louis Raemaekers, 'Thrown to the Swine: The Martyred Nurse,' in *Raemaekers' Cartoons*, p. 25.

Germany did its best to limit Raemaekers's influence over neutral opinion but was largely unsuccessful in this endeavour (even in terms of refuting his and others' claims in dedicated, domestic propaganda organs).[74] This was despite an apparently short-lived success in postponing an exhibition in Madrid in the winter of 1916 and a celebrated court case in Switzerland in early 1918.[75] Most significantly, they were powerless to prevent the effective use of Raemaekers's status as an unbiased neutral observer in the most important neutral context of all: the United States.[76] American cartoonists had been ridiculing the Kaiser for some time before official belligerence began in April 1917.[77] The likes of Boardman Robinson (1876–1952) – a declared socialist – had produced remarkable Kaiser Cartoons, such as showing Wilhelm about to impale feminised Peace on his sabre, at the same time as protesting that he had always striven hard for peace 'even though war was inevitable'.[78] Nevertheless, Raemaeker's impact was of great importance. David Lloyd George personally invited Raemaekers to travel to the United States and Canada in July 1917 (and not, as is sometimes reported, before the US entered the war in April of that year, in order to convert Americans to the cause of the Entente).[79] Once Raemaekers embarked on his tour of North America, William Randolph Hearst saw particular value in recruiting the Dutchman to his vast newspaper empire, and from September 1917, readers of the New York *Puck* magazine obtained either weekly reprints of classic hate cartoons, or new products aimed directly at Americans.[80]

Although Raemaekers's time with Hearst was relatively short (*Puck* itself folded in September 1918), Raemaekers's association with the Northcliffe of the New World did just as much for his reputation as had his original collaboration with the press baron of London.[81] He met with President Woodrow Wilson at the White House, and former President Theodore Roosevelt waxed lyrical about his cartoons as 'the most powerful of the honourable contributions made by neutrals to the cause of civilization'.[82] In addition to his cartoons being reprinted in newspapers and magazines, as stand-alone prints and in specially-edited

---

74 Lasswell, *Propaganda Technique*, pp. 161 ff.

75 Horne and Kramer, *German Atrocities*, p. 298 (the references supplied by Horne and Kramer with regards to Spain are difficult to substantiate – these may relate to a different evening or morning edition of the paper); Charles Vuille, *L'Affair Raemaekers. Compte-rendu d'un process intenté à Me Charles Vuille devant la Haute Cour Pénale Fédérale* (Neuchâtel: Attinger frères, 1918).

76 Louis Raemaekers, 'Seven Cartoons,' *The North American Review* 203, no. 723 (1916); Stewart Halsey Ross, *Propaganda for War: How the United States was Conditioned to Fight the Great War of 1914–1918* (London: McFarland, 1996), p. 43–4.

77 'A Scathing Article – Germany Denounced – American Cartoon of Kaiser,' *Barrier Miner* (Broken Hill), 12 October 1914, p. 2; 'American Opinion – Austro-German Position Hopeless – The Kaiser Ridiculed,' *The West Australian*, 25 July 1916, p. 7.

78 Boardman Robinson, 'I . . . Strove Hard for Peace Even Though War as Inevitable,' *Puck* (1915), accessed 21 March 2014, http://www.granger.com/results.asp?image=0027377&stockindexonline.com=1&screenwidth=1426.

79 M.L. Sanders and Philip M. Taylor, *British Propaganda during the First World War, 1914–18* (London: Macmillan, 1982), pp. 176–7; H.R. Westwood, *Modern Caricaturists* (London: Lovat Dickson, 1932), p. 62; Bevis Hillier, *Cartoons and Caricatures* (London: Studio Vista, 1970), p. 118.

80 'Raemaekers and Hearst,' *Cartoons Magazine* 11, 1917, p. 718.

81 'Raemaekers to Quit Hearst,' *Cartoons Magazine* 11, 1917, p. 862; Scully, 'Kaiser Cartoons,' p. 36.

82 Thomas Fleming, *The Illusion of Victory: American in World War I* (New York: Basic, 2003), p. 57; Theodore Roosevelt, 'The Genius of Raemaekers,' *Land & Water*, 7 June 1917, p. 19.

books, the British War Propaganda Bureau based at Wellington House ensured that there were millions of Raemaekers's cigarette cards and postcards in circulation at any one time (by one estimate, some 50 million postcards were ordered for distribution in the United States alone).[83] This was particularly the case once Lord Beaverbrook and John Buchan had assumed control over propaganda in February 1918, as part of the remit of the new Ministry of Information. The remarkable thing about Raemaekers's success prior to this, therefore, was that his propaganda had managed to reach a global audience without official British government assistance.[84]

Cartoonists in America did receive significant assistance – and guidance – of a similar kind to that provided by Wellington House in Britain. The Committee on Public Information (CPI) established and administered a Bureau of Cartoons quite separately from the Division of Pictorial Publicity.[85] So important was the cartoonists' art in the minds of US propaganda officials, that this was supervised directly by the executive of the CPI. A weekly *Bulletin for Cartoonists* was issued to provide guidance on how best to convey appropriate wartime messages, listing 'fitting subjects' and coming close to 'providing the pictorial ideas themselves'.[86] James Montgomery Flagg's cover for *Bulletin* no. 20 (Figure 3.7) is a nice illustration of the perceived role of the cartoonist: a heroic self-portrait of Flagg himself – dressed in an artist's smock, with a huge folio under his arm – forces Wilhelm II to examine his reflection in a dressing-table mirror. Staring back at the Kaiser is a grinning deaths-head.[87] What is most interesting to the modern scholar is the way the caption of the cartoon – 'The Cartoonist Makes People See Things' – potentially contains a double-meaning: does the image imply that the cartoonist reveals the truth about a situation or individual, or does it imply that the cartoonist makes people hallucinate, and see things that are not there?

By the time these official organs of state took note of the power of the cartoon, much of their impact had already been felt. So prevalent were such images, and so familiar their imagery, that in a short story produced for *McClure's* monthly, Wallace Irwin could describe a propaganda flier to his readers – as depicting Wilhelm II as 'a sort of machine-made dragon, created of steel and iron and armour-plate, with forty-two centimetre guns belching flame from his nose' – without the need for any illustration.[88] However, as Anne Rasmussen has noted in relation to journalists more broadly, while cartoonists 'did what they could to control public opinion', their impact 'diminished in proportion to the discredit that fell on propagandist rhetoric'.[89] It would therefore be a mistake to imagine Kaiser Cartoons being of sustained appeal across the whole 1914–1918 period, and yet in terms of sheer published

---

83 John Fraser, 'Propaganda on the Picture Postcard,' *The Oxford Art Journal* 3, no. 2 – Propaganda (1980): p. 43.

84 Gary S. Messinger, *British Propaganda and the State in the First World War* (Manchester: Manchester University Press, 1992), p. 92; Messinger, *The Battle for the Mind: War and Peace in the Era of Mass Communication* (Amherst: University of Massachusetts Press, 2011), p. 23.

85 Axelrod, *Selling the Great War*, p. 94.

86 Hess and Northropp, *American Political Cartoons*, p. 82.

87 James Montgomery Flagg, 'The Cartoonist Makes People See Things!,' *Bulletin for Cartoonists* 20, 26 October 1918, p. 1.

88 Wallace Irwin, 'One of Ten Million,' *McClure's* 50, no. 2, December 1917, p. 15. The story did include one illustration by Clarence Underwood, showing the Kaiser, with sword drawn, threatening the female protagonist of the story in her dreams.

89 Rasmussen, 'Mobilising Minds,' p. 408.

WARS AND FOREIGN RELATIONS

COMMITTEE ON PUBLIC INFORMATION

GEORGE CREEL, Chairman
THE SECRETARY OF STATE
THE SECRETARY OF WAR
THE SECRETARY OF THE NAVY

Bureau of Cartoons *Bulletin No. 20*

BULLETIN FOR CARTOONISTS

OCTOBER 26, 1918

Figure 3.7　James Montgomery Flagg, 'The Cartoonist Makes People See Things!', 1918

Source: *Bulletin for Cartoonists*

weight, it seems unlikely that belief in their utility had diminished by the last year of the conflict.

Raemaekers had by 1918 become 'the single most influential individual figure in projecting the Allied vision of the German enemy to home audiences and to the rest of the world'.[90] But he was only the most prominent of a whole army of cartoonists the world over who seemed to spend every waking moment demonising Wilhelm II and all he stood for. Just as Raemaekers was being lauded in the United States, so too the work of 'that other genius whose pencil war has turned into a sword' – the Australian, Will Dyson (1880–1938), who worked in Britain – was also heavily promoted across the Atlantic, most notably by the British-American Committee.[91] *Kultur Cartoons* was 'first class propaganda', and its contents were featured prominently in the New York *Sun* newspaper.[92] Interestingly, although Dyson tended to depict symbolic Germans – such as the professor, the vulture-like German eagle, apes bombing British cities, or the arms manufacturer – it was his 'Dysonised Kaiser' that most stood out for the *Sun*'s publicists (see Figure 3.8). Adrian Gregory has noted how Dyson's cartoons often went beyond the standard cultural explanation for German frightfulness, positing a biological, racial explanation for the actions of 'the Hun'. The Kaiser's minions were not merely conditioned by a militarist culture to commit atrocities and forced to do so by the dictates of a military aristocracy; rather, Dyson imagined that 'the Germans as a people were intrinsically flawed, probably depraved, and possibly evil'.[93]

Dyson's presence in London is a useful indicator that Kaiser Cartoons also flowed from the imperial periphery to the metropole, rather than just the other way around.[94] Dyson himself had been in the metropolis since 1910 (and departed the *Daily Herald* to act as Australia's official war artist in 1916), but other Australian cartoonists were soon making an impact of a comparable kind. Official government sanction was given to an exhibition of cartoons from the Melbourne *Punch* that opened at Arthur Tooth and Son's Gallery, Bond Street, on 25 February 1917.[95] This had originally been a Melbourne-based exhibition but had proved so successful that it was taken to London.[96] There, the High Commissioner, and former Prime Minister, Andrew Fisher, was on hand to make explicit the connection between the assembled cartoons and Australia's loyalty to Britain, the empire, and the war effort.

---

90 Horne and Kramer, *German Atrocities*, p. 297.

91 G.K. Chesterton, 'Satan's Partner,' in *Raemaekers' Cartoons*, p. 22.

92 Ross McMullin, *Will Dyson: Australia's Radical Genius* (Carlton North, VIC: Scribe, 2006), p. 154; '"Kultur Cartoons" . . . By Will Dyson,' *The Sun*, 27 June 1915, p. 2.

93 Adrian Gregory, 'A Clash of Cultures: The British Press and the Opening of the Great War,' in *A Call to Arms: Propaganda, Public Opinion, and Newspapers in the Great War*, ed. Troy R.E. Paddock (London: Praeger, 2004), p. 38.

94 For example, J.H. Dowd's, 'Playing the Game: The Kaiser's Cricket' (published in the Sydney-based sports paper *The Referee*, 21 July 1915, p. 13) was originally published in *The Illustrated Sporting and Dramatic News* (London). Australian reprinting of British cartoons was relatively common.

95 'Exhibition of "Punch" (Australia) War Cartoons in London,' *Punch* (Melbourne), 28 April 1917, p. 659.

96 Timothy S. Benson, *Over the Top: A Cartoon History of Australia at War* (Brunswick, VIC: Scribe, 2015), p. 40.

Figure 3.8 Will Dyson, 'Dysonised Kaiser', 1915

Source: The Sun

The opening of the exhibition received considerable publicity from the *Times*, *Daily Telegraph*, *Weekly Graphic*, *Morning Post* and *Daily News*, with the senior paper singling-out the foresight of George Henry Darcey (1865–1922), whose treatment of the Kaiser in the past seemed very much in keeping with his wartime output.[97] 'In cartoon after cartoon', Dancey heaped scorn upon the Kaiser, seeing Wilhelm as either a figure of ridicule, or as one committing 'brutal atrocities in many scenes of violence'.[98] Dancey had already been introduced to British audiences in 1915, when the *Review of Reviews* dedicated their regular column 'Caricatures of the Month' to his work, and the *Weekly Graphic* went so far as to

---

97 'Australian Cartoons of the Kaiser – An Artist's Foresight,' *The Times*, 22 February 1917, p. 9.
98 'Australian Cartoons,' *The Times*, p. 9.

call him 'the Bernard Partridge of Australia', but his lesser known colleague James Charles Nuttall (1872–1934) was also praised for his 'great power of moulding public opinion' and ability to 'speak with the voice of Imperialist Australia'.[99]

The exhibition was significant enough for the London-based art magazine *The Connoisseur* to pick up the story and connect it to another exhibition by Raemaekers.[100] The proprietor of the *Melbourne Punch*, Alex McKinley, was particularly careful to thank another former Prime Minister, Alfred Deakin, for his role in supporting the exhibition in the course of a high-profile visit to Britain.[101] By the time Deakin returned home, Will Dyson's brother-in-law, Norman Lindsay (1879–1969) was adapting the kind of work he had done for *The Bulletin* to the poster format and contributing even more strongly to the worldwide convergence of Kaiser Cartoon imagery (Lindsay's famous '?' of 1918 both reflected H. R. Hopps's imagining of Wilhelm II as a 'Mad Brute' and inspired other American and British imitations).[102] This transnational network of cartoonists would soon also provide Britain with the next generation's greatest exponent of the art, David Low (1891–1963), the New Zealander whose work for the Australian press attracted the attention of the editor of the London *Star* in late 1918.[103]

As was the case with Raemaekers's cartoons, the exhibition of high-quality prints or originals, as well as the reprinting of Kaiser Cartoons in various papers and periodicals, was only one form of dissemination that characterised this global cartoon genre. In many ways a far more direct means by which such images were distributed was via the postcard; a format that – if sent via international mail – was inherently transnational in nature. Though in his work, Jeff Keshen has emphasised their Canadian context, Kaiser Cartoon postcards were circulated globally, and mingled with both more serious images of battlefields 'littered with German dead', as well as other cartoons 'trivializing the dangers of combat'.[104] As well as utilising its wartime output, the London *Punch* recycled many of its pre-war Kaiser Cartoons in postcard format, including 'Cook's Crusader' by Linley Sambourne (1844–1910), which depicted a ridiculous Wilhelm II in the garb of a Teutonic Knight, sympathising with the Ottoman Sultan.[105] These were printed by Jerrold and Sons

---

99   'Caricatures of the Month,' *Review of Reviews* 52, July–December 1915, p. 115; 'Exhibition of "Punch",' p. 659; 'Australian Cartoons,' p. 9.

100 C. Reginald Grundy, 'Current Art Notes,' *The Connoisseur* 47, no. 188, April 1917, pp. 230, 233.

101 Alex McKinley letter to Alfred Deakin, 21 March 1917. Papers of Alfred Deakin, MS 1540, Subseries 1.36 (Correspondence, 1917), National Library of Australia, Canberra.

102 Norman Lindsay. '. . . . .?,' *The Cause of the War*, 1918; H.R. Hopps, *Destroy This Mad Brute – Enlist*, 1917; Peter Stanley, *What Did You Do in the War Daddy? A Visual History of Propaganda Posters* (Oxford: Oxford University Press, 1983), p. 10; Nicolette F. Gullace, 'Barbaric Anti-Modernism: Representations of the "Hun" in Britain, North America, Australia, and Beyond,' in *Picture This*, ed. James, p. 72.

103 David Low, *Low's Autobiography* (London: Michael Joseph, 1956), pp. 76 ff.

104 Jeffrey A. Keshen, *Propaganda and Censorship during Canada's Great War* (Edmonton: University of Alberta Press, 1996), p. 162.

105 Scully, *British Images of Germany*, p. 314; Stefan Goebel, *The Great War and Medieval Memory: War, Remembrance and Medievalism in Britain and Germany, 1914–1940* (Cambridge: Cambridge University Press, 2007), p. 118. The complete set of wartime *Punch* postcards can be viewed (in low resolution) online: Paul Hageman and Jerry Kosanovich, '"Punch" Cards (GB), 1999–2010,' accessed 18 March 2014, http://www.ww1-propaganda-cards.com/; 'Punch Postcards,' *World War I Postcards from the Bowman Gray Collection*, Rare Book Collection, University of North Carolina, Chapel Hill, accessed 18 March 2014, http://dc.lib.unc.edu/cdm/ref/collection/graypc/id/8912.

of London but were soon available as far away as Australia.[106] In France, a remarkable series of six postcards by Charles Fontaine showed all the atrocities of which the Germans were accused, and when arranged together in the form of a picture-puzzle, the images were revealed to be aspects of Wilhelm II.[107] It is worth noting that this important cartoon genre was not without its real-world consequences: by late 1914, it was decided by both French and British authorities that postcard Kaiser Cartoons would not be forwarded to the front.[108] It was feared that should the Germans find such images in the possession of men taken prisoner-of-war, this might result in mistreatment by the enemy, even summary execution.

Mention of the real-world consequences of Kaiser Cartoons brings one to a final, though critically-important issue: as propaganda weapons, what was their actual impact on the conduct and outcomes of the war? In many ways, this must remain a great unanswered – and perhaps unanswerable – question, though a few comments can be made. Because of their visual, popular nature, it was believed that cartoons in particular were best able to convey simple and acceptable messages to the vast majority of a belligerent population. As George J. Hecht asserted in the preface to a 1919 survey of United States war cartoons:

> Editorials are read by few, news stories by more, feature articles by more, headlines by more, and perhaps cartoons by most of all. Because they contrast with the printed material surrounding them, they stand out; they require little thought for their complete digestion.[109]

It is perhaps true that, as Jay Winter has asserted, in wartime, 'images overwhelm words', and 'what people see affects them more than what they read'.[110] Of course, when viewing a cartoon, people do both, and thus in an additive sense, this makes the cartoon particularly powerful.

There was also a widespread belief in the importance of such images to sustain hatred of the enemy and all they stood for. One (ideologically-suspect) German scholar claimed that in the cartoons of Raemaekers, 'a dreadful, boundless hatred was paired with a great artistic talent and an inexhaustible imagination', and that the result 'had more propaganda value than several volumes of English propaganda pamphlets put together'.[111] Similarly, the two leading lights of the inter-war German right – Erich Ludendorff and Adolf Hitler – both believed that visual propaganda was of far greater effect than the written word and that Allied visual propaganda had been instrumental in the defeat of the Central Powers.[112] Such claims can be relatively easily dismissed as the ravings of embittered men, as can exaggerated claims for the impact of such a campaign in actually winning the war (such as

---

106 'The Kaiser in Cartoon,' *Newcastle Morning Herald & Miners' Advocate* 2, December 1914, p. 5.

107 Tony Allen, 'Kaiser Bill Postcards,' n.d., accessed 21 March 2014, http://www.worldwar1postcards.com/kaiser-bill.php.

108 'Kaiser Cartoons Unwise,' *Geelong Advertiser*, 7 December 1914, p. 3.

109 George J. Hecht, *The War in Cartoons: A History of the War in 100 Cartoons by 27 of the Most Prominent American Cartoonists* (New York: E.P. Dutton, 1919), p. 3.

110 Jay Winter, 'Imaginings of War: Posters and the Shadow of the Lost Generation,' in *Picture This*, ed. James, p. 37.

111 Hermann Wanderscheck, *Die englische Propaganda im Weltkrieg gegen Deutschland 1914–1918* (Berlin: E. S. Mittler, 1935), p. 171.

112 Erich Ludendorff, *My War Memories, 1914–1918*, vol. 1 (London: Hutchinson & Company, 1919), pp. 349, 360–9, 381; Adolf Hitler, *Mein Kampf*, vol. 1, 23rd ed. (Muenchen: F. Eher, 1933), p. 204.

those by Roosevelt as regards Raemaekers's impact).[113] It is possible to make a reliable claim that Kaiser Cartoons helped to sustain the Allied war effort when it might otherwise have faltered. One other, final consideration must be whether, after such a sustained campaign of character assassination through cartoons and other media, Wilhelm II would ever have been able to remain on the throne of Germany and Prussia (or possess a realistic chance of regaining that joint status as part of a restoration). The answer surely must be no; the men whose will to fight had been sustained for so long by an image of their enemy that was constantly reinforced in cartoon after cartoon would simply not have stood for it.

There remains much to be said about the global genre of Kaiser Cartoons during the Great War. This chapter has tended to focus on the cartoons that appeared in Europe, North America and Australasia, but an appreciation of the African, South American and Asian contributions to the genre awaits the dedicated historian. In South Africa, for instance, Herbert Wood 'Mac' MacKinney (1881–1953) produced a number of amusing Kaiser Cartoons for the *Cape Times*, while from the Indian context, the contribution by various imitators of the *Punch* tradition is still being researched by a number of active scholars. Intriguing Chinese and other East Asian examples also await the dedicated researcher, in a field of considerable (and increasing) interest to scholars.[114] Regardless of future developments, it is important to see the Great War of 1914–1918 as being just as much a 'war of the cartoonists' as it was a war of posters, or even of nations and empires. That conflict was fought – as Eberhard Demm noted two decades ago – 'over the status of personalities as much as it was over ideological principles', and the cartoon Kaiser was the biggest personality of all.[115]

---

113   J.M. Winter, 'Propaganda and the Mobilization of Consent,' in *The Oxford Illustrated History of the First World War*, ed. Hew Strachan (Oxford: Oxford University Press, 1998), p. 224.

114   Mac, *Cartoons of the Great War, 1914–1916* (Cape Town: The Cape Times Limited, 1916); Mac, *Cartoons of the Great War, 1917–1918–1919* (Cape Town: The Cape Times Limited, 1919); [Chinese Text with Image of Kaiser Wilhelm II of Germany and Marshal Foch of France], c.1918, accessed 24 March 2014, http://www.iwm.org.uk/collections/item/object/31589.

115   Demm, 'Propaganda and Caricature,' p. 178.

Chapter 4
Musical entertainment and the British Empire, 1914–1918

Emma Hanna

Music and the British Empire, from the end of the nineteenth century to the period after the Second World War, has been the subject of a handful of histories in the last fifteen years.[1] In the midst of the war's centenary, historians are now carrying out detailed research into the various modes of musical entertainment during the period of the First World War.[2] This chapter will provide an overview of the provision of musical entertainment for the troops of the British Empire during the conflict of 1914–1918. It will show how British composers, musicians and entertainers worked to take music of all kinds to those serving the British Empire, demonstrating how music was used to maintain the morale of servicemen on the fighting fronts. This chapter will also survey the work of the leading wartime organisation: the Young Men's Christian Association (YMCA), who saw the war as an opportunity to utilise their own brand of Christian philanthropic education, and of the significant efforts they made to provide musical entertainment to soldiers wherever they were serving King and Country.

War, music and morale

During the First World War musical entertainment was an important component in recruitment, fundraising and the maintenance of both civilian and military morale. The importance of music and all kinds of entertainments intensified during the course of the conflict, and in 1917, Lord Derby (Minister of War) said:

> [t]he people's amusements ... should go on ... Let those who come home be met with cheerful faces. Let them feel that their leave from the trenches should be marked by amusements that will abstract them from all the anxieties and dangers.[3]

---

1 See Jeffrey Richards, *Imperialism and Music: Britain 1876–1953* (Manchester: Manchester University Press, 2001); and Nalini Ghuman, *Resonances of the Raj: India in the English Musical Imagination, 1897–1947* (Oxford: Oxford University Press, 2014).

2 This area was initially opened up by works such as J.G. Fuller, *Troop Morale and Popular Culture in the British and Dominion Armies, 1914–1918* (Oxford: Clarendon Press, 1990); and Glenn Watkins, *Proof Through the Night: Music and the Great War* (London: University of California Press, 2003); but there have been more detailed studies by John Mullen, *The Show Must Go On! Popular Song in Britain during the First World War* (Ashgate: Farnham, 2015); Toby Thacker, *British Culture and the First World War* (London: Bloomsbury, 2014); Jason Wilson, *Soldiers of Song: The Dumbells and Other Canadian Concert Parties of the First World War* (Ontario: Wilfred Laurier University Press, 2012).

3 Lord Derby (Minister of War from 1916) quoted in *The Era*, 31 January 1917; as cited in Mullen, *The Show Must Go On!*, p. 37.

Historians are now recognising the power of music and its validity as an area of research in the years 1914–1918. The emotional potency of sound and melody surpasses the capabilities of visual images or written texts; it is an intrapersonal process, a social phenomenon and a product of cultural influences and traditions. As John Mullen recently pointed out, 'songs and musical activities can give us a unique insight into popular attitudes during the Great War . . . as documents of which one can analyse the content, the reception and the social meaning.'[4]

In Britain, and its imperial outposts, music was a staple of family and community life across the social spectrum. At a time before widespread gramophone ownership, people provided their own amusement and entertainments; singing and the playing of instruments were appreciated, and there was an expectation that those who were capable should entertain. Having a piano in the parlour was the mark of a cultured household. In 1914 there were 2–4 million pianos in Britain (one for every fifteen people), as well as the Pianola, an automatic piano, which never reached the level of popularity in Britain as it did in America. Musical performance was an established part of everyday life, and street singers were commonplace. The late Victorian years saw an expansion in choirs and brass bands, often subsidised by local employers. There were competitions from the 1880s, and repertoires included classical song and opera as well as music hall hits. By 1900 there were more than 30,000 brass bands in the UK.[5] In Britain the music hall was the most popular form of mass entertainment, and music hall stars such as Marie Lloyd, Vesta Tilley and Harry Lauder were the celebrities of their day (Tilley and Lauder would become deeply involved in the war effort). In 1914 a new style of music called 'ragtime' was only starting to get established and had not yet developed into jazz, and a dance called the 'foxtrot' became popular. Variety shows and revues were performed twice a night in most towns and cities with a mixture of comic and sentimental songs.

The British Empire's declaration of war against Germany on 4 August 1914 had an immediate impact on British musical life. It was an established practice for notable events to be commemorated with a song, so the search for a new hit soon started with a competition for new wartime songs run by Francis & Day publishers. This was won by 'Pack Up Your Troubles in Your Old Kit Bag', a song that enjoyed great popularity in the earliest months of the war and is now emblematic of the period in our contemporary memory of 1914–1918. Many musicians joined the forces, which left house orchestras in cinemas, music halls and concert venues short of players. On a more positive note, British piano manufacturers, who had been recovering ground against their German competitors, found buoyant opportunities with the removal of new German pianos from the market.[6] The first of the annual Promenade Concerts organised by the composer and conductor Sir Henry Wood was scheduled on Saturday 15 August 1914, and the work of Richard Strauss and all other 'enemy' composers was removed from the programme. The tradition of the following Monday's concert being 'Richard Wagner night', the play list was re-programmed to feature French, Russian and British works including the *Nutcracker* suite and *L'Après-midi d'un faune*. However, after Chappell – the music publishing house which ran the Promenade concert series at the Queen's Hall – announced that '[t]he greatest examples of Music and Art are world possessions and unassailable even by the prejudices and passions

---

4 Mullen, *The Show Must Go On!*, p. 4.
5 Ibid., p. 9.
6 Arthur Jacobs, *Henry J. Wood: Maker of the Proms* (London: Methuen, 1994), p. 148.

of the hour' the works of Strauss, Wagner and other Germanic composers would feature in the remaining wartime Promenade concerts.[7]

The empire and British culture

The elite musical scene in Britain became ever more internationalised as many Belgian musicians arrived in London – such as Joseph Jongen – in addition to artists from other nations including Pablo Casals, Karol Szymanowski and Vaslav Nijinsky. Music and musicians from the allies of the British Empire were welcomed and actively encouraged to perform in Britain, although the rising number of Belgian and French musicians moving into local house orchestras was a cause of some concern to musicians' unions. The Japanese soprano Tamaki Miura did sing a Giuseppe Verdi aria in January 1915 but music from Britain's other ally Russia was easier to programme, especially that by Modest Petrovich Mussorgsky, Sergei Rachmaninoff, Igor Stravinsky and Sergei Prokofiev. From 1915 onward travel was very difficult for foreign instrumentalists and no performers of German, Austrian or Hungarian origin were allowed into Britain. While French music was already popular, in early 1916 a group of leading British composers formed a Russian Music Committee to promote the use of Russian music in Britain.

The nineteenth century had been the century of musical nationalism. Many countries developed a musical style that was seen to reflect their national identity, but there was considerable prejudice against English music in Britain; Italian music dominated opera, German composers led the orchestral field and French the operetta.[8] In 1914 *The Strad* magazine hoped that the war would serve to rectify this position, that the 'easy-going Briton, with all his genius for colonizing and for government', would be encouraged to develop a recognisably British elite musical style:

> War, except so far as it crushes individual talent, is not in principle inimical to art. The present war is arousing the best and truest feelings of our race; and from such a condition an enhanced feeling for the beautiful and the true is likely to spring. A more earnest and profound view of life and its joys and sorrows cannot but be productive of a worthier conception of Art. We may hope to have a more really national music . . . a better educated democracy will perhaps solve the problem of the establishment of a national opera.[9]

In 1914 the British Empire was at its height. In the earliest years of the twentieth century, one of Britain's principal concerns was 'the great show of empire' where writers, travellers and artists 'brought the sounds of tales of distant lands ever closer to home'.[10] Jeffrey Richards has underlined that '[e]very aspect of popular culture contrived to instil pride in the British imperial achievement' and that the empire

---

7 Ibid., p. 149.
8 Richards, *Imperialism and Music*, p. 10.
9 F.A. Hadland, 'Music and the Great War,' *The Strad*, April 1916, p. 2.
10 Nalini Ghuman, *Resonances of the Raj: India in the English Musical Imagination, 1897–1947* (Oxford: Oxford University Press, 2014), p. 2.

was Britain writ large . . . the embodiment and expression of a British character comprising of individuality, stoicism, a sense of duty, a sense of humour and a sense of superiority; that Britain was in the Empire for the good of its native peoples.[11]

This sense of purpose can be seen in the work of the organisations, who worked with the British armed forces during the First World War. A 'Music in War-Time Committee' was established by leading composers of the day including Henry Wood, Ralph Vaughan-Williams and Henry Walford Davies.[12] The Committee organised a number of concerts, such as the performances for approximately 8,000 territorial soldiers on 15 December 1914 at White City Stadium. The Soldiers' Entertainment Fund (SEF) was established in 1915 led by the writer and composer Lyell Johnston. The SEF had two aims: to entertain the troops and also to provide work for performers. Starting in hospitals in February 1915, by May 1919, 750 artistes had performed 2,000 concert parties in London and the surrounding area. The SEF sponsored one excursion to a naval base in Malta in 1916, followed by a visit to a large hospital garrison for those injured on the Eastern Front.[13]

During the early stages of the war, efforts were made to ensure that soldiers' morale was maintained through the provision of a variety of entertainments, particularly in the form of concert parties. These gatherings performed the same vital functions as sports; they brought all ranks together in a spirit of community, gave rest from autonomy and obedience and helped to displace anxiety. Several battalion officers recognised the value of concert parties early on and groups evolved spontaneously amongst the soldiers at rest, in YMCA huts or around the established system of divisional canteens. The regular units of the British Army already had canteens as an established feature of service life, which helped soldiers' pay go further by selling tobacco, beer, soft drinks, books, newspapers, candles, tinned food, biscuits and chocolates at cost prices. The Army acknowledged the need for canteens in all battalions in February 1915, and the Expeditionary Force Canteens (EFCs) was amalgamated as 'EFC Section ASC' (Army Service Corps) in July 1915.[14] The divisional canteens were supplemented by civilian organisations like the YMCA, the Church Army, the Salvation Army, the Dominion Comforts Fund, the Church of England Soldiers' Home, Army Scripture Readers, the Navy Mission Society and the British Soldiers Institute. Many Army divisions had their own troupe of entertainers, and these groups held official brigade or divisional concert parties. The performances owed a large debt to the music hall with a combination of singing, reciting, conjuring, comedy, ventriloquism and ensemble sketches. The light-hearted nature of these groups can be seen from the ensembles' names such as The Whizz Bangs (5th Division), The Cheerios (2/6th Battalion King's Liverpool Regiment), The Very Lights (12th Battalion) and High Tension Entertainers (Army Service Corps). A small admission fee was charged and the events were very well attended.

By the end of 1916 most Army divisions had an official concert party, and by the end of 1917 they were universal.[15] British troops loved to sing, and this was very much encouraged by the Army because 'singing connotes belonging'.[16] The composer Henry Walford Davies had long been involved in the provision of music and singing amongst the troops, and in

---

11 Richards, *Imperialism and Music*, pp. 2, 16.
12 L.J. Collins, *Theatre at War, 1914–18* (Oldham: Jade, 2004 [1998]), p. 81.
13 Ibid., p. 82.
14 Michael Young, *Army Service Corps, 1902–1918* (London: Leo Cooper, 2000), pp. 86–7.
15 Fuller, *Troop Morale and Popular Culture*, p. 96.
16 Richards, *Imperialism and Music*, p. 6.

1918 he was appointed as the first Director of Music in the newly formed Royal Air Force, his primary task being to organise choral singing which he believed reinforced the team spirit of fighting men:

> A brass band is all very well in its way, but it does not come near the male voice choir in the production of the best music . . . Get the men to do something together and you have started an *espirit de corps* among them which will have a tremendous influence for good, and will do more than any of us imagine to make life in camp, in barrack, or billet, or in the outpost more tolerable.[17]

The YMCA

The YMCA quickly became the largest and most far-reaching organisation whose red triangle emblem illustrated its mission to nourish the minds, bodies and spirits of the men fighting for Britain's Empire, wherever they may be. Public appeals were also launched to fund the building of large wooden huts wherever soldiers were stationed which could hold up to 500 soldiers.[18] These huts provided a space for soldiers to rest and listen to musical talks and recitals, as well as for their own music-making, such as informal sing-songs around one of the pianos which were provided for exactly that purpose. YMCA huts quickly became known as places that would provide soldiers with food and a wholesome place to rest on the front line or at home in military camps and railway stations. A widespread education programme for soldiers was started, which became the Army Education Corps in 1920. By October 1914 the charity had erected 400 large marquees in Britain. The British Army invited the YMCA to establish base camps in Le Havre and along the lines of communication down to the Mediterranean. Expansion to the Eastern Front and other areas of the British Empire was swift: YMCA facilities would be found wherever the soldiers were sent.

Music was an integral component of YMCA programmes, as 'in the Army of each of our Allies the same thing is found. The need for music is universal.'[19] The organisation distributed 20,000 copies of a selection of popular songs for in-hut entertainment, and in the autumn of 1914 the YMCA established its own Music Department, which carried the motto 'Whatever Cheers the Warrior Helps to Win the War'.[20] Led by the composer Percy Scholes, those involved with the department identified a 'tremendous awakening of interest . . . in music . . . both from the point of view of performance and appreciation'.[21] It was thought that it was the organisation's duty to do this work, and that 'an Association which has no sign of such activity should question itself very seriously as to whether it is being left behind and becoming hopelessly old-fashioned'. The YMCA Music Department was very well resourced. Amongst its activities was the ability to organise speakers for

---

17 Major H. Walford Davies, 'Music and Arms,' *The Red Triangle*, vol. 1, September 1917–August 1918, YMCA/K/6/1, Cadbury Special Collections, p. 97.

18 Collins, *Theatre at War*, p. 82.

19 Percy A. Scholes, 'Music and the Fighting Man,' *The Red Triangle*, vol. 2, September 1917–August 1918, YMCA/K/6/1, p. 192.

20 'The Music Department and Its Resources,' *The Red Triangle*, vol. 6, September 1917–August 1918, YMCA/K/6/1, p. 207.

21 Ibid.

talks on composers and on subjects such as 'how to form an orchestra', providing a list of musicians, lecturers and entertainers available, maintaining a music library and the sale of instruments at reduced prices through deals with suppliers. The Music Department also started a 'Competition Festival Movement' because they 'afford excellent opportunities for the neighbourly exchange of ideas and for the testing and improving of local standards'.[22] The value of morale-boosting music in wartime was seen as central to the YMCA Music Department's activities. Scholes wrote in 1917:

> "Will music help us to beat the Boche?" The University Extension lecturer was just beginning his talk on 'The Story of British Music', when that question was hurled at him. He looked round the crowd of men squatting around on the floor of the marquee, men just out of the trenches the day before, and replied: "The first hundred thousand crossed the Channel singing 'Tipperary'. How much did their good spirit and courage owe to that tune? Then came the period of the mouth organ, and one musical paper alone sent a thousand pounds' worth as the gift of its readers. Then followed 'Pack Up Your Troubles in Your Old Kit Bag' – a song that has been worth six divisions to the British Army. After that gramophones in their thousands, Miss Ashwell's concert parties, visits to the front of crack Army bands, and now University Extension lectures on Music. Are these things helping you 'to beat the Boche'?" And every man shouted "Yes".[23]

'Every camp its own theatre'

The Music Department was keen to encourage Tommy Atkins to appreciate classical music, and saw the war as an opportunity to civilise men who, if not for the war, would have little exposure to the grand masters. However, it was the popular actress-manager Lena Ashwell who first approached the YMCA to suggest that performers should be utilised to help boost soldier's morale by putting on concert parties for soldiers whose divisions were yet to organise their own ensembles, in wherever part of the empire they were fighting. In October 1914 Ashwell made every effort 'to get the entertainment of troops put on national lines, and was interviewed several times on the scheme of "every camp its own theatre", and the organising of work by professional actors, but there was little interest shown'.[24] Ashwell led the formation of a Representative Committee, a gathering of noted musicians and actors 'with representatives of the Church as a guarantee of respectability and good faith', and an appeal was formulated and sent to the War Office that 'recreation should be organised, that the movement should be national, as national as the Red Cross' but their offer was refused.[25] Somewhat 'sad and disheartened', Ashwell continued her work with the Women's Emergency Corps which was extending their operations from London to Bristol and Newcastle, running fifteen branches by March 1915. Then,

> on one never-to-be-forgotten day, when I had quite lost hope of the drama and music of the country being regarded as anything but useless, Lady Rodney called on behalf of the Women's Auxiliary Committee of the YMCA. She had returned from France, and

---

22 Scholes, 'Music and the Fighting Man,' p. 192.
23 Ibid., p. 192.
24 Lena Ashwell, *Modern Troubadours* (London: Gyldendal, 1922), p. 5.
25 Ibid.

came from Her Highness Princess Helena Victoria, Committee Chairman, to ask if it was possible for a concert party to go to Le Havre.[26]

These royal connections helped smooth the way with the War Office, and Ashwell arranged to cover the expenses privately. It was argued that

> owing to the very suffering state of men at Base Camps who had passed through a very difficult period of fighting, and were to be at Base for rest and further training, this experiment of sending recreation should be made.[27]

Those involved understood this to be a one-off arrangement. Conditions were put in place that there should be no advertising and that the performers would not use the event to increase their professional popularity. A further stipulation was that all members of the concert party had to be known to Ashwell and become known to Her Highness as the latter was to be responsible for their persons and conduct:

> They were to work with the YMCA, who would look after the billeting arrangements in France, and places, times, etc, for the concerts ... There were grave doubts on behalf of the YMCA ... I think some expected us to land in France in tights, with peroxide hair, and altogether to be a difficult thing for a religious organisation to camouflage. Some good things did come to us through the war, and one of them was the breaking down of barriers due to misunderstanding.[28]

Ashwell became a leader of concert parties, the first of which was held at No.15 Camp, Harfleur Valley, on 18 February 1915. The company set the pattern for soldiers' concerts that would follow throughout the war: a soprano, contralto, tenor, baritone/bass, instrumentalist and entertainer. The success of the venture led the YMCA to appoint a committee to oversee Ashwell appointing other artists, promoting the concerts and also raising money to continue putting them on. By the summer of 1916 it was reported that Ashwell's groups had put on around 2,000 concerts in hospitals or YMCA huts. A party had been despatched to entertain British troops in Malta, and many concerts were being put on for the Royal Navy as 'sailors perhaps need it more than any other people, seeing that they have far fewer chances of recreation and entertainment.'[29] Described as 'one of the greatest assets of the YMCA at this time', Ashwell was praised for 'affording the men diversion and recreation when they might be tempted to spend their time unprofitably were there no concerts ... thus exerting a strong and noble influence over the thought and life of the men'.[30]

Ashwell was a formidable fundraiser. In one article she gave her address and wrote, 'I want you to give me your new hat, your new carpet, your new teacups, everything you thought you were going to buy next week, and to give it to me for the sake of the boys at the front and the boys in the Navy.'[31] The YMCA concert party tour of Malta, coordinated

---

26 Ibid.
27 Ibid.
28 Ibid., p. 7.
29 'Have You Given Your New Hat?: A Suggestion by Miss Lena Ashwell,' *The YM*, 30 June 1916, p. 602.
30 Ibid.
31 Ibid.

by Ashwell, began on 23 February 1916. The party was very popular, particularly with the YMCA representatives who 'have had the joy of knowing that everything the party did was done in the most perfect taste and to the honour of the ideals for which the YMCA stands'.[32] By early May ninety-nine concerts had been performed in convalescent camps, hospitals, hospital ships and some small outlying forts. It was reported:

> These concerts were a real mission of mercy. In the early days of the tour the party had the privilege of singing to men broken in health by arduous months on the Gallipoli Peninsula. No one, except those who have themselves gone through the experience, can fully appreciate what such concerts mean to men who heard little music save the sounds of the guns during these months of hardship and suffering.[33]

Indeed, the positive reception and effect on the soldiers in Malta led the YMCA to suggest that concert parties be put on the troop transport ships which passed the island. Several concerts were arranged and to great effect, and 'the reader's imagination can perhaps realise the unique circumstances of a concert given on thronged decks to men for whom, after a rough passage in an over-crowded boat, a good entertainment was a veritable Godsend.'[34] The reception the Navy gave to the concert parties led the YMCA to suggest further entertainments should be provided on board, helped by Lady Limpus, the wife of the Admiral Superintendent, who was a principal YMCA liaison in Malta. Thursdays were devoted to concerts in the naval hospitals or the large naval canteen for men serving on warships or the Merchant Navy:

> Those of us who have carefully watched the progress of the Lena Ashwell party are trying to make up our minds as to which of the two services supply the most enthusiastic audiences. The body of opinion favours the Navy, thought the reason may not be, not that the men of the Navy are of higher musical taste that the Army, but that so much less is done by way of entertaining them.[35]

Concert parties were also given for the survivors of torpedoed or mined vessels, including the *Simla*, the *Minneapolis*, and later *HMS Russell*. These were for the performers 'happy and sad events – happy because the gladdened faces of the men made their programme so obviously a mission of mercy, and sad because thoughts of the men who had lost their lives inevitably came to their minds'.[36]

A club for servicemen of the British Empire

Once the *Lena Ashwells* were established as touring companies, the actress helped the YMCA's next venture: to provide a centre of respectable musical entertainment for soldiers of the empire in central London. In the spring of 1917 the management of Ciro's restaurant

---

32 'On Tour in the Mediterranean,' *The YM*, 9 June 1916, p. 519.
33 Ibid.
34 Ibid.
35 Ibid.
36 Ibid.

offered their premises in Orange Street, Central London, to the YMCA, free of rent until the end of the war. It was felt that the concert parties had been so successful that the YMCA's Emergency War Committee awarded a further £100 to Ashwell's funds and a sum of £350 for equipment at the venue.[37] The YMCA announced its tenancy of the restaurant in May 1917. Under the headline 'What We Are Doing at Ciro's' the Hon. Mrs Stuart-Wortley reported that the premises 'will open its doors to the men of H.M.'s Forces and their lady friends':

> This means that a man can take his mother, his wife, or his sweetheart to these luxurious reception rooms for recreation and refreshment. He can meet his friends of either sex and enjoy with them a cup of tea while listening to music under the most ideal conditions . . . It has been a reproach to London that hitherto the stranger – the man who has come thousands of miles from his home across the seas – within its gates, unless well provided with funds and connections who will introduce him, has found so few opportunities of a social kind that a soldier back for a few days' leave from the trenches may wander forlornly round the town and never get the chance of happy friendly intercourse with the class he would like to meet . . . just the things a man misses so poignantly in the existence to which the war condemns him remorselessly for so many months on end.[38]

Ciro's proved to be a huge success. It was reported in June 1917 that in twelve days the premises were used by 1,780 men and 300 women.[39] The composer John Foulds was also in residence at Ciro's, and the YMCA funded his salary.[40] Foulds had fallen short of Army fitness requirements, and he served as Musical Director of the Central YMCA during the latter stages of the war.[41] Foulds dedicated a large part of his time to the musical activities of the Central YMCA in London from 1917 until 1923, where he had a leading role which he is said to have carried out with an 'altruistic spirit'.[42] His mission was

> to create and sustain an interest in the highest walks of the musical art where none was previously existent, to men who in the main must be considered as non-musical. . . . this branch of the Association is now known throughout London, not to mention the provinces, as being the keenest musical centre of any in the whole kingdom.[43]

Foulds was one of many composers who worked for the YMCA. Another notable example is the composer Gustav Holst who went to organise musical entertainment and education to British and Imperial troops on the Eastern Front on behalf of the YMCA's Music Department. Like Foulds, Holst had tried to enlist during the first months of the war, but he was rejected as unfit for military service. In 1918, as the war neared its end, Holst responded to the

---

37 Minutes of the Finance and War Emergency Committee, 24 April 1917 and 22 May 1917, YMCA/K/1/8/31.
38 Hon. Mrs Stuart-Wortley, 'What We Are Doing at Ciro's,' *The Red Triangle*, 25 May 1917, p. 467.
39 *The Red Triangle*, 15 June 1917, YMCA/K/6/1.
40 Minutes of the Finance and War Emergency Committee, 1 October 1918, YMCA/K/1/8/31.
41 Borthwick: MacCarthy-Foulds, Box 9: Letter from Maud to her mother, 3 May 1918, ACC 51/2008. This was written on YMCA 'HM Forces of Active Service' headed notepaper.
42 Letter from Frank Carter, general secretary of London Central Y.M.C.A., to the principal of Cape Town University, 2 March 1921, 56482, British Library Manuscripts (BLM).
43 Ibid.

YMCA's Music Department request for volunteers to work with British troops stationed in Europe awaiting demobilisation.[44] Holst enjoyed his time in Salonica, from where he was able to visit Athens, which greatly impressed him.[45] His musical duties were wide ranging and even obliged him on occasion to play the violin in the local orchestra.[46] Holst returned to England in June 1919. Both Foulds and Holst are examples of the many British composers who, from around 1910, had been deriving a great deal of inspiration from the empire, particularly India. After a lecture-recital to the newly-founded India Society in 1910, Holst contacted the pioneering musician Maud MacCarthy for guidance on Indian scales.[47] Nalini Ghuman has underlined that while a great deal of Holst's music, notably the pieces of military band, the choral folk songs, and suites for strings undeniably has deep roots in English traditions, 'it was through his intense engagement with Indian culture that his modernist, highly personal voice took shape.'[48] Of Holst's best-known work *The Planets*, which he composed 1914–1916: 'Once the words "I vow to thee my country" had been attached to the *andante maestoso* of "Jupiter" it quickly began to vie with "Land of Hope and Glory" for the place of a second national anthem with which to hymn imperial England.'[49]

The YMCA spent around £18 million in today's money on supporting the troops of the British Empire through the provision of free stationery, games, sports, concerts, educational work and lectures, and hospitality to relatives of the wounded. In total the YMCA's wartime expenditure was equivalent to £5.1 billion today, the majority raised by charitable subscriptions and donations. A total of £166,672 [£7.2 million] was spent on free concerts and entertainments, in addition to £45,000 [£1.95 million] supported work for Indians in France and £75,696 [£3.3 million] for men serving the British Empire in India and Mesopotamia.[50] By the early 1900s the YMCA had branches in many countries all over the world. This naturally included India, which at the time was still perceived as the jewel in the crown of the British Empire. At the YMCA tent in Nowshera, in 1910 – the camp farthest north in India – typical facilities were provided such as games, papers, magazines, also references to tennis and badminton, as well as debates, music and the bioscope [cinema].[51]

The YMCA in India

The YMCA had started working with the British Army in India shortly before the outbreak of war. In the Indian Army in 1914 there were approximately 240,000 serving officers and men. By the end of the war India had deployed over 1 million men overseas in both combat and supporting roles. The majority of the Indian Army had been recruited from the north

---

44 Michael Short, *Gustav Holst: The Man and His Music* (Oxford: Oxford University Press, 1990), p. 159.
45 Ibid., p. 171.
46 Ibid.
47 Ghuman, *Resonances of the Raj*, pp. 123–5.
48 Ibid., p. 139.
49 Ibid.
50 Green Book No. 5, Photographs Illustrating the emergency war work of the YMCA (Germany, Holland, India, Italy), YMCA/K/1/7.
51 Green Book No. 5, Photograph of YMCA tent in Nowshera, 1910, YMCA/K/1/7.

and in Nepal for Gurkha units; but the manpower shortages during the war meant that recruits increasingly came from groups once thought unsuitable for military service. India's largest campaign was in Mesopotamia, where over 657,000 men served; 144,000 were sent to Egypt and Palestine, 138,000 fought in France and Belgium, and smaller numbers were sent to Aden, East Africa, Gallipoli and Salonika. In August 1914 there were three YMCA centres for the British Army in India. Mostly due to the arrival of British Territorial regiments in India by January 1915, there were ten centres, but despite scarce resources in May 1919 there were eighty-two Army centres in India run by the YMCA, managed by forty British and American and thirty-four Indian secretaries.

In Calcutta, the eleven YMCA workers who arrived in India at the end of 1915 were said to have had

> a very trying time at the start, in an atmosphere of suspicion very naturally, but the work once established soon dispelled all difficulties by its very obvious worth, and as for its popularity one only needed the sight of the sports gathering on Christmas Day to convince one that this unprecedented departure for the Indian Army had been there since the Mutiny, so much were the men at home.[52]

The YMCA's mission in India, for both British and Indian troops, was the same as it was nearer home: the red triangle emblem symbolising that they aimed to care for men's' minds, bodies and spirits. It is important to note that despite the Christian nature of the organisation it stated from the outset that 'no religious work or proselytising of any kind is done'.[53] Indian YMCA work was based in rented houses, tents supplied by the Army and specially erected buildings. Subsidies from national funds included the salary of the 'Secretary of Secretaries in Charge' but funds were also obtained by fundraising for example, subscriptions, donations, supper clubs and concerts.[54]

As on the Western and Home Fronts, musical entertainments were always provided in military hospitals and convalescent camps. In Bombay the YMCA funded the appointment of a 'Special Entertainment Secretary' to ensure that 'extensive entertainment work is carried on several British and Indian hospitals at the Alexandra Docks, Brigade Office and Mechanical Transport Centre'.[55] At the Dadar Labour Corps War Hospital and Convalescent Camp a full-time Indian Secretary was in charge of a 'Special Recreation Hut' that would house musical entertainments and cinema shows.[56] An illustration from a YMCA publication is particularly atmospheric and serves to demonstrate that the organisation was acting to maintain Indian musical culture by providing suitable instruments:

> The Indian YMCA: On the banks of the Tigris at Amarah this YMCA hut built of mud with palm trees growing through the roof, making part of the superstructure, is picturesque enough. Here Indian regiments of various creeds enjoy their evenings in their own fashion. Here they have their tamashas, tom-toms and reed musical instruments being supplied by

---

52 J.G. Harley (Calcutta), 'With the Indian Troops in Travel,' Reports, Work of the YMCA for British and Indian Troops in India, 1914–1919, 16 January 1916, YMCA/K/2/7.
53 Reports, Work of the YMCA for British and Indian Troops in India, 1914–1919, YMCA/K/2/7.
54 Ibid.
55 Ibid.
56 Ibid.

the YMCA who cater to all tastes, and a man can always be sure of a good hot meal well turned out.[57]

India sent over 140,000 men to the Western Front: 90,000 served in the infantry and cavalry and 50,000 as non-combatant labourers. They came from the length and breadth of India and represented a very diverse range of religious, linguistic and ethnic cultures. The officer corps was mainly composed from men of European descent. All armies depend on a number of essential support units and the work of the labour corps, particularly those made up of men from China and India, were vital to keep the war effort going and releasing men for front line service. By the last stages of the war there were fifty-four labour corps each made up of 1,150 men, and six syce (grooms) companies of 210 men served on the Western Front.[58] Indian porters were also indispensable in Mesopotamia where the lack of transport infrastructure was a serious threat to the British war effort. Conditions on the Western Front were very hard for all concerned but particularly so for the labourers who were serving in a land so different from their own. To ensure that these men were kept reasonably content, Indian music would be played on gramophones and cinema shows would be provided.[59]

The war brought together a wide variety of musical cultures from around the British Empire and beyond. The experience of hearing and seeing the music and instruments of other cultures captivated Percy Scholes. On YMCA business at a French port in 1917 he recalled:

> Dieppe is the place where the greatest mixture of races is to be seen. There I have noticed an Algerian, sitting at an open window of one of the big hotels, now used as a hospital, and playing on a flute the same little phrase over and over again. Not much of a tune, perhaps, but it brought to the windows all the brother Algerians, who stood or sat, quietly listening so long as the playing continued. Then, in the same place I have seen a group of coal-black Senegalese walking through the streets to the sound of a one-stringed instrument with a parchment body and a plectrum consisting of the tooth of some animal fastened to the finger of the performer on a leather loop. I stopped them, and examined the instrument, and should have liked to buy it, but it would have been cruel to deprive these men, so far from their home, of the tones and tunes that remind them of it, and took them in memory back to their inland swamps or the silver sands of their Atlantic shore. How often, too, have I watched our Chinamen at work to music about the docks at Dieppe, with their blue costumes and their little round brown caps. The foreman gives the order by a little phrase and the coolies respond by rhythmic movements, in lifting or pulling, or whatever the task may be, singing as they do so.[60]

Musical entertainments and the other services provided by the YMCA were greatly appreciated by all troops of the British Empire. A private soldier from Kent serving in India wrote:

> [w]e are also running a good concert party which has made a great name, "The Shara-Bandits". The[y] are probably going to Bagdad at the end of next week and should make

---

57 Green Book No. 5, Photographs Illustrating the emergency war work of the YMCA (Germany, Holland, India, Italy), YMCA/K/1/7.

58 Gateways to the First World War, 'Indians in the British Army,' exhibition by Professor Mark Connelly, Spring 2015.

59 YMCA War Work in France, 1915–18 – Work for Indians in France, YMCA K/2/4.

60 Scholes, 'Music and the Fighting Man,' p. 192.

a hit there. Our sports include the "Buffs Race Meeting" on Boxing Day and they should provide some good racing.[61]

Another conveyed:

> We are looked after very well here we have games here namely the good old English game cricket – crocket and Bammington [sic] & we also have a band come on the grounds & play music. Bombay ladies & also YMCA men come round every Tuesday & Thursday & bring writing material – cards – papers, books & post-cards . . . they put the only shop near as out of bounds, so we have to be satisfied with the things they give us.[62]

While many British soldiers serving in India had to stay within their own camps, some servicemen could venture into nearby towns. One private soldier serving in the 'Near East' reported that they could 'get into the town of an evening. Theres [sic] plenty of amusements, the Divisional Pantomine, picture palaces and a circus. So you see we're having a fairly good time'.[63] Many British soldiers serving in hotter climes recognised that they were 'fortunate in having the sand & not mud & are correspondingly grateful. But we sigh for the green fields of home as we can put up with the elements better there'.[64] The sense of home-sickness is palpable in the millions of soldiers' letters home, but their duty to the empire regularly shines through:

> How proud we are to know that so many have left our own small village to serve with the forces in some capacity or other. . . . what little we are able to do here to keep the Empire still bound in the same bond of unity.[65]

Another soldier wrote:

> The consolation of knowing that my serving out here, is part & parcel, as one might roughly term it, of the defence of the Empire & thus indirectly showing a little gratitude in helping to defend you, & the dear old home, of course. . . . we are still posted on the sandy desert, & civilization seems a thing of the past.[66]

One soldier put his fond thoughts of home into verse:

> There's a village in the Homeland that to many a lad is dear,
> It dwells in all our memories each day throughout the year.

---

61 Letter from Private Charles V Byford, India, 9 July 1915, Great Chart Papers, Kent History and Library Centre (KHLC).
62 Letter from Private Douglas Skinner, Bombay, 3 October 1916, Great Chart Papers, KHLC.
63 Letter from Private Arthur Cramp, Near East, 26 January [no year given], Great Chart Papers, KHLC.
64 Letter from Corporal Samuel Brunger, Egypt, 30 December 1916, Great Chart Papers, KHLC.
65 Letter from Company Sergeant-Major William Brunger, India, 8 July 1915, Great Chart Papers, KHLC.
66 Letter from Corporal Samuel Brunger, 2/5th Suffolk Rgt,, 12 August 1916, Great Chart Papers, KHLC.

We know we're not forgotten by the true kind friends at home,
And that thought uplifts and cheers us wherever we may roam.

There are laddies in the trenches, Salonika and the West,
On the Tigris and in Palestine giving of their best;
In all the various Fronts, Great Chart Men are called to fight,
Soon we hope will come the ending – God will show that Right is Might.

Then our Boys are on the Ocean, keeping clear the wide North Sea,
Some in far off India busy, doing well what is duty,
And like a magnet drawing comes the thought to every heart:
"They're thinking of me there at home, the dear Friends of Great Chart".[67]

Music was often found to be a way in which soldiers could reconnect with fond memories of home and family. This was particularly marked at times of intense fighting when men, the majority of whom were between ages 18 and 30 years old, felt in need of comfort. One young soldier wrote to his parents that physical danger 'is but one part of the trial of war. Quite as bad, to many a man, is the boredom of the Base':

> There is no Y.M. hut here, and nowhere to go and nothing to do. Yesterday I felt in despair, and the others were just as bad. Then I caught sight of a box lying on the ground in the middle of the camp, and some impulse made me jump on it and begin singing, "There's a land, a dear land." Everyone gathered round and cheered at the end. *After that we all felt better.*[68]

The existence of instruments, particularly the piano, was widely known to help provide a relaxing atmosphere in the rest areas. Scholes recalled that in some huts 'the piano is hardly ever silent. . . . The piano and the gramophone have done great service to *morale* in this war.'[69] The cellist Helen Mott was one of many musicians who went to play and teach troops with the YMCA. Of the servicemen she encountered she wrote that

> they used to come up afterwards and ask questions – or tell us that they liked so-and-so (usually Beethoven), because their mothers or sisters used to play it; or could we oblige next time we came by playing Grieg's *Peer Gynt* Suite (or generally something classical), as it was such a long time since they had heard it. Always they spoke of the *peace* and *rest* it gave them to hear good music, and those who were not quite so accustomed to it evidently found plenty of interest and enjoy [*sic*], for they came more than once, and our audiences grew rapidly.[70]

The musical entertainments that accompanied the troops wherever they were posted show that the emotional link with the home they were fighting for was a constant theme. This expanded to the existing dominant narrative of British imperial achievement, which certainly applied to musical activities on the Home Front. The composer Charles Villiers

---

67 Poem written by Rifleman Sydney H. Bates, 30 July 1917, Great Chart Papers, KHLC.
68 Scholes, 'Music and the Fighting Man,' p. 192. Emphasis in original.
69 Ibid.
70 Helen Mott, 'Good Music and the Soldier,' *The Red Triangle*, vol. 1, September 1917–August 1918, YMCA/K/6/1, pp. 367–8.

Standford had written in 1916 that during a national emergency as dire as war that music's most potent role was that of a rallying cry.[71] This is particularly pertinent to the work of the composer Edward Elgar, who in 1924 the critic and composer Cecil Gray would call 'the self-appointed Musician Laureate of the British Empire'.[72] Elgar was actively involved in composing music that supported the British war effort. Jeremy Crump has said that 'the years from 1914 until the beginning of 1918 . . . saw him as much involved in performance and composition as at any time and enjoying an unrivalled position in English musical life.'[73] Indeed, the *Sheffield Daily Post* commented that '[w]hen the history of the Great War comes to be written the name of Edward Elgar will stand out as the one native composer whose music truly expressed the spirit of our people.'[74]

Elgar's wartime compositions included *Polonia*, which he dedicated to the Polish pianist Paderewski; *Carillon: Une Voix dans le Desert* and *Le Drapeau Belge* as a response to events after the invasion of Belgium; *The Fringes of the Fleet*, a setting of four Kipling poems which toured Oswald Stoll's music hall circuit; and *The Saguine Fan*, a ballet composed for charity. His most well-known work up to this point – *Land of Hope and Glory* – was a staple of wartime concerts. Although Elgar's music was even at that time perceived as rather dated, his music was still popular with mass audiences for its ability to convey a sense of English identity. As Crump underlined, apart from large-scale orchestral performances Elgar's music was played by ensembles such as the Black Dyke Mills Band who played over forty engagements with brass band arrangements of Elgar's symphonies.[75] Elgar emphasised that the Great War was an imperial war – underlined when he conducted a peace pageant at the Coliseum Theatre in July 1919 – *Land of Hope and Glory* and the *Imperial March* were played with Britannia seen to acknowledge the colonies and dependencies.[76]

As far as popular music is concerned sentimentality was a more powerful force than nationalism, and humour was very important. As L. J. Collins has observed, patriotism 'had to be done with humour rather than with solemn seriousness. This was the way they did it in the music hall and this was where the common soldier went for his entertainment'.[77] Some in the upper echelons of the music industry were concerned about the baser nature of popular music. The composer Sir Charles Villiers Stanford tried to get military bands to play old folk songs such as *Lillibulero* – a song made popular during the Marlborough Wars, and the Oxford University Press published six patriotic *Songs of War*, all of which, according to the *Times* 'ought to have a sure place in every camp repertory'.[78] However, the most popular musicals performed on the stages of the West End tell us a great deal about the mood of wartime audiences composed of military personnel and civilians. Fantastical productions such as *Maid of the Mountains*, *A Little Bit of Fluff* and the oriental spectacular

---

71   Charles Villiers Stanford, 'Music and the War,' in *Interludes, Records and Reflections* (London: Murray, 1922), pp. 102–3.
72   Cecil Gray, *A Survey of Contemporary Music* (London: Oxford University Press, 1924), pp. 78–9.
73   Jeremy Crump, 'Identity of English Music: The Reception of Elgar, 1898–1935,' in *Englishness: Politics and Culture, 1880–1920*, ed. Robert Colls and Philip Dodd (London: Croom Helm, 1986), p. 171.
74   *Sheffield Daily Post* quoted in Crump, 'Identity of English Music,' p. 175.
75   Crump, 'Identity of English Music,' p. 175.
76   Richards, *Imperialism and Music*, pp. 71–2.
77   Collins, *Theatre at War*, p. 10.
78   Ibid., p. 13.

Chu Chin Chow each ran for more than 1,000 performances in the war years. What the majority of audiences wanted was colour:

> [A]n antidote to the dreariness of brown mud and khaki uniforms . . . a temporary release from the agonies of war; and for this escape they looked, on the whole, to musical comedy and to the music hall with its songs, farcical one act- sketches and revues . . . for reasons which were both psychological and practical.[79]

Popular music, in addition to the theatre and music hall, were too powerful not be made relevant and purposeful. Music was soon utilised for the purposes of recruitment, propaganda, fundraising, and the need for servicemen to protect the interests of the British Empire would feature strongly. The fashion for warlike songs at the start of the war in 1914 has reignited a long-standing debate about the nature and extent of popular support for British imperialism. Andrew Thompson's study of the popular impact of imperialism has underlined the difficulties in ascertaining public attitudes towards the empire, and he has rightly stated that 'what the Empire meant to the masses cannot simply be read from the words of a music hall song.'[80] It is however important to underline that Britain's annual celebration of Empire Day from 1904, and of the imperial connotations of organisations such as the Scout Movement founded in 1907, are evidence of continued public imperialist discourse which led to frequent demonstrations of patriotic sentiment. John Mullen's survey of one thousand one hundred and forty-three songs published in Britain during the First World War identified seven songs, which referenced 'Empire' in their title:

The Empire's Rally (1914)
John Bull's Empire (1914)
For Empire and For England (1915)
Sons of the Empire (1915)
The Song of Empire (1915)
Our Empire (1916)
Tommy Atkins Saved His Empire From the Hun (1917)[81]

The relatively low proportion (0.6 per cent) of songs about the empire suggests that the general reputation of the British wartime music hall as warlike and imperialistic is not entirely justified as the most popular songs 'sang more about mother than the empire, and far more about Tommy than Kitchener'.[82] Nevertheless, as a corrective to a mythologised vision of the chirpy British Tommy going singing to his death, wartime sources such as regimental journals provide genuine insights into the music and mentality of British servicemen:

> Don't believe these stories that he's [*sic*] always singing "Tipperary" and that he's always ready for a fight or a frolic. There's no frolic about it and very little music. His frolic and his music is awaiting him at his castle somewhere in the Empire, if he ever sees it

---

79 Ibid., pp. 2–3.
80 Andrew Thompson, *The Empire Strikes Back? The Impact of Imperialism on Britain from the Mid-Nineteenth-Century* (London: Pearson, 2005), p. 39.
81 The author wishes to thank John Mullen for his assistance with this list of titles. Copies of the music and lyrics are available in the British Library.
82 Mullen, *The Show Must Go On!*, p. 89.

again. He came out here to fight, and he's in dead and serious earnest. He wasn't always singing "Tipperary" while he was doing his day's duties in peace times or while he was commuting to and from work; no more does he do it now . . . the frolic and the music may come after the job is done.[83]

The Royal Engineers Band was one of the most active military ensembles during the war. They played at a number of high-profile concerts, for example on 25 November 1914 at the Queen's Hall, London, in front of Queen Alexandra for the Royal Engineers' Comforts Fund. They would later play at the memorial service for the Minister of War, Lord Kitchener, after his death at sea in 1916. The programme on that occasion was traditionally classical featuring many works by Tchaikovsky, and the concert ended with the national anthems of the Allied Nations: Belgium, Japan, Serbia, Russia and France.[84] Other flagship military bands included the Royal Artillery and a number of Guards regiments who gave thousands of concerts at home and abroad during the war. For example, the Band of the 1/5th Battalion, East Surrey Regiment gave regular performances while on active service in India, and in the archive of the National Army Museum there are a good number of concert programmes from Cawnpore, Nowshera as well as sports events, which were held under the auspices of YMCA. Concerts took place at the Garrison Theatre, Nowshera where a 'selection of songs, dances, illusions, recitations, imitations, sketches and caricatures' were given in January 1917. Other programmes can be seen from events held at Robert's Memorial Institute at Cawnpore – one on 12 May 1917 says it is 'in part aid of the YMCA huts in France'. The Nomads concert party of the 1/5th Batt East Surrey Regiment also appeared in addition to The Aerials and The Darktown Coons.[85]

What we can see from these programmes is that the musical entertainments on offer are identical to those performed on the Western Front. The songs listed are largely either sentimental ballads, or humorous and rather raucous tunes with lyrics full of in-jokes and *double-entendre*, which most soldiers would join in to sing. Many programmes are put together in a style that parodies the British local newspaper, echoing the humour of the now well-known British trench publication *The Wiper's Times*. An illustrated programme for a Grand Fête in aid of the Artists' Rifles' VAD hospital in June 1917 features an advert for The Caffir Craawl:

> Come and see the untrained man and his squaw-d . . . Marvellous Mikers from Mashonoland! Wild Narks from Nyassa! The Show That Made Kiralfi Kry!
> Tommies and Tom-toms
> The donkeys may be rode easy, but this is Rhodesia.[86]

That the fighting fronts were full of music and humour may come as a surprise. However, in the midst of so much fear and death there was a great deal of life amongst the servicemen of the British Empire. Music of all kinds prompted the emotional remembrances of home

---

83 William G. Shepherd, 'At the Front: An American Opinion of Us,' *The Sapper*, June 1915, Royal Engineers Museum, p. 301.

84 'Concert at the Queen's Hall,' *The Sapper*, December 2014, Royal Engineers Museum, p. 111.

85 Programme for concert at The Garrison Theatre, Nowshera, 20 January 1917, 8411–103, National Army Museum.

86 Programme for Grand Fête in aid of the Artists' Rifles' VAD hospital at Hare Hall camp, 2 June 1917, NAM: 9512–170–3.

by linking back to the sound worlds of comfort and family. Whether it was a bawdy music hall tune, the strains of a Chopin piano piece, or the sound of their own native instruments, soldiers were reminded of the home – and empire – they were fighting for. The power of music to console, educate and inspire was particularly effective when the work of individual musicians and performers combined with the logistical might of the YMCA, who were able to generate the resources to take musical entertainment to soldiers of the British Empire wherever in the world they were fighting. Music was truly one of the most powerful weapons in the armoury of the British Empire during the First World War.

Chapter 5
"We New Zealanders pride ourselves most of all upon loyalty to our Empire, our country, our flag"
Internalised Britishness and national character in New Zealand's First World War propaganda

Gregory Hynes

For all the Great War's frequently cited centrality in the story of New Zealand's historical development, the related historiography remains noticeably underdeveloped, with outdated cultural nationalist readings still influential. Especially in public understandings, Gallipoli still reigns supreme, read as a moment of ideological disjuncture from the British Empire, towards independent New Zealand nationalism.[1] Despite overarching challenges to this sort of teleological approach to New Zealand identity by the likes of James Belich,[2] and more specific recent challenges in First World War historiography[3] – most important,

---

1   See Keith Sinclair, *A Destiny Apart: New Zealand's Search for National Identity* (Auckland: HarperCollins Publishers Ltd., 1986), pp. 170–3; see also, Erik Olssen, 'A Nation: 1914–1918,' in *The People and the Land: An Illustrated History of New Zealand, 1820–1920*, ed. Judith Binney, Judith Bassett and Erik Olssen (Wellington: Bridget Williams Books, 1990), pp. 319, 322; Olssen, 'Waging War,' in *The People and the Land*, p. 313; Christopher Pugsley, *Scars on the Heart: Two Centuries of New Zealand at War* (Auckland: David Bateman, 1996), pp. 70, 75.

2   James Belich, *Replenishing the Earth: The Settler Revolution and the Rise of the Anglo-World, 1783–1939* (Oxford: Oxford University Press, 2009); Belich, 'The Rise of the Anglo-World: Settlement in North America and Australasia, 1784–1918,' in *Rediscovering the British World*, ed. Phillip Buckner and R. Douglas Francis (Calgary: University of Calgary Press, 2005), pp. 39–57; Belich, *Paradise Reforged: A History of the New Zealander from the 1880s to the Year 2000* (Auckland: University of Hawaii Press, 2001); see also, Phillip Buckner, 'Whatever Happened to the British Empire?,' *Journal of the Canadian Historical Association* 4, no. 1 (1993): pp. 8–32; Carl Bridge and Kent Fedorowich, 'Mapping the British World,' in *The British World: Diaspora, Culture and Identity*, ed. Carl Bridge and Kent Fedorowich (London: Routledge, 2003), pp. 1–15; Stuart Ward, 'Imperial Identities Abroad,' in *The British Empire: Themes and Perspectives*, ed. Sarah Stockwell (Oxford: Wiley-Blackwell, 2008), pp. 219–43.

3   Steven Loveridge, *Calls to Arms: New Zealand Society and Commitment to the Great War* (Wellington: Victoria University Press, 2015); Loveridge, 'A German Is Always a German?: Representations of Enemies, Germans and Race in New Zealand c. 1890–1918,' *New Zealand Journal of History* 48, no. 1 (2014): pp. 51–77; Loveridge, '"Soldiers and Shirkers": Modernity and New Zealand Masculinity during the Great War,' *New Zealand Journal of History* 47, no. 1 (2013): pp. 59–79; Loveridge, 'Seeing Trauma as Sacrifice: The Link between "Sentimental Equipment" and Endurance in New Zealand's War Effort,' in *Endurance and the First World War: Experiences and Legacies in New Zealand and Australia*, ed. David Monger, Sarah Murray and Katie Pickles (Cambridge: Cambridge Scholars Publishing, 2014), pp. 49–63; Gwen Parsons, 'The New Zealand Home Front during World War One and World War Two,' *History Compass* 11, no. 6 (2013): pp. 419–28; Parsons, 'Debating the War: The Discourses of War in the Christchurch Community,' in

challenges to the concept of soldiers' rejection of imperial identities[4] – Gallipoli continues to dominate cultural understandings of the war in New Zealand. We certainly should not understate the importance of Gallipoli as a, perhaps even the, key moment of New Zealand's war experience. As contemporary F. C. Rollett explained:

> It was not until the cables announced that great landing on Gallipoli, and the long lists of killed and wounded were made public, that they realised to the full that their own country was taking part in the war.[5]

However, as an overarching cultural and historical framework, Gallipoli alone is insufficient in understanding the broader New Zealand response to the war. Part of the reason for the continued orthodoxy of the Gallipoli-centric narrative is a neglect of wider source material. New Zealand's official wartime propaganda, one such overlooked area, reveals the breadth of New Zealand's cultural experience of, and response to, the war. The little attention that New Zealand's official propaganda has received tends to dismiss it as demonstrating New Zealand's naïve and passive reliance on British imperial authority.[6] This assumes that British identity was externally imposed, rather than internalised and self-sustaining in New Zealand. Instead, a close examination of New Zealand's wartime propaganda shows that while New Zealand's official propagandists certainly eagerly utilised and built on British rhetoric and justifications for war, they maintained authority in this process, and in doing so, expressed a confident, internalised Britishness, as a marker of Dominion pride and identity. Expressions of wider British identities in New Zealand's official propaganda were not so brittle, and imposed, as to be easily thrown off after Gallipoli, but were homespun, internalised, and adapted to express New Zealand's particular wartime experience through the lens of shared imperial Britishness. Exploring both the organisation and content of New Zealand's wartime propaganda campaign illustrates the subtlety of this process, revealing a complexity to Dominion British identities too easily ignored by cultural nationalist readings.

Beyond the broader questions of Gallipoli and New Zealand identity, the scholarly neglect of New Zealand's official propaganda is perhaps not surprising given the evaluation by James Allan Thompson, director of New Zealand's Dominion Museum in 1920, that 'no war posters of artistic value were issued by the New Zealand Government.'[7] Indeed, New Zealand produced little if any of the original, illustrated poster propaganda created in Britain

---

New Zealand's Great War: New Zealand, the Allies and the First World War, ed. John Crawford and Ian McGibbon (Auckland: Exisle Publishing, 2007), pp. 550–68; Parsons, 'Challenging Enduring Home Front Myths: Jingoistic Civilians and Neglected Soldiers,' in *Endurance and the First World War*, pp. 66–85; Graham Hucker, '"The Great Wave of Enthusiasm": New Zealand Reactions to the First World War in August 1914,' *New Zealand Journal of History* 43, no. 1 (2009): pp. 59–75.

4 Charles Ferrall, 'Maurice Shadbolt's Gallipoli Myth,' pp. 94–108; Jock Phillips, 'Lest We Forget: Remembering, and Forgetting, New Zealand's First World War,' in *How We Remember: New Zealanders and the First World War*, ed. Charles Ferrall and Harry Ricketts (Wellington: Victoria University Press, 2014), pp. 228–40,

5 F.C. Rollett, 'New Zealand and the War,' in *Countess Liverpool's Gift Book of Literature and Art*, ed. A.W. Shrimpton (Christchurch: Whitcombe and Tombs, 1915), p. 24, AY14 COU, Auckland War Memorial Museum (AWMM), Auckland.

6 Stephanie Gibson, 'First World War Posters at Te Papa,' *Tuhinga* 23 (2012): pp. 70, 74; David Grant, *Field Punishment No.1: Archibald Baxter, Mark Briggs, & New Zealand's Anti-Militarist Tradition* (Wellington: Steele Roberts, 2008), p. 15.

7 Thompson to Under Secretary of Department of Internal Affairs, 20 July 1920, Department of Internal Affairs – World War One (Part One), MU 000002/073/0004, Te Papa Archives (TPA), Wellington.

New Zealand's First World War propaganda 83

Figure 5.1   'Military Service Act, 1916', August 1916

Source: Alexander Turnbull Library, Wellington

and the three other Dominions, which dominates the historiographical legacy of First World War propaganda.[8] The character of the majority of New Zealand's governmental poster propaganda was basic and letterpress, such as posters advising regulations of enlistment, and eventually of military service once conscription was introduced (Figure 5.1), betraying

---

8   Jim Aulich and John Hewitt, *Seduction or Instruction? First World War Posters in Britain and Europe* (Manchester: Manchester University Press, 2007), p. 36.

very little of the wider cultural impulses that informed New Zealand's wartime experience.[9] Conforming to the conception of 'propaganda' as information from the late nineteenth century, these posters prioritised clarity and specific detail over rhetoric and emotion.[10] Even in official New Zealand posters – focussed more on rhetoric than instruction, such as the Defence Department's 'Halt!' recruiting poster of 1915,[11] or the Treasury's evocative war loans posters – the advertising-style illustration, so prevalent elsewhere in the propaganda of the British world, is completely absent.[12] This was of course partly a practical issue – New Zealand's advertising and printing industries were not as developed as Britain's, or those of the other Dominions, which meant that New Zealand could not utilise and mobilise these techniques and materials as readily as a Dominion the size of Canada could.[13]

To fill out New Zealand's campaign, poster designs by British propaganda bodies such as the early Parliamentary Recruiting Committee (PRC), and illustrated posters from Australia, were importuned and displayed by both official bodies and private volunteers.[14] The PRC's Arthur Wardle–designed 'Lion poster' (Figure 5.2), featuring an adult 'British lion' calling to four younger 'Dominion lions' to fight for the empire, was frequently reproduced and displayed, for instance.[15] This supplementary borrowing approach has led to an assumption amongst the few who have explored New Zealand propaganda that New Zealand naïvely relied on particularly British propaganda to provide the emotional content of New Zealand's propaganda campaign, or at its most extreme, was cynically manipulated by British propaganda, accepting an external British line.[16] To a certain extent, Stephanie Gibson is correct in arguing that British propaganda rhetoric was used to support New Zealand's efforts;[17] however, this process was not as simple as a basic reliance, not practically, nor ideologically. Instead, as the organisation and content of New Zealand's official propaganda campaign more broadly illustrates, New Zealand retained agency in this process, to determine its propaganda needs and utilise British rhetoric accordingly.

It is not enough to simply note the presence of British-designed posters in New Zealand to claim their significance either way. Instead, in line with what visual historians Elizabeth

---

9 See 'Military Service Act, 1916,' August 1916, Government Printer, Eph-D-WAR-WI-1916-01, Alexander Turnball Library (ATL), Wellington; 'Liberty Loan,' August 1917, Government Printer, Eph-D-WAR-WI-1917-01, ATL, Wellington; see also, Gibson, 'Posters,' pp. 70–4.

10 Gerard J. De Groot, *Blighty: British Society in the Era of the First World War* (London: Longman, 1996), pp. 174–5; Nicholas Reeves, *Official British Film Propaganda during the First World War* (London: C. Helm, 1986), p. 10; M.L. Sanders and Phillip Taylor, *British Propaganda during the First World War, 1914–1918* (London: Crane, Russak & Company, 1982), p. 3.

11 The 'Halt!' poster reproduced in Paul Baker, *King and Country Call: New Zealanders, Conscription and the Great War* (Auckland: Auckland University Press, 1988), p. 22. The poster is mentioned frequently in New Zealand's Defence Department correspondence with museums and wartime poster collectors towards the end of the war; see Allen to Liverpool, 12 May 1919, R 22432788, Archives New Zealand (ANZ), Wellington.

12 'At 12 o'clock to-day Stop,' 1917, Treasury Department, R 22504945, ANZ, Wellington.

13 Gibson, 'Posters,' pp. 73–4.

14 See 'The Call for Men: Recruiting Board's Fresh Enterprise,' *Poverty Bay Herald*, 15 April 1916, p. 4; Massey to Robinson, 6 March 1916, Parliamentary Recruiting Committee, R 10075020, ANZ, Melbourne.

15 Arthur Wardle, 'The Empire Needs Men!, 1915,' *New Zealand Herald*, (Auckland) R 22444232, ANZ. Gibson, 'Posters,' p. 75.

16 Gibson, 'Posters,' pp. 70, 74; Grant, *Field Punishment*, p. 15.

17 Gibson, 'Posters,' pp. 70, 74.

Figure 5.2 Arthur Wardle, 'The Empire Needs Men!', 1915

Source: New Zealand Herald (Auckland), R 22444232, ANZ

Edwards, Janice Hart and Ludmilla Jordanova have argued, it is important to interrogate the 'social life' of such visual and material sources – to explore how they were adapted, transmitted and adopted in their historical contexts.[18] In the case of British-designed posters

---

18 Elizabeth Edwards and Janice Hart, 'Introduction: Photographs as Objects,' in *Photographic Objects Histories: On the Materiality of Images*, ed. Elizabeth Edwards and Janice Hart (London: Routledge, 2004), p. 2; Ludmilla Jordanova, 'Approaching Visual Materials,' *Research Methods for History*, ed. Simon Gunn and Lucy Faire, (Edinburgh: Edinburgh University Press, 2012), pp. 41–2; Jordanova, *The Look of the Past: Visual and Material Evidence in Historical Practice* (Cambridge: Cambridge University Press, 2012), pp. 4–5.

that ended up in New Zealand, the question of adaptation is subtle but important. Wardle's 'Lion poster', for instance, was not reproduced exactly from the original design but was adapted for its eventual display in New Zealand by the Defence Department. The most significant detail is the switch from a more general call from Britain to 'the Overseas States' of the empire, to explicitly addressing the call to three Dominions, Australia, Canada, and New Zealand, along with India.[19] It is unknown exactly when and where these changes occurred, with similar changes made to the design in Canadian copies,[20] and while the switch is not dramatic, it does show a general Dominion perspective that British propaganda could be adapted for local audiences. Likewise, another notable poster reproduced in New Zealand, titled 'Why Britain is at War' (Figure 5.3), was adapted more radically – at least in a formal sense – from a British design found in the *Times*. Rather than a poster, it is reformatted, colourised, and stamped with the New Zealand coat of arms, on the initiative of New Zealand businessman Frederick Ferriman.[21] Viewed in isolation, these changes are

Figure 5.3   'Why Britain Is at War', 1915

Source: Lyttelton Times Company, R 22444093, ANZ, Christchurch

---

19   Gibson, 'Posters,' p. 75.

20   Ibid.

21   Ferriman to Allen, 15 December 1915, R 22432762, ANZ; Ferriman to Allen, 22 December 1915; see also, Gibson, 'Posters,' p. 76; specific phrases were also directly borrowed, such as from the 'Daddy, What Did You Do in the Great War?' poster, see, Baker, *King and Country Call*, p. 41; Nicholas Hiley, '"Kitchener Wants You" and "Daddy, What Did You Do in the Great War?": The Myth of British Recruiting Posters,' *Imperial War Museum Review* 11 (1997): p. 42.

indeed subtle and do little to dislodge the assumption of New Zealand's passivity to British propaganda. However, broadening the exploration of the social life of these posters to their initial arrival in New Zealand complicates this relationship.

Crucially, the nature of the relationship between Britain and New Zealand during the war, and more specifically of their propaganda interactions, was such that New Zealand could not passively rely on British propaganda to be forthcoming in a strictly practical sense. Continuing the story of the 'Lion poster', far from imposing propaganda on New Zealand, Britain's propaganda bodies were hesitant and used a light touch. While the 'Lion poster' was widely displayed in New Zealand,[22] it initially arrived in New Zealand only after specific requests by the New Zealand government for such material, and only then in a small number of copies, both to limit British printing material expenditure, due to ongoing paper shortages,[23] and to put the control of printing and distribution on New Zealand authorities.[24] The 'Why Britain is at War' poster, meanwhile, was almost entirely a private initiative, only endorsed later by New Zealand's wartime Minister of Defence James Allen.[25] Far from being the passive recipients of a concerted British propaganda campaign, New Zealand propagandists had to actively seek British propaganda material.

This apparent disconnection between Britain and New Zealand's propaganda campaigns is partly explained by practical factors. Britain's wartime propaganda campaign was consistently overstretched, due to its rapid improvisation, and its wide remit, which resulted in constant complaints of inefficiency.[26] This limited capacity, compounded by continued wartime paper shortages in Britain, the prohibitive cost of sending large amounts of material to New Zealand, and the particular wartime dangers of long-distance shipping to New Zealand for non-essential items meant extensive propaganda donations from Britain were unsustainable and unrealistic.[27] In sum, Britain simply did not have the capacity to actively engage New Zealand in propaganda for most of the war. This was also a question of approach and priority. The two initial priorities and reasons for Britain's propaganda campaign were countering Germany's sophisticated attack propaganda and influencing opinion in neutral

---

22 Gibson, 'Posters,' p. 75.

23 For British wartime paper shortages see, Sanders and Taylor, *British Propaganda*, pp. 167–8; Brock Millman, 'HMG and the War against Dissent, 1914–18,' *Journal of Contemporary History* 40, no. 3 (July 2005): p. 431; Millman, *Managing Domestic Dissent in First World War Britain* (London: Frank Cass, 2000); Simon J. Potter, 'Communication and Integration: The British and Dominions Press and the British World, c.1876–1914,' in *The British World: Diaspora, Culture and Identity*, ed. Carl Bridge and Kent Fedorowich (London: Routledge, 2003), pp. 195–6.

24 Mackenzie to Massey, Memorandum No.7223, November 1918, MU000207/001/0001, TPA; for paper shortages in Britain see, Millman, *Managing Domestic Dissent*, p. 431.

25 'Why Britain Is at War,' 1915, Lyttelton Times Company, Christchurch, R 22444093, ANZ; Ferriman to Allen, 15 December 1915, Allen to Ferriman, 22 December 1915, R 22432762, ANZ.

26 Sanders and Taylor, *British Propaganda*, p. 15; Gary Messinger, *British Propaganda and the State in the First World War* (Manchester: Manchester University Press, 1992), p. 12; De Groot, *Blighty*, p. 174.

27 Sanders and Taylor, *British Propaganda*, pp. 167–8; Millman, 'HMG,' p. 431; Millman, *Managing Domestic Dissent*; Potter, 'Communication and Integration,' pp. 195–6; see also, Ian McGibbon, 'Shaping New Zealand's War Effort,' in *New Zealand's Great War*, pp. 65–6; Glen O'Hara, 'New Histories of British Imperial Communication and the "Networked World" of the 19th and Early 20th Centuries', *History Compass* 8, no. 7 (2007): pp. 611–13; Duncan Bell, 'Dissolving Distance: Technology, Space, and Empire in British Political Thought, 1770-1900', *The Journal of Modern History* 77, no. 3 (September 2005): pp. 524–5.

nations, especially the United States. Domestic propaganda even took a backseat to these initial priorities.[28] As such, the Dominions were deferred. Initial propaganda bodies like the Neutral Press Committee and the News Department of the Foreign Office took no interest in the Dominions, while they were only one of many general 'national' categories in the work of the War Propaganda Bureau at Wellington House.[29] Naturally trusted, and seen as reliable and loyal allies, the Dominions were far from priorities to Britain's propaganda organisations early in the war. More broadly, however, this approach demonstrates wider Colonial Office policy of 'responsible imperialism' with regard to the Dominions.

This 'hands-off' approach to Dominion propaganda by the British government in one sense was an extension to the British domestic approach. Modern connotations of the term 'propaganda' tend to denote lies, misrepresentation and even a degree of psychological manipulation enforced downward by the state, that have often wrongly bled into historiographical approaches to the subject.[30] However, the contemporary First World War understanding of the term was much more benign, leaning more towards 'information' or 'publicity'. As David Monger has argued, while there was certainly a degree of 'black', or knowingly deceitful, distorted propaganda in Britain's campaign, in general propagandists could not manipulate the public into believing ideas that were not already generally favourable and entrenched. British propagandists recognised the substantial risks in overplaying or exaggerating their case, with the general approach far from malevolent.[31] By extension, British propagandists did not seek to control or dictate propaganda to New Zealand audiences, and left control to local authorities. When Britain did send propaganda material to New Zealand it was limited, and seldom, if ever, sent with any formal direction or instruction. A good example of this is the distribution of photographic propaganda. In 1917, for example, Britain's Department of Information sent a large number of lantern-slide collections of official war photographs through the Victoria League to branches in New Zealand. While the narrative of these collections conformed to wider themes of British propaganda, they were not accompanied with instructions suggesting how they were to be used or presented.[32] Again, echoing Britain's domestic approach, it was believed that propaganda messages would be more palatable and have more impact if delivered by eminent local speakers, a principle also used by the National War Aims Committee

---

28   M.L. Sanders, 'Wellington House and British Propaganda during the First World War,' *The Historical Journal* 18, no. 1 (1975): p. 119.

29   Ibid., p. 121.

30   Millman, *Managing Domestic Dissent*, pp. 7–29; Millman, 'HMG,' pp. 413–40; Phillip Knightley, *The First Casualty: The War Correspondent as Hero and Myth-Maker from Crimea to Iraq* (Baltimore, MD: Johns Hopkins University Press, 2004), pp. 83–120; see also, Katie Pickles, *Transnational Outrage: The Death and Commemoration of Edith Cavell* (New York, NY: Palgrave Macmillan, 2007), pp. 60–1; Cate Haste, *Keep the Home Fires Burning: Propaganda in the First World War* (London: Allen Lane, 1977), p. 107.

31   David Monger, *Patriotism and Propaganda in First World War Britain: The National War Aims Committee and Civilian Morale* (Liverpool: Liverpool University Press, 2012), esp. pp. 5–7.

32   For more on these photographic collections see, Greg Hynes, 'Picturing the Empire: Enduring Imperial Perceptions and Depictions in British First World War Photographic Propaganda,' in *Endurance and the First World War*, pp. 215–35; Greg Hynes and Erin Kimber, 'Imperial Identities: Revealing the Victoria League's First World War Images,' exhibition website, accessed, http://www.canterbury.ac.nz/imperial/.

(NWAC), later in the war.[33] This principle was even more important in dealing with the Dominions. In any question of propaganda, the Colonial Office (CO) emphasised the authority of Dominion Governors General in deciding whether British propaganda should be sent to their Dominion.[34] This hesitancy characterised Britain's propaganda exchanges with the Dominions.

Colonial Office officials were strident in their efforts to restrict British propaganda from influencing the Dominions. For instance, it vehemently opposed Britain's War Propaganda Bureau at Wellington House ambitions, despite practical limitations, to increase its propaganda efforts throughout the empire. These differing positions were made clear in a joint conference held between Wellington House and the Colonial Office in 1916:[35]

> Wellington House feel themselves bound by the terms of their appointment to press their propaganda to the fullest possible extent not only abroad but also throughout the Empire . . . We [the CO] feel that propaganda in the Empire is, except in a few special cases, sheer waste of public money, and want to damp it down so far as we can.[36]

Wellington House's main proposal was to increase contact and coordination between British and imperial propagandists.[37] The Colonial Office's first objection clarified the aforementioned practical limitations; it argued that the proposal was unnecessarily wasteful, would choke already clogged telegraph lines and distract governors from their work with 'idle propaganda'.[38] The Colonial Office also considered such efforts redundant, as Colonial Secretary Andrew Bonar Law, a Canadian, stated, 'loyalty as a general rule need[ed] no spur, to justify the trouble and expenditure involved' in the Dominions.[39] Specifically to New Zealand, one Colonial Office official likewise stated 'opinion in Aust[ralia] and NZ needs no spur.'[40] Only South Africa, with its delicate and potentially explosive internal politics, was deemed unstable enough to justify light propaganda efforts from Britain.[41]

However, this was not simply a question of imperial governance more broadly, but specifically of Dominion status. Tellingly, the Colonial Office was much less restrictive regarding propaganda towards the crown colonies and protectorates. Though perceived to be pointless, the Colonial Office was happy for Wellington House to circulate pamphlets

---

33 Monger, *Patriotism and Propaganda*; Monger, 'Transcending the Nation: Domestic Propaganda and Supranational Patriotism in Britain, 1917–1918,' in *World War I Propaganda*, ed. Troy R.E. Paddock (Leiden: Brill, 2014), pp. 22–7.
34 'Propaganda in the Colonies,' 17 November 1916, CO 323/733-55353, Public Record Office (PRO), The National Archives (TNA), Kew, pp. 27, 30.
35 'Propaganda in the Colonies,' 17 November 1916, CO 323/733-55353, TNA:PRO, p. 22.
36 Ibid.
37 'Propaganda in the Colonies,' 17 November 1916, PRO, CO 323/733-55353, TNA, p. 22.
38 Ibid.
39 Ibid.; see also, Parsons, 'Debating the War'; Baker, *King and Country Call*, pp. 15–23; W. David McIntyre, *Dominion of New Zealand: Statesmen and Status, 1907–1945* (Wellington: New Zealand Institute of Internal Affairs, 2007), pp. 60–1; Ron Palenski, 'Malcolm Ross: A New Zealand Failure in the Great War,' *Australian Historical Studies* 39, no. 1 (March 2008): pp. 20–1.
40 'Raemaekers' Cartoons,' 15 December 1915, PRO, CO 323/693-58573, TNA, p. 639.
41 Ibid.; see also, George Robb, *British Culture and the First World War* (Basingstoke: Palgrave Macmillan, 2002), p. 17; T.R.H. Davenport, 'The South African Rebellion, 1914,' *The English Historical Review* 78, no. 306 (January 1963): pp. 73–4.

and papers in both 'European' and 'native' languages throughout the colonies as it had been doing, as long as it was at the local Governor's discretion.[42] The approach towards the Dominions was much more restrictive. In the resolution of the conference, Wellington House's future policy towards the Dominions was firmly established:

> The Governments of the self-governing Dominions are the sole responsible Authorities for their respective territories, and for this reason no propagandist publications of any description shall be circulated in Australia, Canada, South Africa or New Zealand without the concurrence of those Governments.[43]

The term 'responsible authorities' is significant. The Colonial Office's anxiety to avoid any undue or unregulated propaganda material finding its way to the Dominions relates to a broader understanding of responsible imperial government. The generally held perspective, especially in the Colonial Office, was that Britain should not dictate or interfere with the self-governing Dominions.[44] The Colonial Office was so concerned with maintaining this non-interference policy that it vetted all interactions between the Dominions and Wellington House.[45] 'Responsible government' was a central concept to the general understanding of Dominion status. The achievement of 'responsible government' was one of the assumed requirements and, as W. David McIntyre claims, the 'backbone' of Dominion status, though this was not its limit or the definition.[46] Thus, it was not for Britain to dictate Dominion domestic policy. Accordingly, the Colonial Office was anxious to keep Wellington House well within the boundaries of responsible government and Dominion status, in its attempts to direct propaganda in the Dominions. Echoing Britain's hesitancy to directly 'coerce' domestic opinion, the Colonial Office took a similar 'hands-off' approach to Dominion propaganda.[47] Close imperial interaction, particularly on propaganda, was more often facilitated by public initiative, and patriotic societies, especially during the early years of the war, which made up for the gaps left by official organisation.[48]

---

42 'Propaganda in the Colonies,' 17 November 1916, PRO, CO 323/733-55353, TNA, p. 22.

43 Ibid., p. 29.

44 Buckner, 'Whatever Happened,' p. 11; John Darwin, 'Britain's Empires,' in *The British Empire*, p. 3; McIntyre, *Dominion of New Zealand*, p. 20; McIntyre, *The Britannic Vision: Historians and the Making of the British Commonwealth of Nations, 1907–48* (New York, NY: Palgrave Macmillan, 2009), pp. 77–9; Andrew Stewart, 'The "Bloody Post Office": The Life and Times of the Dominions Office,' *Contemporary British Histor* 24, no. 1 (2010): p. 44; see also, Richard Jebb, *Studies in Colonial Nationalism* (London: Edward Arnold, 1905), pp. 101–3, 334.

45 'Propaganda in the Colonies,' 17 November 1916, PRO, CO 323/733-55353, TNA, p. 30.

46 McIntyre, *Britannic Vision*, p. 73; Douglas Cole, 'The Problem of "Nationalism" and "Imperialism" in British Settlement Colonies,' *Journal of British Studies* 31, no. 4 'Britishness and Europeanness: Who Are the British Anyway?' (October 1992): p. 171; McIntyre, *Dominion of New Zealand*, pp. 19–20, 67; Bridge and Fedorowich, 'Mapping the British World,' p. 6.

47 For Britain's 'hands-off' approach to domestic propaganda see, John Horne, 'Remobilizing for "Total War": France and Britain, 1917–1918,' in *State, Society and Mobilization in Europe during the First World War*, ed. John Horne (Cambridge: Cambridge University Press, 1997), pp. 196–7; for Britain's 'hands off' approach to imperial governance see, Buckner, 'Whatever Happened,' p. 11; Darwin, 'Britain's Empires,' p. 3.

48 Katie Pickles, *Female Imperialism and National Identity: Imperial Order Daughters of the Empire* (Manchester: Manchester University Press, 2002), pp. 4–8, 16–17; Pickles, 'A Link in "The Great Chain of Empire Friendship": The Victoria League in New Zealand,' *The Journal of Imperial and*

All this is to say that the interaction between Britain and the Dominions in terms of wartime propaganda distribution was more complex than critical readings of the purpose of British propaganda might assume. While New Zealand propagandists certainly utilised British propaganda, it would have been difficult to 'rely' on British propaganda, due to significant practical and ideological boundaries to doing so. Accordingly, the presence of such British posters in New Zealand is striking, and must be understood in this context of isolation.

Quite apart from representing a form of passive reliance, or conversely of active propagandisation of the Dominions by Britain, the presence of British propaganda material and rhetoric in New Zealand's campaign reflects active engagement with British ideals in the New Zealand government. This is clearer through an examination of the impact of British propaganda rhetoric on New Zealand's campaign beyond material evidence of imported propaganda. Crucially, the narrative and central themes of New Zealand's propaganda campaign show an obvious borrowing from Britain's campaign. This is not surprising. As Steven Loveridge argues, it was not a contradiction at this time for New Zealanders to see themselves as both naturally 'British' in the broad sense, and distinctly 'New Zealand'. British language and ideals were naturally New Zealand's own, with enough licence to adapt and shape them to the particularities of the New Zealand experience.[49]

New Zealand's engagement with the specifics of Britain's justification for war is a clear example of this internalisation of British rhetoric. Understandably, this was achieved first by explicitly reiterating New Zealand's Britishness, portraying vaunted British morals and ideals equally New Zealand's. A speech by James Allen towards the end of the war emphasised this, characterising New Zealanders as Britons, upholding particularly 'British' characteristics of honour, fair play and values of civilisation:

> We British people were determined at the start to play the game, but our opponents did not play the game and, as the Mayor has said, we had to retaliate. It was against our nature, and constitution, but we had to do it for our own safety, and when a Briton has to adopt retaliation I hope that he does so promptly and thoroughly.[50]

By extension, and in a more practical sense, this also meant that New Zealand naturally extended British motivations for joining the war as its own. This is plain in the extension of Britain's treaty commitments to Belgium as its main motivation for joining the war, to be equally New Zealand's. This was conceptualised both in a vague legal sense, and more rhetorically, due to the shared moral ideals of imperial Britishness.[51] One of New

---

Commonwealth History 33, no. 1 (2005): pp. 29–32; John M. Mackenzie, *Propaganda and Empire: The Manipulation of British Public Opinion, 1880–1960* (Manchester: Manchester University Press, 1984), p. 3; Matthew C. Hendley, *Organised Patriotism and the Crucible of War: Popular Imperialism in Britain, 1914–1932* (Montreal: McGill-Queen's University Press, 2012), pp. 3–4, 7–10.

49 Loveridge, *Calls to Arms*, esp. pp. 29–30.

50 'Reprisals: Sir J. Allen's Speech,' *Ashburton Guardian*, 18 September 1918, p. 8; see also 'Trafalgar Day,' *Dominion*, 22 October 1914, p. 8.

51 Nicoletta Gullace, '*"The Blood of Our Sons": Men, Women and Renegotiation of British Citizenship during the Great War* (New York: Palgrave Macmillan, 2002), p. 36; see also, Nicola Lambourne, 'Production versus Destruction: Art, World War I and Art History,' *Art History* 22, no. 3 (September 1999): pp. 352–3; Katie Pickles, 'Mapping Memorials for Edith Cavell on the Colonial Edge,' *New Zealand Geographer* 62 (2006): p. 14.

Zealand's very few non-instructional, but equally plain, propaganda posters, 'To New Zealand's Manhood', issued by New Zealand's Parliamentary Recruiting Board (PRB) in 1916, illustrates this, stating that New Zealand would not stop fighting until 'Belgium's wrongs have been righted',[52] while New Zealand Prime Minister William Massey called for vengeance for German atrocities as New Zealand's moral and religious duty.[53] Building on this foundation, the other keystones of British propaganda rhetoric were replicated in New Zealand's propaganda narrative. By virtue of its imperial Britishness, New Zealand was accordingly drawn into the wartime dichotomy (constructed in British atrocity propaganda) of moral, just and peace-loving Britishness at odds with militaristic, aggressive and expansionist Germany, most clearly distilled and expressed in British atrocity propaganda regarding the German invasion of Belgium in the Bryce Report.[54] Popular stories of German atrocities from Britain's campaign received traction in New Zealand, such as the story of the German destruction of a medieval library in Louvain, publicised in *Countess Liverpool's Gift Book*, a fundraising book of patriotic stories, poems and artworks, created by Lady Liverpool, the wife of wartime New Zealand Governor Lord Liverpool.[55]

Again echoing Britain's propaganda rhetoric, these concepts were anchored by a central concept of duty and sacrifice, with service at the front, and endurance and contribution to the war effort at home characterised as patriotic duty.[56] New Zealand's posters put this point succinctly, such as the rare non-instructional New Zealand government poster, 'Halt!', created by the Defence Department in 1915. This poster emphasised duty, stating: 'Every man of the required age who is a British subject and is medically fit owes a duty to Empire.[57] Allen applied the concepts of duty and sacrifice in the same way, first characterising service, and particularly death, at the front as heroic patriotic duty,[58] but also calling for

---

52 'To New Zealand's Manhood,' 1916, Government Printer, UB 325.N45 NEW, AWMM, Wellington.

53 'Recruiting Rally,' *Dominion*, 1 November 1915, p. 6; see also, 'To Aid Recruiting,' *Ashburton Guardian*, 14 May 1915, p. 7.

54 Monger, *Patriotism and Propaganda*, pp. 86, 115–16; Jessic Bennett and Mark Hampton, 'World War I and the Anglo-American Imagined Community: Civilisation vs. Barbarism in British Propaganda and American Newspapers,' in *Anglo-American Media Interactions, 1850–2000*, ed. Joel H. Wiener and Mark Hampton (Basingstoke: Palgrave Macmillan, 2007), p. 159; Gullace, *Blood of Our Sons*, pp. 25, 31; Pickles, *Transnational Outrage*, pp. 60–6; Peter Buitenhuis, *The Great War of Words: Literature as Propaganda 1914 and After*, (London: B.T. Batsford, 1989), pp. 27–8; Pickles, 'Mapping Memorials,' p. 14.

55 M.A. Sinclair, 'The Sack of Louvain,' in *Countess Liverpool's Gift Book of Literature and Art*, ed. A.W. Shrimpton (Christchurch: Whitcombe and Tombs, 1915), p. 72, AY14 COU, AWMM; Johannes C. Andersen, 'In Memory of Gallipoli,' in *Countess Liverpool's Gift Book of Literature and Art*, p. 46; see also, Pickles, *Transnational Outrage*, pp. 60–6; Alan Kramer, *Dynamic of Destruction: Culture and Mass Killing in the First World War* (Oxford: Oxford University Press, 2007), p. 13; Lambourne, 'Production versus Destruction,' p. 353; Megan C. Woods, 'Re/producing the Nation: Women Making Identity in New Zealand, 1906–1925' (MA Thesis, University of Canterbury, Christchurch, New Zealand, 1997), pp. 82–4; Olssen, 'Waging War,' p. 302; Keith Scott, *Dear Dot, I Must Tell You: A Personal History of Young New Zealanders* (Auckland: Activity Press, 2001), pp. 423–4.

56 Baker, *King and Country Call*, p. 36; For Britain's use of 'duty' as a central concept see, Monger, *Patriotism and Propaganda*, pp. 85–6.

57 Baker, *King and Country Call*, p. 22; Allen to Liverpool, 12 May 1919, R 22432788, ANZ.

58 '"Done Their Duty" – Memorials for New Zealand Soldiers,' *Evening Post*, 4 November 1918, p. 8; see also, L.S. Fanning, 'The Soldier's Dream,' in *Countess Liverpool's Gift Book of*

the same sacrifice and duty on the home front, through sacrifice and work to assist the war effort.[59] This equation of domestic service with military service also highlights the concept of equality of sacrifice, a vitally important and contentious concept on the New Zealand home front, which further echoed the British home front, in discussions of what Adrian Gregory terms 'economies of sacrifice'.[60] Gendered dimensions of this call to duty, present in British rhetoric, were also replicated in the New Zealand narrative, specifically the concept of women shaming and emasculating men unwilling to serve,[61] or calls to the defence of mothers, sisters, women and children, as a motivation to fulfil masculine duty.[62]

To this point, these rhetorical lines were merely extended from British propaganda, to overlay and frame New Zealand's wartime experience and illustrating the degree to which New Zealand's propaganda throughout the war utilised 'British' rhetoric, shared Britishness and British cultural constructions of the war. However, delving deeper, it is clear that this language was flexible, with New Zealand propagandists adapting it to local needs and experiences suiting its own needs. New Zealand certainly utilised British propaganda but did not simply or passively rely on it to explain New Zealand's entire wartime experience.

While New Zealand shared this language of 'British' imperial patriotism and propaganda, this facilitated, rather than inhibited, unique local responses to the war. As with physical British propaganda, New Zealand retained authority and initiative in its interaction with 'British' rhetoric, and adapted and re-oriented certain aspects to make it more closely relevant to the New Zealand experience of the war, and to insert the New Zealand identity into wider constructions of Britishness. Far from being an imposed identity, this was something New Zealanders were encouraged to take pride in.

As Loveridge argues, the key to resolving any possible tension between membership of an extended British family, and expression of New Zealand nationhood, was an expression of a distinct, perhaps even superior, New Zealand brand of Britishness.[63] Accordingly, New Zealand propaganda rhetoric often not only expressed a New Zealand ownership of British history, but also New Zealand's responsibility in protecting, guarding and, most important, furthering that 'British' historical glory and tradition in its own right. The 'To

---

Literature and Art p. 57, AY14 COU, AWMM; for sacrifice in the British context see, Adrian Gregory, *Last Great War: British Society and the First World War* (Cambridge: Cambridge University Press, 2008), chaps 4–6, esp. p. 113.

59 'The Overseas Dominions,' *Grey River Argus*, 10 May 1915, p. 2; see also, Gwen Parsons, 'The New Zealand Home Front during World War One and World War Two', *History Compass* 11, no. 6 (2013), pp. 419–22.

60 Baker, *King and Country Call*, p. 36; Gregory, *Last Great War*, pp. 112–13; see also L.S. Fanning, 'The Soldier's Dream,' in *Countess Liverpool's Gift Book of Literature and Art*, p. 57; for equality of sacrifice in a French context see, John Horne, '"L'impôt du sang": Republican Rhetoric and Industrial Warfare in France, 1914–18,' *Social History* 14, no. 2 (May 1989): pp. 201–23.

61 E.g. Joseph Ward's call to women in 1915, in 'A Recruiting Rally,' *Wairarapa Times*, 1 November 1915, p. 4.

62 'The Call for Men,' *The Press*, 18 April 1916, p. 6; see also, 'To New Zealand's Manhood,' 1916, Government Printer, UB 325.N45 NEW, AWMM, Wellington; see also, Gullace, *Blood of Our Sons*, pp. 36, 38–40, 44–5; Monger, *Patriotism and Propaganda*, p. 88; Susan R. Grayzel, *Women's Identities at War* (Chapel Hill, NC: The University of North Carolina Press, 1999), p. 113; Baker, *King and Country Call*, p. 27; Paul Ward, '"Women of Britain Say Go!": Women's Patriotism in the First World War,' *Twentieth Century History* 12, no. 1 (2001): p. 26; Pickles, *Female Imperialism*; Pickles, 'Victoria League,' p. 195; Woods, 'Re/producing the Nation,' p. 80.

63 Loveridge, *Calls to Arms*, esp. pp. 29–30.

New Zealand's Manhood' poster characterised this in racial terms, as a 'sacred heritage', which New Zealanders had to live up to.[64] Allen expressed this even more clearly in a speech advocating the Military Service Act in 1916:

> It is a privilege to share in the traditions of the Motherland. She has helped to make us what we are; we inherit much from the past, and we are confident that our New Zealand men and women serving at the front, with their comrades from other parts of the Empire, are securing for us something now which will make our own country and the Empire and our people nobler and better in the days that are to come.[65]

Within this emphasis on New Zealand carrying British history forward, a distinctive Dominion and New Zealand settler character and identity was also emphasised. Allen stated in a speech in 1915: 'The blood of the pioneers of this country still beats in the veins of our boys to-day.'[66] Deeply associated with this emphasis was the concept of 'Better Britain', which held that British heritage, combined with the 'pioneer spirit', had made New Zealand an elite and heroic fighting force, stressing New Zealand's distinctiveness and dynamism within the wider British identity.[67] This impulse for New Zealand glorification was most evident in discussions of the Gallipoli campaign, such as in J. L. Mortimer's 'The Men of the Dardanelles', from *Countess Liverpool's Gift Book*:

> Men of the Dardanelles! Ah, that great name is writ forever on the scrolls of fame. Thy fame, New Zealand! Do thou make it well, thou hast a story now which thou may'st tell to thrill the heart and give tongue release more than the oft-told tales of Rome or Greece.[68]

In this light, Gallipoli represents not necessarily a break with British ideals, but an opportunity to extend and re-orient them, to assert New Zealand's contribution to the broader British struggle, and to contribute not only to historical British military successes, but give New Zealand its own military glory to rival those of the ancient world.[69] The campaign accordingly re-oriented the concept of duty to furthering New Zealand's legacy in the wider British military tradition, with the heroic New Zealand dead of the Gallipoli campaign being utilised to call for more men to protect and capitalise on their heroic sacrifices.[70] This too was a British, and as John Horne notes, also French, concept of service as a blood

---

64 Manhood poster, see also, the New Zealand Defence Department's 'Halt!' poster from 1915 in, Baker, *King and Country Call*, p. 22; F.C. Rollett, 'New Zealand and the War,' *Countess Liverpool's Gift Book of Literature and Art*, p. 24.

65 'To Win the War,' *NZ Truth*, 3 June 1916, p. 6; see also, 'Trafalgar Day,' *Dominion*, 22 October 1914, p. 8; 'Recruiting Rally,' *Dominion*, 1 November 1915, p. 6.

66 'N.Z. and the War,' *Dominion*, 20 September 1915, p. 2; see also, 'The Call for Men,' *The Press*, 18 April 1916, p. 6.

67 Belich, *Paradise Reforged*, p. 21; see also, M.A. Sinclair, 'The Beginnings of Colonial Nationalism: Richard Jebb in New Zealand, 1899,' in *The Rise of Colonial Nationalism*, ed. John Eddy and Deryck Schreuder (Sydney: Allen and Unwin, 1988), pp. 124–5.

68 J.L. Mortimer, 'The Men of the Dardanelles,' p. 151; Charles F. Salmond, 'Fallen at Gaba Tepe,' p. 113, both in, *Countess Liverpool's Gift Book of Literature and Art*.

69 See, Loveridge, *Calls to Arms*; Baker, *King and Country Call*, pp. 23–5.

70 'Mr. Allen's Visit,' *Fielding Star*, 27 March 1916, p. 3; 'New Zealand's Part,' *Poverty Bay Herald*, 11 July 1917, p. 4.

sacrifice.[71] Once again, this concept, though European, was adopted with authority in New Zealand to illustrate and glorify Gallipoli as a distinctly local experience of the war, and to draw New Zealand more obviously into the narrative of war sacrifice.

The twin concepts of duty and sacrifice were further re-oriented in New Zealand, to make the calls more immediately relevant to New Zealand. Specifically, the concept of duty was expanded to include concepts of imperial loyalty and responsibility. Allen expressed this in a speech in 1917, responding to emerging feelings of war weariness, arguing that defence of empire and New Zealand's domestic interests were intertwined, and if anything, imperial interests were more important during the war:

> It is unfortunate, of course, that the broader interests of New Zealand, as a dominion of the British Empire, should pull in a direction contrary to what we may term her domestic interests, but there is no question which of the two should be regarded as the more important at a time like this. The paramount consideration for New Zealand, as for every part of the Empire, must be the successful prosecution of the war.[72]

This demonstrates how tensions between local New Zealand interests and identities, and broader British loyalties, were resolved through the concept of duty towards 'loyalty' and 'responsibility'. Allen argued New Zealand owed service not only to itself, but also to Britain, and as a loyal Dominion, it had a responsibility to respond to the Motherland's pleas, expanding self-sacrifice to a national level. This was not portrayed as a reluctant responsibility but a duty that New Zealand could take pride in as a developed and important member of the British imperial community, through an emphasis on New Zealand's duty to its British heritage. This was partly achieved by an appropriation of 'British' heroes, for instance, the government's 'Halt!' poster includes the phrase, 'Your Empire Calls You, and – England Expects!',[73] a repurposing of Viscount Horatio Nelson's famous plea at the Battle of Trafalgar, 'England expects that every man this day will do his duty.'[74] The evocation of the cult of Nelson suggests it mirrored deep significance to national identity in New Zealand, as in Britain, through shared imperial Britishness,[75] and a clear sense of New Zealand ownership of British history and its heroes. This concept was also delivered in more sympathetic ways, less as a demand from Britain, and more as a desperate plea from 'Old England' or the 'Mother Country', such as in the 'To New Zealand's Manhood' poster:[76] 'The Motherland, which has made many sacrifices on our behalf, appeals to her sons across the sea for their assistance and cooperation.'[77] In response to these calls, it was argued that New Zealand could not maintain its honour by refusing Britain's pleas in its time of need. As such, a similarity was drawn between Germany's betrayal of its treaty with Belgium as a 'scrap of paper', arguing that New Zealand would be no better than Germany

---

71 Gregory, *Last Great War*, p. 113; Horne, 'L'impôt du sang,' p. 202.
72 'The Obligation of Service,' *Otago Daily Times*, 12 July 1917, p. 4.
73 Baker, *King and Country Call*, p. 22.
74 'Trafalgar Day,' *Dominion*, 22 October 1914, p. 8.
75 Cynthia Fansler Berhman, *Victorian Myths of the Sea* (Athens, OH: Ohio University Press, 1977), pp. 96–7.
76 'To New Zealand's Manhood,' 1916, Government Printer, UB 325.N45 NEW, AWMM, Wellington.
77 See also, 'Recruiting Rally,' *Dominion*, 1 November 1915, p. 6.

if it did not honour its duty to Britain.[78] This complicated strictly 'familial' associations into something more formal, but nonetheless, illustrates the complexity of New Zealand's sense of internalised Britishness, tempered with a sense of both duty and loyalty to 'Home' in New Zealand's propaganda.

'British' rhetoric was also actively shaped in New Zealand's propaganda to account for specific New Zealand difference, or local New Zealand concerns. In particular was the need to account for New Zealand's distance from the war. Bart Ziino argues that distance from the front, while a feature of the home front experience throughout the empire, made the wartime experiences of grief and mourning in the antipodean Dominions distinct, as Australia and New Zealand were furthest from any part of the empire's front.[79] In some cases this distance was portrayed as a virtue, making New Zealand's sacrifice particularly morally admirable, as men were going to a war that had not yet impacted the New Zealand home front, as another extract from *Countess Liverpool's Gift Book* by W. H. Triggs, explains:

> Such sacrifices are being made throughout the Empire, but of the mothers of New Zealand it may be said that their devotion is the more to their honour because while the Motherland is almost within the sound of the enemy's guns, we in these happy, prosperous isles are far from the scene of the conflict to all appearances wrapped in complete security, and therefore the need for sacrifice, although just as real as in England, is less apparent.[80]

Gallipoli was also conceptualised in terms of distance, as a way to bring the immediate significance of the war to the New Zealand home front, as Rollet's quote from *Countess Liverpool's Gift Book* suggests.[81] Once again, in this light, Gallipoli was comfortably folded into a broader shared British narrative, rather than disrupting it.

These varied renegotiations of 'British' rhetoric illustrate the degree to which New Zealand had authority, control and initiative in shaping its conception of the war, and its own identity, due to a generally accepted broader British identity. However, there were, of course, limitations to this flexibility. New Zealand's conscription debate intensified the need to readjust British rhetoric for local conditions; however, in this case a degree of awkwardness is evident in the renegotiation. Specifically, British, and to an extreme, 'Anglo-Saxon' histories, were used to justify New Zealand's introduction of conscription. It was argued that New Zealand was still keeping to British ideals of anti-militarism, as New Zealand was simply following Britain's lead. The complexity of this issue is revealed, however, by Allen's decision to evoke both Oliver Cromwell as an example of British use of military conscription and the U.S. President Abraham Lincoln's use of the system in the American Civil War as evidence of its use in an 'Anglo-Saxon' context. Both were contentious examples, showing the difficulty of reconciling conscription with the

---

78 'To Win the War,' *NZ Truth*, 3 June 1916, p. 6; 'New Zealand's Part,' *Evening Post*, 11 July 1917, p. 6.

79 Bart Ziino, *A Distant Grief: Australians, War Graves and the Great War* (Crawley, WA: University of Western Australia Press, 2007), p. 29.

80 W.H. Triggs, 'New Zealand Mothers and the War,' *Countess Liverpool's Gift Book of Literature and Art*, p. 73; see also, 'Keep Sport Going,' *Evening Post*, 29 October 1915, p. 3; 'Recruiting Rally,' *Wanganui Chronicle*, 6 November 1916, p. 4.

81 F.C. Rollett, 'New Zealand and the War,' *Countess Liverpool's Gift Book of Literature and Art*, p. 23; Ziino, *Distant Grief*, p. 59.

established British ideal of anti-militarism.[82] This illustrates the potential for the US to be included in constructions of otherwise 'British' heritage, though it was more problematic and uncomfortable.[83]

Naturally, however, British propaganda rhetoric could not speak for the entire New Zealand experience of the war, as it notably excluded certain groups, most notably non-white and indigenous populations of the empire. Despite the potential fluidity of concepts such as the 'British world', Phillip Buckner argues that an inherent belief in the superiority of 'white Britishness' remained common,[84] particularly in the Dominions, where distance from 'Home' and close contact with native populations made identifications of white 'racial Britishness' even more pronounced.[85]

This issue of 'racial Britishness' and 'whiteness' took on a new dimension and relevancy in New Zealand, due to the place of Māori. Māori were not uniformly against the war. Initially, despite the eager support of certain tribes, or *iwi*,[86] Māori were initially excluded from the war effort as a whole: offers to send a Māori battalion were refused and only accepted due to the precedent set by the use of Indian troops to hold the Suez Canal.[87] This was due to the British principle of the undesirability of having black or native soldiers fighting a white enemy.[88] Though the Māori offer was eventually accepted, cultural characterisations of the war along British lines still led to issues of ideological exclusion and disillusionment, and a sense that Māori did not have an interest in the war. This is illustrated well in a letter from a Māori citizen, E. Karetai, to the *Otago Daily Times* in 1915:

> The Maori understands that England has gone to war for honour's sake – that Germany violated a 'scrap of paper', which her representative had signed for the protection of a

---

82 'To Win the War,' *NZ Truth*, 3 June 1916, p. 6; see also, Bennett and Hampton, 'Anglo-American,' pp. 155, 157; see also, 'Military Service,' *The Press*, 12 June 1916, p. 7.

83 Bennett and Hampton, 'Anglo-American,' p. 157; Belich, *Replenishing the Earth*, p. 5.

84 Buckner, 'Whatever Happened,' pp. 27–8; see also, Alan Lester, 'British Settler Discourse and the Circuits of Empire,' *History Workshop Journal* 54 (Autumn 2002): p. 25; Catherine Hall, 'What did a British World Mean to the British?: Reflections on the Nineteenth Century', *Rediscovering the British World*, ed. Phillip Buckner & R. Francis Douglas (Calgary: Calgary University Press, 2005), pp. 25–6, 29; see also, Bridge and Fedorowich, 'Mapping the British World,' p. 3; Phillip Buckner and R. Francis Douglas, 'Introduction,' *Rediscovering the British World*, ed. Phillip Buckner & R. Francis Douglas, (Calgary: Calgary University Press, 2005) p. 14; Douglas Lorimer, 'From Victorian Values to White Virtues: Assimilation and Exclusion in British Racial Discourse, *c.* 1870–1914,' *Rediscovering the British World*, pp. 110–11.

85 Buckner and Douglas, 'Introduction,' p. 15; Ward, 'Imperial Identities,' p. 219; Bridge and Fedorowich, 'Mapping the British World,' p. 3; Robb, *British Culture*, p. 11; David Cannadine, *Ornamentalism: How the British Saw Their Empire* (London: Oxford University Press, 2001), p. 5.

86 'Pamphlet on the Subject of Conscription,' 17 June 1918, PRO, CO 209/297-29649, TNA, p. 439, 513–20; Ashley Gould, '"Different Race, Same Queen": Maori and the War,' in *One Flag, One Queen, One Tongue*, ed. John Crawford and Ian McGibbon (Auckland: Auckland University Press, 2003), p. 120.

87 Gould, 'Different Race, Same Queen,' pp. 119–20; P.S. O'Connor, 'The Recruitment of Maori Soldiers, 1914–1918,' *Political Science* 19, no. 48 (1967): p. 49.

88 Christopher Pugsley, 'Images of Te Hokowhitu A Tu in the First World War,' in *Race, Empire and First World War Writing*, ed. Santanu Das (Cambridge: Cambridge University Press, 2011), p. 197; O'Connor, 'Recruitment of Maori Soldiers,' p. 49; see also, Robb, *British Culture*, p. 8; Franchesca Walker '"Descendants of a Warrior Race": The Maori Contingent, New Zealand Pioneer Battalion, and Martial Race Myth, 1914–19,' *War and Society* 31, no. 1 (March 2012): p. 2; Gould, 'Different Race, Same Queen,' p. 120.

small country. So far so good. But the mere Maori mind cannot help asking, where is Britain's honour? What about the 'scrap of paper' Britain signed for the protection of a small people, and the promises contained therein? Why has Britain allowed the New Zealand Government to violate that 'scrap of paper', called the Treaty of Waitangi? Did I hear the Minister say those injustices were past? No; they live to-day, and will live for ever, a blot on New Zealand's history, and – shall I say it? – on Britain's honour and her much-vaunted fairplay.[89]

This clear Māori dislocation from the 'British' rhetoric was a significant barrier to Māori enlistment, particularly in the implacable Waikato region, which refused attempts at enlistment and even conscription of Māori.[90]

Showing the limitations of this flexible, extended British rhetoric, Māori were only significantly drawn into New Zealand's wartime rhetoric through the British Victorian racial discourse of the 'martial race myth', which asserted that certain races were genetically suited to battle and warfare as 'warrior races'.[91] The characterisation of Māori as particularly warlike was a long-standing yet reflexive discourse; during the war it was considered a positive and inclusive characterisation, instead of the negative, aggressive connotations it often carried in the nineteenth century.[92] Newspaper illustrations, for instance, depicted Māori in an 'exotic', warrior-like manner, with tongues out and eyes flaring, in hand to hand combat with the enemy, a scenario which was very different from the reality of the Gallipoli campaign (Figures 5.4 and 5.5).[93] Such depictions emphasised Māori as inherently brave and skilled in battle, channelling their warrior ancestors, and further expanding the mythology of the Gallipoli campaign by co-opting traditional symbols of Māori dress and warfare in this First World War context. This concept was also utilised by Māori MPs, such as Apriana Ngata, also a member of the government's Māori Recruiting Board. Ngata stated that Māori involvement in the war would be beneficial, rather than jeopardising the survival of the race, as it was the lack of battle in recent memory that had led to the decline of the naturally martial Māori race:

The Maori race had declined because it was only very recently that they had stopped fighting, and it took more than half a century for some of the Maori warrior tribes to suit themselves to the requirements of peace. When the Maoris first volunteered it was not patriotism – that and other things of the sort came afterwards as excuses . . . But they went first for a sheer love of adventure, and because the spirit of their fathers were calling them to battle.[94]

---

89   'Maori Loyalty,' *Otago Daily Times*, 6 September 1915, p. 2.
90   Walker, 'Warrior Race,' p. 4; O'Connor, 'Recruitment of Maori Soldiers,' pp. 49, 65–7.
91   Walker, 'Warrior Race,' pp. 2, 15.
92   Christina A. Thompson, 'A Dangerous People Whose Only Occupation Is War: Maori and Pakeha in 19th Century New Zealand,' *The Journal of Pacific History* 32, no. 1 (June 1997): pp. 109, 111–14.
93   William Blomfield, 'The Spirit of His Fathers,' *New Zealand Observer*, 25 December 1915, ATL, A-312-1-088; 'The Maoris at Gallipoli,' *Dominion*, 15 November 1915, D 526.2 MAO, AWMM.
94   'Maoris and the War,' *Auckland Star*, 2 June 1916, p. 2; Walker, 'Warrior Race,' p. 13; see also, Ernest Denis Hoben, 'Ake, Ake, Kia Kaha,' *Countess Liverpool's Gift Book of Literature and Art*, p. 130.

Figure 5.4 William Blomfield, 'The Spirit of His Fathers', 25 December 1915

Source: New Zealand Observer, A-312–1–088, ATL

100   *Gregory Hynes*

Figure 5.5   'The Māoris at Gallipoli', 15 November 1915

Source: Dominion, D 526.2 MAO, AWMM

This is a telling representation of the martial race myth. It illustrates that the exclusive nature of the shared British imperial discourse of patriotism, which appealed so naturally to white, or *pakeha*, New Zealanders, could not speak for the entirety of New Zealand's wartime experience, and necessitated finding new ways to accommodate and include Māori in New Zealand's war effort and its mythology. However, as a British intellectual and racial discourse in its own right, it also shows the continuing influence of British cultural discourses in formulating New Zealand's cultural perceptions and identities, at the expense of Māori identity.[95] This speaks to a wider, and more problematic, use of British intellectual language

---

     95   Walker, 'Warrior Race,' p. 20; Pugsley, 'Images of Te Hokowhitu A Tu,' pp. 196, 200.

and ideals to conceptualise New Zealand society and experience, towards cultural attempts at re-conceptualisation of Māori to align as an 'acceptable' race within New Zealand's proto-British society.[96] In the context of the First World War, Māori were normalised in this militaristic identity, though clearly many Māori themselves still felt alienated by this heavy reliance on 'British' rhetoric during the war.

This exploration of the impact of British wartime propaganda rhetoric on New Zealand understandings and representations of the First World War suggests the subtlety and complexity of the interaction between broader British and local New Zealand identities. For the most part, these were not in opposition but perceived to be naturally complimentary. First World War propaganda provides a particularly clear picture of this process, demonstrating the ways that British rhetoric was used as a tool to both conceptualised events, and assert a particular New Zealand identity and contribution to the war. It is only through close examination of the ways in which the relationship between metropole and Dominion operated during the war that these subtleties emerge. Viewing New Zealand engagement with British wartime rhetoric not as a passive process, but as complicated and contending with significant barriers to cultural connection and exchange during the war, demonstrates the continued resonance of British ideals and identities in New Zealand during the war, and the local desire to engage with them. Of course, in spite of this, fractures in this neat consensus are clear, as an examination of the isolated place of Māori in New Zealand's wartime propaganda makes clear. Dismissing the influence of British identities after Gallipoli only undercuts the importance of such complexities to New Zealand's response to the First World War.

---

96   Belich, *Paradise Reforged*, pp. 189–90, 106–207; see also, Tony Ballantyne, *Orientalism and Race: Aryanism in the British Empire* (Basingstoke and New York, NY: Palgrave Macmillan, 2002).

Chapter 6
Heligoland
Between the lion and the eagle

Jan Asmussen

Introduction

Heligoland (*Helgoland*) was occupied by the British during the Napoleonic wars in 1807. In 1890 the island became part of a deal that lead to German acceptance of British sovereignty over Uganda, Kenya and Zanzibar, for which Germany received Heligoland in exchange. At that time the Heligoland-Zanzibar Treaty, arranged by Lord Salisbury, was seen as a net gain for the Empire, and only a few British observers viewed the 'sale' of British subjects to Germany as a problem. The islanders were never asked but neither did they express overt opposition to the change. During the Great War the island's significant fortification did not play any significant role though the islanders themselves were evacuated for the duration of hostilities. Upon their return there were calls for the island to revert to British rule. This chapter examines the local identity of Heligolanders' by analysing British imperial politics and strategy, before, during and after the Great War. It will be demonstrated that the idea of imperial identity and unity was subjugated to real politics and we shall observe how imperial pro-British sentiments were steadily replaced with German national leanings.

Historical foundations

Heligoland is located in the North Sea 46 km off the German coastline. It consists of a triangular Main Island (*Hauptinsel*) to the west, measuring 1 square km, and a sandbank (*Düne*) to the east measuring 0.7 square km. The Main Island is inhabited and is divided into the Lower Land (*Unterland*) at sea level and the Upper Land (*Oberland*) at higher elevations. The Upper Land includes a plateau about 50 m above sea level which is surrounded by rocky cliffs.[1] It has been inhabited since late Palaeolithic times (15,700–11,000 years BCE)[2] and has a population which, until the late nineteenth century, spoke a special Frisian dialect: the *Halunder*. This was gradually replaced by German as the main language. Ownership of the island has shifted over the centuries between Denmark and the Duchy of Schleswig. It came under Danish rule again in 1714 but remained under the influence of both the Duchies of Holstein and Schleswig. Its main business contacts through trade and piloting also resulted in frequent interactions with the port towns of

---

1 Today the island has an additional *Mittelland* (Middle Land) formed as the result of a giant bomb explosion carried out by British forces in 1947.
2 Niedersächsisches Institut für historische Küstenforschung, ed., *Flint von Helgoland – Die Nutzung einer einzigartigen Rohstoffquelle an der Nordseeküste* (Rahden: VML Vlg Marie Leidor, 2014).

Elbe and Weser, and notably with Hamburg and Bremen.[3] Administration was divided between a Bailiff (*Landvogt*) delegated by the Duke of Schleswig or the Danish King who made all legal decisions and the country board (*Landschaftsvorstand*), a body of local self-administration that consisted of six councillors and eight quarter men.[4]

British occupation and Heligoland identity under British rule

The British occupied Heligoland during the Napoleonic wars in 1807 in order to break the 'continental system', and its Danish garrison surrendered without a shot fired. The Instrument of Capitulation contained the provisions that the island's internal government remain unchanged and that islanders were exempt from serving in the Royal Navy.[5] Indeed, under British rule the islands continued to enjoy self-rule,[6] and in 1814 Denmark formally transferred the 'full and unlimited sovereignty' of the island to Britain in the Treaty of Kiel.[7] The island remained British for the next seventy-six years during which relations between the British government and the islanders remained generally amicable. On only one occasion did the British attempt to change the Heligoland constitution in favour of the administration, and this met with fierce resistance from the Heligoland population who in turn refused to pay their taxes.[8] The British government reacted swiftly by transferring all executive and legislative powers to the governor who was empowered to introduce new laws single-handedly by Order in Council. A newly installed force of half a dozen coast guards quickly silenced all further resistance.[9] Despite nationalistic support in some German circles, the Heligolanders did not fight long against the new state of affairs nor did they make any appeal for a change of status in national (German) terms.[10] The British Governor Henry Berkeley Fitzhardinge Makse (1863–1881) subsequently managed to improve the administration and the revenue which led to notable improvements in the local living conditions. As tourism prospered – the number of guests more than doubled from 4,000 in 1880 to 8,320 in 1886 – the Heligolanders became increasingly content with the administration.[11] Education and church affairs were mainly conducted in German. Teachers were hired, and school books were imported, principally from the German mainland.[12] As Germany unified in 1871 school books (and teachers) on the island celebrated.

---

3 Michael Herms, *Flaggenwechsel auf Helgoland: Der Kampf um einen militärischen Vorposten in der Nordsee* (Berlin: Ch. Links Verlag, 2002), pp. 21–4.

4 Ibid., p. 20.

5 Letters from Commanders-in-Chief, North Sea: Including Admiral Russell, 1807, ADM 1/557, The National Archives of the UK (TNA).

6 Governor Corbet D'Auvergne to Admiralty, 201, 1807, ADM 1/557, TNA.

7 Herms, *Flaggenwechsel auf Helgoland*, p. 34.

8 Order in council making provisions for the government of Heligoland and declaring powers of the Governor thereof, 7 January 1864, 174–114 Landschaft und Britische Kolonie Helgoland, Verfassung, SHLA.

9 Heligoland. Memorandum on the changes in 1868 as made by order in council, n d., 174–170 Landschaft und Britische Kolonie Helgoland, Helgoländer Ordinanzen des Gouverneurs Henry Fitzharding, SHLA.

10 Ibid.

11 Herms, *Flaggenwechsel auf Helgoland*, p. 46.

12 Kurt Friedrichs, *Umkämpftes Helgoland, Leidensweg eines Inselvolkes* (Helgoland: Maren Knaus, 1988), p. 18. It should be noted that English language was taught in the highest classes.

Transition: fortress from tourism

In 1890 Britain decided to exchange Heligoland for wide-ranging German concessions in Africa as the island was of little military or commercial interest to the empire. The treaty itself was signed on 1 July 1890 and contained border adjustments in East, West, and South-West Africa. Germany ceded claims to Witu and the Somaliland coast and acknowledged the British protectorate of Zanzibar. Britain agreed to cede Heligoland to Germany. Article XII of the treaty regulated the cession of Heligoland. It reads:

1. Pending approval by the British parliament, Her British Majesty shall grant sovereignty over the Island of Heligoland and all its facilities to His Majesty the German Kaiser.
2. The German government shall grant natives of the ceded territory the right to choose British citizenship by a declaration to be made by themselves or, in the case of underage children, by their parents or guardians before January 1, 1892.
3. Natives of the ceded territory and their children born before the day on which this treaty is signed shall be exempt from compulsory military service in the German army and navy.
4. The currently valid local laws and practices will remain unchanged wherever possible.
5. The German government agrees not to raise, until January 1, 1910, the customs tariffs currently in force in the ceded territory.
6. All property rights acquired by individuals or existing corporations in Heligoland under the British government shall remain intact. Any obligations linked to these shall pass to His Majesty the Emperor of Germany. The term 'property rights' includes Lloyd's signalling rights.
7. The rights of British fishermen shall remain unaffected, including the right to anchor in all weather, take on provisions and water, make repairs, trans ship goods, sell fish, land and dry nets.[13]

In Heligoland the news of the imminent change was learnt from the German press. No hearings were held to inquire about the views of the Heligolanders, and soon Governor Arthur Cecil Stuart Barkly could report that the locals who generally didn't desire change had two main concerns: first that the Germans might turn the island into a military base which would have a negative impact on tourism, and second that they would be simply treated as a Prussian or Schleswig-Holstein island. No other opposition was noted. Barkly conveyed that the islanders would prefer to be treated as a province under direct rule of the empire similar to Alsace Lorraine (*Elsass-Lothringen*).[14]

The official ceremony of cession took place on 9 August 1890 in the garden of Government House between German Secretary of State Karl Heinrich von Boetticher and Governor Barkly.[15] During the official banquet one of the island's dignitaries, the Bath

---

13 Paper C. 6046. FO, TNA.
14 Heligoland Register, CO 346/6, TNA; Malet to Barkly, 1 July 1890, 174–417 Landschaft und Britische Kolonie Helgoland, Kopialbuch von Schreiben des Gouverneurs (Letterbook), SHLA; and Barkly to Malet, July 1890, CO 346/6, TNA.
15 'The Cession of Heligoland,' *The Times*, 11 August 1890, p. 5.

Director stood up to express a few simple words: 'Our present rulers will not think ill of us if, in bidding farewell to the Queen of England, who has ruled us so kindly, we do so with heavy hearts.'[16] The Heligolanders had previously sent a petition to Queen Victoria that read: 'In parting from your Majesty, we shall never forget the manifold reasons we have experienced to feel content and happy under you Majesty's government.'[17] On 10 August 1890 Emperor Wilhelm II landed in Heligoland to take over the island. In a proclamation to the Heligolanders, he declared:

> Heligolanders! In consequence of an Agreement concluded with Her Majesty The [sic] Queen of Great Britain and Ireland the sovereignty over Heligoland and its dependencies has been ceded to me. Thus you return in a peaceful manner to that relation to the German Fatherland which is indicated by history and by the position and conditions of communications of your island. By community of race, of language, of customs and interests you have always had much in common with your German brothers. Thanks to the benevolent wisdom of the Government which has hitherto ruled over you this has not been altered during the period in which you belonged to the mighty British Empire. With all the more joy does every German welcome with Me [sic] your re-union with the German people and Fatherland. . . . I assure to you my protection and my care for yourselves and for your rights. I shall take care that Right and Justice shall be administered equally among you and that your native laws and customs shall, as far as possible, remain unchanged.[18]

Representatives of the Heligolanders responded with declarations of loyalty to the Emperor.[19] A souvenir was presented to him by a committee and a number of girls in national costume presented a tribute of flowers in the shape of an immense floral anchor in the Heligoland colours of green, red and white.[20] The wish to be treated as an imperial territory did not materialise, and instead Heligoland became annexed to the Prussian province Schleswig-Holstein on 18 February 1891 where it was treated as a rural municipality within the county of Süderdithmarschen.[21] School education was conducted according to German national curricula.[22]

Only a few Heligolanders actually remained British. A small number had served in the British navy, and the UK National Archives list thirteen Heligolanders in their medal cards.[23] Eleven opted for British citizenship, and of these five immigrated to England and

---

16 'A Visit to Helgoland: Island Tired of Injustice: Memories of British Rule,' *The Times*, 24 November 1919, p. 9.

17 Petition of the Heligolanders to Queen Victoria, 21 July 1890, CO 346/6, TNA.

18 German Emperors Proclamation given on 10 August 1890, translation British Embassy Berlin, Malet to Marquis of Salisbury, 12 August 1890, CO 537/70, TNA.

19 Herms, *Flaggenwechsel auf Helgoland*, p. 54.

20 George Drower, *Heligoland: The Story of German Bight and the Island That Britain Betrayed* (Stroud: Sutton, 2002), pp. 120–1.

21 Herms, *Flaggenwechsel auf Helgoland*, p. 54.

22 Schule auf Helgoland, 1902–1909, 320.22–108, SHLA.

23 Registry of Shipping and Seamen: Index of First World War Mercantile Marine Medals and the British War Medal, Medal Card of Kruz, William, Place of Birth: Heligoland, Date of Birth: 1863, BT 351/1/78429, TNA; Medal Card of Ross, William, Date of Birth: 1861, BT 351/1/122533, TNA. Medal Card of Stackmann, Harry, Date of Birth: 1860, BT 351/1/133395, TNA. Medal Card of Krause, Charles, Date of Birth: 1865, BT 351/1/78368, TNA. Medal Card of Temple, James, Date of Birth:

other parts of the Empire. At the beginning of the Great War only two remained.[24] This was probably because the German Colonel (*Oberst*) Leo had personally invited all those who wished to remain British and had informed them that in future only German citizens would be employed in the profitable municipal tourism business.[25]

The German military regarded Heligoland as vital for the defence of the Kiel Canal, and subsequently the island saw the build-up of a major fortress and naval harbour.[26] Despite the fact that more and more military installations were built on the island, there seemed to be no adverse effect on tourism. Quite the contrary – many tourists came purposely to see the military base. Subsequently for the rest of the pre-war years the Heligoland people did not voice nostalgic dreams of a return to British rule.

Heligoland, the Great War and temporary exile

Heligoland didn't see any direct action during the war. None of the large military installations were used, and the island served mainly as a submarine base. As I have demonstrated elsewhere, Britain considered invasion – a potentially disastrous plan as the military planning grossly underestimated the military strength of the fortress.[27] Nevertheless, the war brought about substantial disruption to the Heligoland inhabitants. The military commander Rear Admiral (*Konteradmiral*) Leo Jacobson decided on 1 August 1914 that all civilians had to leave the island within twenty-four hours and allowed them to carry only personal luggage and refreshments. The implementation order read:

> All Heligolanders are to be transferred to the mainland at outbreak of war. Should the mouth of the (German) rivers (Elbe and Weser) be blocked by the enemy, the population is to be transferred to the dune; no Heligolander will remain on the island. In cases of disturbances or resistance weapons are to be used.[28]

The actual evacuation ran smoothly, and on 2 August 1914, 3,427 Heligolanders were brought to Hamburg on two steamboats. Most were settled there and in the towns of Altona

---

1879, BT 351/1/138789, TNA. Medal Card of McCray, James, Date of Birth: 1867, BT 351/1/91643, TNA. Medal Card of Englehardt, Henry, Date of Birth: 1853, BT 351/1/41612, TNA. Medal Card of Geige, Peter, Date of Birth: 1861, BT 351/1/50040, TNA. Medal Card of Wright, John. Date of Birth: 1864, BT 351/1/155402, TNA. Medal Card of Schmit, Frank, Date of Birth: 1858, BT 351/1/125606, TNA. Medal Card of Smith, Fred, Date of Birth: 1850, BT 351/1/130644, TNA. Medal Card of Miller, Frank Henry, Date of Birth: 1863, BT 351/1/97372, TNA.

24 Anni Peters, 'Der Anschluß der Insel Helgoland an das Deutsche Reich,' in *Helgoland. Ein Mitteilungsblatt für Hallunder Moats*, ed. James Krüss no. 36–7, 1951.

25 Friedrichs, *Umkämpftes Helgoland*, pp. 35–6. Complains and German official denial can be found in Heligoland: Despatches, Offices and Individuals, 1890–1910, CO 537/17, TNA.

26 See Claus Fröhle und Hans-Jürgen Kühn, *Hochseefestung Helgoland: Eine militärgeschichtliche Entdeckungsreise* (Herbholzheim: Fröhle-Kühn Verlagsgesellschaft, 1998).

27 For a treatment on Heligoland's military value during the Great War see Jan Asmussen. 'Heligoland and the Great War: A Major Theatre of War That Never Was,' in *Re-Visiting World War I: Interpretations and Perspectives of the Great Conflict*, ed. Jaroslaw Suchoples and Stephanie James (Frankfurt: Peter Lang, 2016), pp. 385–419.

28 Quoted by Friedrichs, *Umkämpftes Helgoland*, p. 43, trans. by Jan Asmussen.

and Wedel.[29] The remaining British subjects were interned in a camp at Ruhleben, close to Berlin.[30] This time in exile meant distress for many who had never left the island and now lived in totally alien neighbourhoods of big cities. All of the islanders could speak German, but to use their *Hallunder* Frisian mother-tongue raised the suspicions of the local German population. Mina Borchert, who as a child was evacuated first to Hamburg and then to Bremen, recalled a telling incident:

> In Bremen my mother and I once took the tram into town. As always we spoke Heligolandish with each other. Unrest broke out among the passengers. I asked my mother. 'Why do the people look at us this way?' At that moment the conductor came and told us to leave. As we were out, my mother explained that people had thought we were English. To me this incident remained present and I have long only spoken very silent in public.[31]

Back on the island there remained between three and four thousand military personal. Later in the war eighty fishermen and some additional Heligoland service providers were allowed to return.[32] Those Heligolanders born before 1890 were exempted from military service and so only few served in the German Imperial Army. A plaque of honour at the Heligoland St. Nicholas Church lists twenty-three Heligoland sons that died in the war.[33] The famous uprising of the German naval seamen that started in Wilhelmshaven and Kiel in November 1918 also had its repercussions in Heligoland, where a soldier's council took control. Before leaving the island, soldiers ransacked and plundered many Heligoland homes, leaving them in a wrecked condition.[34]

The return of the Heligolanders to their island was organised by the Heligoland municipality and took place from 6–15 December 1918.[35] The British War Cabinet decided in March 1919 that both the fortifications and the harbour of Heligoland should be destroyed.[36] This decision, if carried out, could have meant the end of fishery and tourism on the island and accordingly the islanders responded with a petition calling for the retention of a small harbour in the north-east side of the island.[37] This call was ultimately successful. On 7 October 1919 the Head of the Naval Inter-Allied Commission of Control (Heligoland Sub-Committee) reported that the small boat harbour would remain.[38] Article 115 of the

---

29 Henry P. Rickmers, Frank Woosnam and Beate Griese, *Helgoland: Eine Insel auf dem Weg nach Europa* (Otterndorf: Niederelbe-Verlag, 1992), p. 60.
30 Friedrichs, *Umkämpftes Helgoland*, p. 43.
31 Mina Borchert, *Das alte Helgoland. Kindheit und Jugend zwischen 1918 und 1930* (Helgoland: Verlag der Kirchengemeinde St. Nicolai, 2003), pp. 10–11, trans. by Jan Asmussen.
32 Herms, *Flaggenwechsel auf Helgoland*, p. 68.
33 Ibid.; Friedrichs has forty-eight dead without giving any references. Friedrichs, *Umkämpftes Helgoland*, p. 43.
34 Anni Peters, 'Der Wiederaufbau des Gemein- und Badewesens nach dem 1. Weltkrieg,' *Mitteilungsblatt für Haluner Moats*, ed. James Krüss, no. 40–1, 1952.
35 Gemeindevorsteher. Vorläufige Mitteilung an die Helgoländer, 26 November 1918, 320.22-98, SHLA; according to Friedrichs the return was already concluded by 12 December; Friedrichs, *Umkämpftes Helgoland*, p. 44.
36 Extract from War Cabinet 546, 19 March 1919, WO 32/5382, TNA.
37 Bürgerverein Helgoland, Petition, 15 August 1919, FO 608/132, TNA.
38 Naval Inter-Allied Commission of Control (Heligoland Sub-Committee) to Admiralty, 7 October 1919, ADM 1/8568/260, TNA.

Treaty of Versailles nevertheless regulated the demolition of all military installations on the island, and the work was supervised by seventeen Royal Engineers and around five hundred to six hundred German personnel. The process was completed in June of 1922.[39]

Return to Britain (or Denmark)?

In October of 1919 the Heligolanders made an appeal to the British to return to the island – an action which some have interpreted as a desire to return to British rule. British author George Drower certainly interpreted it as such.[40] Upon hearing these rumours, the German press attacked the islanders, calling them traitors. Had years of German school education (even in British times) and German national indoctrination from 1890 had no impact? In fact, as described earlier, upon return to the island the Heligolanders found their houses in a terrible state and many of their belongings stolen.[41] Moreover, the economic prospects were grim, as fishing grounds were almost empty and tourism suffered from the deep economic crisis now taking grip in Germany. The Heligolanders demanded compensation for the damage caused by the naval soldiers and after some struggle received two million *Reichsmark*.[42] Given the rapid inflation the value of this money rapidly declined through 1923.[43] On top of the economic troubles the Heligolanders were aroused by the 24 January 1919 decision of the Prussian Parliament that equal voting rights should be granted in all Prussian municipalities. Before this only property owning men had voting rights on the island. Now, everybody residing there for more than six months would be eligible to vote. In addition, it became known that the Prussian government intended to impose all government taxes and tariffs on the island from which it had been exempted since 1890. The Fünfundzwanziger Kommission, an assembly of leading Heligoland notables that had already negotiated with the German Government about the compensation, led by the tailor and merchant August Kuchlenz, went to the Ministry of Interior in Berlin in order to change these decisions.[44] All demands were rebutted. The commission then turned to the Entente-Commission in Berlin where the head of the Naval Inter-Allied Commission of Control, Admiral Edward Charlton expressed sympathy. This might have encouraged Kuchlenz to draft the appeal which was sent in October 1919 to the Supreme War Council at Versailles. It was signed by former British subjects of Heligoland and complained about the 'many injustices of the Prussian regime [that should] be examined and abolished'. It claimed that

---

39   J.C. Matheson, 'The Dismantling of Heligoland,' *The Royal Engineers Journal* 37, (December 1923): pp. 547–51; Heligoland. Admiralty: Architectural and Engineering Works Department, later Civil Engineer in Chief's Department: Photographs of Works, 1921, ADM/195/52.

40   Drower, *Heligoland*, p. 178.

41   Landgemeinde Helgoland. Erster Weltkrieg, 1914–1920, 131–10, SHLA. This includes several complaints about the conditions of houses.

42   Inselkreis Helgoland, Vergleichsausschuss für Kriegsschäden 1918–1921, 320.22-99, SHLA; Entschädigungen für die militärische Nutzung privater Häuser, Boote und Einrichtungen während des Krieges, 1918–1921, 320.22 101, SHLA.

43   Herms, *Flaggenwechsel auf Helgoland*, p. 70.

44   Eckhard Wallmann, *Eine Kolonie wird deutsch: Helgoland zwischen den Weltkriegen* (Bredstedt: Nordfriisk Instituut, 2012), p. 13. The Kuchlenz family had migrated to the island from Schleswig in the beginning of the nineteenth century. August Kuchlenz (1878–1961) was married to an English woman.

'under the long and blissful administration of the great British nation, all our rights and customs were always most loyally upheld.' It concludes:

> We Heligolanders, on our little island in the middle of the seas, far from all the world's commotion, form the very smallest nation which has for centuries maintained its independence and its local customs. We seek neither wealth nor ostentation, but desire and hope to live in our lonely home upon the rocks, in peace and contentment, as our forefathers did before us.[45]

At that time a number of petitions were also created by unknown Heligolanders to both the German Constitutional Assembly at Weimar demanding that the island should remain German and to the British Prime Minister demanding that the British flag be hoisted again in Heligoland. Unlike the Kuchlenz petition those addressed to the British government were sent anonymously for fear 'that in case of our request finding no favour with the British Government, our present government on being informed of our memorial would punish us severely and make us pay a heavy penalty'.[46] One of the petitions stated that in the case of a negative reply from the British government, the island should return to Denmark:

> Should the British government, however, entirely oppose taking back Heligoland ... then, Sir, let us became part of the Danish kingdom and in either of these cases we beg you to grant us a free decision.
>
> (plebiscite)[47]

However, the wish to become Danish again was not widely communicated at the time. On 10 February 1919 Kuchlenz had sent a confidential message, signed by nine Heligolanders, to the Danish Embassy in Berlin in which they expressed the wish to become Danish. Sensing signs of an annexation to Denmark they wanted to assure the Danish government that 'the Heligoland people, who had always used their own mother-tongue and used their own green, red, white flag, would be delighted, if they could unite with the Danish kingdom.' They didn't seek a seat in the Danish Parliament (*Folketing*) but would appeal for their 'ancient rights and traditions'. In order to avoid 'any troubles with our present government' they asked to keep the entire affair secret for the time being. Apparently the Danish government didn't consider the petition seriously and simultaneously Britain had also decided that Heligoland was not to become British again.[48] Winston Churchill, the Minister of Munitions, in a speech on 4 December 1918 answered a question regarding

---

45 'A Visit to Heligoland: Island Tired of Injustice: Memories of British Rule,' *The Times*, 24 November 1919, p. 9.

46 Peace Conference. British Delegation Petition send by 'Yours faithful Heligolanders' via Seaman R.S. Stanley to Lloyd George, 19 January 1919, FO 608/141, TNA; Letter from Mr. W.G. Black informing about anonymous communication from Heligolanders urging annexation by Great Britain, 2 March 1919; Letter from R.S. Stanley forwarding a communication from Heligoland, protesting against Petition sent to Weimar by certain Germans who are not natives of the Island, appealing for the continued union of Heligoland with Germany, 19 March 1919.

47 Petition send by 'Yours faithful Heligolanders' via Seaman R.S. Stanley to Lloyd George, 19 January 1919, FO 608/141, TNA; translated by Jan Asmussen.

48 Thomas Steensen, *Die friesische Nationalbewegung in Nordfriesland im 19. und 20. Jahrhundert* (Neumünster: Wachholtz, 1986), p. 309; (UM, 6. C.47) translated by Jan Asmussen.

the future of Heligoland saying: 'The Admiralty experts have come to the conclusion that it is not necessary to demand it.'[49] Some Heligoland petitioners noted this speech with regret.[50] The British parliament finally decided in November 1920 that it would not use Article 289 of the Paris Peace Treaty in order to revoke the 1890 Anglo-German agreement and that it considered the entire Heligoland question an internal matter for Germany.[51] The Heligolanders were subsequently accused of treason by the German press, and this was further exacerbated by the 'Appeal on the British Nation' that a Heligoland delegation brought to London in spring 1920.[52] This time it contained the declaration:

> We would have preferred to remain under the British Flag exercising our liberties under British justice; we would prefer it to stay. It might be claimed by us that if the Agreement is declared void we revert to Great Britain, but if this is no longer possible we appeal to Great Britain to support our just claims to the rights she guaranteed to us at the time of our cession to Germany.[53]

Lord Sydenham (Conservative peer) took the matter up in the House of Lords and claimed that the 1890 agreement had lapsed and that it had been a mistake to surrender the island to Germany in the first place. He thought the island could have been put under League of Nations control or become Danish again. The chancellor of the Duchy of Lancaster (The Earl of Crawford) answered that Lord Sydenham was correct in assuming that the Agreement of 1890 had lapsed, but that the treaty 'relating to Heligoland of 1890 dealt not merely with Heligoland but with Africa and other important subjects in relation to the comprehensive Agreement made with Germany in that year'. The fact that the Agreement had lapsed didn't imply that German sovereignty over the island had disappeared: 'The status of Heligoland is clearly laid down in Article 115 of the Treaty of Versailles. That Article provides for the destruction of the fortifications of the island.'[54]

It is debatable whether Kuchlenz and his supporters really wanted to return to British rule or if they used the British threat to gain a better bargain with Berlin. Initially they had not actually asked for a return of the island to British rule, but rather sought in vain to gain the support of the British for the protection of their ancient rights. Later, as the conflict became tougher, the *Appeal on the British Nation* still rather vaguely expressed the desire for a return to British rule, rather than openly demanding it. In this conflict they didn't consider the German people, but rather Berlin bureaucrats, as their adversaries. This became apparent in their subsequent petitions. It is impossible to assess how much support the idea of return to British or Danish rule actually had. Today Heligolanders claim that it

---

49 Winston Churchill, 'A Fair Trial and No Favour,' in *Winston S. Churchill: His Complete Speeches, 1897–1963, vol. 3, 1914–1922*, ed. Robert Rhodes James (London: Atheneum, 1974), pp. 2,646–7.

50 Petition sent by 'Yours faithful Heligolanders' via Seaman R.S. Stanley to Lloyd George, 19 January 1919, FO 608/141, TNA.

51 For a treatment on the British reasons see Asmussen, 'Heligoland and the Great War.'

52 Wallmann, *Eine Kolonie wird deutsch*, pp. 16–17.

53 Hansard, Heligoland. HL Deb, 10 November 1920, vol. 42, cc 238–43; 'Lonely Islanders Heligoland Appeal. Prefer British Flag,' *The Sydney Morning Herald* (NSW: 1842–1954), 25 December 1920, p. 10.

54 Hansard, Heligoland. HL Deb, 10 November 1920, vol. 42, cc 238–43.

was never meant seriously while others have asserted that it was merely a sign of coquetry.[55] Eckhard Wallmann regards the Heligolanders' wishes to change nationality as a rather more serious business born out of the frustration with Prussian bureaucracy and surmised that nothing came out of it solely because the British and Danish governments had refused to follow suit.[56] The example of Schleswig might show how difficult such evaluations are. Schleswig's 1920 referendum shows clear national majorities in Zones one (Danish) and two (German) of the plebiscites.[57] In 1939 the Danish minority south of the new border numbered only 2,500 members[58] yet after the Second World War membership of the Danish minority sky-rocketed to 74,683 in 1948,[59] declining again to a mere 39,348 in 1956.[60] These statistics indicate that national leanings can be affected by economic troubles as well as by economic recovery. Taking this into consideration Heligoland might not seem so exceptional. Thomas Steensen was probably right in stating that the Heligolanders fluctuated between irredentist aspirations, separatist approaches, ambitions for self-administration and loyalty towards Germany.[61]

Next, Kuchlenz assembled an even stronger association of Heligoland inhabitants, the so-called *Zweiundsechziger Kommission*, consisting of sixty-two leading Heligoland individuals representing various Heligoland associations. This commission now took up the fight for changes in the Prussian and German laws in Heligoland. In July 1921 the *62er Kommission* circulated the first very strongly-worded petition titled 'Memorandum on the reasons for the desire for independence of the island of Heligoland' that was mainly geared towards public consumption. It accused the Prussian-Berlin administration of constantly ignoring their opinions and needs, while the press raised unjustifiable accusations about the motives of Heligolanders (such as treason). The memorandum called for the preservation of ancient Heligoland rights, saying 'What Heligoland wants, is its autonomy, its own administration, freedom in the utilisation of its economic abilities!' It reiterated that they would do nothing that would 'amount to a material or moral damage for Germany', but nevertheless concluded reluctantly

> that they had nothing to expect from Germany than further humiliations of their delegations... The Heligolanders [were] sick and tired of catching flies in the audience rooms of Berlin ministries. [They sensed] that the German government has learned nothing from the damage that faulty policies had done in Alsace Lorraine, Upper-Silesia

---

55 Kurt Jürgensen, 'Helgoland, 1890–1990,' *Zeitschrift der Gesellschaft für Schleswig-Holsteinische Geschichte*, no. 116 (1991): p. 196.

56 Wallmann, *Eine Kolonie wird deutsch*, p. 17.

57 The Referendum was conducted in February and March 1920 in accordance with the Paris Peace Treaty paragraphs 109–14. 75 per cent of the voters in the northern zone voted for Denmark; 75 per cent in the southern zone for Germany; Erich Hoffmann, 'Historische Voraussetzungen für die Herausbildung der heutigen deutsch-dänischen Staatsgrenze', *Zeitschrift der Gesellschaft für Schleswig-Holsteinische Geschichte*, no. 106 (1981): p. 10.

58 Johan Peter Noack, *Det danske mindretal i Sydslesvig, 1920–1945* (Abenrade: Institut for Grænseregionsforskning, 1989), p. 580.

59 Kurt Jürgensen, 'Schleswig-Holstein nach dem Zweiten Weltkrieg.' Kontinuität und Wandel, in *Geschichte Schleswig-Holsteins. Von den Anfängen bis zur Gegenwart*, ed. Ulrich Lange (Neumünster: Wachholtz, 1996), p. 630.

60 Membership declined further 2005: 14,000. SSF Statistics.

61 Steensen, *Die friesische Nationalbewegung in Nordfriesland*, p. 308.

and Poland. .... We appeal for a last time, not to the offices "unter den Linden" [the road in Berlin were most of the ministries were situated] but to the German people, to the German public, who despite everything are something different than administrative material of ossified and historical orientated bureaucrats. We turn as smaller brother to the big [brother], as repressed smaller people to the suffering bigger [nation] and trust to hope, to find understanding and help with them.[62]

What was conspicuously absent from the memorandum was any reference to a possible change in sovereignty of the island from Germany to Britain or Denmark. Some of the islanders' demands had been taken up positively in the German press and even the so-viciously-attacked Berlin administration started to send out reconciliatory signs.[63] This was positively noted by the *62er Kommission* that now drafted a far more conciliatory 'Memorandum on the clarification of (Heligoland's) legal relationships with the German Empire and Prussia' in which the Heligoland municipality, the *62er Kommission* and fourteen other associations listed their demands for local elections, administration and taxation. The petitioners begged that 'in the desire to design Heligoland's relations and its inhabitants with the German Empire and the Prussian state in a way that they are not burdened with disagreements in essential questions now and in future' their

applications would be benevolently evaluated and positively approved. ... The smallest, but not the worst tribe (*Volksstamm*) appeals to representatives of the great German people for their benevolent understanding.[64]

The use of the word *Volksstamm* (literally: peoples strain) is telling as it departs from the notion of an independent Heligoland nation. This opened the way for the German government to regard the memorandum as a sign that the Heligolanders regarded themselves as an integral part of the nation. On 10 March 1922 a meeting took place in the Prussian Ministry of the Interior between a Heligoland delegation and Secretary (*Ministerialdirektor*) Oskar Mulert in which most of the demands that were listed in the memorandum were addressed in a manner that proved satisfactory to the Heligoland representatives.[65] The Imperial Electoral Law (*Reichswahlgesetz*) of 1920 was amended by a Heligoland-clause that made five years residency a pre-condition for voting rights. The island was disconnected from the county of Süderdithmarschen and became an independent county (*Landratsamt*) with a county chief executive (*Landrat*) and two elected councillors.[66] Some taxes were lowered or delayed, while the income tax was introduced on 1 April 1921. The duty free privilege,

---

62 Die 62er-Kommission der Insel Helgoland, *Denkschrift über die Gründe des Selbstständigkeitswillens der Insel Helgoland*, October 1921, 131–7, SHLA; translated by Jan Asmussen.
63 Regierungsrat Dr. Franz Rathenau, 'Helgoland,' *Vossische Zeitung*, 5 October 1919, p. 3.
64 Gemeinde Helgoland und 62-Kommission. Denkschrift der Helgoländer über Klarstellung ihrer Rechtsverhältnisse zum Deutschen Reiche und Preußen in Anbetracht ihrer Reservate, October 1921, 131–7, SHLA; trans. by Jan Asmussen.
65 Abschrift Mulert, 'Besprechung Mulert mit Abordnung der Helgoländer,' 10 March 1922, 131–7, SHLA.
66 Herms, *Flaggenwechsel auf Helgoland*, p. 71.

an important factor for day-trip tourism, remained.[67] It continues as a special Heligoland right to this day.

During the 10 March 1922 meeting with the Heligoland representatives it was decided that the position of *Landrat* would be held by a person who would know the conditions of the island well and would be prepared to stay there for as long as possible in order to acquaint themselves with its peculiarities.[68] Unfortunately, as the suspicion amongst the Prussian bureaucracy about possible Heligolander moves towards independence or secession remained strong, civil servants were selected for the post, and this turned out to be an unsatisfactory arrangement. In fact, most of the *Landrat*s came from Silesia where they had previous experience of fighting separatism.[69]

The island recovered economically and tourism reached the pre-war figures of 1911 in 1924, when 36,119 guests arrived.[70] No further efforts for separation were made, but suspicions continued to appear in the German press. In 1926, for example, Kuchlenz threatened that Heligolanders could use their domiciliary rights (*Hausrecht*) to eject Prussians from the dune. This conflict revolved around the proper preservation of the dune and its finances and was widely reported in the German press with references to the previous Anglo-Danish ambitions of Kuchlenz.[71] He had no hidden agenda for secession from Germany but attempted to use 'free Frisian people' in order to put more weight behind his arguments. By the same token he did get in touch with the North-Frisian association in Schleswig that was seeking minority status without any concrete political agenda in mind. The North-Frisians asked him to sign a petition of 'All Frisians' to demand minority rights, but he declined. The Heligoland Frisian effort was mainly economically motivated.[72] Kuchlenz headed the Unity-List H (*Einheitsliste Helgoland*) that would dominate Heligoland politics for most of the Weimar-Republican era. The *Einheitsliste* was linked to the German National group in the Prussian Parliament (*Landtag*) and would not propagate any secessionist policies.[73] On the contrary it became increasingly nationalist as its pivotal role in the erection of a statute for German Colonial pioneer Carl Peters in 1930 demonstrates.[74] The Heligolander author Kurt Friedrichs claimed that the Heligoland people had been almost immune to Nazi propaganda because their manifold fate had never encouraged nationalism let alone greater German ideas. Moreover, any kind of coercion, especially of the military kind, would have been a mortal enemy to the Heligolander's love for freedom.[75] This rather idle characterisation has been disproven by the research of Eckhard Wallmann who analysed how gradually but steadily the island came under the influence of German party politics. Nationalist German education contributed to the

---

67 Friedrichs, *Umkämpftes Helgoland*, p. 48.
68 (Oskar) Mulert, Besprechung Mulert mit Abordnung der Helgoländer.
69 Herms, *Flaggenwechsel auf Helgoland*, p. 71.
70 Ibid., p. 72.
71 Helgoländer Sonderrechte; Das grenzt an Hochverrat. Helgoländer wollen zu England,' *Berliner Morgenpost*, 7 February 1929; 'Helgoländer Querköpfe. Ein Zwischenfall im Preußischen Landtag,' *Berliner Morgenzeitung*, 7 February 1929, newspaper clips in: 131–7 Helgoländer Sonderrechte, SHLA.
72 Steensen, *Die friesische Nationalbewegung in Nordfriesland*, p. 311
73 Wallmann, *Eine Kolonie wird deutsch*, p. 50.
74 Ibid., p. 70.
75 Friedrichs, *Umkämpftes Helgoland*, p. 54.

inability of Heligolanders to detach themselves from political developments in the *Reich*[76] and so as the last truly free elections were held for the *Reichstag* on 1 August 1932 the Nazi party (NSDAP) scored 42.7 per cent of the Heligoland votes. The average in Germany was 37.8 per cent.[77] The free Frisian spirit was hence-forth upset on the island, and soon racism and anti-semitism prevailed as Jewish people were banned from travelling there. In 1945 a group tried to plot the surrender of the island to the British in a last-ditch effort to save the island from a final Allied air-attack, but they were betrayed and arrested. Heligolanders called them traitors and spit at them while they were under arrest in the bomb-shelter.[78] This didn't mean that the Heligolanders were more prone to Nazi propaganda than other Germans. It merely suggests the extent to which they had finally integrated into German political culture.

Heligoland itself was almost destroyed by a British air strike on 18 April 1945.[79] On 12 May 1945 the entire population was evacuated to the mainland. The British Air Force then used the island as a bombing range. The intent was for the island to never be resettled. On 18 April 1947 the British Army carried out the operation 'Big Bang' when 6,700 tonnes of explosives were ignited in what amounted to, until then, the biggest non-nuclear explosion in history.[80] The Heligolanders who were settled in Schleswig-Holstein, Lower-Saxony and Hamburg fought a long political struggle until they could finally return to their island on 1 March 1952.[81] The Homeland Association *Hallunder Moats* stated in 1950: 'We are Frisian and will never deny our Frisian culture . . . but, we may not forget, that we are German Frisians, in the same way as there are Dutch and Danish Frisians.'[82]

Conclusion

Heligoland has always been an isolated island imbued with a sense of uniqueness – *The Land* (*Deät Lun*). British occupation did not lead to the development of a special Heligoland British spirit. The islanders, rather, regarded British rule as a welcoming guarantee of security for their developing tourism economy. By the same token the swing towards German rule was not resisted, so long as old privileges were respected and tourism – that was predominately German – continued to prosper. The German nationalist education

---

76 Anna Symicek, *So war es damals: Meine Kindheit, Jugend und Rückkehr auf den roten Felsen* (Helgoland: Verlag der Kirchengemeinde St. Nicolai, 2011), p. 80.

77 Wallmann, *Eine Kolonie wird deutsch*, p. 142.

78 Astrid Friederichs, *Wir wollten Helgoland retten: Auf den Spuren der Widerstandsgruppe von 1945* (Helgoland: Verlag der Kirchengemeinde St. Nicolai, 2010), p. 38.

79 See Elisabeth Wallmann, ed., *Die Zerstörung Helgolands durch die Bombardierung am 18. April 1945: Helgoländer erinnern an diesen Tag vor 50 Jahren*, 4th ed. (Helgoland: Verlag der Kirchengemeinde St. Nicolai, 2001).

80 Demolition of fortifications on Heligoland: (operations Big Bang and Little Bang), PRO 30/26/197, TNA.

81 See Elisabeth Wallmann, ed., *Helgoland ist frei! Zum 1. März 1952: Helgoländer erinnern sich an die Evakuierung, Freigabe und die Rückkehr in ihre Heimat* (Helgoland: Verlag der Kirchengemeinde St. Nicolai, 2007).

82 James Krüss, ed., *Helgoland. Ein Mitteilungsblatt für Halluner Moats*, 22–23, 1950; trans. by Jan Asmussen.

started to have a real impact at the beginning of the Great War when young Heligolanders joined the German Imperial Army and Navy and this was then tempered with four-and-a-half years of exile which had a sobering effect on Heligolander Germanic feelings. Upon return to the island calls for a return to British rule appeared that could largely be attributed to the desperate economic conditions on the island and in Germany. No such calls reappeared after the Heligoland tourism industry recovered. The success of the Nazi Party in Heligoland showed that the island had finally, for better or worse, integrated into the wider German political society.

Chapter 7

Imperial Austerlitz

The Singapore Strategy and
the culture of victory, 1917–1924

Wm. Matthew Kennedy

For millennia, historical accounts of armed conflict between people and states has been narrated primarily through an analysis of the aims, means and ends of its orchestrators – generals, admirals and politicians. Historiographies of warmaking, perhaps more than most, have remained focussed on such figures – the assumption being that – like in some strains of political history, the acts of 'great men' play out on a distinct and higher historical register. Unlike the substantial challenges to such narrative conventions in political history by social and cultural historiographies that aim to repatriate the subaltern into accounts of politics, historiographies of warmaking, and particularly of its intellectual dimension – strategy formation – have been slower to respond critically to this practice. Many scholars who are exceptions to this rule have provided chapters for this volume.[1] This chapter also aims to contribute to this effort as well by reflecting on how we might re-think our treatment of military leaders in histories of warmaking that are willing to consider the often substantially different world of those whose fates they are assumed to control.

In exploring this problem, a number of profound challenges to the nature of historical knowledge itself become apparent. Chief amongst them is the relationship between the realm of thought and the realm of political action. To what extent ideas of the world, and especially of potential actions in the world, are shaped by material realities, and in turn alter conceptions of those realities, is a common point of contention between intellectual, social and political historians.[2] This dilemma is especially apparent when considering military strategy, relying as it does on the capability of plans to transcend this divide – an epistemological claim that separates the pre-modern 'prophecy' from modern, scientific

---

1 See W.G. Sebald, *A Natural History of Destruction* (New York: Random House, 2003). In particular, some histories of the First World War have taken up the interesting problem of the war in public memory, articulating a kind of 'natural history', in W.G. Sebald's words. For this approach in the First World War historiography, see, Jay Winter, ed., *The Cambridge History of the Frist World War* (New York: Cambridge University Press, 2014); Paul Fussell, *The Great War and Modern Memory* (New York: Oxford University Press, 2013); and Jay Winter, *Remembering War: The Great War between Memory and History in the Twentieth Century* (New Haven, CT: Yale University Press, 2006).

2 See Patrick Joyce, 'What Is the Social in Social History?,' *Past and Present* 206, no. 1 (2010): pp. 213–48; For an insightful essay on these distinctions. Also, W.G. Sewell, *The Logics of History: Social Theory and Social Transformation* (Chicago: University of Chicago Press, 2005). For a review of what intellectual history claims to be, see Quentin Skinner, 'Meaning and Understanding in the History of Ideas,' *History and Theory* 8, no. 1 (1969): pp. 3–53; and an insightful review essay by John E. Toews, 'Intellectual History after the Linguistic Turn: The Autonomy of Meaning and the Irreduciblity of Experience,' *American Historical Review* 92, no. 4 (October 1987): pp. 879–907.

'prediction'.[3] Secondary to this is the nature of political and military leadership, a position so integral to what some scholarship has called the 'official mind' of government, but also one fundamentally entangled with certain institutional, social and cultural knowledge, statuses and practices. Especially after assuming the status as one such 'great man' of history, and therefore deserving of access to the 'official mind' of policy making bodies, it seems ill-advised to forget that individuals performed and inhabited these roles, very conscious of the cultural valence and social stature of their heroic positions. Strategic thought, therefore, might be approached with the combination of intellectual, cultural and social historical methodological sensitivities with which historians approach its political corollary.

One of the most substantial beginning points for a study of self-awareness amongst those that history invests with a particular greatness, because of its narrative conventions, is Leo Tolstoy's seminal work, *War and Peace*.[4] In a brilliant essay exploring Tolstoy's masterpiece, Isaiah Berlin claims that the work is substantially devoted to critiquing the then nearly universal practice of 'great man' historical narratives as well.[5] Military leaders are little more than embodied delusions, Tolstoy claims, but necessary ones, for they allow those whom they lead to forget the merciless complexity of battle, a metaphor for life in general. Heroes claim to be and make themselves into a standing proof of the possibility of rising above the mire, to transcend their immediate circumstances. In such vanity, martial leaders serve as founts of hope, direction and perhaps purpose, even though Tolstoy believes that hope ultimately to be false. History, because of its practitioner's belief in the myth of 'great men', is full of such characters, so Tolstoy explains. All of them, historians included, he regards as pitiable in their own deluded beliefs to 'command', whether troops or facts, but equally contemptible for such destructive vanity.

My purpose in writing is to take up Tolstoy's challenge and apply it to a particularly apt moment in the history of strategic thought and politics of the post–Great War British Empire. In particular, I examine the conversations that were had and decisions made by British and Australian political and military leaders from 1917 to 1924. As principle partners, their actions and thought led to the construction of a large naval base at Singapore and the development of a war plan for action against the Japanese Empire based upon it – the Singapore Strategy. Of course, much has been written on both the base and the strategy. Roger Louis's landmark study of Britain's defence policy in Asia suggests that planning each necessarily involved an element of strategic groupthink.[6] W. David McIntyre's superb examination of the inter-service and inter-party rivalries, which persisted from the base's inception to capitulation, reveals the increasingly toxic relationship even amongst junior

---

3 Reinhardt Koselleck, 'Historical Prognosis in Lorenz von Stein's Essay on the Prussian Constitution,' in *Futures Past: On the Semantics of Historical Time*, trans. Keith Tribe (New York: Columbia University Press, 2010), pp. 58–71.

4 Leo Tolstoy, *War and Peace*, trans. Constance Garnett (New York: Modern Library, 2002). There is a significant controversy as to which translation of the masterwork is the best. I have relied on this conventional translation.

5 Isaiah Berlin, *The Hedgehog and the Fox: An Essay on Tolstoy's View of History* (London: Weidenfeld and Nicolson, 1953).

6 Wm. Roger Louis, *British Strategy in the Far East, 1919–1939* (Oxford: University Press, 1971).

officers and politicians from differing branches and parties.[7] Singapore as an object in a wider imperial iconography has also been discussed by historians Neville Meaney, David Day and Ian Hamill, as well as the extent to which the next war's heroes like Winston Churchill owe their glory, or infamy, to the events of 1942.[8] Whole new mythologies have indeed sprung up around the people, place and plan in fiction. Building on this scholarship, I consider how Tolstoy's challenge might contribute to these analyses, examining how some of the 'great men' of Britain's Empire were influenced in their policy making by the role of hero that they both cultivated for themselves during the Great War and how they were expected to perform in the subsequent peace.

The Singapore Strategy might be thought of as the product of the advising mission of former First Sea Lord of the British Admiralty, Lord John Jellicoe of Scapa. Although he once occupied the senior-most fighting rank in the Royal Navy, he was specifically chosen for the mission by the Admiralty and British Government because of the influence he had garnered after winning the war's only major naval engagement off the Norwegian Coast at Jutland. Such influence, so the Admiralty thought, would win over dominion strategic thinkers, and would perhaps lead to their adoption of the Admiralty's preferred strategic doctrine – Imperial Naval Cooperation in which dominion navies would be placed under Admiralty command to be distributed as the British Government saw fit to protect Imperial shipping and territory.

He drew up a lengthy report with this ultimate goal in mind.[9] In particular, he felt the need to convince reluctant Australian and New Zealand governments to commit firmly to the new cooperative Imperial defence strategy. Targeting Australia specifically, he went on to suggest lines along which Australian military thought should develop during the next twenty years:

> Owing to the small population the local military forces cannot be numerically strong . . . The very fact of this numerical weakness of the military forces increases the vital importance of naval defence as a deterrent to invasion . . . *It must be recognized that Australia is powerless against a strong naval and military power without the assistance of the British Fleet.*[10]

Playing off of Australia's long-standing strategic concerns, Jellicoe's words reiterate an older imperial government expression, but gave it a new face – Imperial Defence Cooperation now had the victor of Jutland behind it.[11]

---

7 W. David McIntyre, *The Rise and Fall of the Singapore Naval Base* (London: Macmillan, 1979).

8 Neville Meaney, *Australia and World Crisis: A History of Australian Defence and Foreign Policy, 1901–1923* (Sydney: Sydney University Press, 2009); David Day, *The Great Betrayal, Britain, Australia, and the Onset of the Pacific War* (London: Angus & Robertson Publishers, 1988); Ian Hamill, *The Strategic Illusion: The Singapore Strategy and the Defence of Australia and New Zealand, 1919–1942* (Singapore: Singapore University Press, 1982).

9 'Naval Defence: Report of Admiral of the Fleet Viscount Jellicoe of Scapa, on Naval Mission to the Commonwealth of Australia' (hereafter Jellicoe Report), May–August 1919, vol. 1, A5954 1080/1, National Archives of Australia (NAA).

10 Jellicoe Report, May–August 1919, A5954 1080/1, NAA; the emphasis is Jellicoe's.

11 David Walker, *Anxious Nation: Australia and the Rise of Asia, 1850–1939* (St. Lucia: Queensland University Press, 1999); for Australia's anxieties about Asia.

In particular, Jellicoe's solution to the apparent problem of Australian dependence upon the Royal Navy for security lay in a cooperative naval building programme. He suggested 'that the naval interests of the Empire are likely to demand within the next five years, a Far Eastern Seagoing Fleet of considerable strength'.[12] This fleet would consist of 130 new ships; of these 8 would be battleships and another 8 battle-cruisers. Central command would be vested in an Admiral headquartered at Singapore, 'the naval key to the Far East'.[13] But, in a gesture to Australian government officials concerned with maintaining control over their own forces, Jellicoe reminded them that the doctrine was to be followed only in times of crisis. In peace, each dominion would be allotted its own squadron:

> The Far Eastern Fleet should be provided by those constituent parts of the Empire, including Great Britain, for which it is of vital necessity, and that there should be the closest co-operation with unity of direction in war, between the various squadrons composing that Fleet.[14]

This programme was hardly an inexpensive venture, especially for post-war economies. Once again Jellicoe stressed the cooperative nature of the programme – the projected maintenance expenditure stood at £19,704,700, of which Australia's contribution was 20 per cent, or £3,940,940.[15] It presented a formidable challenge to the Australian government, whose 1913–1914 defence expenditure for all services amounted to £3,000,000.

As the scheme went to the Australian parliament, it became clear that the rhetorical contest was to be between financial common sense and faith in Jellicoe's strategic projections. Signalling his own view of his role, perhaps, Jellicoe delivered his report on 21 October 1919, Trafalgar Day. As a result of a combination of an increasing strategic anxiety, and the positive impression left by Jellicoe on many of Australia's defence planners, Jellicoe's plan was quickly canonised in Australian military circles.[16]

Indeed, Jellicoe's posturing as a modern Nelson may have worked too well. As David McIntyre writes, his self-representation as a strategic celebrity led many in the Dominions to ask him to reform other aspects of naval organisation in New Zealand and Australia. Being taken in by the admiration he was receiving, Jellicoe more than obliged – he essentially dictated naval war plans, policy, and a programme of armament to the Royal Australian Navy. Not realising the sensitive and wholly unsanctioned advice Jellicoe was giving, dominion parliaments published debates concerning his suggestions, and even details of his 1919 report, revealing highly sensitive information to anyone with access to a daily newspaper in Sydney, Melbourne and Wellington. Amongst these sensitive details was the Admiralty's wish to develop the port of Singapore to house a brand new Far Eastern Fleet for operations against Japan, still an ally of Great Britain under the ten-

---

12   Jellicoe Report, May–August 1919, A5954 1080/1, NAA.
13   Ibid.
14   Ibid.
15   Ibid. Interestingly, four of these ships were to be aircraft carriers.
16   'Expenditure under Ordinary Votes and Appropriations,' [table], 13 October 1920, vol. 94, col. 5588, Commonwealth Parliamentary Debates (CPD). A more illustrative example of the financial strain placed on Australia is the comparison in total Commonwealth of Australia expenditure. In 1913–1914, this number was £23,160,733. By 1919 it was £45,135,876, of this £23,530,960 alone was war expenditure and expenses related to the war (such as old-age and disability pensions).

year Anglo-Japanese Alliance of 1911.[17] The Admiralty, motivated by diplomatic urgency, hotly protested this assumption. According to officials in Britain, Jellicoe 'had entered into a sphere never contemplated by the Admiralty, and far beyond his terms of reference'.[18] The publication of the report was suppressed, but Jellicoe, the victor of Jutland, was only obliquely chastised by the Admiralty, and quietly dismissed. His strategic doctrine was not revised, however, and he remained unapologetic for the potential blunder, repeating the assertion during a visit to New Zealand.[19]

The doctrine itself was wholly impracticable as it called for massive outlays of expenditure over the course of several years. His plan would radically increase financial pressure on already burdened post-war imperial economies and would surpass even wartime building programmes in an era of peacemaking. Few as they were, Australian critics of Jellicoe's scheme of Imperial defence cooperation mounted a vigorous opposition. Their chief objective was to undermine Jellicoe's heroic authority. Radical Labour member Frank Antsey, always keen to attack Australia's dependence on British Imperialism generally, took especial exception to this:

> No true Australian will ever have an opinion of his own ... Who can be responsible when we import a British General or Admiral to assist us? What need is there to have a judgement of our own when we have paid an imported expert for his opinion, and act blindly upon it, only to find afterwards that he knows no more about it than we ourselves do? If he is not responsible, who is? Of course, the fact that it was said in England is sufficient.[20]

But over the course of several planning meetings held by British and Dominion naval representatives, Jellicoe's assumptions and consequent recommendations were upheld, and particularly the decision to base all imperial defence plans on the non-existent Singapore naval base. In the first weeks of January 1920, the Admiralty completed their official draft plan for war in the Pacific, should that contingency arise. It began with a basic rephrasing of Jellicoe's formerly offending point:

> The Anglo-Japanese Alliance may not be renewed on its expiration in 1921. British interests in the Pacific and Far East generally are likely to be more closely allied to those of the United States than Japan. Racial differences and the exclusive commercial policy of

---

17 As Jellicoe writes in his final report, 'Information obtained from the Foreign Office, my own knowledge of the recent course of events in the Pacific, information obtained from official quarters in India and Australia of the actions and aspirations of the Japanese, and the known and oft proclaimed policy of a "white Australia" pointed to Japan as the nation with which trouble might conceivably arise.' Final report on whole mission, 3 February 1920, ADM 116/1831, The National Archives of the United Kingdom (TNA); as quoted in Hamill, *The Strategic Illusion: The Singapore Strategy and the Defence of Australia and New Zealand 1919–1942* (Singapore: Singapore University Press, 1982), pp. 19–20.

18 Admiralty to First Lord, 31 October 1919, ADM 116/1834, TNA; as quoted in John McCarthy, *Australia and Imperial Defence, 1918–1939* (St. Lucia: University of Queensland Press, 1976), p. 9.

19 Leading to another leak of sensitive details of the proposed fleet. McIntyre, *The Rise and Fall*, p. 23.

20 CPD, vol. 94, 14 Oct 1920, col. 5677.

the latter may eventually tend to estrange Great Britain from Japan as they already have the United States.[21]

These assumptions worked into imperial cooperative war plans, drafted as a whole into the infamous War Memorandum Eastern of the following year.[22]

The plan itself largely relied upon an initial victory by attrition, operations which the Admiralty considered themselves expert in after Jutland. This was the first stage of a remarkably vague three-point strategy, the first of which was only possible if the proposed naval base at Singapore was also made impregnable. An anticipated Japanese landing force on the Malay Peninsula would be unable to take it with Singapore made impregnable by virtue of the future fortifications and an imperial garrison, so the plan asserted, and naval forces would be deterred by large batteries emplaced across the island. A rescue fleet would arrive some time later, and provide naval cover for an advance to the South China Sea, based out of Hong Kong, satisfying the second part of the plan. And thirdly, would be the 'Phase of Victory', so self-explanatory that the section barely surpassed a paragraph in length.

This was the origin of the basis for strategic planning conferences, first for imperial flag officers in Penang in 1920, and second amongst imperial prime ministers in 1921, each of who were heroes in their own right. Like Tolstoy's account of the war council of the Emperors of Austria and Russia before Austerlitz, the conference of Imperial leaders that met from 1917 to 1924 to discuss war plans in the pacific were certainly not short of titles. Around the table in 1921 sat Canadian Prime Minister Robert Borden, South African General Louis Botha (a veteran and hero of the Anglo-Boer war), New Zealand Prime Minister William Massey, the Australian Prime Minister William Morris Hughes, Admiral David Beatty, the victor of Jutland's more daring subaltern, Lord Curzon – the prime ministerial hopeful, former viceroy of India and current Foreign Secretary – Colonial Secretary Viscount Alfred Milner and the redoubtable British Prime Minister David Lloyd George. Canadian Robert Meighen, South African Jan Smuts and Winston Churchill would join the conference in 1924.

Unlike 1919, in 1921 the dominion prime ministers were anything but acquiescent in things said by English experts, and made claims from their own heroic authority. Most famous is Australian Prime Minister Billy Hughes.[23] It was not his first time on this kind of stage – he had already gained some infamy for his performance at the 1919 Paris Peace Conference and his very public defiance of U.S. President Woodrow Wilson. The two wrangled constantly in meetings. Wilson tried to circumvent Hughes's stubborn resistance to insertion of racial equality clauses in the configuration of the League of Nations Mandated Territories, but Hughes thwarted him.[24] At the end of one particularly exasperating session, Wilson leaned over the table and asked 'Mr. Hughes, am I to understand that if the whole

---

21 'War Memorandum,' 12 January 1920, ADM 116/3124, TNA.
22 Report of Penang Conference, 13 March 1921, ADM 116/3100, TNA.
23 See Laurence Fitzhardinge, *The Little Digger 1914–1952: William Morris Hughes, a Political Biography*, vol. 2 (Sydney: Angus & Robertson, 1979); and Donald Horne, *Billy Hughes* (Melbourne: Black, 1983).
24 See Margaret MacMillan, *Paris, 1919: Six Months That Changed the World* (New York: Random House, 2001) for of the best recent treatments of the Peace Conference; and Susan Pedersen, *The Guardians: The League of Nations and the Crisis of Empire* (Oxford: Oxford University Press, 2015); on the rise of the League of Nations Mandate System.

civilized world asked Australia to agree to a mandate in respect of these islands, Australia is prepared to defy the appeal to the whole civilized world?' Hughes replied, 'after some stage of business with his hearing aid, "that's about the size of it, Mr. President."'[25] Hughes very neatly defeated Wilson in a showdown by threatening to make inflammatory speeches in the western United States, whose constituents, like those in Australia, were deeply distrustful of potential Japanese immigration. The threat led Wilson to remember Hughes as a 'pestiferous varmint'.[26] The *Sydney Bulletin* portrayed him quite differently, as Horatius, single-handedly upholding the 'White Australia' policy.[27]

Hughes was soon to perform this Horatian role again at the Imperial Conference in 1921. Taking with him his popularity amongst some of Australia's returning servicemen, he positioned himself, in his mind at least, as their direct representative as well as that of the government of the Commonwealth. According to Hughes's autobiographical account of his diplomatic life, these years were overshadowed by the previous British strategic failing at Gallipoli. 'For six weeks', he wrote of 1915, 'I went about with the appalling postscript, "Prepare for 49 per cent casualties" burnt into my very soul.'[28] Performing this role, however, meant undermining Jellicoe's authority in particular and that of the empire's strategic thinkers in general. At a time when a sound basis for war plans against uncertain enemies remained tenuous, the need to maintain the authority of heroes was paramount. Hughes's performance at the conference is especially revelatory in this light.

It appears clear from the notes of the meetings that Hughes's and other dominion leaders' faith in the heroes who had developed the Singapore Strategy was sitting awkwardly with the Admiralty's increasingly apparent unwillingness to discuss its assertions. This reluctance stemmed from both the Admiralty's intent to maintain control over imperial planning and concerns that too many questions would smother the only strategic doctrine that had any chance at support. Speaking as the Chairman of the Committee of Imperial Defence, Sir Arthur Balfour's announcement made at the beginning of the sessions dedicated to imperial defence cooperation that the British Government intended to construct a large naval base at Singapore was primarily motivated by this tension. According to Ian Hamill, the decision to a large extent represented the British determination to 'be in a position to tell the Dominion Governments that [Britain] had a Naval Policy'.[29] In the Committee of Imperial Defence's estimation, 'this was even more important than actually commencing the work of developing Singapore at the moment.'[30] Although British Prime Minister David Lloyd George insisted at the opening of the conference that 'to-day the Empire is in charge of Downing Street,' the culture of victory that already surrounded the emerging Singapore strategy translated into the half-hearted evaluation of the fateful plan by all at the conference.[31]

---

25 Horne, *Billy Hughes*, p. 163.
26 Erez Manela, *The Wilsonian Moment, Self-Determination and the International Origins of Anticolonial Nationalism* (Oxford: Oxford University Press, 2007), p. 182.
27 David Low, *Horatius Holds the Bridge*, *Bulletin* (Sydney), 1 May 1919.
28 William Morris Hughes, *The Splendid Adventure: A Review of Empire Relations within and without the Britannic Commonwealth of Nations* (London: Ernest Benn Limited, 1929), p. 77.
29 Cabinet Minutes, 16 June 1921, CAB 23/26, TNA. This is quoted in Hamill, *The Strategic Illusion: The Singapore Strategy and the Defence of Australia and New Zealand, 1919–1942*, p. 25.
30 Ibid.
31 Stenographic notes of Imperial Meetings, 1stmeeting (opening statements), 20 June 1921, CAB 32/2, TNA.

This tension between the need to maintain the public role of dominion or imperial hero on the one hand, and the need to arrive at some kind of implementable strategic consensus on the other, brought Hughes and Admiral Beatty into conflict. Beatty was keen to enhance his reputation as Jellicoe's junior from Jutland by solving once and for all the strategic question first opened by his former superior. His presentation on the disposition of available forces and the general plan of campaign in case of war essentially reiterated Jellicoe's own. The British fleet, being based in Britain, would proceed at full speed at first notice of hostilities in the Far East to Singapore, he explained to the conference. So long as Singapore remained in British Empire hands, there was nothing to fear.[32] Testing the flexibility of the plan, but not wishing to openly disagree with it, Hughes asked his fair share of questions regarding unforeseen contingencies. Observe a telling exchange between Beatty and Hughes:

Mr Hughes: ... but you have not told us yet what we in Australia are anxious to know. What force is it that has to be stationed at Singapore and in the China Seas to ensure the carrying out of this strategy of which you have been speaking?

Lord Beatty: The actual force of ships we should place at Singapore would be a force capable of commanding the seas; that is to say a force superior to that which could be put on the seas by Japan.

Mr Hughes: Will you translate that into terms of ships?

Lord Beatty: You can do that as easy as I can.

Mr. Hughes: What we want to know is this, for we are dealing with the thing itself. Japan now has so many ships, such and such a fleet. We have in the China Seas, how many? By how much have we got to reinforce that China Squadron base in order to give us a chance?

Lord Beatty: We should send the whole fleet we have today to Singapore . . .[33]

'How long would that take?' asked Hughes. Beatty replied that the fleet, whatever its composition, could arrive in Hong Kong in six weeks, or forty-two days.

The line of questioning suddenly shifted. Whereas Beatty thought he had guaranteed that a strong British fleet would be present after a six-week period, when the campaign would begin, dispelling all possible worry, Hughes realised that the Admiralty simultaneously guaranteed that there would be no British naval cover until then. 'Supposing you fail – your six weeks become eight weeks! – if you could not get there in time to save us, could we then look to the United States?' Beatty answered forcefully no, 'we could get there in six weeks, but the United States could not get there at all.'[34] Hughes became strangely silent, perhaps only then realising how completely dependent Australia remained upon the presence of a British Fleet, according to the plan. But, observing the confidence with which the Admiralty's representatives spoke of the Singapore Strategy, no further serious opposition was made. On the motion of Winston Churchill, only one copy of the notes was preserved. The attitude of the discussion, in the opinion of an apprehensive Lloyd George, was 'one which, if reported, would blow up the whole East'.[35] 'As one who lives on the top

---

32 Imperial Conference 1921, 14th meeting (Naval Defence), 4 July 1921, CAB 32/2, TNA.
33 Ibid.
34 Ibid.
35 Imperial Conference 1921, 15th meeting (Military and Air Defence), 5 July 1921, CAB 32/2, TNA.

of a powder magazine', Hughes retorted, 'I agree with you. . . . we cannot afford to live in a paradise of fools.'[36] The appeal to heroic authority had worked. The conference resolved to take the first tenuous steps towards the building of the Singapore base and the adoption of the Singapore Strategy.

In hindsight the war plan – mooted in 1919, made official in 1920 and then upheld in 1921 – was disastrously incomplete and based upon an overestimation of personal and operational capability. It was adopted eventually, even by zealous critics, because of the Admiralty's heroic authority that seemed to ensure its reliability. By the early 1920s, however, the Singapore Strategy had been separated from any single origin. It had become a product of collaborative genius and foresight, and was trusted by one because it was trusted by all. How could so many heroes be wrong, after all? Not much else could have endeared subsequent colonial ministers to accept it, given its complete inability to stand up on its own. Of paramount importance was that there was *a* plan, regardless of what that plan was; the fact that it was shaped by the same men who had secured victory in Europe, peace in Versailles and dominion in the Pacific made it virtually sacrosanct. This was so much as admitted in 1923 by another Australian Prime Minister, Stanley Bruce, who in all other respects repeated the contrarianism of his predecessor except on the Singapore Strategy. Despite this attitude, regarding Singapore, he remarked only, 'While I am not quite as clear as I should like to be as to how the protection of Singapore is to be assured, I am clear on this point, that apparently it can be done.'[37]

While victors may not always write history, they certainly do write policy. As James Q. Whitman has argued, the 'verdict of battle' gives to the winners the right to structure the postwar order.[38] Victors themselves are often key figures in this process, and this is especially apparent in the post-war strategic thought surrounding the development of the Singapore Strategy. Policy made by the empire's heroes, or those regarded as heroes, created within military and political leadership a culture founded on this authority as well. It weighed heavily on the presentation and content of these meetings, and, in the end, contributed to the fateful consensus of the Singapore Strategy and the impregnable fortress on which it relied.

To return to Tolstoy, his criticism of such figures in history is unkind, but significant for historians of policy, law and administration, especially of modern global empires like Britain's claimed to be. For him, these heroes are little more than poseurs, self-aggrandizers and charlatans, far from the treatment they enjoy in histories of imperial strategy, diplomacy and the 'official mind' that they are understood to represent. But, as Berlin argues, Tolstoy does not see them as unimportant. Indeed, as Berlin argues of Tolstoy's vision of such heroes, they are the key actors in the progress of history because they, in positions of political or martial leadership, can shape the fates of so many of their peers and subalterns, yet they are also the most tragic, because they perceive themselves to be effecting their will in the world when even their best-laid plans often devolve into delusion, dragging armies and polities to oblivion. This, he submits, is as true in victory as in defeat. Tolstoy's critique of a historiography based on the progress of the 'great man' suggests a method that is not as fanciful as it seems; the study of the bearing of institutionalised practices on policy making is not a radical notion. Indeed it translates usefully into emerging histories of the cultures of

---

36 Ibid.
37 Imperial Conference 1923, stenographic notes, meeting 11, CAB 32/9, TNA.
38 James Q. Whitman, *The Verdict of Battle: The Law of Victory and the Making of Modern War* (Cambridge, MA: Harvard University Press, 2012).

diplomacy and international relations, and it maps well onto the new tradition of imperial history that examines Britain's Empire in particular as concerned with maintaining a set of cultural codes and practices as well as Britain's geostrategic power.

Although inspired by Tolstoy, I differ from him in aim and in conclusion. It is not my intention to criticise the character, to mar the legacy or to rescue the reputation of any of these individuals. My point is in fact quite the opposite – individuals sometimes are overpowered by their own reputations, shrunk behind their larger-than-life characters, and dwarfed by the roles that they are expected to perform. In this case, imperial and dominion governments relied almost wholesale on the reputation of Jellicoe as the empire's only wartime naval hero to justify the results of a frantic re-thinking of operational plans that suddenly seemed much more urgently needed. Similarly, Hughes, the 'little digger', and Beatty, Jellicoe's Lieutenant, succeeded in performing their roles only by allowing a consensus to form – both of their efforts to arrive at a real understanding at the Conference appear half earnest. Both display a tacit knowledge of the fundamental flaws in the Singapore Strategy, but neither upset the forming resolutions and commitments. As Tolstoy might also have observed, the Singapore plan relied on a collective act of strategic self-deception that all of the empire's leaders eventually vetted in order to retain their status as political or military heroes. Thus, a negative consensus could be created, a flawed plan could be validated by its continued non-rebuttal and living heroes could retain their place of glory after the Great War had claimed the lives of so many others.

Following this method, important elements of how and why the Singapore Strategy became the empire's strategic doctrine despite clear and continuous reservations become clearer. Exploring how some of the 'great men' of imperial strategic thought performed the heroic role that the empire invested them with reveals just how significantly their performance of this role affected the content and consensus of post-war imperial strategy, especially in the context of the creation of official narratives about the meaning of the First World War itself.[39] Indeed, as I have argued earlier, it encouraged the convention of consensus even at the most secret meetings of imperial leaders. From this consensus, or rather, from this mutual desire and the public expectation to succeed in solving the apparently intractable problems of empire, the Singapore Strategy was allowed to become the guiding defence policy of empire. Millions of pounds and hundreds of thousands of lives would be sunk into a project in which few resolutely believed initially. Defeat at Singapore in 1942 therefore undermined far more than the empire's strategic capacity – it greatly crippled a predominantly unspoken but at times outspoken confidence in the authority of imperial leadership and the institutions it had created. This post-war culture of victory, as much as the material shortcomings of the British imperial world system, brought about the empire's Austerlitz in 1942.

---

39 For example, Britain's 109-volume series primarily compiled by Brigadier Sir James Edmonds, *The Official History of the Great War Based on Official Documents* (London: HMSO, 1922–2010); and Australia's 12-volume series compiled by Charles Edward Bean, *Official History of Australia in the War of 1914–1918* (Sydney: Angus & Robertson, 1920–1942).

PART III
Art, memory and forgetting

Chapter 8
'Our warrior Brown Brethran'
Identity and difference in images of non-white soldiers serving with the British army in British art of the First World War

Jonathan Black

There can be no doubt that the peoples of the British Empire made an immense contribution to the British war effort during the First World War. There has been much greater recognition in recent years of the important part played by soldiers from the so-called White Dominions: Anzacs at Gallipoli, and the impressive fighting reputation of the Canadian and Australian Corps, New Zealand Division and South African Brigade, on the Western Front.[1] The wider British general lay public is only just now beginning to appreciate the undoubted heroism of men of the Indian Army – who held the line on the Western Front for a critical period in 1914–1915 and without whom the British could not have defeated the forces of the Ottoman Empire in Mesopotamia and Palestine.[2]

India contributed by far the most non-white combat and support troops to the British imperial war effort, with a total over 1 million. In August 1914 the Indian Army numbered 242,000, and by 1918 a further 862,855 Indians had volunteered. From this a total of 552,000 men served overseas: in France, Palestine, Mesopotamia and at Gallipoli.[3] Approximately 65,000 Indian servicemen were killed during the First World War or died from disease.[4] An estimated 160,000 Indian soldiers served in France and Flanders between October 1914 and November 1915; 25,000 of them became casualties.[5] When the Indian Corps left in November 1915, the 4th and 5th Indian Cavalry Divisions remained in France until February 1918 when they were despatched to reinforce Allenby's Egyptian Expeditionary Force (EEF) in Palestine.[6] At the same time the British Army planned to increase the Indian Army by a further half a million troops by the middle of 1919, in order to meet anticipated combat demands in the Middle East.[7]

Meanwhile, the British West Indies Regiment, numbering some 20,000 men, all volunteers, served in a non-combatant role in France and Flanders, and as combat troops in

---

1   David Olusoga, *The World's War* (London: Head of Zeus, 2014), p. 356.
2   This point has recently been made by: Olusoga, *The World's War*, p. xv; Jeremy Black, *The Great War and the Making of the Modern World* (London: Continuum Publishing, 2011), p. 272; and by William Philpott, *Attrition: Fighting the First World War* (London: Little Brown, 2014), pp. 267–8.
3   David Stevenson, *With Our Backs to the Wall: Victory and Defeat in 1918* (London: Allen Lane, 2011), p. 257.
4   Black, *The Great War and the Making of the Modern World*, p. 548.
5   Richard Holmes, *Tommy: The British Soldier on the Western Front, 1914–1918* (London: Harper Perennial, 2005), p. 13.
6   Stevenson, *With Our Backs to the Wall*, p. 305.
7   Ibid., p. 258.

the Middle East from September 1915.[8] The British Expeditionary Force (BEF) in France and Flanders was also supported in 1917–1918 by some 100,000 non-combatant Chinese Labour Corps of which some 2,000 were killed or died, and with many more succumbing to the Spanish Flu epidemic of 1918–1919.[9] There are, however, only occasional glimpses of the men of the Chinese Labour Corps in official British war art – for example in a drawing Paul Nash made in November 1917 called *Chinese Labourers Working in a Quarry* (see Figure 8.1).

They do not appear regularly either in official photography of the era. This neglect may be explained by a common perception that the Chinese were not essentially a 'martial' people and therefore not deserving of the respect and admiration commonly accorded to combatants belonging to the so-called 'martial' or 'warrior' races of India.[10] Periodically, doubts were expressed as to the fighting ability of the 'West Indian negro' while the commander of the EEF, Sir Edmund Allenby – advised by the British authorities in Egypt – was extremely reluctant to arm any Egyptians who were already serving in a non-combatant role with British and Dominion forces in Palestine.[11] Even though these Egyptians were all volunteers, the growth of anti-British nationalist sentiment in the country led the British

Figure 8.1 Paul Nash, *Chinese Labourers Working in a Quarry*, **November 1917**

Source: © Imperial War Museum

---

8   Olusoga, *The World's War*, p. 294.
9   Stevenson, *With Our Backs to the Wall*, p. 258.
10 Olusoga, *The World's War*, p. 198.
11 Black, *The Great War and the Making of the Modern World*, pp. 240–1.

authorities to doubt their loyalty and the wisdom of giving them access to and training in modern weaponry.[12]

Part of the essential support structure for the British Empire was a belief in the need for well-defined hierarchies that securely located an individual, whether British or 'other', within a carefully stratified world. During the last thirty years of the nineteenth century certain British observers, army officers and administrators, carefully divided the population of India into so-called 'warrior races' and those who were not and, thus, deemed entirely unsuitable for service in the Indian Army. Lieutenant-General Sir George MacMunn, for example, stated in his *The Armies of India* (published in 1911) that the 'warrior races' of India predominantly came from the north of the sub-continent. These 'warriors' include men from along the Himalayas with the fearsome Gurkhas of Nepal, and to the west of their Kingdom, the Garwhalis, while the hardy Dogras were to be found in the hills of Kashmir. Equally formidable were the Punjabis (Sikhs and Jats) and the Rajputs from the north-east of the country and the unpredictable Pathans of the north-west frontier. MacMunn grudgingly acknowledged that men from only certain areas in south-central India – with units such as the Poona and Deccan Horse raised from former Mahratta kingdoms – produce 'good fighting material'.[13]

Eric Kennington (1888–1960), 1917–1918

The first artist under consideration, Eric Kennington, was age 26 when he volunteered to serve as a private in a Territorial battalion of the British Army on 6 August 1914.[14] Between mid-November 1914 and mid-January 1915 he served in the ranks of the 13th Battalion of the London Regiment (known as The Kensingtons) in north-eastern France. In mid-January 1915 he was wounded in the left foot and evacuated back to a military hospital in Britain. In June of the same year he was invalided out of the army on medical grounds. During the latter half of 1915 he painted (using oils in reverse on glass) a remarkable tribute to his platoon *The Kensingtons at Laventie: Winter 1914*. This work caused a sensation when exhibited in central London during April and June 1916. In May 1916, deeply impressed by *The Kensingtons*, Kennington was befriended by the older and more established artist William Rothenstein, who had travelled to India before the war and was fascinated by Indian art and culture.[15]

Towards the end of August 1917 Kennington went to France as an official war artist for the Department of Information (later expanded in February 1918 to a Ministry). While finding his feet in this new post, Kennington was attached to the 3rd Army Corps, in a relatively quiet sector of the front, and encountered men of the 4th Indian Cavalry Division.

---

12 T.E. Lawrence, *Seven Pillars of Wisdom: The Complete 1922 "Oxford" Text* (Fordingbridge, Hampshire: The Seven Pillars of Wisdom Trust, 2004), pp. 584–5. In March 1918, for example, Lawrence reflected in his journal a common prejudice that men of the Egyptian Army cooperating with Arab Bedu forces he was advising in South-East Palestine looked 'handsome on parade' but were perceived as 'too wedded to routine . . . to dare to fight'.

13 Gordon Corrigan, *Sepoys in the Trenches: The Indian Corps on the Western Front, 1914–1915* (Stroud, UK: Spellmount, 2006), pp. 3–6. By the time MacMunn published *The Martial Races of India* in 1930 he was the recognised authority on the subject.

14 Jonathan Black, *The Graphic Art of Eric Kennington* (London: UCL Press, 2001), p. 2.

15 Black, *The Graphic Art of Eric Kennington*, p. 55.

Evidence from the period would suggest that Kennington's perception of the Indian soldiers was considerably shaped by his pre-existing fervent belief in the British Empire and admiration for the writings of Rudyard Kipling. Indeed, arriving in France, he admitted to his friend William Rothenstein that he could not help seeing ordinary British 'tommies', soldiers of the BEF, through the prism provided by Kipling's short stories about British troops in the ranks serving in India: the *Soldiers Three* (first published in 1888) and his *Barrack Room Ballads* (published in two series, 1892 and 1896).[16]

After drawing the portrait of the 3rd Corps' appreciative Corps Commander, Sir William Pulteney, Kennington was able to arrange to spend a fortnight with one of the units comprising the Division: the Jodhpur Imperial Service Lancers. This was a volunteer unit raised within one of the Indian Princely States, under the 'Imperial Service Scheme' by Pratab Singh, the formidable 70-year-old ruler of Jodhpur, who remained attached to the Indian Army for the duration of the war.[17] Pulteney may have suggested the Jodhpur Lancers because he was aware that Pratab Singh admired Kennington's recent pastel portrait of the Corps Commander and was eager to be drawn by the artist.

While staying with the Jodhpur Lancers, Kennington wrote periodically to Rothenstein and admitted he felt '. . . all at sea among these Indians . . .' He could not easily communicate with them and found it difficult to establish who did what. As he later rather sheepishly confessed, one of the first men from the Lancers who sat for a portrait was actually one of the unit's contingent of followers – the latrine wallah. Kennington then asked the 'babu quartermaster sergeant'.[18] The Bengali 'babu' or clerk was a figure of fun even in the Indian Army, a necessary trial with his unquenchable thirst for paperwork and procuring just the right 'chit'.[19] Kennington eventually secured sittings with some of the officers and the 'fighting men' of the Lancers, referring to them admiringly in a letter to Rothenstein as 'our warrior brown brethran'.[20] One of the former was the unit's Indian medical officer who would have stood out because in the regular Indian Army medical officers were British (see Figure 8.2).

As was often the case with his Indian sitters, the artist did not find it easy to communicate with them. However, Kennington later mentioned how he had been impressed by the 'beautiful manners' and 'sensitive face' of the Indian medical officer and by the man expressing a 'halting admiration' for the poetry of William Blake.[21]

On completing his portraits of soldiers at this time, Kennington would habitually ask his sitters, if they were pleased with the results, to sign their name in their own language at the bottom. During August–September 1917 he drew half a dozen portraits of officers and men of the Jodhpur Lancers. He was most upset to discover, after having submitted the drawings to the official censor at General Headquarters, Major Arthur Lee, that he had scrupulously

---

16   Eric Kennington letter to Sir William Rothenstein, n.d., *c*. late August 1917, Papers of Sir William Rothenstein, Houghton Library, Harvard University.

17   Corrigan, *Sepoys in the Trenches*, pp. 22–3. In all 21 Imperial Service Units served overseas with the Indian Army during the First World War.

18   Eric Kennington letter to Sir William Rothenstein, undated (probably mid-November 1917), Papers of Sir William Rothenstein, Houghton Library, Harvard University.

19   Corrigan, *Sepoys in the Trenches*, p. 22.

20   Eric Kennington letter to Sir William Rothenstein, n.d., *c*. early September 1917, Papers of Sir William Rothenstein, Houghton Library, Harvard University.

21   Eric Kennington to Sir William Rothenstein, n.d., *c*. late September 1917, Papers of Sir William Rothenstein, Houghton Library, Harvard University.

Figure 8.2   Eric Kennington, *The Indian Doctor*, 1917, charcoal on paper
Source: Manchester City Art Gallery

rubbed out all the signatures of the sitters as a 'security risk'.[22] Lee also disapproved of Kennington having spent time on Indian portraits because the artist had been specifically despatched to France to draw British soldiers from the ranks.[23] Kennington later wrote to his overall superior at the Department of Information, C.F.G. Masterman, who was in charge of 'visual propaganda', that he felt guilty whenever he sketched a landscape, as he was aware that other artists had been tasked with depicting such subject matter. However, he felt it was only right and proper that the Indian contribution to the British war effort on the Western Front be acknowledged through portraiture of suitable individuals.[24]

---

22   Black, *The Graphic Art of Eric Kennington*, p. 5.
23   Ibid., p. 4.
24   Ibid., p. 36.

William Rothenstein (1872–1945), 1917–1918

Kennington would return to draw the portraits of more Indian soldiers early in 1918, this time from other units within the 4th Cavalry Division and in the company of William Rothenstein, who came out to France as an official war artist. By mid-March 1918 Kennington drew over a dozen Indian soldiers serving in France, about 10 per cent, from a total of nearly a hundred portraits of British soldiers from the ranks. Rothenstein would draw a similar number of Indian cavalrymen in February and March 1918 – before the 4th and 5th Indian Cavalry Divisions were posted to Palestine.[25] It would seem that his view of the sitters was bound up with his existing fascination with Indian culture that dated from a pre-war visit to central India. He also had a general desire to make a contribution to the British war effort and do something to promote what he referred to as 'the glory of the British Empire', as a man who was too old for normal military service and who moreover came from a German-Jewish background.[26] Rothenstein later noted in his memoirs that on visiting the Jodhpur Lancers he was initially given a decidedly frosty reception, on the grounds that some of the men Kennington had drawn from the Regiment had gone on to be killed during the unit's brief involvement in the Battle of Cambrai in November 1917. Many of the surviving Indian officers and men now suspected that sitting for a portrait somehow prejudiced their chances of survival. Rothenstein reflected that Kennington had previously told him that some British soldiers of other ranks had been resistant to having their portraits drawn, on the grounds of the absolute novelty of this experience. However, once it was explained that the portrait would eventually be exhibited in London, potential sitters 'clamoured to be drawn'.[27] When Rothenstein deployed the same explanation prior to drawing Indian cavalrymen of Hodson's and Jacob's Horse in February 1918, he found they quickly warmed to the idea of sitting for a portrait – all suspicion of it being 'bad luck' having evaporated.[28]

While drawing Indian subjects in the small town of Devise in February 1918 Rothenstein suggested to C.F.G. Masterman that since his Department was about to be expanded to become a full ministry, the new organisation commission himself and Kennington to draw a whole series of portraits of Indians in France, and perhaps add examples of the West Indians and Chinese working behind the lines digging trenches and carrying shells and supplies.[29] These would be reproduced in a booklet similar to that planned for the official war artists and called *British Artists at the Front*. Masterman initially welcomed the idea and the India Office was interested, but in the end nothing came of it.[30] Two months before the end of

---

25   William Rothenstein, *Men and Memories, Volume Two, 1900–1922* (London: Faber & Faber, 1934), p. 331.

26   Indeed, such was the level of anti-German prejudice in British society at the outbreak of the First World War that, later in 1914, William's elder brother Charles and younger brother Albert both changed their surnames to the more English-sounding 'Rutherston'. To his credit William felt it would be wrong and contrary to British notions of fair play to anglicise his surname. Rothenstein, *Men and Memories*, p. 361.

27   Black, *The Graphic Art of Eric Kennington*, p. 7.

28   Rothenstein, *Men and Memories*, pp. 331–2.

29   William Rothenstein letter to C.F.G. Masterman, 19 February 1918, Rothenstein First World War File, Department of Art, Imperial War Museum (IWM), London.

30   William Rothenstein, *Since Fifty: Men and Memories, 1922–1938* (London: Faber & Faber, 1939), p. 106.

the war postcards and photographs of some of the Indian soldiers drawn by Kennington and Rothenstein became available for purchase from the Ministry of Information shop on Norfolk Street, just off the Strand.[31]

A few of Kennington's Indian portraits were included in his solo exhibition as an official war artist, held at the Leicester Galleries in June-July 1918. The portraits were well-received by several critics who praised them for possessing a sober dignity that was doubtless true to the character of the sitters depicted.[32]

In the summer of 1918, Kennington fell out with the Ministry of Information when it was seeking to buy his work from the official exhibition at a considerable discount, which Kennington regarded as exploitative and blatantly unfair. During this period he remained in touch with some of the British officers serving with the Jodhpur Lancers and their relatives at home. From them he learnt that in March 1918 the unit had been sent with the rest of the 4th Cavalry Division to serve with the EEF in Palestine. The Lancers were assigned to the new 15th Imperial Service Cavalry Brigade and attached to the 5th Cavalry Division – which itself became part of the EEF. The Regiment would serve with distinction during Allenby's Palestine offensive of September 1918, memorably charging uphill on 23 September to successfully clear Turkish machine gunners from the summit of Mount Carmel, defending the approaches to the key port of Haifa. Seventeen machine guns and over 1,300 Turks were captured.[33] However, Kennington was saddened to discover that at the moment of victory, Colonel Holden, his friend and the unit's commander, had been killed by a Turkish sniper.[34]

As he learnt of Holden's death Kennington was contemplating an offer from the Ministry of Information to travel to Palestine to succeed James McBey, as the official British artist on the spot. McBey made it clear that he did not want to move as yet – especially as the campaign against the Turks was reaching a triumphant climax – while he had the backing of the EEF's commander-in-chief Sir Edmund Allenby.[35]

Eric Kennington, 1919–1920

Shortly after the Armistice in 1918 Kennington went to France to work as an official war artist for the Canadian War Record Scheme. In December 1918 he attached himself to the 16th Canadian-Scottish (Highlanders of Canada), a battalion with a formidable fighting record under its larger than life commanding officer, Lt-Col Cyrus Peck VC.[36] Peck was unusually relaxed about having non-white individuals serving in his battalion. As the unit marched into Belgium and then Germany, Kennington, sketching as they went, was quick to notice the presence of an Inuit soldier, as well as one with unmistakable West Indian features amongst their ranks. Peck had also been keen to establish a first rate band for the battalion, and he selected a bandmaster who was a West Indian from Vancouver (most

---

31   Meirion and Susie Harries, *The War Artists: British Official War Art of the Twentieth Century* (London: Michael Joseph, 1983), p. 73.

32   'The British Soldier at the Leicester Galleries,' *The Times*, 17 June 1918, p. 18.

33   Anthony Bruce, *The Last Crusade: The Palestine Campaign in the First World War* (London: Thistle Publishing, 2013), p. 301.

34   Eric Kennington letter to Sir William Rothenstein, n.d., c. October 1918, Papers of Sir William Rothenstein, Houghton Library, Harvard University.

35   Harries, *The War Artists*, p. 26.

36   Black, *The Graphic Art of Eric Kennington*, p. 52.

of the men had volunteered in British Columbia).[37] The West Indian bandmaster and an Inuit private are prominent in Kennington's subsequent painting *The Conquerors* created between December 1919 and April 1920. The painting was exhibited in a display of work commissioned by the Canadian War Art Scheme and held in Ottawa during July-August 1920. Local newspaper journalists and individuals writing to their editors were more than little taken aback by the 'alien' presence of the West Indian and the Inuit, in a unit which purported to be of Canadian-Highland Scots.[38] Their anxieties over the wisdom of such public 'mixing of the races' appear to be rooted in pre-war controversies in Canada over the rate of immigration into the country by non-whites from within the British Empire.[39]

Percy Wyndham Lewis (1882–1957), 1918–1919

Similar expressions of dismay and alarm can be found in reaction to the prominent appearance of non-white soldiers in another painting on display in the summer 1920 exhibition in Ottawa – *A Canadian Gun Pit* by Percy Wyndham Lewis, which is now housed in the National Gallery of Canada.

In the right foreground Lewis depicted members of a West Indian Labour Battalion involved in the prosaic yet necessary task of 'shell-humping' – moving shells from a depot some distance behind the firing lines to front line artillery positions. At the time the work was first exhibited in London, at Burlington House in January 1919, Lewis stated that the presence of the West Indians, along with men of the Chinese Labour Corps added to the 'Alice in Wonderland' aspect of the Western Front.[40] He further thought many of the West Indians were 'superb in physique', bringing to mind the impressive straining bodies depicted by Signorelli in his murals for Orvieto Cathedral, painted in the early sixteenth century. Moreover, some of their faces had possessed an attractive 'melancholy dignity' as they gravely went about their duties.[41]

However, in later years, the artist's perceptions of the West Indians he observed in France in 1918 became sharply less positive and admiring. In his 1937 autobiography *Blasting and Bombardiering*, Lewis made some extraordinarily racist observations concerning a group of 'West Indian negroes from Jamaica' attached to a battery of the Royal Garrison Artillery he was visiting and adjacent to one in which he was serving in France in the summer of 1917 as a First Lieutenant. He wrote in his autobiography:

> [O]nce, when two of the negroes had started a razor-fight, it devolved upon me to stop it. So to start with I seized them respectively by the shirt-collar and opening my arms abruptly, as you open a pair of scissors, I flung them apart. One drooped to the right of me, one to the left of me, but only for a moment. I supposed I had ended hostilities but then simultaneously each of them scooped up a handful of mud and discharged it across my face at his antagonist. And soon we were all three covered in liquid clay. Kamper [the

---

37   H.M. Urquart, *The History of the 16th Canadian-Scottish Battalion, Canadian Expeditionary Force in the Great War, 1914–1918* (Toronto: Godenrath & Company, 1932), p. 401.
38   Black, *The Graphic Art of Eric Kennington*, p. 10.
39   Olusoga, *The World's War*, p. 5.
40   Paul Edwards, *Wyndham Lewis: Art and War* (London: Lund Humphries and the Wyndham Lewis Memorial Trust, 1992), p. 32.
41   Ibid., p. 34–6.

officer in charge of the nearby West Indian Labour Corps detachment] appeared revolver in hand and, as if by magic the two Blacks vanished and I found myself alone, straddling like a statue of clay, with only a razor at my feet to testify to the fact I had not been dreaming![42]

Later in the same chapter Lewis added, somewhat defensively:

> I never got the right touch with the West Indian negro. At our Nieuport position [where Lewis was serving in August 1917] one dark night the negroes were rolling shells up to the guns – very large ones, since the guns were outsize. This operation had to be affected without so much as a match struck, lest the German air-patrols should spot us. A negro sergeant I noticed was not only stationary, and peculiarly idle, but actually obstructing the work of the dusky rollers. I spoke to him. He neither looked at me, nor answered [any NCO wearing a British Army uniform would normally have promptly come smartly to attention and saluted Lewis as an officer]. I could scarcely see him – it was very dark and he was very dark. I ordered him to do a little rolling. This was a *word of command*. It elicited no response from the dark shape. Whereupon I gave him a violent push. This propelled him through space for a short distance, but he immediately returned to where he had stood before. I gave him a second push. As if made of india-rubber, he once more reintegrated the spot he had just left. After this, I accepted him as part of the landscape and the shells had to be rolled round him since they could not be rolled *through* him.[43]

By this stage in his career his attitude to the West Indians he had depicted in *A Canadian Gun Pit* were bound up with his general lofty dismissal of the value of the official war art he had created for the Canadians. At the same time non-Western individuals were often presented in his writings as somewhat less than human grotesques, not made of comfortingly normal human flesh and blood. *Blasting and Bombardiering* was published after he had made a visit to French colonial North Africa (Morocco and Algeria) which resulted in the publication of a controversial travel book *Filibusters in Barbery* (1932) where Lewis made a number of hostile remarks concerning the Arab inhabitants of the region, their culture, manner of living and religion.[44]

James McBey (1883–1959), 1917–1919

McBey, the sole British official war artist attached to the Egyptian Expeditionary Force during the First World War (from June 1917 to February 1919) had a very different view of the Islamic world to that held by Lewis. He had visited Morocco for a month in late 1912,[45] prompted by the knowledge that Henri Matisse had first visited French North Africa in

---

42 Wyndham Lewis, *Blasting and Bombardiering* (Los Angeles: University of California Press, 1967), p. 152.
43 Ibid., p. 153.
44 Paul O'Keeffe, *Some Sort of Genius: A Life of Wyndham Lewis* (London: Jonathan Cape, 2000), pp. 306–7. To be fair Lewis was just as critical and antagonistic in his presentation of French colonial officials.
45 Harries, *The War Artists*, p. 23.

May 1906[46] and spent nearly a year in French Morocco in 1912.[47] The latter period in particular had proved extremely fruitful in the development of the Frenchman's approach to painting.[48] McBey emerged from this trip with a profound love for the culture and art he had encountered in French North Africa. Moreover, as a working class Scot from Aberdeen, he came from a very different social background than that of the majority of official British war artists who had been born into professional middle class households and been educated at major British public schools – Rugby in the case of Lewis and St Pauls regarding Kennington.[49] McBey had completed his formal education at age 14 and worked as a clerk until he had saved up enough money to study printmaking through part-time evening classes at the local municipal art school.[50]

In poor health at the outbreak of the First World War, partially as a consequence of the harsh circumstances of his growing up in damp Aberdonian housing, McBey failed in a number of attempts to join the Army as a volunteer. Eventually, in the autumn of 1915, he was accepted into the Army Service Corps. By the summer of 1916 he had been commissioned as a Second Lieutenant and posted to work in the Army Postal Service in Rouen. He later wrote of his frustration at the nature of his duties – worthy and yet mind-numbingly tedious. He wanted to make use of his artistic gifts and see something of the 'warriors world' of the war; his wartime service could not be reduced to 'licking stamps for the Empire'.[51] McBey certainly did not look like conventional warrior material being short-sighted, a sufferer from frequent severe bouts of asthma and rather over-weight. However, his determination, past familiarity with Islamic culture and undoubted facility in watercolour persuaded an advisor to the Visual Art Section of the Department of Information, Campbell Dodgson (at the time the Keeper of Prints and Drawings at the British Museum), that McBey would be able to work effectively as a war artist with the British forces in the Middle East.

The Sinai and Palestine theatre of operations for the British Empire in the First World War is sometimes referred to dismissively as a 'sideshow'. It was, however, quite an impressively sized 'sideshow' involving some 1,200,000 British, Dominion and Indian soldiers between 1915 and 1918 – and this total includes the Egyptian Camel Corps, the Egyptian Labour Corps, an Infantry Brigade of Jewish Volunteers and a West Indian Brigade (deployed, unlike its counterpart on the Western Front, as front line combat troops).[52]

McBey was appointed as war artist to the EEF in May 1917, with a brief from the Department of Information to record the activities of British and Dominion soldiers. He arrived at Port Said, Egypt, the following month, though the British authorities in Cairo impeded his efforts to reach the front line in southern Palestine until the early autumn of 1917. As he later observed, his work was made more difficult because of lack of access to a car, or some form of reliable motor transport, and the lack of a translator that would have enabled him to communicate with the Egyptians and Indians prominently at work

---

46   Hilary Spurling, *Matisse: The Life* (London: Penguin, 2009), pp. 143–4.
47   Ibid., pp. 235–8.
48   Ibid., p. 250–2.
49   Rothenstein and Lewis had studied art at the prestigious Slade School of Art, part of University College, London, while Kennington had gone to the reputable Lambeth School of Art and paid for classes at the City and Guilds School in Kennington.
50   Harries, *The War Artists*, p. 24.
51   Kenneth Hare, *London's Latin Quarter* (London: John Lane, 1925), p. 134.
52   John Terraine, *The Smoke and the Fire: Myths and Anti-Myths of War, 1861–1945* (London: Sidgwick & Jackson, 1980), p. 57.

everywhere in the rear areas of the EEF in Sinai. By the time he reached EEF positions south of Gaza in September 1917 he was able to hire a Christian Egyptian Copt as a translator.[53]

Overall, between June 1917 and February 1919, when he returned to London, McBey produced approximately 300 watercolours. Just over 10 per cent, or 34, depict the activities of non-white individuals serving with the EEF. Throughout his time as a war artist in the Middle East, McBey was very much aware that his primary objective was to produce images 'for the people back home', to give them some sort of insight of the tribulations the soldiers had to face in their struggle against the forces of the Ottoman Empire.[54] However, by the time McBey arrived on the Gaza Front, he could not help but be impressed by how many of the support and supply activities vital to the existence of the EEF were carried out by Egyptian non-combatant units. This is evident from such watercolours as *Egyptian Labour Corps Landing Stores at Jaffa Harbour*, *Men of the Egyptian Camel Transport Corps* (November 1917; see Figures 8.3 and 8.4) and *The Egyptian Labour Corps Repairing the Nebi Musa Road* (9 May 1918) (now Collection of the IWM, London). These indicate how closely the Egyptian Labour Corps (ELC) followed behind the fighting units of the EEF after the latter had captured Gaza in November 1917, then moved to take Jerusalem the following month and proceeded to advance deep into central Palestine.

Just over 225,000 Egyptians supported British and Dominion forces in the First World War – almost entirely in a non-combatant capacity.[55] One hundred seventy thousand served

Figure 8.3   James McBey, *Egyptian Labour Corps Landing Stores at Jaffa Harbour, 19 November 1917*

Source: © Imperial War Museum

---

53   Hare, *London's Latin Quarter*, p. 136.
54   Harries, *The War Artists*, p. 124.
55   It is often overlooked that a further 100,000 Egyptians were sent 1917–1918 to work as Labourers for the British Expeditionary Force in France, digging trenches, making roads and bringing supplies up to close to the front line where they often came under shell fire. Stevenson, *With Our Backs to the Wall*, p. 235.

Figure 8.4   James McBey, *Men of the Egyptian Camel Transport Corps*, November 1917
Source: © Imperial War Museum

with the Egyptian Camel Transport Corps (ECTC), founded early in 1916, as camel drivers, while a further 55,000 volunteered for the ELC formed in December 1915. Men from the latter unit laid pipelines to carry vital water supplies to the Front, created new railway lines, unloaded cargo and constructed entire new roads and bridges in a part of the Ottoman Empire which had only possessed meagre infrastructure before the outbreak of war. Some 4,500 of the ECTC and ELC were killed or died in accidents or from disease, while at least one 1,500 were treated for bullet and shell-fragment wounds.[56]

Following the great German offensive on the British lines in March 1918 Allenby, commander of the EEF, lost most of the British troops under his command, as well as some

---

56   Stevenson, *With Our Backs to the Wall*, p. 235.

of his Australians and New Zealanders to the Western Front. McBey noticed that their places were increasingly taken up from the influx of Indian troops, including more infantry, cavalry and engineers. An increasing number of recently formed Sikh units were evident, clearing blocked roads and re-building damaged bridges as is demonstrated in *Sikh Sappers Repairing a Bridge*, 1918 (now Collection of the IWM, London).

By this time, thanks in large part to the support of Allenby, McBey now had a car with a driver (or batman) and, in addition to his Coptic interpreter, an Indian interpreter from one of the Imperial Service regiments that arrived in the theatre of war in March 1918, with the 4th Indian Cavalry Division. The latter made it much easier for McBey to approach groups of Indian servicemen and engage them in conversation. McBey now felt more at ease in sketching individual Indian soldiers while gently probing them with questions concerning home life and past service. Tellingly, Military Intelligence at Allenby's GHQ in March 1918 asked McBey to avoid discussing 'political questions' as much as possible in his conversations with Indian servicemen, while also asking him to take careful note of any unprompted expressions of dissatisfaction with continuing British rule in India.[57] Doubtless McBey had these strictures in mind when he produced a series of highly sensitive and engaging portraits of individual soldiers from a Punjabi battalion in September 1918, such as *Arsuf, A Punjabi Sentry* (see Figure 8.5).

These were drawn just a few days before these same troops took part in Allenby's great offensive, which essentially destroyed three Ottoman Turkish armies in Palestine and Syria.

Though he did not feel technically able or comfortable with depicting such Indian troops in battle, he nevertheless found himself fascinated by the evidence he encountered in September 1918 of the sheer carnage British and Australian fighter-bombers had inflicted on retreating Ottoman columns on 20 September 1918. These resulted in sketches such as *Retreating Turkish Column Machine-gunned and Bombed by the Royal Air Force, Tul Keram Defile*. Two days previously Allenby's attacking troops had cut defending Ottoman forces in two – one section retreated towards the headquarters of the 8th Ottoman Army at Tul Keram but was intercepted en route by the Royal Air Force and Royal Australian Air Force, leaving a trail of dead and wounded Ottoman and wrecked vehicles and carts over six miles long.[58] While making the sketch McBey also noted the 'dispiriting effect' the sight of the destruction at Tul Keram had on passing Indian cavalry units and groups of irregular Beduin horsemen whom McBey believed to be on the side of Britain's Arab ally the Hashemite Sherif Feisal.[59] McBey did not speculate then, or later, as to why the havoc at Tul Keram produced the effect it did on the Indians and Bedu, but it is not too far-fetched to imagine these non-white horsemen reflecting that if the British could unleash their annihilating air power on the Turks, they could just as easily do it again in the future on any other non-white opponent who attracted their wrath.[60]

---

57   Harries, *The War Artists*, p. 124.
58   Bruce, *The Last Crusade*, p. 291.
59   Malcolm Brown, *Lawrence of Arabia, the Life, the Legend* (London: Thames & Hudson and the Imperial War Museum, 2005), p. 43.
60   The Ottoman Army in Palestine in September 1918 did indeed suffer horrendous casualties; by the end of the month some 30,000 of its original strength of 35,000 to 36,000 had been killed or captured. From the beginning of Allenby's September offensive to the surrender of Ottoman forces towards the end of October 1918, the EEF lost 1,064 dead and 4,428 wounded. Bruce, *The Last Crusade*, p. 331. Total Ottoman casualties in the region, 1914–1918, were in the region of 1.5 million: 772,000 dead (304,000 killed in action and 466,000 dead from disease) and 764,000 wounded, Stevenson, 2011, p. 307.

Figure 8.5 James McBey, *Arsuf, A Punjabi Sentry*, September 1918

Source: © Imperial War Museum

Thomas Cantrell Dugdale (1880–1952), 1918–1919

As Allenby's triumphant offensive was coming to a close in 1918, McBey was joined by another war artist, Thomas Dugdale, who had transferred to Palestine from official duties for the Ministry of Information on the Salonika front and had a specific brief to paint some 'stirring cavalry actions' of the type which McBey did not feel equal to recording. By the end of the year Dugdale had selected just such an action from early on 20 September 1918 when the 4th Indian Cavalry Division had broken through the Turkish lines to close in on the strategically important village of El Afule. As dawn rose the Division's leading unit, the 2nd Lancers, known as Gardner's Horse (founded in 1809 in Bengal), encountered some rudimentary Ottoman defences just to the south of El Afule. To prevent Turkish resistance from solidifying the 2nd Lancers immediately charged catching the exhausted defenders, who were fast asleep, completely by surprise. In less than 10 minutes, 46 Turkish soldiers had been speared to death while a further 500 were taken prisoner.[61] Shortly after completing the oil depicting these events, Dugdale wrote in early 1919 to the Imperial War Museum (IWM) in London that he sought to capture the moment when 'Gardner's Horse swept down on "Johnny Turk" spearing many as they slept'. After interviewing one of the unit's British officers, who had taken part in the charge, Dugdale had been greatly impressed by the image conveyed of the sheer cold-blooded professionalism of the Indian cavalrymen when 'his lancers had behaved that morning as if they were putting on a bravura display of tent-pegging; each man chose his Turk and ran him through as they lay firing'.[62]

Dugdale generally displayed a visceral general animus towards the Indian Ottoman, referring to them as less than human, which McBey did not feel. The Scotsman was invariably impressed by the Indian Army combat units advancing deeper into Palestine and Syria in September-October 1918. As with many British and Dominion soldiers of the EEF, McBey was much less taken with what he saw of Allenby's Arab allies. Early in October 1918, McBey reached Damascus and encountered T. E. Lawrence who had just occupied the city with some 3,000 'Arab Irregular Cavalry' of the Howeitat, Rualla and Beni Sakhr tribes, technically loyal to the Hashemite Emir Feisal (1885–1933).[63] McBey later recalled being impressed by Emir Feisal's 'beautiful manners' so different from his men who for all their flamboyant robes struck him as 'just a lot of bandits, jolly bandits but a cutthroat crew all the same'. He found himself unable to resist sketching Feisal's bodyguard for *A Bodyguard to the Emir Feisal* – 'a huge Abyssinian negro with swords, knives and automatic revolvers hung round his neck [who] stood immobile behind the Emir's chair'.[64]

Stuart Reid (1883–1971) and James McBey, 1919

McBey did not warm to Feisal's Bedu supporters, referring to them as 'endearingly scruffy and oddly child-like' one moment and then in a trice capable of turning 'fanatical and murderous'.[65] His view of the Bedu was similar to that of the official war artist Stuart Reid who arrived in Palestine as McBey was planning to leave the area for home. Early in 1919 Reid painted the evocative *Deraa: The Arab Welcome the First Handley Page Machine to Arrive in Palestine, 22 September 1918*, celebrating the moment when a huge twin-engine heavy bomber landed outside Deraa to provide fuel for two British Bristol fighters attached to Sherif Feisal's army as well as small arms ammunition to his cavalry – part of which was technically commanded by T. E. Lawrence.[66] At the time Reid wrote to the RAF section of the Visual Art Department of the Ministry of Information that he hoped the painting would forcefully convey to the viewer the 'childlike wonder' of the Arabs confronted by the Handley Page as the 'last word' in British aerial military might. The Bedu cavalrymen had never seen such a huge aircraft before and speculated whether it could give birth to the

---

61 Bruce, *The Last Crusade*, p. 295.
62 Harries, *The War Artists*, p. 124.
63 Bruce, *The Last Crusade*, pp. 314–15. Damascus appears to have been entered simultaneously by the Arabs and by the Third Australian Light Horse Brigade, part of the 5th Indian Cavalry Division.
64 Hare, *London's Latin Quarter*, p. 137.
65 Ibid., p. 138.
66 Michael Korda, *Hero: The Life and Legend of Lawrence of Arabia* (London: JR Books, 2011), p. 414.

smaller machines with which they were more familiar.[67] Reid noted the excitement mixed with trepidation the Arabs display in front of the Handley Page as if they could have just as easily 'attacked it . . . as worship it'. He relished the fact the machine seemed to have a 'bracing effect' on the Arabs who 'feared Turkish aircraft but then they never had a machine like this [the Handley Page bomber]'.[68]

As Allenby's campaign in the Levant began to wind down, and as the Ottoman Turks signed an Armistice with the British at the end of October 1918, McBey found he had more time than ever with Indian units. No longer on a wartime footing there was also more opportunity for him to chat with Indian soldiers who were now full of thoughts of returning home, as beautifully observed in *Punjabis by a Camp Fire, Tripoli, The Lebanon* (see Figure 8.6).

Figure 8.6   James McBey, *Punjabis by a Camp Fire, Tripoli, The Lebanon*, 4 November 1918

Source: © Imperial War Museum

67   Ibid., p. 415.
68   Stuart Reid letter to Lieutenant-Colonel A.C. MacClean (Royal Air Force Art Section), 11 June 1919, Reid First World War File, 1919, Department of Art, IWM, London. By the time Reid had written this letter RAF Handley Page 0/400s had been deployed to bomb Kabul, during the Third Anglo-Afghan War, and rebellious Kurdish tribesmen in the north of what was to become Iraq. David Loyn, *Butcher and Bolt: Two Hundred Years of Foreign Engagement in Afghanistan* (London: Windmill Books, 2009), pp. 117–18.

Figure 8.7 James McBey, *The Egyptian Cook at No. 10 Mess, GHQ*, December 1918

Source: © Imperial War Museum

With the general relaxation in the atmosphere, McBey felt able to sketch individual Egyptians working as waiters and cooks in the kitchens of Allenby's GHQ, such as the affable Anwar in *The Egyptian Cook at No. 10 Mess* (see Figure 8.7).

McBey had a fairly lengthy conversation with Anwar who told the Scot that 'the English' (McBey was always quick to emphasise in conversation with anyone he encountered in the Middle East that he was 'not an Englishman') had been welcome guests in Egypt and they had done some good things for his country but now 'the time had come for them to go home' as the Turks had been defeated.[69] McBey wondered at the time what would happen to Egypt so abruptly annexed by Britain in November 1914. In March 1919, as he arrived back in London, Egyptians rioted for independence from British control while British troops in

---

69 James McBey letter to A.N. Yockney, n.d., *c.* January 1919, McBey First World War File, 1917–1919, Department of Art, Imperial War Museum, London.

the army of occupation rioted in camps near Port Said demanding to return home. In his capacity as High Commissioner, Field-Marshal Allenby recommended that independence be granted to the Egyptians in a qualified form. In February 1922 he would formally declare Egypt a sovereign state and independent monarchy – though Britain retained control of the Suez Canal and of the Foreign and Defence policies of the British-approved Egyptian King. Egypt would essentially remain firmly within the British sphere of imperial influence until July 1952 when the playboy King Faruq was overthrown by his own army.[70]

Back in London McBey was rather chastened to discover that few of his drawings of the Palestine campaign (that had already reached the Ministry of Information) had been exhibited in public or reproduced in the press. After the Armistice in November 1918 the Ministry had formulated ambitious plans to publish two books of McBey reproductions – one of work produced in Egypt and Sinai, the other of images from Palestine and Syria, but neither were realised by the time the war came to an end. The proposed project was first postponed and then cancelled as the Ministry wound up at great speed early in 1919. As with the Rothenstein project mentioned previously, there was yet interest on the part of the India Office and the Indian chamber of Princes, in publishing something after the war, that would feature images of the exploits of the Indian Army, but there was little enthusiasm for the proposal from the Foreign and Colonial Offices. It was as if the less the British home population knew about the new British Empire in the Middle East, made possible by the decisions of the Paris Peace Conference, the better.[71] Of course, by the spring of 1919 both Egypt and India were wracked by riot and revolt; there were major disturbances in Cairo in March 1919, and the Amritsar massacre took place in the Punjab in April that year. Some Egyptian and Indians were certainly acting in a warrior fashion but very much against, rather than in support of, British Imperial power.

Britain's new Empire in the Middle East, 1919–1921

By the time McBey left for London in February 1919 the British Empire still had over a million men in Palestine, Lebanon, Syria and Mesopotamia.[72] At the close of the year the British military pulled out of Lebanon and Syria to make way for an occupying French force in accordance with the Versailles Treaty of July 1919. The subsequent Treaty of San Remo, in April 1920, awarded Britain League of Nations Mandates for Palestine and stated what were to become the new kingdoms of Transjordan and Iraq.[73] The fine details concerning the future shape of the British Middle East were decided at the Cairo Conference in March 1921. The Hashemite Emir Feisal who had so impressed McBey in October 1918, and had been briskly ejected from Damascus by the French in July 1920, agreed to become King of the new State of Iraq (which was so arranged after a rigged plebiscite in August 1933).[74] Meanwhile, Feisal's elder brother Abdullah somewhat reluctantly accepted an offer brokered by T. E. Lawrence to become Emir of Transjordan, with his capital in Amman.[75]

---

70   David Fromkin, *A Peace to End All Peace: The Fall of the Ottoman Empire and the Creation of the Modern Middle East* (London: Phoenix, 2000), p. 502.
71   Harries, *The War Artists*, pp. 27–8.
72   Fromkin, *A Peace to End All Peace*, p. 404.
73   Ibid., p. 411.
74   Ibid., pp. 502–6.
75   Ibid., pp. 510–12.

Eric Kennington in the Middle East, 1921

Lawrence invited Eric Kennington, whom he had befriended in Oxford in December 1920 after an introduction from Robert Graves, to visit the Middle East and draw portraits of some of the Arabs who had fought alongside Lawrence during the Desert Revolt, and about whom he was writing at the time in an early draft of his epic *Seven Pillars of Wisdom*.[76] Kennington arrived in Cairo in March 1921, but he did not attend the Conference at which Lawrence was working as an adviser on Arab Affairs to the Colonial Secretary, Winston Churchill. The artist spent some time wandering around the city and exploring the Cairo Museum for its collection of Ancient Egyptian artefacts. He did not seem aware of the unrest against British rule amongst the local population. However, after having afternoon tea with Howard Carter at the Semiramis Hotel, he did note that the archaeologist seemed concerned that the 'tense political situation' might prevent him from continuing his search in the Valley of the Kings for an as yet undiscovered and unplundered tomb of a Pharaoh.[77]

From Cairo, Kennington made his way by boat to Beirut, from which he travelled by lorry to Damascus in April 1921. While in Damascus he drew a striking pastel portrait of Nawaf Shalaan of the powerful Rualla tribe. Nawaf and his father had been uneasy allies for Lawrence in 1918 (in fact Lawrence had suspected Nawaf of being in the pay of the Ottomans). At the time Kennington wrote to his brother that it had been a challenge to communicate with Nawaf, even with a competent translator present, but he had eventually been able to persuade the chief to sit motionless for over an hour. He grants that the Chief has a 'presence . . . looking like a lion in a zoo' but this very animalistic quality made him seem remote and detached from normal human concerns. The artist was also surprised that such a powerful chief, who had studiously remained neutral when the French advanced on Damascus in July 1920, was illiterate and seemed to show so little interest in what was happening in Europe – though he had heard of Lloyd George and gave the impression he thought the artist had been sent direct to draw him by the British Prime Minister.[78] Later, Nawaf would, during the great Druze rebellion of July 1925–June 1927, turn on the French. He was arrested and died in prison as the rising was being crushed.

Kennington then made his way to Haifa, where he visited the site of the cavalry charge made by the Jodhpur Lancers in September 1918. He continued to Jerusalem, where he stayed with and drew the Military Governor of the City, Sir Ronald Storrs, then went to Amman where he drew Abdullah (1882–1951) the 39-year-old newly minted Emir of Transjordan. Kennington thought Abdullah not so noble looking, or as gracious as Feisal, but probably a wilier politician with a firmer grasp of the realities of European power politics.[79] By the time the portrait came to be exhibited in London in October 1921, Kennington was aware that Lawrence respected rather than admired Abdullah, who had resisted all of Lawrence's attempts to charm him and was justly suspicious of the hold Lawrence appeared to have established over his younger brother Feisal.[80]

---

76   Black, *The Graphic Art of Eric Kennington*, p. 56.
77   Eric Kennington letter to William Oscar Kennington, n.d., *c.* March 1921, Kennington Papers, Department of Western Manuscripts, Bodleian Library, Oxford University.
78   Ibid.
79   Eric Kennington, 'T.E. Lawrence: An Appreciation,' in *T.E. Lawrence by His Friends*, ed. A.W. Lawrence (London: Jonathan Cape, 1937), p. 268.
80   Scott Anderson, *Lawrence in Arabia: War, Deceit, Imperial Folly and the Making of the Modern Middle East* (London: Atlantic Books, 2014), pp. 195–6.

Abdullah, despite being twice nearly overthrown by incursions from Sunni Wahhabi *Ikwhan riders* despatched by Ibn Saud, in 1922 and 1924 (on both occasions he was saved by a combination of the Royal Air Force and the 750-strong British-officered Arab Legion),[81] proved a successful and enlightened ruler of Jordan. He managed to stay on the throne until he was assassinated in 1951.[82] After Abdullah, Kennington drew a further two dozen Arab sitters who can be broadly divided into two groups. Firstly there were senior chiefs who had befriended Lawrence and with varying degrees of loyalty remained true to the Hashemite cause, such as Ali ibn Hussein, Sherif Shakir and the wonderfully piratical Auda abu Tayi (1874–1924) of the Howeitat of the northern Hejaz (who managed, against all the odds, to die in bed of natural causes in 1924 in a luxurious new home he had built east of Maan in southern Jordan with Turkish POW labour).[83] During the war Auda had commanded approximately 500 mounted tribesmen and was reputed to have killed over 70 Bedu in a single combat (he did not bother to count the number of Turks he had killed). He had been wounded over a dozen times in battle. Lawrence admired his physical bravery and leadership skills and acknowledged that he could not have captured Aqaba in July 1917 without Auda's support.[84]

Then, amongst Kennington's most interesting and challenging Arab sitters, were those in the second group, former members of Lawrence's 1918 bodyguard. These were hard, ruthless killers, often renegades or outcasts from their own tribes who feared no one and were unimpressed by any white man – especially one who was not a soldier but who followed the despised calling of being a *rassam* (an artist).[85] Lawrence later told Kennington that being a member of his bodyguard was no sinecure – only half of the 150 or so men who had served with him during 1917–1918 had survived to see the Ottoman Turks defeated.[86]

Kennington later recalled that he had felt distinctly uneasy in the presence of the 'religious zealot' Saad El Sikeini who within three years would defect to the Wahhabi *Ikwhan* of Ibn Saud. As for the 'runaway negro slave' Abd el Rahman, he had noisily unloaded and then loaded his pistol as the Englishman attempted to draw him, while his friend Mahmas – whom even Lawrence described as a 'homicidal manic' – nearly attacked Kennington with a knife when the artist unwisely disturbed him during their sitting by suddenly reaching for a fresh stick of chalk.[87]

Kennington's pastel portraits of Arabs were exhibited at the Leicester Galleries in London in October 1921. Lawrence wrote a most revealing short essay for the exhibition catalogue in which he boldly asserted that the 'true Arab' was the nomadic Bedu and not those to be found in towns and cities.[88] In their reaction to the portraits, art critics embraced the attractive dichotomy Lawrence provided them. The Arab portraits most admired were

---

81   Fromkin, *A Peace to End All Peace*, pp. 513–14.
82   Ibid., p. 512.
83   Brown, *Lawrence of Arabia*, p. 202.
84   Anderson, *Lawrence in Arabia*, pp. 288–9.
85   Sir Ronald Storrs, *Eric Kennington: Drawing the R.A.F.: A Book of Portraits* (London: Oxford University Press, 1942), pp. 14–15.
86   Anderson, *Lawrence in Arabia*, pp. 413–14.
87   Storrs, *Eric Kennington*, p. 16.
88   T.E. Lawrence, 'Preface,' in *Arab Portraits by Eric Kennington* (London: Leicester Galleries, October 1921), pp. 6–8. Exhibition catalogue.

of independent, free-spirited 'Ishmaels'[89] and forbidding-looking 'desert Messiah-types',[90] as opposed to the 'Jacobs' who were perceived to be wily, treacherous and calculating – little better than despised 'slum Arabs'.[91] The overall verdict was clear: the desert nomad Ishmaels were the 'true Arab warriors' because of, rather than despite, the fanatical and unreasoning nature of their faith, which made them instinctively bridle at conforming to Western European values. They were the Arabs to be cultivated by the British as allies and not their settled relatives who had been exposed to the corruption of Western influence and urban living. Taken to its logical conclusion this argument rather neatly legitimated continuing British involvement in the Middle East. If the 'true' Arabs the British were backing in the region were noble, picturesque and yet backward, then there was every reason for the British to maintain a presence there, to keep a paternally interested eye and controlling gaze upon them.

In many respects the artists discussed here were products of their time, imbued with the prejudices and casually stereotyping assumptions of their class, education and upbringing. Some, such as Reid and Dugdale, did not conceal their contempt for the Arabs and Egyptians they encountered as war artists. However they, along with McBey, Kennington and Rothenstein, were far more ready to respect Indians in uniform – their favourable view of them to a great extent structured by Imperial propaganda they had already absorbed concerning the existence of reputable and admirable 'martial races' on the sub-continent. Kennington and McBey appear to have been genuinely sympathetic towards and interested in the Indian and Arab individuals they sketched as war artists, though both felt true empathy could have only been established with the ability to readily communicate with them. Kennington never returned to the Middle East after his 1921 trip, but he later expressed regret that he had not done so between the wars.[92] As for McBey he would retire to live in Morocco in the late 1940s and die there in 1959.[93] This chapter has merely scratched the surface of a subject that requires further in-depth research; more discussion is required of the imagery of non-white individuals in the service of the British Empire during the First World War, while continued exploration of the vital contribution such individuals made to a war effort all to casually referred to as 'British' is long overdue.[94]

---

89 P.G. Konody, 'Ishmaelites: Mr. Kenningtons Desert Pictures,' *Daily Mail*, 8 October 1921, p. 4.
90 'Mr. Kenningtons New Exhibition,' *The Times*, 11 October 1921, p. 18.
91 Charles Marriott, 'Current Drawings,' *The Outlook*, 22 October 1921, p. 332.
92 Eric Kennington letter to Basil Liddell Hart, n.d., *c.* April 1954, Kennington-Liddell Hart Correspondence, Liddell Hart Archive Centre, Kings College, London.
93 Harries, *The War Artists*, p. 27.
94 Black, *The Great War and the Making of the Modern World*, p. 272.

Chapter 9
The imagining of Mesopotamia/Iraq in British art in the aftermath of the Great War

Tim Buck

On 12 December 1919, *The Nation's War Paintings and Other Records* opened at the Royal Academy in London. Passing through the various rooms of the Academy's home in Burlington House that day visitors may have been overwhelmed by the sheer scale of an exhibition that comprised over 920 pictures drawn from the collection of the Imperial War Museum (IWM).[1] Of these works, just over 90 depicted locations or individuals connected with the hostilities in Egypt, Palestine, Syria, Arabia and Mesopotamia (present-day Iraq). When this figure is further broken down, a mere 15 pictures – 14 of which were relatively small-scale watercolour studies – imagined the 'neglected war' that had been fought in Mesopotamia,[2] where, in the view of an airman who served there, 'forgotten British officers [died] in nameless fights or rott[ed] with fever in distant outposts, unknown, uncared-for, and unsung.'[3] At the Royal Academy in 1919 the Mesopotamian campaign may have seemed to the exhibition's visitors, visually, also unsung.

For most Britons prior to 1914 knowledge of Mesopotamia would likely to have been acquired second-hand, either through writing or images produced by the few Britons who had travelled there or through visits to the British Museum, which held a substantial collection of excavated Assyrian artefacts.[4] Undoubtedly, the war changed this situation and limited though the British presence in Mesopotamia had been during wartime (hence perhaps its numerically minor representation in the exhibition), by 1919 greater first-hand knowledge of the country circulated in Britain. Public interest in Mesopotamia had to some extent been ignited, as a review in the *Manchester Guardian* in 1921 of Richard and Sydney Carline's exhibition of paintings of the East at the Manchester City Art Gallery (an exhibition that included images of Mesopotamia) indicated: 'Because more John Smiths have travelled in the East during the last few years than ever before both they and their friends are interested in the record of what they have seen' and, judging by a number of relevant art exhibitions

---

1 *Imperial War Museum: The Nation's War Paintings and Other Records. Exhibition at the Galleries of the Royal Academy* (London: H.M.S.O., 1919).
2 A.J. Barker, *The Neglected War: Mesopotamia, 1914–1918* (London: Faber and Faber, 1967). The title given by A.J. Barker to his account of the war in Mesopotamia.
3 Lt-Col J.E. Tennant, *In the Clouds above Baghdad: Being the Records of an Air Commander* (London: C. Palmer, 1920), p. 7.
4 See Nadia Atia, 'A Relic of Its Own Past: Mesopotamia in the British Imagination, 1900–14,' *Memory Studies* 3 (2010), p. 233; on British travellers to Mesopotamia prior to 1914. See, Brian M. Fagan, *Return to Babylon: Travellers, Archaeologists, and Monuments in Mesopotamia* (Colorado: University Press of Colorado, 2007), p. 127; on the excavated Assyrian artefacts.

and illustrated books that date to the early 1920s, this interest continued to be stimulated and maintained.[5]

A 'high finish and meticulous rendering of detail' typified much of the painting produced by nineteenth-century Western artists when imagining the Islamic world, of which Mesopotamia was part, and many such works were included in an exhibition, *The Lure of the East: British Orientalist Painting*, held at Tate Britain in 2008.[6] For Nicholas Tromans, the editor of the exhibition catalogue, amongst professional artists, 'transparently truthful' Orientalist painting 'expired after the First World War' as the East came increasingly under the sway of Westernisation.[7] The war, clearly, had made a Western presence all too visible in the East to those who chose to record it. This, for example, is an account of the Mesopotamian city Basra in 1918 by the American war correspondent Eleanor Franklin Egan: 'The smoke came with the British, and it rolls today – in black spirals of industrial abomination – from workshops innumerable, from electric power plants, from many steamboats, and from tall chimneys and funnels of every kind all round the horizon.'[8] As Linda Nochlin has argued, a key defining feature of Orientalist painting is the 'presence that is always an absence: the Western colonial or touristic presence'.[9] When Mesopotamia is imagined by British artists in the aftermath of the Great War, though, that 'absence' is at times made visible. This is easily explained as certain artists were commissioned to produce accounts of British military activity in Mesopotamia during the war. But other works produced at this time echo nineteenth-century Orientalist configurations of the East; a Western presence is filtered out or, more interestingly, obliquely acknowledged, suggestive of an equivocal response by British artists when imagining Mesopotamia during a period of heightened cross-cultural encounter. This chapter reflects upon these differing imaginative configurations and how they may have been perceived in the years immediately following the Armistice; a time when the cost to Britain of maintaining administrative and military personnel in Mesopotamia/Iraq came under intense scrutiny both in parliament and the press[10] and when mere mention of Britain's newly acquired 'de facto colony' had the potential to polarise public opinion.[11]

---

5 'The City Art Gallery: "Lands of the Bible,"' *Manchester Guardian*, 2 May 1921, p. 3. Illustrated art books featuring Mesopotamia published in the early 1920s include Donald Maxwell, *A Dweller in Mesopotamia* (London, 1921); and *Mesopotamia (Iraq) Watercolours by Edith Cheesman* (London: John Lane, 1922).

6 Mary Anne Stevens, 'Western Art and Its Encounter with the Islamic World, 1798–1914,' in *The Orientalists: Delacroix to Matisse (European Painters in North Africa and the Near East)* (London: Thames and Hudson, 1984), p. 21.

7 Nicholas Tromans, 'Introduction: British Orientalist Painting,' in *The Lure of the East: British Orientalist Painting*, ed. Nicholas Tromans (London: Tate Publishing, 2008), p. 20.

8 Eleanor Franklin Egan, *The War in the Cradle of the World: Mesopotamia* (New York and London: Harper and Brothers, 1918), p. 104.

9 Linda Nochlin, 'The Imaginary Orient,' in *The Politics of Vision: Essays on Nineteenth Century Art and Society*, ed. Linda Nochlin (New York: Westview Press, 1991), p. 36.

10 See Priya Satia, *Spies in Arabia: The Great War and the Cultural Foundation of Britain's Covert Empire in the Middle East* (Oxford: Oxford University Press, 2008), p. 291.

11 At the San Remo Peace Conference in April 1920 Britain was granted protective mandates for Palestine and Mesopotamia. See Charles Tripp, *A History of Iraq* (Cambridge: Cambridge University Press, 2000), pp. 30–65; for an account of the British Mandate in Iraq. See Niall Ferguson, 'A World on the Brink of Violence' in 'The Second World War, Day 1: Origins,' *Guardian*, 5 September 2009, p. 1. Niall Ferguson uses the term 'de facto colonies' to describe the mandated territories acquired by Britain at the end of the First World War. See Satia, *Spies in Arabia*, p. 287; on Mesopotamia's capacity to polarise opinion in the early 1920s.

Richard and Sydney Carline's paintings of the RAF in Mesopotamia/Iraq: imagery and perception

On 18 July 1918, Colonel MacLean, President of the Royal Air Force (RAF) Section at the IWM, wrote to the Secretary of the museum informing him that he had 'secured the services' of 2nd Lieutenant Richard Carline 'and hope[d] to also obtain the services of his brother [Sydney Carline]'.[12] Initially, MacLean sent Richard Carline to France to 'undertake a series of pictures of noteworthy localities, taken from the air',[13] but in October 1918 he informed Carline that 'I [now] wish to push you off to the Holy Land or to Mesopotamia . . . to return say in 6 months time with . . . sketches and really get down to turning out masterpieces.'[14] By January 1919, both Carline brothers were in Egypt. So what were they looking for as they flew above the Middle East? As Richard Carline later recalled, their objective was 'to paint the main scenes of battle in the air, obtaining the details before all record was lost'.[15] To this end, when moving on to Palestine that same month, they made sketches during flights over Jerusalem, the Dead Sea, and Gaza for use in their pictorial reconstructions of air battles that had taken place over the country. In reconstructing events to which they had not been party, the Carlines, however, were not granted imaginative licence. As Lt Insall, the curator of the IWM's RAF section, stated in a letter dated May 1919, their 'sketches are first criticised by the authorities out there, and on their return home their work will [also] be strictly supervised'.[16] And if they pictorially overstepped the mark, the Carlines were quickly brought to book:

> Would you please note that the RAF Section is not prepared to exhibit, in the Museum, pictures showing any extreme forms of art. It should be borne in mind that only true records, faithfully depicting places, incidents, etc., will be accepted. All extremes should be carefully avoided, it being essential not to overlook the fact that the impression of one individual may perilously clash with the impression of others. With the photographs at your disposal, you should be able to produce absolutely correct records of the various places selected for your pictures. A point which has been criticised by flying people visiting the [Royal Academy] is the hard appearance of anti-aircraft smoke in those pictures by [Sidney (sic) Carline], and the treatment of this anti-aircraft smoke in the Damascus picture suffers from the same fault, vis – a hardness and unnatural formation.

---

12 See Burgh House and Hampstead Museum, accessed 10 December 2015, http://www.burghhouse.org.uk and Tate, Art and Artists, 'Sydney Carline,' accessed 10 December 2015, http://www.tate.org.uk/art/artists/sydney-carline-863. Sydney Carline (1889–1926) studied at the Slade from 1907 to 1910 and later at Tudor-Hart's Academie de la Peinture in Paris. Richard Carline (1896–1980) also trained at Tudor-Hart's in Paris in 1913, at the Academie's new Hampstead address from 1913 to 1915 and at the Slade between 1921 and 1924.

13 'Colonel MacLean, President, Air Force Section, IWM to Secretary, IWM,' 18 July 1918, First World War Artists Archive: Richard Carline 81/3 (hereafter R. Carline Archive), IWM. Richard Carline produced one aerial view of wartime France and Sydney Carline three oils depicting the aerial war in Italy. See Richard Carline, 'Introduction,' in *Richard and Sydney Carline* (London: Imperial War Museum, 1973), p. 7. All four oils were displayed in 'The Nation's War Paintings' exhibition.

14 'MacLean to R. Carline,' 18 October 1918, R. Carline Archive.

15 Carline, 'Introduction,' p. 7.

16 'Lt Insall, RAF Curator to Miss H.F. Hall,' Finance Dept., 15 May 1919, R. Carline Archive, IWM.

If these points are not lost sight of, it will save a lot of further work when your pictures come before my Committee.[17]

When the Carlines eventually arrived in Mesopotamia in June 1919 Sydney Carline believed that their 'experience of the East in Palestine' would enable them to quickly complete their aerial views of the country as they now knew 'what to look for'.[18] In a later interview he detailed a modus operandi that involved flying 'to and fro over the selected view till one had sufficient details to complete the picture on landing'.[19] Dozens of sketches in pencil and watercolour resulted from this process enabling the Carlines to produce unique impressions of wartime Mesopotamia and of the country's topography and people.[20] In accordance with their commission, the Carlines memorialised specific actions undertaken by the RAF in the wartime campaign. Both, for instance, produced paintings that imagined confrontations between RAF and German aeroplanes over the city of Kut al-Amara, where around 10,000 British and Indian troops under General Sir Charles Townshend were besieged by Ottoman forces from December 1915, before surrendering at the end of April 1916. It perhaps appears surprising that a site of British military humiliation (this was the first time a British army had surrendered since 1781)[21] should be chosen as a subject of painted record, yet less so when recalling the Carlines' raison d'être in imagining the war in the Middle East: the role performed by the RAF in its execution. Accordingly, Sydney Carline's *British Maurice Farman Attacked by German Fokker while Dropping Sacks of Corn on Kut-el-Amara During the Siege of 1916*, as the title suggests, imagines the RAF's attempt to alleviate the hunger of those in the besieged city.[22] The youngest of Britain's three armed services, the RAF would have been keen to promote the added dimension that it could bring to military confrontation. 'Sieges', for instance, as Antoine Capet has argued, 'would never be the same again . . . since air forces radically altered their nature'.[23]

The symbolic significance of Kut in the Mesopotamian campaign can be measured by the inclusion of three paintings of the city at the Academy exhibition.[24] In 1916, the date of the events depicted in Sydney Carline's oil, the name 'Kut' was, for the British public, synonymous with military defeat, but after its recapture by the Mesopotamian Expeditionary

---

17 Chairman, RAF Section, IWM to S. and R. Carline, 6 February 1920, IWM, First World War Artists Archive, Sydney Carline 73/3 (hereafter S. Carline Archive).

18 Sydney Carline to MacLean, 25 June 1919, S. Carline Archive.

19 '"Painting in the Air Artists" Tour of the Middle East,' *The Times*, 30 April 1921, p. 7.

20 Seven oils resulted from the Carline's time in Mesopotamia; three views of Baghdad, Kut and Samara, by Richard, and four paintings; A pilot approaching his objective over Hit; A dog-fight over Kirkuck; An aircraft returning in the evening, and An aircraft dropping food on Kut during the siege, by Sydney. See Sydney Carline to MacLean, 11 July 1919, S. Carline Archive.

21 Nadia Atia, 'A Wartime Tourist Trail: Mesopotamia in the British Imagination, 1914–1918,' *Studies in Travel Writing* 16, no. 4 (2012): p. 404.

22 See www.iwm.org.uk/collections/item/object/4532 to view this painting.

23 Antoine Capet, 'Views of Palestine in British Art in Wartime and Peacetime, 1914–1948,' in *Britain, Palestine and Empire: The Mandate Years*, ed. Rory Miller (Farnham: Ashgate Publishing, 2010), p. 90.

24 Sydney Carline, *The River Front, Kut, Mesopotamia*; Richard Carline, *Kut-el-Amara and the Tigris*; and J.D. Revel, *Kut Town. Imperial War Museum: The Nation's War Paintings and Other Records. Exhibition at the Galleries of the Royal Academy* (London: H.M.S.O., 1919). The paintings are listed in the catalogue as 760, 219 and 737 respectively. J.D. Revel, 124/4, First World War Artists Archive, IWM. Revel was a salaried war artist attached to the Mesopotamian Expeditionary Force.

Force (MEF), under the command of General Sir Stanley Maude in February 1917, its name acquired new meaning.[25] The renowned Middle Eastern traveller and writer Gertrude Bell had, as a member of the British administration in Mesopotamia, described Kut in a letter to her parents as that 'poor tragic little place' with 'its shelled walls and shattered palm trees' in April 1917, as she journeyed to Baghdad in the wake of the MEF's entry into Baghdad on 11 March 1917. Then, the city was empty, but Bell was determined that 'we [the British] are going to clean it out and build it up as soon as possible.'[26] Writing not long after Bell, Franklin Egan considered:

> Kut el-Amara will always be sacred to the British. At Kut their pride was crucified, and at Kut their pride was eventually redeemed and rose triumphant, a shining thing which shines in Mesopotamia today in the finest demonstration of high morality and right purpose that I have ever seen.[27]

Having established rule in Baghdad, the British authorities, as Bell predicted, rebuilt Kut, and it was views of the resurrected city that were exhibited by the Carlines at the Academy in 1919. Sydney Carline's watercolour, *The River Front, Kut, Mesopotamia, 1919*, shows an eye-level view of a peaceful riverside scene.[28] A local sailing vessel is depicted mid-river whilst moored up against the far shore are a number of other boats. Behind these are seen the low-lying buildings of the city, including an arcaded bazaar that had been built by the British authorities as part of Kut's regeneration.[29]

Richard Carline's watercolour, *Kut-el-Amara and the Tigris, Mesopotamia* offers an aerial view of a mud-built city devoid of twentieth-century technology and innovation.[30] In his painting though there are none of the 'shelled walls' witnessed by Bell two years previously, and the palm trees now appear to be thriving, as generally is life in the city, evidenced by the numerous figures Carline depicts going about their daily business. These two paintings demonstrated that Kut, laid waste by the forces of the Ottoman Empire, had been restored to rude health by those of the British Empire,[31] and thus may have been viewed by visitors to the Academy in a manner redolent of the opinions expressed by Franklin Egan, as demonstrations of the 'high morality and right purpose' of British rule in Mesopotamia.

The imagery in other works by the Carlines, for instance, Sydney Carline's *Flying over the Desert at Sunset, Mesopotamia*, would, too, have retained topical relevance if viewed

---

25 See Charles Townshend, *When God Made Hell: The British Invasion of Mesopotamia and the Creation of Iraq, 1914–1921* (London: Faber and Faber, 2010), pp. 337–59.

26 Gertrude Bell to Florence and Hugh Bell, 15 April 1917. Gertrude Bell Archive, Newcastle University Library, www.gerty.ncl.ac.uk/letters.php. Her sentiments chimed with a commonly held belief, especially amongst those of the elite political class, that it befell Britain to help develop the countries under its jurisdiction.

27 Egan, *The War in the Cradle of the World*, p. 242.

28 See www.iwm.org.uk/collections/item/object/4384 to view this painting.

29 Georgina Howell, *Gertrude Bell Queen of the Desert, Shaper of Nations* (New York: Farrar, Straus and Giroux 2006), p. 288.

30 See www.iwm.org.uk/collections/item/object/4301 to view this painting.

31 The imperial dimension to the war in Mesopotamia was recognised at the Academy exhibition by the inclusion of Richard Carline's *Indian Camp, Mesopotamia*, a watercolour depicting soldiers of the Indian Army in front of tents pitched amongst the palm trees of a Mesopotamian desert oasis.

in the early 1920s.[32] Beneath the radiating light of an evening sun that has turned the sky amber and mauve, Carline's painting shows an RAF biplane flying over a monotonous, seemingly barren, desert landscape that is puddled by a lake's glistening surface and cut by two zigzagging rivers. His vision of the desert at sunset matches that of Franklin Egan who wrote, in 1918, of 'far horizons' comprising 'slashes and banks of burning orange . . . at sunset'.[33] For an earlier visitor, Louisa Jebb, the desert horizon despite having 'nothing to show and nothing to tell you' remained captivating because its 'emptiness' was 'full of secret possibilities and hidden wonder'.[34] The privileged aerial view accorded to Carline enabled him, in his painting, to disclose the desert's obvious 'hidden wonders', namely the lake and rivers, but generally the darker marks that blemish the flatness of his picture's surface conceal, rather than reveal, information about the scene. Is, for example, the dark tone that shadows the river's course suggestive of vegetation growing in more fertile ground? We can speculate as to this being so, but cannot say categorically. For Carline, twilight has turned a landscape (that in wartime the RAF was photographing daily in order to produce accurate squared maps)[35] into something largely indecipherable, one that perhaps corresponded to the 'bare desolated ground' of the European battlefields that he had also viewed from above.[36] His choice of scene and favouring of an abstracted and opaque mode of expression over a more legible, topographical rendering was perhaps born out of this earlier experience, for as Richard Carline later recalled, 'the bare stark crudity of the landscape constituted new visual material' for those artists familiar with the devastating effects of modern warfare.[37]

The formal characteristics of Carline's painting link it to some degree with modernist practices evident in British art at this time, but it is his depiction of an RAF biplane that also engenders the picture's topicality in the early 1920s. A year after the painting's execution in 1919 a revolt against the widening of British rule in Mesopotamia erupted amongst some of the country's tribal groups. This was not quelled until mid-October 1920 at a cost of over 300 Indian and British lives and many millions of pounds, with the consequence that hereafter military spending in Mesopotamia was 'guided by the overarching motive of financial stringency'.[38] To reduce the size of a military garrison, that in 1919 had still stood at approximately 80,000 Indian and 25,000 British troops, and thereby expenditure, a policy of air policing by the RAF was inaugurated in Iraq (as the British government now named Mesopotamia) on 1 October 1922.[39] For Sir Samuel Hoare, the Secretary of State for Air, the use of aircraft rather than land forces was not only cheaper and more efficient but enabled control to be maintained without occupation.[40] Some commentators in Britain,

---

32 See www.iwm.org.uk/collections/item/object/4527 to view this painting.
33 Egan, *The War in the Cradle of the World*, pp. 201.
34 Louisa Jebb, *By Desert Ways to Baghdad* (Boston: T.F. Unwin, 1909), pp. 63, 260; cited in Satia, *Spies in Arabia*, p. 65.
35 Tennant, *In the Clouds above Baghdad*, p. 145.
36 Carline, 'Introduction,' p. 5.
37 Ibid.
38 Kristian Coates Ulrichsen, 'The British Occupation of Mesopotamia, 1914–1922,' *The Journal of Strategic Studies* 30, no. 2 (April 2007): p. 375.
39 See David E. Omissi, *Air Power and Colonial Control: The Royal Air Force, 1919–1939* (Manchester and New York: Manchester University Press, 1990), pp. 21, 31.
40 'The Royal Air Force in Irak,' *The Near East*, 22 March 1923, p. 286.

however, were less positive about the implementation of air power in Iraq. The journalist Sir Percival Phillips, for one, quietly, but devastatingly, condemned its use:

> It would surprise the British taxpayer to know the extent to which bombing has prevailed in the country districts of the new state of Iraq ... British aeroplanes have been utilised to extract overdue revenue and in general to impress the Mesopotamians with their responsibilities as an independent nation. Of course innocent people have been killed. That cannot be helped. The subjugation of an unruly village or district involves the punishment of old women as well as recalcitrant head men.[41]

Published in the mass-selling *Daily Mail*, Phillips's comments would, potentially, have reached a wide readership. Other commentators, though, albeit in less populist forums, attempted to counter his condemnatory remarks. The weekly newspaper *The Near East*, which covered politics and commerce in countries that now constitute the Middle East, considered that

> other visitors to Iraq who set greater store on accuracy and fair play where British honour and prestige are involved, would tell us that this particular form of punishment [RAF bombing] is used only under compulsion, and after all the circumstances have been carefully considered by the responsible authorities.[42]

Into this mix of views concerning the deployment of the RAF could be added the account of Lt-Col J. E. Tennant, whose record of his role as an air commander in Mesopotamia during the war had been published in 1920. Tennant described with a cold matter-of-factness how,

> If a tribe got out of hand a raid could leave the next morning and bomb and machine-gun any village within a 100 mile radius. Such immediate and drastic action inspired terror in the Arabs; once hunted down by machine-guns from the air they never wished a second dose, and a bomb having blotted out the happy home there was nought left but surrender.[43]

The biplane depicted by Carline flying over the desert therefore had the potential to conjure up differing imaginative responses from those who viewed the painting in the aftermath of the war. For some, the destructive potential of this modern technology, 'celebrated as a vindicating testament to Western superiority over the world's backward peoples',[44] would perhaps have epitomised the polarity of the cross-cultural encounters that played out daily in Iraq at this time. Others, though, would possibly have seen beyond the aeroplane's policing role in Iraq, imagining instead its commercial potential and use in extending Britain's Imperial communications.[45] Still more may have imaginatively concurred with Robert Brooke-Popham, who served as an air commander in Iraq and romantically believed there was 'a sort of natural fellow-feeling between nomad[ic] Arabs

---

41 'Government by Bomb: From Our Special Correspondent Sir Percival Philips,' *Daily Mail*, 18 November 1922, pp. 7–8.
42 'Anti-Iraq Propaganda,' *The Near East*, 23 November 1922, p. 654.
43 Tennant, *In the Clouds above Baghdad*, p. 163.
44 Toby Dodge, *Inventing Iraq: The Failure of Nation Building and a History Denied* (New York: Columbia University Press, 2003), p. 149.
45 'The RAF in the Middle East by H.T. Montague Bell,' *The Near East*, 8 June 1922, p. 770.

and the Air Force', based upon a mutual feeling that 'both feel that they are at times in conflict with the vast elemental forces of nature'.[46]

Tennant, too, made reference to the elemental quality of the Mesopotamian desert: 'A hundred feet up and everything was obvious, but once on the ground even the pilot who had just descended might lose his bearings'.[47]

A Sydney Carline watercolour, *Forced Landing in the Desert of a British BE2E near Nasarije, Mesopotamia, September 1919*, lays bare the possible implications when the technology that enabled a British occupying force to lord it over an alien country and people fails.[48] Carline shows two airmen who, having stepped out of their stricken aircraft, appear isolated and vulnerable on the desert floor. Each airman is shown looking in opposite directions as if disorientated by their surroundings. The curtailed shadows, cast by the aeroplane and by the men, suggest an oppressive, noonday sun beats down. On the horizon, to the left of the aircraft, a plume rises into the sky; sand whipped up by a fierce desert wind, perhaps? Or, more sinisterly, drifting smoke from the campfire of a possibly hostile nomadic tribe? Carline's painting offers an image of the RAF that, it could be argued, contrary to their objective, fails to present the service in a positive light. The picture is replete with negative inferences – failed technology, a forbidding environment, unforgiving elements and, perhaps, a possibly hostile foe – that may have caused viewers of the picture at this time to reflect upon the fragility of British rule in Iraq, dependent as it was to some extent on an infant technology prone to breaking down.

Orientalising Iraq after the Great War

Beyond the confines of an exhibition commemorating the empire's wartime activities and achievements, the views of Kut shown by the Carlines at the Academy fit within an early twentieth century vogue in Britain for romantic and topographical landscape painting depicting scenes at home or abroad. Oliver Brown, director of the Leicester Galleries in London, recalled how English taste in the 1900s favoured such work, and the market for it appears to still have been strong in the 1920s.[49] For example, of the eighty-one exhibitions staged at Walker's Galleries in New Bond Street, London, between 1920 and 1922, thirty-nine were artist-traveller shows.[50] A number of these exhibitions featured 'the Muslim Mediterranean' which constituted the Orient for British artists. 'The hinterland well beyond the coasts [of which Mesopotamia was part] remained the province of soldiers and explorers' and was seldom visited by British artists,[51] though an earlier exception was the Scottish painter Arthur Melville who, in a letter sent to his brother from Baghdad in 1882, reported the completion of sixty 'big sketches of the Mesopotamian city'.[52] So, in

---

46   Quoted in Satia, *Spies in Arabia*, p. 242.
47   Tennant, *In the Clouds above Baghdad*, p. 64.
48   See www.iwm.org.uk/collections/item/object/4379 to view this painting.
49   See Oliver Brown, *Exhibition: The Memoirs of Oliver Brown* (London: Evelyn, Adams and Mackay, 1968), p. 16.
50   See Walker's Galleries catalogues, National Art Library, Victoria and Albert Museum, London.
51   Tromans, 'Introduction,' pp. 10–11.
52   National Galleries Scotland, 'Arthur Melville: The Eastern Journey,' accessed 21 October 2015, www.nationalgalleries.org/collection/arthur-melville/the-eastern-journey.

the early 1920s, the pictorial imagination of Mesopotamia would thus have had a certain novelty value.

Many of the paintings of the East shown by the Carlines in Manchester in May 1921 had originally been displayed at the Goupil Gallery in London in March 1920. The IWM, which had first call on the pictures, 'placed at the disposal' of the brothers a 'few ... examples [of] no war interest',[53] and it was these that the Carlines exhibited, presumably with the intention of supplementing their income from the IWM, but also perhaps to establish their names within the art world.[54] A report in the *Times* detailed that the Carlines had sought 'to express changes of character in peoples, scenery, and conditions by a judicious choice of subjects and places' in their studies of the Middle East.[55] This, arguably, was the intention of most artist-travellers in the 1920s, as there remained a relatively strong market for pictures of this ilk. The descriptive accuracy expected of such work may not have been unequivocally stated, as it had been to the Carlines by the IWM, though there was a demand for authenticity in travellers' accounts at this time.[56] To this end, evidenced by the review in the *Manchester Guardian* of their Manchester exhibition, which informed readers that the pictures' major attraction was that 'they ... satisfy curiosity and ... give information as to what the East is like,' the Carlines' work was up to the mark.[57]

The market had determined the type of image expected of artist-travellers – generally a naturalistic study of exotic, picturesque or topographical material – and though, in the 1920s, not garnering many enthusiastic critical plaudits, such pictures continued to feature in the exhibition programmes of commercial galleries.[58] Disregarding the conventions established by the market, for example, departing, however slightly, from a naturalistic idiom, possibly meant risking commercial failure. Aware that on occasions the formal character of the Carlines' work diverged from the patently naturalistic (those 'hard' edges that had provoked criticism from the IWM), Lawrence Haward, in the 'Prefatory Note' of the Manchester exhibition catalogue, felt obliged to warn the exhibition's audience that 'One or two of the oils to some slight extent sacrifice representation to decorative effect but are neither abstract nor abstruse,' adding, as if by way of compensation, that 'the watercolours

---

53 Yockney to Insall, 23 January 1920, R. Carline Archive.

54 During wartime, the Carlines received their service pay as war artists and an additional £77 per annum from the IWM to cover studio rent and the cost of artist materials. After demobilisation they were paid £700 per annum to paint for the IWM. See MacLean to Secretary, 18 July 1918, IWM; and Memo dated 12 December 1918, R. Carline Archive. The London and Manchester exhibitions were the Carlines' first solo shows.

55 'Painting in the Air,' *The Times*, 30 April 1921, p. 7.

56 An editorial in *Wide World Magazine* – a travel journal that began publication in 1917 welcomed submissions from 'travellers, explorers, tourists, missionaries and others' under the proviso that narratives be 'strictly true in every detail'. Paul Fussell, *Abroad: British Literary Travelling between the Wars* (New York: Oxford University Press, 1980), p. 60.

57 'The City Art Gallery: "Lands of the Bible,"' *Manchester Guardian*, 2 May 1921, p. 3.

58 'Mr Wyndham Lewis: "Haunting Images of an Alien Art",' *The Times*, 14 April 1921, p. 8. In April 1921, Robert Burns' 'Watercolours of Morocco' was one of two exhibitions (the other, Wyndham Lewis' 'Tyros and Portraits') simultaneously staged at the Leicester Galleries. Most of a review in the *Times* was dedicated to Lewis' work whilst Burns' pictures, considered to 'skilfully give us tourist impressions of unfamiliar scenes', received scant attention. Five years later in February 1926, the *Times* considered that Miss A.F. Wood's watercolours of Palestine, then being exhibited at Walker's Galleries, 'never get beyond a certain level attained by most topographical painters', and were 'interesting only because of their subject'. 'A Painter in Palestine,' *The Times*, 9 February 1926, p. 9.

are simple, direct and literal.'[59] As the two commercial exhibitions largely comprised these more 'literal' watercolours, formally, the Carlines' pictures failed to fundamentally challenge one of the parameters that had helped define the market for artist-travellers' work. This may have been a contributing factor to the commercial success of their pictures when shown at the Goupil Gallery. In total 138 paintings were exhibited in London, but when the exhibition transferred to Manchester a year later, only 87 of the original pictures were featured.[60] The reduced scale of the Manchester exhibition suggests that possibly as many as fifty-one sales were achieved in London, signifying a relatively successful show.

The commercial success of the Goupil show, and the positive critical comments extended to the pictures exhibited in Manchester, may in part also have been due to the Carlines' imaginative configuration of the East in works deemed of no 'war interest'. Edward Said has defined Orientalism as 'a library or archive of information commonly ... held' – an archive into which Orientalists could delve, as in the nineteenth century when perceptions of the Orient were 'nourished by earlier accounts which ... provided the vocabulary, imagery and rhetoric'.[61] The consequence, as Tromans has pointed out, is a 'susceptibility to repetitious habits of representation that end up taking on a spurious authority'.[62] So with Tromans's comment in mind, the description in the Manchester exhibition catalogue of the Richard Carline watercolour *Baghdad: The City of the Arabian Nights* requires careful evaluation. Present-day Baghdad, it is said, 'consists largely of narrow covered-in bazaars and alleyways'.[63] It was this claustrophobic street pattern that British visitors to the city seemed to have found especially compelling – Gertrude Bell describes 'incredibly narrow crooked streets' where 'the eaves almost touch overhead' – for, as the picture title alludes, it allowed them to imagine themselves within the world of Scheherazade's ancient folk tales.[64] The catalogue hints, however, at modernity's incursion into this seemingly timeless setting when it relates that Baghdad 'hitherto had no street down which a motor could pass'.[65] And indeed under Ottoman rule – and contrary to British characterisation of it as un-dynamic – a radical urban transformation of Baghdad had been instigated early in the twentieth century. A wide, straight avenue, Al-Rashid Street, or New Street as it was known under British rule, was cut through the existing city in 1914 to improve traffic flow, resulting 'in the establishment of a different street life [with] a character totally different from the traditional urban fabric'.[66] New Street was described by a British visitor, Zetton Buchanan, in 1920 as 'the one broad main street of the place' and 'the only road suitable for traffic in our sense of the word', which consisted 'mostly [of] Ford cars [and] donkeys with most cumbersome

---

59 Lawrence Haward, 'Prefatory Note,' in *Lands of the Bible: Pictures by Richard and Sydney Carline* (Manchester: City Art Gallery, 1921), p. 5. James Wood, in the 'Prefatory Note' of *the Goupil Gallery's* exhibition catalogue, similarly referred to the 'direct manner' of the Carlines' sketches. James Wood, 'Prefatory Note,' in *'"The East": Egypt, Palestine, Mesopotamia, Persia, India: A Series of Paintings by Sydney W. and Richard Carline* (London: William Marchant and Co, 1920).
60 See Wood, *The East*; and Haward, *Lands of the Bible*.
61 Edward Said, *Orientalism* (London: Penguin Books, 2003), p. 41.
62 Tromans, 'Introduction,' p. 14.
63 Haward, *Lands of the Bible*, p. 12.
64 Gertrude Bell to Hugh Bell, 15 February 1918, Gertrude Bell Archive.
65 Haward, *Lands of the Bible*, p. 12.
66 Hoshiar Nooraddin, 'Globalisation and the Search for Modern Local Architecture: Learning from Baghdad in Planning Middle Eastern Cities,' in *Planning Middle Eastern Cities: An Urban Kaleidoscope in a Globalising World*, ed. Yasser El-Sheshtawy (London: Routledge, 2004), p. 64.

loads'.[67] Judging by the catalogue description of the painting though, it was not signs of Baghdad's nascent modernity that appealed to Richard Carline in his visual evocation of the city. And for Sydney Carline the East's allure, when seen from the air, rested on the permanency of its 'historic places . . . since one's attention is not disturbed by the modern and incidental details'.[68] For the Carlines, and for many early twentieth-century British visitors to Mesopotamia, 'its contemporary reality [was] a mere obstacle to be overcome in the pursuit of greater knowledge of its history'.[69]

If Richard Carline's imagining of Baghdad replicated the configuration of the East in much Western art of the nineteenth century as a static and isolated world through its avoidance of obvious signs of modernity or of an alien presence, then a little-known British artist, Edith Cheesman, who visited Mesopotamia late in 1921, obliquely imagined the presence of both there.

Cheesman's watercolour, *The Site of the New Maude Memorial, Baghdad*, was reproduced in *The Near East* in August 1922 within an article titled 'A Bit of New Baghdad', and it discretely conveys the British presence within the city. Her painting depicts the boundary wall and gates of the Residency (the home of the British High Commissioner), behind which sprout a number of palm trees. In front of the wall is shown a large stretch of barren earth, presently occupied by a number of figures in Arab dress, but in the future, as the article informs, destined to be the site of the 'new Maude Memorial'.[70] Franklin Egan described Mesopotamia as 'a sacred land . . . filled with shrines'.[71] Directed only by the picture's title, viewers of Cheesman's discrete evocation of the British presence in the city – one that remained enmeshed within a picturesque configuration of Baghdad – were compelled to imagine a shrine to the British general who 'liberated' Baghdad.[72]

The title of Cheesman's watercolour, *New Street, Baghdad*, exhibited at Walker's Galleries in November 1922, indicates that the Baghdad she encountered was also not an ossified entity. Her painting shows the wide thoroughfare that had 'swept old and new away together' when cut through the city,[73] but Baghdad's exotic allure is retained through her depiction, on one side of the street, of a mosque with an elaborate green-tiled dome and minaret, and its picturesqueness, through the ramshackle market stalls shown lining the other. Two of Buchanan's cumbersomely loaded donkeys entering the foreground of the picture are granted pictorial prominence, but notably lacking is any indication of the motorised transport she had also associated with New Street. Cheesman offers, then, only a tentative evocation of Baghdad's modernity, one that, like the 'Maude' picture, remained ensconced within an exotic and picturesque purlieu, but bearing in mind the taste of the market at which her work was aimed this was perhaps understandable; too overt a depiction of prosaic modernity had the potential to jeopardise the accepted configuration of an exotic or picturesque East.

---

67 Zetton Buchanan, *In the Hands of the Arabs* (London: Hodder and Stoughton, 1921), p. 13.
68 'Painting in the Air,' *The Times*, 30 April 1921, p. 7.
69 Atia, 'A Relic of Its Own Past,' p. 233.
70 'A Bit of New Baghdad,' *The Near East*, 31 August 1922, p. 278.
71 Egan, *The War in the Cradle of the World*, p. 242.
72 'General Maude's Statue,' *The Near East*, 16 March 1922, p. 362. A one-and-a-quarter life size bronze equestrian statue of Maude was executed by Sir William Goscombe John R.A., and, according to a report in *The Near East*, was to 'stand on an imposing pedestal and platform . . . in front of the gates of the British Residency'.
73 Gertrude Bell to parents, 27 April 1917, Gertrude Bell Archive.

When P. G. Konody reviewed Cheesman's exhibition in the *Daily Mail* he referred to the 'picturesqueness' of her work.[74] Konody's description was, though, politically loaded. The opening of Cheesman's exhibition on 15 November coincided with the general election victory of the Conservatives under Bonar Law, who whilst campaigning had lamented Britain's role in Mesopotamia – 'I wish we had never gone there' – and came amidst a strident campaign in the *Daily Mail* damning the financial cost of Britain's continuing presence in Iraq.[75] So Konody's hope 'that the picturesqueness of [Cheesman's] scenes . . . will not be pleaded as an additional reason for the continued occupation of Arab lands at the expense of the British taxpayer' – an argument suggesting that others believed only a British presence in the region could ensure the survival of the Arab world's picturesqueness – not only toed his newspaper's editorial line, but thrust – by this date – a hackneyed visual configuration of the East into the midst of contemporary British politics.[76]

In May 1921, it was enough for the *Manchester Guardian* that the Carlines' picturesque images of Mesopotamia satisfied 'curiosity' and gave 'information as to what the East is like'. Edith Cheesman's similarly picturesque studies of Iraq, though, were considered by P. G. Konody in the *Daily Mail*, in November 1922, in much less neutral terms. Now, Konody hoped, Cheesman's evocation of Iraq's 'picturesqueness', would not be used as propaganda by those supporting Britain's continuing occupation of the country. That in the space of a mere eighteen months picturesque views of Iraq could serve such different purposes offers a hint as to the volatile atmosphere surrounding Mesopotamia/Iraq that existed in Britain in the years following the Armistice. This chapter has highlighted the various imaginative configurations of Mesopotamia/Iraq seen in British art at this time and has elaborated on the reasons for their construction, be they to meet the specific demands of a commissioning patron, such as the IWM, or the less explicit, though by the 1920s well-established requirements of a market especially geared to picturesque or exotic images produced by artist-travellers. This chapter has argued that how this work was perceived may have been influenced by the often polarised attitudes, then circulating in Britain, towards Mesopotamia/Iraq; a country at this time that, to use Said's felicitous phrase, was being 'prod[ded] into active life [and] made to enter history'.[77]

---

74 P.G. Konody, 'Nature's Palette: Pictures Made with Leaves and Vegetable Matter,' *Daily Mail*, 21 November 1922, p. 5.
75 'I Wish We Had Never Gone There – Mr Bonar Law on Mesopotamia, November 7th 1922,' *Daily Mail*, 18 November 1922, pp. 7–8.
76 Konody, 'Nature's Palette'.
77 Said, *Orientalism*, p. 240.

Chapter 10
Spaces of conflict and ambivalent attachments
Irish artists visualise the Great War

Nuala C. Johnson

Introduction

Ireland was simultaneously a bulwark of the Empire, and a mine within its walls. Irish people were simultaneously major participants in Empire and a significant source of subversion.[1]

The status of Ireland as kingdom or colony within the larger British imperial realm, after the Act of Union in 1800, has generated considerable historiographical debate over the last few decades.[2] Moreover it is only since the 1980s that the general literature on settler colonialism and imperialism has made anything other than very scant reference to Ireland as part of this story. However, from claims that, if economic exploitation was a condition of colonialism, Ireland could not be conceived as a financial asset to Britain in the nineteenth century,[3] to suggestions that the Irish Constabulary became a model of policing in most colonial police forces,[4] or that the National Education system introduced in 1831 was an exercise in cultural imperialism that marginalised the Irish language,[5] all studies indicate that Ireland's position within Britain's Empire was complex, at times contradictory, and operated on a number of diverse registers. As David Fitzpatrick puts it:

> The imprint of Ireland may thus be detected in virtually every colonial institution, ranging from schools and police forces to land law, fraternities, political parties, and churches.

---

1 Alvin Jackson, 'Ireland, the Union, and the Empire, 1800–1960,' in *Ireland and the British Empire*, ed. Kevin Kenny (Oxford: Oxford University Press, 2004), p. 123.
2 Terence McDonough, *Was Ireland a Colony?: Economics, Politics and Culture in Nineteenth-Century Ireland* (Dublin: Irish Academic Press, 2005); Stephen Howe, *Ireland and Empire: Colonial Legacies in Irish History and Culture* (Oxford: Oxford University Press, 2005); Pamela Clayton, *Enemies and Passing Friends: Settler Ideologies in Twentieth Century Ulster* (London: Verso, 1996); Liam Kennedy, *Colonialism, Religion and Nationalism in Ireland* (Belfast: Institute of Irish Studies, 1996).
3 Oliver McDonagh, *States of Mind: A Study of Anglo-Irish Conflict, 1780–1980* (London: Allen and Unwin, 1983).
4 David Anderson and David Killingray, eds, *Policing the Empire: Government, Authority and Control, 1830–1940* (Manchester: Manchester University Press, 1991).
5 John Coolahan, 'The Irish and Others in Irish Nineteenth-Century Textbooks,' in *The Imperial Curriculum: Racial Images and Education in British Colonial Experience*, ed. J.A. Mangan (London: Routledge, 1993), pp. 54–63; John Coolahan, *Irish Education: Its History and Structure* (Dublin: Institute of Public Administration, 1981); Nuala C. Johnson, 'Building a Nation: An Examination of the Irish Gaeltacht Commission Report of 1926,' *Journal of Historical Geography* 19 (1993): pp. 157–68.

Likewise, the imprint of Britain may be found in every Irish institution, signifying the ambiguity of Ireland's location in the Empire.[6]

Clayton has argued for the value of describing Ireland as a 'mixed colony', reflecting the religious, political and geographical diversity of the island, with Ulster representing the 'Imperial Province', while the remainder of the island represented 'Rebel Ireland'.[7] Others have claimed that Ireland's geographical proximity to Britain meant it was too near to be left alone, but rather than proposing an exceptionalist explanation of Ireland's place in the empire, they have alternatively suggested that all parts of the empire were in their own way distinctive, and that 'Ireland's defining peculiarity was that it stood at the world's metropolitan centre; but it was no less a British possession for that.'[8] Moreover, this location in part helps us understand the role of Irish people as both imperial subjects and active participants in the construction, management and maintenance of Britain's non-European empire. As Jackson observes, 'the Empire was simultaneously a chain and a key: it was a source both of constraint and of liberation.'[9]

While historians and others continue to investigate the complex relationship between the two islands, by the summer of 1914 nationalist and unionist forces in Ireland were sufficiently mobilised for the Cabinet in London to spend time in July poring over a map where '[t]he fate of nations appeared to hang upon the parish boundaries in the counties of Fermanagh and Tyrone'.[10] That the destiny of millions might hinge on the assassination of Archduke Ferdinand and his consort in Sarajevo was less obvious at the time. The declaration of war by Britain, however, did have significant implications for the crisis in Ireland. The Home Rule Bill would be placed on the statute book but Asquith made two provisos: the bill would not take effect until the First World War ended, and special amending legislation would provide the opportunity to make special provision for Ulster. While the bill was given Royal Assent on 1 September, Lyons observes '[t]he Irish problem had been refrigerated, not liquidated. Nothing had been solved and all was still to play for.'[11] The recruitment of Irish men and women into the war effort was influenced by alliances at home. The home front and battlefront were intimately connected and with volunteer military movements already mobilised in Ireland, partly trained and certainly motivated, the Great War provided an occasion for each side to display its political and strategic allegiances. The existence of 'private armies', including the Ulster Volunteer Force (UVF), the Irish Volunteers and the Citizen Army, with a collective membership of over a quarter of a million people, was

---

6 David Fitzpatrick, 'Ireland and the Empire,' in *The Oxford History of the British Empire: The Nineteenth Century*, ed. Andrew Porter (Oxford: Oxford University Press, 1999), p. 520.

7 Pamela M. Clayton, 'Two Kinds of Colony: "Rebel Ireland" and the "Imperial Province",' in *Was Ireland a Colony?: Economics, Politics and Culture in Nineteenth-Century Ireland*, ed. Terence McDonough (Dublin: Irish Academic Press, 2005), pp. 235–46.

8 Kevin Kenny, 'Ireland and the British Empire: An Introduction,' in *Ireland and the British Empire*, ed. Kevin Kenny (Oxford: Oxford University Press, 2004), p. 3.

9 Alvin Jackson, 'Ireland, the Union, and the Empire, 1800–1960,' in *Ireland and the British Empire*, ed. Kevin Kenny (Oxford: Oxford University Press, 2004), p. 136.

10 Paul Fussell, *The Great War and Modern Memory* (Cambridge: Cambridge University Press, 1975), p. 21.

11 F.S.L. Lyons, 'The Revolution in Train,' in *A New History of Ireland*, vol. 6, ed. W.E. Vaughan (Oxford: Oxford University Press, 2010), p. 144.

both an opportunity and a threat for the Crown.[12] Moreover 'the outbreak of war among the civilized nations of Europe promoted the view that violence was a legitimate, indeed necessary, means of attaining political ends.'[13] Recruitment campaigns proceeded apace as Unionists, Home Rulers and those with no explicit political affiliation responded to the call to arms.[14] This reflected a longer trajectory of Irish men, of all religious persuasions and social classes, who had joined the armed services and served in various corners of Britain's Empire during the nineteenth and early twentieth centuries. While military commissions were common amongst the Irish gentry, they were rare for the middle class or Catholic population. It is estimated that 150,000 men were raised in Ireland between 1865–1913, serving in imperial wars from South Africa to Bengal.[15]

The onset of war in Europe not only precipitated a renewed recruitment campaign for Irish military personnel but farmers also saw growth in production as British consumers relied more heavily on Irish agricultural output to compensate for the disruption of transoceanic trade. The munitions industry also expanded on the island as demand for armaments deepened as the war progressed.[16] However, as well as the military and economic role of Ireland in the First World War, the arts were also enlisted to record, represent and generate ideological support for the war effort. It is through art that we gain some insight into how the conflict was visually translated and how space and place were symbolised in the different arenas in which the war was conducted. One dimension of this was the recruitment poster campaign, which with the establishment of a separate recruiting board, the Central Council for the Organisation of Recruiting in Ireland in early 1915, provided a new, particularly Irish dimension to the use of visual imagery for recruitment.[17] War posters appealed to what were regarded as universal principles of duty and masculinity and domesticated them to specific national or imperial contexts. In the Irish case this included themes such as the duty of Irishmen to protect their agricultural homeland from invasion;

---

12 David Fitzpatrick, 'Militarism in Ireland, 1900–1922,' in *A Military History of Ireland*, ed. T. Bartlett and K. Jeffery (Cambridge: Cambridge University Press, 1996), pp. 379–406.

13 L.P. Curtis, 'Ireland in 1914,' in *A New History of Ireland*, vol. 6, ed. W.E. Vaughan (Oxford: Oxford University Press, 1996), p. 180.

14 There are several studies examining recruitment patterns in Ireland, including D. Howie and J. Howie, 'Irish Recruiting and the Home Rule Crisis of August–September 1914,' in *Strategy and Intelligence: British Policy during the First World War*, ed. M. Dockrill and D. French (London: Hambledon Press, 1996), pp. 1–22; Keith Jeffery, *Ireland and the Great War* (Cambridge: Cambridge University Press, 2011); Nuala C. Johnson, *Ireland, the Great War and the Geography of Remembrance* (Cambridge: Cambridge University Press, 2007), chap. 2; T. Bowman, 'Composing Divisions,' *Causeway* 2 (1995): pp. 24–9; Terence Denman, 'Sir Lawrence Parsons and the Raising of the 16th (Irish) Division, 1914–15,' *Irish Sword* 17 (1987): pp. 90–104; N. Perry, 'Nationality in the Irish Infantry Regiments in the First World War,' *War and Society* 12 (1994): pp. 65–95; P. Callan, 'Recruiting for the British Army in Ireland during the First World War,' *Irish Sword* 17 (1987): pp. 42–54.

15 Fitzpatrick, 'Ireland and the Empire,' pp. 511–12.

16 Jeffery, '*Ireland and the Great War*,' Catherine Pennell, *A Kingdom United: Popular Responses to the Outbreak of the First World War in Britain and Ireland* (Oxford: Oxford University Press, 2012).

17 C. Haste, *Keep the Home Fires Burning: Propaganda in the First World War* (London: Viking, 1977); for general overviews of the use of posters in the First World War. Also see: M. Rikards, *Posters of the First World War* (London: Evelyn, Adams and MacKay, 1968); J. Darracott, *The First World War in Posters* (London: Dover Publications, 1974).

positive stereotypes of a brave 'national character', where aggression would be fittingly channelled in the cause of a just war; and gendered appeals to volunteer in defence of the nation through allegorical representations of Ireland embodied in the figure of Hibernia.[18] These posters were primarily used to capture the imagination of the nationalist population as appeals to king, country and empire were sufficient stimuli to serve amongst unionists. Although it is notoriously tricky to provide precise numbers of Irish men and women who volunteered, it is estimated that around 50,000 men transferred from the 'private' armies already in existence at the outbreak of war, mainly from the UVF and Redmond's National Volunteers. A further 80,000 were recruited outside of these channels, and adding to the existing cadre of servicemen, the total number of Irish men in the wartime forces is estimated at 210,000. This excludes Irish people serving in the armies recruited in mainland Britain or from across its empire.[19] As well as the recruitment poster campaign, however, there were initiatives to enlist the visual arts more deeply as a means of representing the war to wider audiences at home. The fine arts provided a visual record of the war that could represent and interpret the various spaces in which the war was prosecuted, both in the fields of battle and in the factories, homes, training camps and hospitals located across the home front.

Recruiting the arts

Shortly after the war's outbreak, Chancellor of the Exchequer, David Lloyd George, was tasked with establishing the British War Propaganda Bureau, better known as Wellington House, the building in which it was headquartered in central London. Responding to the knowledge that Germany already had established a propaganda agency, the imperative to channel Britain's propaganda effort through an official department was realised, and Liberal MP Charles Masterman headed up the bureau.[20] Initially Wellington House devoted its time, in secrecy, to publishing and distributing pamphlets and books that promoted the government's view of the war. Enlisting some of the most significant writers of the day to support and work with the agency, including people such as Arthur Conan Doyle and Henry Newbolt, it produced over 1,100 pamphlets during the course of the conflict. These pamphlets supported Britain's role in the war and were directed at neutral states around the globe, particularly the United States.[21] A pictorial section was established in the bureau in 1916 in order to visually capture some arresting imagery of the conflict as experienced at the front and at home. This visual propaganda included the production of lanternslides, postcards, calendars, photographs, bookmarks and line drawings for worldwide distribution. The appetite for images, especially of the sites of battle, was intense, particularly amongst the editors of newspapers and illustrated publications. Photographs, however, were not meeting this huge demand for a pictorial record of the conflict. By 1916 newspapers were exploring

---

18 Johnson, *Ireland, the Great War and the Geography of Remembrance*; M. Tierney, P. Bowen and D. Fitzpatrick, 'Recruiting Posters,' in *Ireland and the First World War*, ed. D. Fitzpatrick (Dublin: Lilliput, 1988), pp. 47–58.

19 Fitzpatrick, 'Militarism in Ireland,' p. 383.

20 M.L. Sanders, 'Wellington House and British Propaganda During the First World War,' *The Historical Journal* 18 (1975): pp. 119–46.

21 P.M. Taylor, *British Propaganda in the 20th Century* (Edinburgh: Edinburgh University Press, 1999).

ways to procure new images for use in their publications and were offering monetary rewards to soldiers on the front to supply suitable line drawings. Moreover Masterman had learnt in the summer of 1916 that the renowned Scottish etcher and watercolourist, Muirhead Bone, had been called up for military service. He thought that the services of Bone might be better utilised by capitalising on his artistic talent rather than serving as an infantry officer. Consequently Bone was recruited as the first official war artist. He was sent to France and by October had produced over 150 drawings of life on the front.

Bone's drawings were published in ten monthly parts, beginning in 1916, and they proved very popular with the public, as they were both affordable and accompanied by an explanatory essay.[22] Collecting visual war memorabilia had begun. Moreover their popularity confirmed Masterman's view that drawing from the front would serve 'as a novel adjunct to the programme of pictorial propaganda'.[23] France and Germany had already recruited war artists to the battlefront, so the appointment of Muirhead Bone as the first official war artist meant that Britain was following a wider trend amongst combatant states to develop a painterly record of the conflict.[24] War art would also provide a permanent and influential visual evocation of the Great War in the imagination and memory of the public in the post-war period.

The move to establish an official war artist scheme also gained momentum when Eric Kennington's painting *The Kensingtons at Laventie* (1915) received critical and popular acclaim when it was exhibited in London in April 1916.[25] The *Times* reviewer captured the essence of the painting's impact: 'The picture convinces us that it is real life, but it is not at all like a photograph of the actual scene.'[26] Such adjudication indicated the potential for art to provide a visual record of the war that both engaged the viewer with the material dimensions of war but also, significantly, with the emotional and moral landscape of the conflict. Painting was seen to have the potential to generate an affective response to the battlefront that could be more compelling and transparent than photographic reproduction. As such, the capacity of art to elicit popular support for the war was increasingly recognised at the official level. The decision to establish a new Department of Information in February 1917, headed by the diplomat, historian and novelist John Buchan, and drawing on the expertise of key figures in the London arts scene, reinforced the state's commitment to using the visual arts to represent the war, and to re-deploying many existing artists who were serving as soldiers as specifically dedicated official war artists.

Whilst the initial intention of the scheme was to create a pictorial record, the appointment of Lord Beaverbrook, William Maxwell Aitken, as Director of the new Ministry of Information in March 1918 (which replaced the Department of Information) brought the longer-term commemorative role of war art to the fore. Beaverbrook, with his business and newspaper experience, aimed to make the artistic representation of the war serve a wider purpose as a memorial legacy to the conflict for future generations to

---

22 S. Malvern, *Modern Art, Britain and the Great War* (New Haven and London: Yale University Press, 2004).

23 P. Gough, *A Terrible Beauty: British Artists in the First World War* (Bristol: Sansom and Company, 2010), p. 23.

24 S. Hynes, *A War Imagined: The First World War and English Culture* (London: Bodley Head, 1990).

25 A. Weight, 'The Kensingtons at Laventie: A Twentieth Century Icon,' *Imperial War Museum Review* 1 (1986): pp. 14–18.

26 *The Times*, 20 May 1916, p. 4.

appreciate. Beaverbrook brought this ambition with him from his experience of leading the Canadian War Memorials scheme. He sought to guide the Ministry towards a wider remit of deploying the visual arts as an act of commemoration, the performance of which would have long-lasting effects on the public's imagination.[27] War art would become an archive as well as a propaganda tool and thus become part and parcel of a wider memorialising effort. As Gough explains, '[a]rguably the greatest legacy of the war's art was the scheme itself: under Beaverbrook's tutelage the Ministry for Information protected and promoted emerging artists, brought intellectual coherence to a previously haphazard programme of commissioning.'[28] It was within this political and cultural context that many of the most significant names in British war art were to emerge. From John and Paul Nash to Stanley Spencer, artists produced a large collection of exceptionally alluring and, at times, harrowing images of life on the battlefront. These works went on to become some of the most iconic visual images of the First World War, and their longevity is confirmed by their recirculation and reproduction in books, films, websites and galleries devoted to interpreting the material and cultural context of the war and its afterlife. In particular, but not exclusively, this archive is housed at the Imperial War Museum in London.[29] It is also within this official context that three Irish-born artists would make their contribution to the visual memory of the conflict but who would also be torn, to varying degrees, emotionally and ideologically, by the turbulent politics of Ireland in the second decade of the twentieth century. It is to the contribution of William Orpen, John Lavery and William Conor to the canon of war art that I now wish to turn and, in particular, to the spatial dynamics underpinning their pictorial encounter with the war both on the home front and in the arenas of battle. As Irish-born artists, working within a wider imperial realm, each contributed significantly but differently to representing the spaces of conflict. This reflected both their individual biographies as artists as well as the wider political and cultural environment in which they worked.

Confronting the theatre of battle: William Orpen, 1878–1931

By the outbreak of war William Orpen was one of the most acclaimed society portrait painters in Britain but as Upstone observes, '[t]he Great War marked a watershed in Orpen's life; he was never the same after it.'[30] As a celebrated and popular artist, with significant connections to the British establishment, in December 1915 Orpen enlisted for the Army Service Corps with a commission as Second Lieutenant and was stationed at the Adjutant's Office in Kensington Barracks. The Dubliner was born in 1878 into a wealthy, Protestant family and lived his early years at Oriel House in Stillorgan, a well-to-do suburb of the city. Although his father was a successful solicitor, both his parents and his eldest brother Richard were accomplished amateur artists, and Orpen's drawing talent was quickly recognised and nurtured by his parents. He enrolled in the Dublin Metropolitan School of Art at age 12, and although the art school specialised in industrial design, his painting skills

---

27 M. Harries and S. Harries, *The War Artists: British Official War Art of the Twentieth Century* (London: Michael Joseph, 1983).

28 Gough, *A Terrible Beauty*, p. 31.

29 Malvern, *Modern Art*; G. Kavanagh, 'Museum as Memorial: The Origins of the Imperial War Museum,' *Journal of Contemporary History* 23 (1988): pp. 77–97; Imperial War Museums's Art Collection, http://www.iwm.org.uk/collections-research/about/art-design.

30 R. Upstone, ed., *William Orpen: Politics, Sex and Death* (London: Philip Wilson, 2005), p. 34

were quickly recognised. In 1897 he moved to the Slade School in London (1897–1899) where he flourished, and it was during these years that his skills in portraiture developed and which 'may have derived from [t]his early impulse to commemorate and comment in paint upon those around him'.[31] In 1900 he exhibited – to much critical acclaim – his early oil paintings at the New English Art Club. He married Grace Knewstub, the daughter of a London art dealer, in 1901, but he was to have numerous extra-marital affairs with society ladies whom he painted and with the models he used in his studio.

As his reputation was building in Britain, Orpen also spent time teaching at the Dublin Metropolitan School of Art (1902–1914), at yearly or bi-yearly sessions. This brought him back to the home of his birth and into dialogue with friends and students with political allegiances different from his own. During these years Orpen met students of a nationalist persuasion, in particular Sean Keating, who became, for a time, his studio assistant in London. Keating discouraged Orpen from any involvement in the Great War.[32] At the school he also became friends with a gifted Protestant art student Grace Gifford, whom he captured in the portrait titled *Young Ireland*. She supported the increasingly influential nationalist movement, joined Sinn Féin, converted to Catholicism, and became an active promoter of the Irish cultural revival. She became engaged to Joseph Plunkett, one of the leaders of the Easter Rising 1916, and married him in his prison cell on the eve of his execution.[33] Despite their political differences she maintained her friendship with Orpen, now domiciled in England. While Foster claims that 'Protestant families like the Orpens lived at a distance from their Catholic neighbours, even those of the same class,'[34] it is clear that well-to-do Protestants did come into close personal and professional contact with Catholics and with those of differing political persuasions to themselves. Orpen was a close friend, for instance, of the collector and art dealer Hugh Lane and shared his ambition to create a museum of modern art in Ireland, while at the same time he supported the socialist James Larkin and his campaign to improve the employment conditions of the Irish working class. Many of Orpen's Irish paintings, however, reflected his critique of puritanism, piety and his view of the Catholic Church's influence in stifling progress towards modernity. This ambivalence towards Catholic culture is expressed in his painting *The Holy Well* (1915). His friend Sean Keating was modelled as the quintessential Connemara man, overlooking, with an air of disgust, the naked, head-bowed figures below him approaching the well of absolution which is overseen by a priest. While Orpen's pre-war engagement with Ireland was complex and ambivalent, it is notable that after 1915 he never visited the island again apart from one day-visit in 1918. Sean Keating had quit Britain prior to conscription and advised Orpen to '[c]ome back with me to Ireland. This war may never end . . . I am going to Aran. There is endless painting to be done,'[35] but Orpen decided to remain. If Ireland was in the throes of political turmoil Britain too was undergoing radical social and cultural upheaval on the eve of the war, and the conflict itself would transform the ideological

---

31 Ibid., p. 10.
32 J. Turpin, 'William Orpen as Student and Teacher,' *Studies: An Irish Quarterly Review* 68 (1979): pp. 173–92.
33 Upstone, *William Orpen*.
34 R. Foster, 'Orpen and the New Ireland,' in *William Orpen: Politics, Sex and Death*, ed. R. Upstone (London: Philip Wilson, 2005), p. 63.
35 S. Keating, 'William Orpen: A Tribute,' *Ireland Today* 2 (1937), p. 5.

landscape of the country.[36] With the introduction of the war artists' scheme, Orpen quickly secured himself a position and was posted to France. During this time he produced one of the largest collections of paintings of any of the official war artists and subsequently donated all his war work to the state.

In April 1917 Orpen arrived in France and stayed until March 1918. Unlike other war artists who were permitted three-week stints in France to prepare their work, Orpen was set no time limitations. He was provided with an official car and a chauffeur, and he personally employed a batman and a private secretary. While these special privileges reflected his status within British society, they also put him under pressure to produce effective images. The painter Paul Nash had observed that the look of the front was 'utterly indescribable',[37] and thus the visual arts might be more effective than texts to translate the landscape of war. The first phase of Orpen's work in France included portraits of Sir Douglas Haig and General Trenchard, mirroring his commercial success as a portrait painter and providing material that appealed to those in charge of the propaganda machine. He recorded his experiences at the front in a memoir titled *An Onlooker in France 1917–1919*. His first impressions of the Somme focussed on the physical destruction of the landscape:

> I shall never forget my first sight of the Somme battlefields. It was snowing fast, but the ground was not covered, and there was this endless waste of mud, holes and water. Nothing but mud, water, crosses and broken Tanks; miles and miles of it, horrible and terrible.[38]

For the Department of Information war artists' primary concern should be to document and record the war. As well as producing portraits of senior military personnel during the early months of his arrival in France, Orpen also produced some line sketches and watercolours of individual soldiers on the front line. *Man in the Glare: Two Miles from the Hindenburg Line* (1917) represents one of these moving studies of a young soldier facing his potential mortality on the battlefield and reflects a wider societal concern that the war was destroying a whole generation. While other war artists were delivering more interpretive representations of the front through reconstructed landscapes of destruction,[39] and with soldiers 'going over the top', Arnold observes, 'Orpen concentrated on the direct and factual encounter.'[40] When he returned to the Somme in the late summer of 1917 the landscape had transformed:

> Never shall I forget my first sight of the Somme in summer-time. I had left it mud, nothing but water, shell-holes, and mud – the most gloomy, dreary abomination of desolation the mind could imagine; and now in the summer of 1917, no words could express the beauty of it. The dreary, dismal mud was baked white and pure – dazzling white. White daisies,

---

36 Paul Fussell, *The Great War and Modern Memory* (Oxford: Oxford University Press, 1975); M. Higonnet, J. Jenson, S. Michel and M. Collins Weitz, eds, *Behind the Lines: Gender and Two World Wars* (New Haven: Yale University Press, 1989); M. Eksteins, *Rites of Spring: The Great War and the Birth of the Modern Age* (New York: Mariner Books, 2000).

37 Quoted in Fussell, *The Great War*, p. 170.

38 W. Orpen, *An Onlooker in France, 1917–1919* (Fairford and Glouchesterhire: Echo Library, 2010 edn). Originally published in London: Williams and Norgate, 1921, p. 16.

39 Malvern, *Modern Art*.

40 B. Arnold, *Orpen: Mirror of an Age* (London: Jonathan Cape, 1981), pp. 322–3.

red poppies and a blue flower, great masses of them, stretched for miles and miles ... It was like an enchanted land; but in the face of fairies there were thousands of little white crosses, marked 'Unknown British Soldier' for the most part.[41]

This transmogrified landscape drove Orpen to transform his approach to representing the battle zone. He altered his palette of colours to include mainly pastel shades: white, pea greens, soft lavenders, mauves, and clear blues for depicting the skies. This change of mood in his work enabled him to express pictorially nature's capacity to rejuvenate itself amidst a landscape of human destruction. As Gough observes:

> [A]n unusually piercing, acute and intense light that deflected off the seared white chalk casting bizarre shadows and extreme shifts in tone and colour. To an artist accustomed to the dusky opulence of cavernous Edwardian drawing rooms it came as a revelation.[42]

Dispensing with half tones and deploying shadowing and foreshortening to create effect, Orpen evoked this summer scene. *Dead Germans in a Trench* (1917) gives a flavour of the theatricality produced by this technique as the two long-dead German soldiers appear as if lit with artificial light beams, occupying the base of the trench and conveying the stark demarcation of a world divided between life and death. During this period Orpen produced at least eighteen oil paintings of the summer Somme landscape and although '[t]he evidence of death was all around him ... so was the evidence of life. Skulls and flowers were side by side ... Death is even more inscrutable in the face of beauty.'[43] The tension between the aesthetics of nature and the ugliness of warfare characterised much of his work in this period.

As the war wore on, 125 of his war works were exhibited at Agnew's gallery in London in May 1918, to considerable popular acclaim but mixed critical response. Some commentators regarded them as lacking sufficient sentiment, drama or action. It was during this exhibition that Orpen offered to donate all his war paintings to the state under the proviso that they were kept as a single collection. While the exhibition travelled to Manchester and the United States, any thoughts of showing the paintings in Dublin's National Gallery were shelved amidst fears about how such war paintings might be received in the aftermath of the 1916 Rising. These fears were exacerbated by the artist's close personal friendship with Colonel Lee who oversaw the execution of the rebellion's leaders in Dublin.[44]

Suffering from continual ill health, possibly from syphilis, and becoming increasingly depressed by the war, Orpen returned to France in July 1918. During this sojourn Orpen's work moved from the realism of his earlier paintings towards a more symbolic or allegorical approach to the conflict. In *The Mad Woman of Douai* (1918), perhaps one of his most disturbing war paintings, he evokes the destructive impulse on the civilian as well as the military population ushered in by the war (see Figure 10.1). In the midst of a devastated landscape sits a woman, seemingly having lost her reason, as wearied soldiers and local villagers appear either incapacitated or disinclined to comfort her.

The image represents the aftermath of a rape, a metaphor for German brutality that had circulated throughout the war. The violation, however, resides not solely in the body

---

41 Orpen, *An Onlooker in France*, p. 31.
42 Gough, *A Terrible Beauty*, p. 173.
43 Arnold, *Orpen: Mirror of an Age*, p. 320.
44 S. Dark and P.G. Konody, *Sir William Orpen: Artist and Man* (London: Seeley Service, 1932).

Figure 10.1 William Orpen, *The Mad Woman of Douai*, 1918

Source: © Imperial War Museum

of the woman herself but also on the ruined countryside enveloping the group. The warweary soldiers occupying the space display no appetite for sympathising with the woman's experience as they too, perhaps, have endured the ravaging of their bodies and minds over the course of four years of conflict. The psychological, as well as the corporeal, cost of war depicted in this painting represents as increasingly wide recognition that the war's effects were mental as well as physical.[45] The affective response to the war was not only felt by the

---

45 J. Bourke, *Dismembering the Male: Men's Bodies, Britain and the Great War* (Chicago: University of Chicago Press, 1996); J. Meyer, *Men of War: Masculinity and the First World War in Britain* (Basingstoke: Palgrave Macmillan, 2012); L. Zuckerman, *The Rape of Belgium: The Untold Story of World War I* (New York: New York University Press, 2004).

Spaces of conflict and ambivalent attachments 173

Figure 10.2 William Orpen, *To the Unknown British Soldier in France*, 1921–1928

Source: © Imperial War Museum

grieving families of dead soldiers but the emotional toll permeated civil society in wider ways and infiltrated the heads of soldiers who managed to survive the conflict. War art, as well as creative writing, attempted to capture some of these effects on men and reveal 'how spurious were their visions of heroism, and – by extension – history's images of heroism'.[46] The high incidence of shellshock, estimated as 40 per cent of casualties in the war zones by 1916, challenged earlier interpretations of male hysteria, and painting presented uncomfortable and dislocating representations of the effects of modern, mechanised and industrial warfare.

---

46 S. Gilbert, 'Soldier's Heart: Literary Men, Literary Women, and the Great War,' in *Behind the Lines: Gender and Two World Wars*, ed. M. Higonnet, J. Jenson, S. Michel and M. Collins Weitz (New Haven: Yale University Press, 1987), p. 201.

When the war ended Orpen remained in Paris, commissioned to document the peace negotiations on canvas. This culminated in the controversial memorialising painting *To the Unknown British Soldier in France* (1921–1928; see Figure 10.2).

Initially he methodically painted the principal politicians and servicemen involved in the conference, a total of thirty-six figures, gathered in the luxurious surroundings of the Hall of Peace. But then, without notifying the War Museum, he erased them all and replaced them with a coffin draped in the Union Jack and guarded by two semi-nude soldiers and cherubs in the air above. This painting was exhibited at the Royal Academy in 1923. Ridiculed by the establishment and the conservative press, the painting was hailed a triumph by the public who voted it the picture of the year. The left wing press concurred with such a view, with the *Daily Herald* claiming it 'a magnificent allegorical tribute to the men who really won the war'.[47] The Trustees of the Imperial War Museum rejected it though, and this prompted the *Liverpool Echo* to opine 'Orpen declines to paint the floors of hells with the colours of paradise, to pander to the pompous heroics of the red tab brigade.'[48] The painting evoked an embodiment of the heroism of the common soldier in the face of a hollow victory and seemed to touch a nerve amongst popular English audiences in the immediate post-war period where the memory of the conflict was still fresh. To mark the death of his friend, Earl Haig, in 1928, Orpen edited the painting. He erased the soldiers, the cherubs and the floral tributes and left only the coffin, the gilded marble façade framing it and the beam of light leading to the cross in the painting's background. The Imperial War Museum accepted the revised painting.

Orpen's final years were spent often estranged from his family and friends. A hugely successful artist during his lifetime, his work entered relatively obscurity in the aftermath of his death in 1931, only to be resurrected by retrospective exhibitions from the 1970s onward including two staged in the National Gallery of Ireland in 1978 and 2005. William Orpen initially confronted life on the Western Front with some enthusiasm and with the imprimatur of key establishment figures. His talent as a portrait painter in London was mirrored in his early paintings of key military leaders. As the war progressed, however, his approach became bleaker, as he attempted to capture the landscape at the front as experienced by ordinary soldiers. While his war work did not achieve the critical acclaim of other official artists, the impact of the conflict on his painting and on his health more generally, would have enduring effects on his life that proved more potent than any patriotic connections he might have had to his place of birth. Independent Ireland was to remain increasingly remote from either his personal or professional life as an artist.

Capturing the home front: John Lavery's war, 1856–1941

In contrast to William Orpen, John Lavery, the son of a struggling wine and spirit merchant, was born in 1856 in North Queen Street, Belfast and baptised in St Patrick's Catholic Church on Donegall Street. His father Henry Lavery was drowned three years later on a voyage onboard the American vessel the *Pomona*, when it struck a sandbank off the coast of Wexford, and his mother Mary Donnelly died shortly afterwards, leaving him and his two siblings orphans. He was sent to live with his uncle on his farm near Moira, County Down

---

47   Gough, *A Terrible Beauty*, p. 196.
48   Ibid., p. 197.

before moving, at age 10, to more prosperous relatives in Saltcoats Ayrshire. His creative talents began with a three-year apprenticeship at J. B. McNair's photographic studio in Glasgow where he developed his drawing skills as he touched up negatives and colour prints. In 1874 he started taking classes at the Haldane Academy of Arts in Glasgow, with the aim of becoming a portrait artist. Over the next few years he continued to work with photographers, and when a studio he was renting was gutted by fire, he received £300 from the insurance company. He then moved to London where he enrolled in 1879 in the Heatherley School of Art before travelling to Paris to study at the Académie Julian.[49] It was in Paris that some of his early paintings were first exhibited and where he met James McNeill Whistler. On returning to Glasgow he became increasingly associated with the emerging Glasgow School, a group of artists noted particularly for their use of Impressionist and Post-Impressionist techniques.[50] In 1888, in a stroke of good fortune, he obtained a prestige commission to record Queen Victoria's visit to the International Exhibition in the city. This provided him with the platform to become a significant society painter and, after spending some time in Morocco, he returned to Glasgow and married, in 1889, Kathleen McDermott, a local flower-seller. They had one child, Eileen, before Kathleen died of tuberculosis in 1891.

In the years following Lavery travelled Europe extensively and his work was gaining recognition amongst continental artists and galleries. Moreover his artistic reputation was also gaining traction at home. He was elected to the Royal Scottish Academy in 1896 and moved to 5 Cromwell Place, Kensington, in 1896. This address would remain significant as both his home and the studio in which some of his most well-known works, including war paintings, were produced.[51] In 1903 he met the Irish American artist, socialite and heiress, Hazel Martyn Trudeau, and they married in 1909 in a union that would see her become the most significant model-muse of his artistic career. She appears in over 400 of his paintings both as the subject of portraits but also as the model for other works. 'The Artist's Studio' (1910–13), produced just before the war, features Hazel, Eileen (John's daughter from his first marriage) and Alice (his stepdaughter) and illustrates the continued influence of Velázquez's *Las Meninas* (The Maids of Honor) in early twentieth-century art. The painting also underscores the significance of Hazel Lavery to his career – where she would exert a long-term influence on his work.[52] The Laverys took trips to Tangier and other North African locations between 1910–1914, and John painted these 'exotic' landscapes and people, following on from the Orientalist tradition of the nineteenth century.[53] McConkey claims that through such excursions '[c]olourfully clad Moors, Berbers and Nubians became the painter's antidote to society ladies, who habitually arrived in the studio [in London] dressed in black and grey'.[54] Tours to Venice and Wengen, where he also painted *en plein air*, provided an additional escape from the routine of portraiture that occupied much of his time at his London studio.

---

49 T. Snoddy, 'Sir John Lavery,' *Dictionary of Irish Biography* (2010), accessed 10 November 2015, http://dib.cambridge.org/viewReadPage.do?articleId=a4701.

50 R. Billcliffe, *The Glasgow Boys* (London: Frances Lincoln, 2009); J. Burkhauser, *Glasgow Girls: Women in Art and Design, 1880–1920* (Edinburgh: Canongate Press, 1993).

51 Snoddy, 'Sir John Lavery'.

52 S. McCoole, *Hazel: A Life of Lady Lavery* (Dublin: Lilliput Press, 1996).

53 K. McConkey, 'The White City: Sir John Lavery in Tangier,' *Irish Arts Review* (1989–90): pp 55–63.

54 K. McConkey, *Sir John Lavery: A Painter and His World* (Edinburgh: Atelier, 2010), p. 117.

In 1913 the Laverys visited the picturesque lakes beside Killarney House, in County Kerry, where John was to paint a portrait of Lady Dorothy Browne. But it was here that he started to develop the idea for his religious triptych *The Madonna of the Lakes* (1917). The Killarney mountain landscape and its lakes formed the backdrop for the painting while Hazel represented the Madonna; Alice, the young St Patrick; and Eileen as St Brigid. The composition was emblematic of the devotional significance of Our Lady to Irish Catholicism and the increasingly iconic status of these two saints to Irish identity. Their friend Edwin Lutyens was commissioned to design the frame using Celtic spiral motifs. When exhibited at the Royal Academy in 1919 it was hailed as 'an enormous advance on anything to be seen in modern religious painting'.[55] Lavery donated it to the church in Belfast where he was baptised; and it consolidated his wife's iconic status in his work. The painting's execution during the years between the start of the Great War and the Easter Rising illustrates the complex loyalties the family had between his success as well-respected portrait painter in London and their strong Irish affiliations. Indeed the Laverys spent increasing time in Ireland, and at the outbreak of the war in 1914 they were visiting Dublin and Wicklow. Hazel Lavery's Galway ancestry, alongside her husband's Catholic Belfast roots, prompted him 'to ponder more deeply the question of national allegiance'.[56] Moreover their social circle in Dublin brought him into direct contact with many of the key supporters of the Home Rule movement.

However on their return to London in the late summer of 1914 the impact of the war was immediately apparent. Lavery set about depicting the war's destructive force in his early painting *The First Wounded, London Hospital August 1914* (1915). The picture was exhibited at the Royal Academy and won critical and popular acclaim from a public increasingly hungry to see the effects the war at home.[57] The composition, set in a London military hospital, appealed to a large audience because it conveyed the immediate wounds of war and domesticated the conflict for those at some distance from the sites of battle. Moreover it also provided an insight into the medical and nursing care provided to these early casualties of the war. Unlike Orpen, Lavery's chronicling of the Great War was to be from the perspective of the home front.[58] He joined the Artists' Rifles in 1915 but because of his age and health was advised by his doctor that his contribution to the war effort should be made through visually depicting the conflict rather than fighting in it. Initially he continued with his portrait commissions, painting political leaders including Winston Churchill, John Redmond (leader of the Irish Parliamentary Party) and Edward Carson (leader of Ulster Unionists). His immediate attitude to the Easter Rising in April 1916 is difficult to discern, but it is acknowledged that he supported the idea of introducing conscription to Ireland, although the Military Service Act (1916) never applied to the island.

While Lavery was anxious to travel independently to the Front to witness the war first-hand, under military restrictions there was no possibility of him securing permission. While he spent some time in early 1917 in St Jean de Luz and painted its harbour, he was never to get close to the action at the front lines, and consequently his war paintings evoked conditions on the home front. In July 1917 twenty-one German Gotha biplanes carried out

---

55   Ibid., p. 30.
56   Ibid., p. 124.
57   M.P. Park and R.H.R. Park, 'Art in Wartime: The First Wounded, London Hospital, August 1914,' *Medical Humanities* 37 (2011): pp. 23–6.
58   P. Cooksley, *The Home Front: Civil Life in World War One* (London: The History Press, 2006).

an aerial bombardment of London. These were clearly visible from Lavery's Cromwell Place studio and provided inspiration for one of his most iconic war paintings. He captured the scene on canvas depicting Hazel, with her back to the viewer, kneeling before a statue of the Madonna as the sky outside erupted in the aerial battle between German bombers and British defence forces (see Figure 10.3).

Figure 10.3   John Lavery, *Daylight Raid From My Studio Window*, 1917

Source: © National Museums Northern Ireland Collection Ulster Museum

Depicting this attack on the capital by combining the domesticity of their interior world of home and studio, with the aerial war being conducted outside their window conveyed to the public that the conflict was not just conducted in spaces afar across the English Channel but that it was intimately bound up with the lives of those who remained at home.[59]

Lavery was increasingly keen to play an official role in representing the war, and with the establishment of the new Department of Information under the stewardship of John Buchan, his opportunity arose to become an official war artist. His desire followed the wider motivation of artists 'to witness, interpret and leave some form of personal testimony was a powerful incentive to those who needed to come to terms with their violent muse'.[60] However Lavery, now in his early 60s, was restricted to home front duty and was issued with a Special Joint Naval and Military Permit. He initially went to Scotland to draw the fleet at anchor in the Firth of Forth and made several paintings including *The Forth Bridge 1917, Bluejackets Landing* (1917; see Figure 10.4).

The image depicts the bridge itself, the grand fleet of the Royal Navy at some distance in the background and in the foreground naval personnel disembarking from a vessel moored at a jetty. While much of the work of the official war artists captured life of the infantry soldier at the front, this image highlighted the significant role of the navy in the prosecution of this conflict. On his way to Edinburgh he stopped at Newcastle-upon-Tyne

Figure 10.4 John Lavery, *The Forth Bridge 1917, Bluejackets Landing*, 1917

Source: © Imperial War Museum

---

59 T. Chapman, *IWM: The First World War on the Home Front* (London: Andre Deutsch, 2014).
60 Gough, *A Terrible Beauty*, p. 32.

and visited the munitions factories at Elswick. Lavery portrayed this interior space as a visual representation of the industrial scale of production underpinning the industrial speed of killing along the battlefronts. In *Munitions, Newcastle, 1917* the size of the machinery and weaponry of war dwarfs the workforce responsible for their production. The vast girders, the armaments themselves, under the high ceilings in which they were contained, conveyed the enormous human and technological effort invested to provide the infrastructure of what would later be described as the first modern war. The transformation in gender roles that the war precipitated as women became centrally involved in the manufacture of weapons is also highlighted.[61] His final commission, as the war ended in 1918, was to provide the Imperial War Museum with a series of paintings for their Women's Work collection, including *The Cemetery, Etapes* (1919). Lavery's contribution to the corpus of war art earned him a knighthood.

In the years after the war Lavery's connections to Ireland deepened as he produced numerous paintings of politicians and churchmen on both sides of the political divide. The family established a strong friendship with the nationalist leader Michael Collins, and they provided their London house as a retreat for the Irish delegation that arrived in England to negotiate the terms of the Anglo-Irish Treaty. After independence Lavery continued his close connections with Ireland. He completed several portraits of Irish Free State politicians and donated many of his works to the Hugh Lane Municipal Gallery in Dublin and the Belfast Museum. Moreover Hazel Lavery served as model for John when commissioned to produce an allegorical image of Ireland, an image that was subsequently used on Irish banknotes from 1928–1975 and became the watermark on Euro notes introduced in 2002. Lavery died in 1941 in Kilkenny, where he was the guest of his stepdaughter, and was buried beside his wife in Putney Vale cemetery.

The Irish home front: William Conor, 1881–1968

If Orpen and Lavery were both artists of the British establishment living mainly in London by the time war broke out in 1914, William Conor's feet were more firmly placed in Ireland. Moreover he was not an official war artist, so his response to the conflict was not mediated through the lens of the Department of Information. Conor was born in 1881 in north Belfast to a working class Presbyterian family. His father William Connor – who spelled his surname with a double n – was a sheet-metal worker and a gasfitter. Conor's mother, Mary Wallace, bore seven children, and William was fourth. He attended the local primary school in Avoca Street and although the family frequently moved house they remained in the same neighbourhood in the north of the city. At school Conor's drawing talent was recognised, and he was accepted into the Belfast Government School of Design, the forerunner to the Belfast College of Art, at the age of 13. These provincial schools aimed to train their pupils in design and drawing for industry and commercial enterprises rather than in fine art. In Belfast trainees were employed mainly in the linen industry to design damasks and wrappings or in lithographic and poster companies. In 1904 Conor joined the firm of David Allen and Son as an apprentice lithographic poster designer. He became

---

61 S. Ouditt, *Fighting Forces, Writing Women: Identity and Ideology in the First World War* (London: Routledge, 1994); A. Woollacott, *On Her Their Lives Depend: Munitions Workers in the Great War* (Los Angeles: University of California Press, 1994).

known as the 'black man', as his job entailed using black ink and lithographic chalk applied directly onto a lithographic stone for the production of posters. Poster design required the conveying of clear messages that could be easily read at a distance and thus the training instilled Conor with a disciplined approach to his craft, in terms of the balance and legibility of the posters. Through the constant use of the greasy lithographic chalk Conor developed a liking for using crayon as a drawing medium, a method he would employ through the rest of his career.[62]

While lithography provided Conor with a living and developed his skills in poster design, his artistic ambitions outweighed the experience gained at David Allen, and so he gave up the job around 1910 and devoted himself full-time to painting. He began to exhibit his work at the Belfast Art Society, a forerunner to the Royal Ulster Academy, and he regularly visited the Central Reference Library in Belfast city centre to study art books – in particular, works devoted to physiognomy. It is thought that he intended to focus on portraiture. As the Irish Literary Revival gathered pace, Conor was exposed to it through plays by Yeats and Synge staged in Belfast's theatres.[63] Moreover he visited the Blasket Islands, in County Kerry, which had been the focus of much scholarly inspiration of the Gaelic Revival.[64] In 1912 Conor, following the other Belfast artist Paul Henry, visited Paris for several months during which he may have spent some time working in the studio of the Cubist painter André Lhote.[65] He returned to Belfast having absorbed some of the atmosphere of the Parisian art scene.

At the outbreak of war Conor visited munitions works and army training camps in Belfast and at Ballykinlar in County Down. Jeffery observes that '[f]rom the start of the war Conor painted the mobilization of the Protestant Belfast working class.'[66] In 1914 he visited the military training camp at the Clandeboye estate in County Down where he witnessed first-hand the training of the 36th Ulster Division. Conor's war was very much based on the home front – the intimate spaces of community – where the war's effects were being simultaneously translated to military and civilian populations. One his most celebrated images was the mobilisation in 1915 of the 36th Ulster Division before their transportation to England and onward to the Western Front (see Figure 10.5).

He produced it on paper, using his customary charcoal and chalk technique, and evoked three young men heading off to battle. Neatly decked out in their Division's uniform, two of the young men appear happily and nonchalantly marching off towards their destiny. This characterisation mirrored the languages of duty, adventure and heroism evident in most early literary interpretations of the conflict.[67] The older-looking soldier, carrying a bayonet over his shoulder and gazing towards the artist in a more determined and serious manner, tempers the innocence of the youthful generation of men behind him. The prospect of fighting for 'King and Country' and in defence of the Union, which motivated much of the mobilisation of the 36th Ulster Division, seems to have had a strong impact on Conor's

---

62 M. Anglesea, *William Conor: The People's Painter* (Belfast: W&G Baird in association with the Ulster Museum, 1999).

63 J.L. Pethica, 'The Irish Literary Revival,' in *A Companion to British Literature*, ed. R. DeMaria, H. Chang and S. Zacher (Oxford: Wiley, 2014), pp. 160–74.

64 I. Lucchitti, 'The Blasket Islands and the Literary Imagination,' *Shima* 7 (2013): pp. 1–10.

65 Anglesea, *William Conor*.

66 Keith Jeffery, 'William Conor's People's War,' *History Ireland* 22 (2014): p. 43.

67 Fussell, *The Great War*; Hynes, *A War Imagined*; R.M. Bracco, *Merchants of Hope: British Middlebrow Writers and the First World War, 1919–39* (Oxford: Berg, 1993).

Spaces of conflict and ambivalent attachments 181

Figure 10.5 William Conor, *Off, the Ulster Division*, 1915

Source: © The Estate of William Conor Collection Ulster Museum

interpretation of the war's effect on the home front.[68] For Ulster Protestants fighting in the Great War was never disentangled from political events at home and from their opposition to Home Rule. Conor would have been well aware of these debates in his hometown of Belfast.

---

68 P. Orr, *The Road to the Somme: Men of the Ulster Division Tell Their Story* (Belfast: Blackstaff, 1987); R. English and G. Walker, *Unionism in Modern Ireland: New Perspectives on Politics and Culture* (Dublin: Gill and Macmillan, 1996); A.T.Q. Stewart, *The Ulster Crisis: Resistance to Home Rule, 1912–14* (London: Faber & Faber, 1967); G. Doherty, ed., *The Home Rule Crisis, 1912–14* (Cork: Mercier Press, 2014).

During Christmas 1916 Conor's crayon drawings of the Ulster Division's military camps were exhibited at Belfast City Hall and auctioned to raise money for the UVF hospitals. They made over £100. He also illustrated the Ulster Division's charge at Thiepval on 1 July 1916, which was reproduced as prints and sold for 6d and as Christmas postcards retailing at a penny each. Conor's experience as a commercial lithographer continued to inform his work during the war and provided much-needed funds for the UVF's hospitals. This work also highlighted the significant practical role that war art could play in supporting Britain's war effort at home and abroad, and for Ulster unionists, it underwrote their loyalty to monarch and empire.

As well as portraying military personnel, Conor also produced images of civilian life on the home front and especially the contribution of women to the war. While Pašeta points out that munitions factories were not as widespread in Ulster as in other regions of the United Kingdom,[69] James Mackie, Chairman of the Belfast engineering works Mackie and Sons, employed Conor in 1917 to record the munitions workers he had recruited for war work. The factory in west Belfast produced about 75 million shells during the war and, as was customary elsewhere, Mackie hired 'foundry girls' to supplement his predominantly male workforce.[70] Conor based his drawing on Madeleine Ewart, fourth daughter of William Ewart (who owned one of the linen factories in the city). She had worked in munitions until her marriage in 1917. In *Munition Worker at Mackies* (1917), she is portrayed operating a turret lathe which manufactured 18-pound shrapnel shells. The image was produced on paper using watercolour. As Jeffery observes, Conor's war art embodies a more localised and domestic approach to the conflict: '[i]ndividual people soldiers, nurses, workers – caught up in the cataclysm of the war are at the core of his images'.[71] It is precisely the intimacy of his drawings and paintings and, at times, their naïve quality that transports the viewer into the ordinary spaces of activity that the Great War produced for the residents of Belfast.

After the war Conor briefly spent time in London where he met Orpen, Lavery, and Augustus John amongst others. In 1921 he returned to Belfast and was commissioned, at the suggestion of Lavery, to paint the *Opening of the First Northern Ireland Parliament* at City Hall. But it was his commitment to drawing the life of the ordinary people of his native city that would remain his most enduring legacy – as he continued to paint life in the shipyard, the bustling street, the factory, the cinema until his death in 1968.

Afterlife: drawing support in the decade of centenaries

The contribution of three Irish painters – two Belfast men and one Dubliner – to immortalising the war effort on canvas is attracting more attention in discussions of Ireland's role in the Great War. The visual arts provide an enduring and provocative insight into how the spaces of war were calibrated by those not directly involved in combat. In the case of Ireland's 'war' artists, both Lavery and Orpen shared some similarities, most notably, enjoying highly successful careers in England as portrait painters of the social elite of the day. Both men were also keen to serve in the war effort and the official war artists' scheme afforded them

---

69 S. Pašeta, 'Women and War in Ireland, 1914–18,' *History Ireland* 22 (2014): pp. 24–7.
70 Woollacott, *On Her Their Lives Depend*.
71 Jeffery, 'William Conor's People's War,' p. 44.

such an opportunity. Their difference in age, however, coupled with Orpen's significant contacts with the political establishment, meant that he would paint at the war front while Lavery would be confined to depicting the war's impact at home in mainland Britain. They both produced portfolios of work that contained many arresting images of the human and physical costs of war, and each, in their own way, spoke to the emotional and moral questions raised by four years of conflict. They were both rewarded with knighthoods. William Conor, by contrast, was far more connected literally and allegorically to the city of his birth and to the working class Protestant, Ulster background from which he came. His war paintings were created – both from the lithographic training he received in his youth and the commercial potential of postcard drawings, posters and prints – to raise funds in support of the war effort and the UVF hospitals in particular. Moreover his depictions of soldiers in training and munitions personnel at work spoke to the localised effects of war on the day-to-day life of Ulster's industrial city. The Dubliner Orpen, who had many personal connections with Irish nationalists, over time, distanced himself from the political turmoil that enveloped Ireland during the war. His retreat in the post-war years from family and friends, both in England and Ireland, perhaps is emblematic of the significant long-term impact serving as a war artist on the front had on his psychological and physical well-being. By contrast, the Belfast man Lavery maintained a longer and deeper relationship with the island of his birth, and whilst his ultimate political views remain below the surface, the legacy of his artistic output indicates a highly nuanced set of geographies of allegiance. It is precisely the complexity of these loyalties, mirrored in his paintings, that renders his work, symbolic of the entangled topologies of identity and memory, prevalent on these islands from the First World War to the present. Conor remained in the city of his birth and witnessed first-hand the emergence of Northern Ireland and some of the sectarian divisions that would characterise life in the city, particularly in its poorer neighbourhoods. All of these artists performed the war through visual rather than verbal media. The communication of life in the trenches and at home, under wartime conditions, was translated through the vocabulary of the painterly image, evoking landscapes of death and domesticity that reflected both their personal experiences and the wider geographies of identity each held. Their paintings and drawings reinforce the significance of space in the conduct of war and demonstrate the interconnectedness between soldiers fighting in the trenches in France and the infrastructural, economic and political support chains that supported this effort at home. The emotional registers that the Great War provoked for each painter speak to the deeper complexities of their ideological and affective commitments to Ireland, before, during and after the First World War.

Chapter 11
Empire and nation in Canadian and Australian First World War exhibitions, 1917–1922

Jennifer Wellington

In Britain the First World War is entrenched in popular culture as a futile tragedy in which incompetent leadership led to countless, purposeless deaths.[1] This perception of the war is in marked contrast to the entrenched view in both Canada and Australia – culturally similar British settler societies that fought as part of the British Imperial forces during the war. In Australia and Canada, the war is popularly remembered as, while tragic, the site of the birth of the modern nation.[2] This chapter will discuss one way in which this divergent view began to be produced, by briefly sketching how Canadian and Australian officials in London, both independently and in interactions with British government and military bodies, collected and exhibited war representations and material. In particular, this chapter will focus on the construction, promotion and consumption of Canadian and Australian official war photograph exhibitions and how these exhibitions capitalised on popular desires for an 'authentic' connection with the experience of war. Curators used this desire to connect with the front line experience to emotively impress upon audiences the heroism and grit of Australian and Canadian soldiers when faced with the dramatic 'reality' of war. Thus, exhibitions stressed the significance of the dominions' role in the war, and by implication, buttressed Australian and Canadian claims to a greater stature within the empire.

Britain, Canada and Australia all founded national war museums during the First World War, creating large collecting apparatuses and commissioning officers to write histories, collect artefacts and organise artists and photographers to record the conflict. During the war, they all exhibited war photographs, war art and war trophies in London and various

---

1 For commentary on this perception, see Adrian Gregory, *The Last Great War: British Society and the First World War* (Cambridge and New York: Cambridge University Press, 2008), p. 4; Dan Todman, *The Great War: Myth and Memory* (London: Hambledon Continuum, 2005); and generally Paul Fussell, *The Great War and Modern Memory* (Oxford: Oxford University Press, 1975).

2 For extended commentary on the absence of such a 'futility wave' of interpretation of the Great War in the British Dominions, see Mark David Sheftall, *Altered Memories of the Great War: Divergent Narratives of Britain, Australia, New Zealand and Canada* (London and New York: I.B. Tauris, 2009); Mark Sheftall, 'Mythologising the Dominion Fighting Man: Australian and Canadian Narratives of the First World War Soldier, 1914–39,' *Australian Historical Studies* 46, no. 1 (2015): pp. 81–99; Jonathan Vance, *Death So Noble: Memory, Meaning and the First World War* (Vancouver: University of British Columbia Press, 1997); Tim Cook, 'Battles of the Imagined Past: Canada's Great War and Memory,' *The Canadian Historical Review* 95, no. 3 (2014): pp. 417–26; John F. Williams, *The Quarantined Culture: Australian Reactions to Modernism 1913–1939* (Cambridge: Cambridge University Press, 1995); Marilyn Lake, 'Mission Impossible: How Men Gave Birth to the Australian Nation – and Other Seminal Acts,' *Gender & History* 4, no. 3 (1992): pp. 305–22; Robin Gerster, *Big-Noting: The Heroic Theme in Australian War Writing* (Carlton: Melbourne University Press, 1992).

provincial centres around Britain. These exhibitions were organised by government bodies and were aimed at encouraging a sense of connection and commitment to continue prosecuting the war, as well as promoting enlistment and financial support for the war via buying war bonds.

The story of collecting and exhibiting the war was not, however, one of blunt state coercion. The public, be they civilians or members of the armed forces, *wanted* to see images and objects which provided them with as authentic a connection to the war as possible. War relics, particularly objects from the battlefield, provided this sense of authenticity through their apparent proximity to the experience of war. Direct contact – viewing them or touching them – created a sense of connection to the dramatic events of the war, and to friends, sweethearts and family members at the front. Soldiers themselves collected with great enthusiasm (some more enthusiastically than others) as a way of staking a claim to and remembering their own experiences.[3] State agencies capitalised on these genuine popular desires, with officials encouraging soldiers to contribute items they had 'souvenired' to national collections for display after the war.[4] For their part, soldiers mocked these official collecting efforts in their own publications (see Figure 11.1). In September 1918, for example, the authors of the Australian Imperial Force 6th Battalion's trench newspaper contended that after the war, a dialogue between a visitor and a local might proceed as follows:

Visitor in Aussie:	'Can you tell me what that tremendous great big building is?'
The Aussie:	'Yes, it's this way, the War Museum they built wouldn't hold all the 6th Bn trophies, so they built an Annex, then after the 2nd of August stunt, they built this place as an Annex to the Annex to hold the trophies the 6th Bn captured then.'
Visitor:	'And what is that little place across the street?'
Aussie:	'Oh, that's where we're goin' to billet the 6th Bn when they get back.'[5]

Canadian officials asserted control over collecting and representing the war very early on. This was partially a matter of logistics – Canada was much farther from where its armed forces were fighting than Britain was, Canadian troops unlike their British counterparts

---

3 For literature on soldiers and souvenir or trophy collecting, Paul Cornish, '"Just a Boyish Habit" . . .? British and Commonwealth War Trophies in the First World War,' in *Contested Objects: Material Memories of the Great War*, ed. Nicholas J. Saunders and Paul Cornish (New York: Routledge, 2009), pp. 11–25; Cook, Tim. '"Tokens of Fritz": Canadian Soldiers and the Art of Souveneering in the Great War,' *War & Society* 31, no. 3 (2012): pp. 211–26; Denis Winter, *Death's Men: Soldiers of the Great War* (London: Penguin, 1979), p. 206; Nicholas J. Saunders, *Trench Art: Materialities and Memories of War* (Oxford and New York: Berg, 2003). On dehumanising the enemy and trophy hunting in the Pacific War, see James J. Weingarter, 'Trophies of War: U.S. Troops and the Mutilation of Japanese War Dead, 1941–45,' *Pacific Historical Review* 61, no. 1 (1992): pp. 53–67.

4 For contemporary accounts of these activities, see for example C.E.W. Bean, 'The Australian War Records: An account of the present development overseas and a suggestion of course necessary to be taken at the end of the War,' 38 3DRL 6673/362, Australian War Memorial (AWM); 'National War Museum,' 31 August 1917, Origins & Scope 1917, EN1/1/MUS/25/2 A3/3, pp. 2–3, Imperial War Museum (IWM), London.

5 *Ça Ne Fait Rien*, 6 Bn. A.I.F. Newspaper, September 4, 1918, near Hamel. Held in the collections of the AWM.

Figure 11.1 An image cropped from *Ça Ne Fait Rien*, 6 Bn AIF newspaper, 4 September 1918

Source: Australian War Memorial

could not easily go home on leave, and far fewer objects were able to move from France and Belgium to Canada than to Britain. It was also partly the result of the energetic efforts of a few influential Canadians. Although these well-connected Canadians initiated their collecting and recording activities prior to the formal articulation of central government policy, there was little question such endeavours would soon become part of an official undertaking. Very early in the war, the Canadian newspaper baron, Sir Max Aitken (styled Lord Beaverbrook from 1917) appointed himself Canadian Eye Witness, obtained the honorary rank of lieutenant-colonel in the Canadian militia and received authorisation to attend GHQ in France.[6] Having subsequently acquired official backing, Aitken opened the Canadian War Records Office in January 1916. As early as August 1915, the Dominion Archivist Sir Arthur Doughty suggested to the government that it establish a policy for

---

6 See A.J.P. Taylor's energetically worded account of Beaverbrook's activities in A.J.P. Taylor, *Beaverbrook* (London: Hamish Hamilton, 1972), p. 87.

collecting war trophies.[7] By the spring of 1916, Doughty, who also acted as the Deputy Minister of Public Records, had travelled to Europe on business for the Public Archives and acquired a large collection of war trophies as a gift from the French Government.[8] Doughty ensured that war trophies continued to be collected and began to be shipped to Canada for exhibition. In October 1917 the government staged its first show, in aid of the Red Cross, in Halifax, Nova Scotia, where the war mementos had been brought ashore.[9] Officials framed such projects as components of a multifaceted and exhaustive attempt to record 'Canada's entire connection with the war'.[10]

In contrast to the more official impetus for collecting in Canada, in February 1917, a group of civilian men with connections to both the English museum world and the British government proposed the idea of a National War Museum in London. Amongst these self-styled cultural patriots were Charles ffoulkes, Curator of the Tower Armouries; Lord Harcourt, a backer of the London Museum; and Ian Malcolm, a Conservative Member of Parliament.[11] In March 1917, the War Cabinet approved the proposal, asserting control over the detritus of war.[12] The War Office 'issued circulars and orders to the various Fronts asking the several Commanding Officers to note Museum requirements and collect specimens that may be of value'.[13] The same year, the Australian official war correspondent (and later official historian) Charles Bean conceived the idea for an Australian War Museum and lobbied for the creation of an Australian War Records section to oversee the collection of a comprehensive war record and museum collection. By October 1917, the Australian government, acting on C.E.W. Bean's advice, committed itself to an Australian War Museum.[14] Initially, the museum focussed on the physical tools of war. Several thousand of its earliest collected objects were guns – mostly German artillery pieces and machine guns

---

7   A.G. Doughty, Report on War Trophies, n.d. (*c.* December 1919), RG 37 vol. 366, Library and Archives Canada (LAC). See also the description of the beginnings of Canadian official trophy collection in Donald E. Graves, 'Booty! the Story of Canada's World War One Trophy Collection,' *Arms Collecting* 23, no. 1 (1985): pp. 3–10; and in Jonathan F. Vance, 'Tangible Demonstrations of a Great Victory: War Trophies in Canada,' *Material History Review* 42 (Fall 1995) [*Revue d'histoire de la culture materielle 42 (automne 1995)*]: pp. 47–56.

8   Report on War Trophies, RG 37, vol. 366, folder 1A, LAC.

9   'Business and Advisory,' transcripts of the history of the Red Cross in Nova Scotia during World War I, Canadian Red Cross Society, MG 20, vol. 321, Public Archives of Nova Scotia.

10   'The Record and Commemoration of the War (From A Correspondent)' [reprinted from *the Quebec Chronicle*, 20 July 1918], Edmund Walker Papers, Box 30, Fisher Rare Book Library, University of Toronto.

11   Charles ffoulkes, Memorandum, 'Origin and Beginnings of the National War Museum,' 15 March 1917, The Origin of the IWM 1917, EN1/1/MUS/25/1 A3/3, IWM. Note also Diana Condell's description of same in *The Imperial War Museum 1917–1920: A Study of the Institution and its Presentation of the First World War* (MPhil, 1985), pp. 13–14.

12   War Cabinet, 87, 'Minutes of a Meeting of the War Cabinet held at 10, Downing Street, on Monday, March 5, 1917, at 11.30 a.m. / Proposed National War Museum. 15. The War Cabinet approved the proposal made by the First Commissioner of Works to for a National War Museum, as set forth in his memorandum dated the 27th February, 1917 (Paper G.T.-83), (Appendix VI.), and authorised.' The Origin of the IWM 1917, EN1/1/MUS/25/1 A3/3, IWM, London.

13   'National War Museum,' 31 August 1917, pp. 2–3, Imperial War Museum Origins and Scope 1917, EN1/1/MUS/25/2 A3/3, IWM, London.

14   K.S. Inglis, *Sacred Places: War Memorials in the Australian Landscape*, 3rd ed. (Carlton, VIC: Melbourne University Press, 2008), p. 334.

captured by Australian troops in the course of the war.[15] Bean also oversaw the creation of a scheme to collect and commission official war art as well as official photographs. Offices and depots were established in France and in London to hold collected objects.[16]

Initially, the Imperial War Museum assumed that the London museum would have first pick of *all* war trophies captured by Imperial forces. The Dominions, and especially Canada and Australia, protested vociferously. While the dominion collecting efforts were quite clearly attempting to operate within an imperial framework, they were also proclaiming that they owned a piece of imperial history. In enthusiastically creating exhaustive collections of objects and documentation relating to their national experiences, each of the dominions declared that their distinctive character was a vital part of the imperial story. Such postures were evident, for instance, in the following cable sent to the Secretary of State for the Colonies by the Australian Department of Defence making the case for Australia's right of first refusal:

> Another viewpoint is that Britain already has a history and traditions and relics and trophies extending back for centuries and the present war however great is only adding to a long record and collection whereas Australia has none here other than what she draws from the mother country. A nation is built upon pride of race and now that Australia is making history of her own she requires every possible relic associated with this to help educate her children in that national spirit thereby ensuring her loyal adherence to and defence of the Empire of which she forms part.[17]

Likewise, in Canada objects for exhibition formed part of a larger museum preservation and exhibition project, which in turn constituted a foundation for a comprehensive national scheme of records collection. Reports from the Canadian War Records Office, overseen by the ubiquitous Lord Beaverbrook, repeatedly asserted that their primary aim was the creation of a permanent record of Canada's achievements. The Canadian War Records Office argued in a memorandum addressed to the Overseas Military Forces of Canada that it, 'exists for the benefit of the Canadian people', as '[i]n the years following the war Canadians will expect to be told what Canadians have done in the war. They will want the younger generation to be taught the glory of Canada.'[18] Another report claimed that everything 'of permanent value'

---

15 For the committee's activities in distributing the trophies, see 170 1/1, AWM. This process is also described in detail in R.S. (Bill) Billett, *War Trophies: From the First World War* (East Roseville, NSW: Kangaroo Press, 1999). The Memorial also kept a cutting book of public references to the distribution of trophies: 93 12/12/4, AWM.

16 Michael McKernan, *Here Is Their Spirit: A History of the Australian War Memorial, 1917–1990* (St. Lucia, Queensland: University of Queensland Press in association with the Australian War Memorial, 1991), p. 37. The Australian War Records Section (AWRS) commenced operations on 16 May 1917, when John Treloar began his posting as its Officer-in-Charge. For an account of the AWRS's early collecting efforts, see C.E.W Bean, 'Report on the Formation and Operations of the B.E.F. Subsection Australian War Records Section,' 10 March 1918 to 31 October 1918, and embracing the period from 7 August 1917 to 9 March 1918, prior to the formation of the subsection, 38 DRL 6673/66, AWM.

17 Cable despatched to the Secretary of State for the Colonies from the Secretary of Defence, Melbourne, quoted in Copy of Cable from Secretary of Defence Melbourne to Administrative Headquarters AIF London, 3 March 1918, 38 3DRL 6673/364, AWM.

18 'The Canadian War Records Office,' Reports – Origin of Records, 1915–1918, RG 9 III-D-1, vol. 4746. Folder 175, Folder 5, LAC.

collected during the war was intended to 'show what the Canadian factor is itself and how it works in connection with the Imperial and Allied factors' and to 'eventually find its place in the national war museum, just as every document produced by the war will eventually find its place in the national war archives, every picture in the national war gallery, and so on.'[19] This need to create a distinct national story, albeit one framed within a greater imperial narrative, resulted in different collecting and exhibiting priorities in the Dominions than was the case in Britain.

Having their own official photographers was one way in which Canada and Australia facilitated the creation of a particular national record. After a *laissez-faire* beginning in which numerous officers carried Vest Pocket Kodaks to the front in 1914, in June 1915 the War Office directed that each battalion be allowed only one camera.[20] After Britain appointed its first official photographer in early 1916, the Canadians quickly commissioned their own first official photographer that March.[21] Australia rapidly followed suit. Photographs produced by these official photographers were displayed in a series of exhibitions in Britain, France, the United States and Canada in the last two years of the war.

During the war, exhibitions of Australian war art, war photographs and war trophies were staged in Britain. Like exhibitions staged by the British government for domestic consumption, Australian displays sought to remobilise an exhausted British populace for the continued prosecution of an arduous and costly war. Australian exhibitions, however, also served a second purpose: they were a testament to the importance of the Dominion's contribution to the imperial war effort. It was to this end – the promotion of Australia's war effort in Britain – that in 1918, an Australian official war photograph exhibition was staged in the Grafton Galleries, London. It featured a wealth of images by the Australian official photographer, Frank Hurley, depicting the war as something exotic and far away, removed from ordinary existence, as well as a number of composite enlargements he created to dramatise battle or aestheticise the front. Hurley was already famous (unusual for an official war photographer), having been the photographer on both Sir Douglas Mawson's and Sir Ernest Shackleton's Antarctic expeditions between 1911 and 1917.[22] The exhibition attracted around 600 visitors a day, with a military band playing throughout the day and colour slides of scenes 'on the Western Front, Flanders, and also in Palestine' 'elicit[ing] applause at every showing.'[23] These colour images were projected onto a

---

19 'The Record and Commemoration of the War (From A Correspondent),' [reprinted from the *Quebec Chronicle*, 20 July 1918], Edmund Walker Papers, Box 30, Fisher Rare Book Library, University of Toronto.

20 Peter Barton, *The Battlefields of the First World War: The Unseen Panoramas of the Western Front* (London: Constable and Robinson, 2005), p. 49; Jane Carmichael, *First World War Photographers* (London and New York: Routledge, 1989), p. 16.

21 Carmichael, *First World War Photographers*, p. 17.

22 See Frank Hurley, *Argonauts of the South, By Captain Frank Hurley . . . Being a Narrative of Voyagings and Polar Seas and Adventures in the Antarctic with Sir Douglas Mawson and Sir Ernest Shackleton; with 75 Illustrations and Maps* (New York, London: G.P. Putnam's sons, 1925); for Hurley's account of his Antarctic adventures. See also Frank Hurley, *South with Endurance: Shackleton's Antarctic Expedition 1914–1917: The Photographs of Frank Hurley* (London: Bloomsbury, 2001); for images of the Shackleton expedition.

23 Frank Hurley, 'Diary Entry for 25 May 1918,' *The Diaries of Frank Hurley*, ed. Robert Dixon and Christopher Lee (London and New York: Anthem Press, 2011), p. 104. See also 'Australian Battle Pictures in Natural Colour: Exhibition at the Grafton Galleries,' *The Times*, 22 May 1918, p. 3.

screen at intervals – their luminous, transient quality heightening the sense of the exotic. The *Times* described these as follows:

> The deep colour of the East comes out with rich effect. The marble glory of the Mosque of Omar is conveyed as vividly as the hue of the wild purple iris of Palestine or that anemone which brightens the road to Jerusalem. Many who will never visit them can gather a true notion of the Judean hills from these pictures.[24]

Hurley arrived in Palestine in January 1918 to record the activities of the Australian Light Horse. In addition to numerous exotic landscapes, he turned to creating staged images of military dash and excitement. For example, in February 1918, Hurley observed '[i]t is amusing what the troops will do for the camera,' and described how with the keen participation of the troops and battalion commanders, he 'had the 2nd Regiment paraded through the narrow laneways and in many other pictorial settings'.[25] He made a 'programme of stunts which I require doing' and photographed them, including a 'battery going into action, machine-gun drill and ambulance turnout' and 'two regiments turned out and reenacted their famous charge at Beersheba.'[26] The images he created of 'stunts', 'action' and 'pictorial settings' were highly romanticised and particularly glamorised the Australian Light Horse and the Flying Corps, groups whose dashing reputation persisted long after the war. The landscapes of the Holy Land amidst which these events took place were replete with Biblical and medieval (crusader) associations. Hurley's fascination with the Middle East, and with the symbolic resonance of the landscape, derived partly from a sense that the Holy Land was part of the cultural heritage of the British peoples.[27] The symbolic associations of the Holy Land fired Hurley's imagination and were also later reflected in Australia's official history of the conflict. In this narrative, the Australians who partook in this action were part of a hardier British colonial type who could invigorate the empire. In the official history of Australia's participation in the war in the Sinai and Palestine published in 1923, official historian Henry Gullett depicted the campaigns 'as a

---

24 'Colour Photographs: Capt. Hurley's Work in Palestine,' *The Times*, 6 June 1918, p. 9. Hurley's colour photographs were also reported as of interest because they were 'natural colour photographs, as distinct from prints which have been "sprayed"', and were being 'shown for the first time'. 'Australian Battle Pictures in Natural Colour: Exhibition at the Grafton Galleries,' *The Times*, 2 May 1918, p. 3.

25 Hurley, 'Diary Entry for 25 May 1918,' p. 91. 'The exotic locations and multicultural character of the Middle East also provided Hurley with unlimited opportunities to indulge his interest in travelogue photography, a genre that might be characterised as Great War Orientalism.' Robert Dixon, *Photography, Early Cinema and Colonial Modernity: Frank Hurley's Synchronized Lecture Entertainments* (London and New York: Anthem Press, 2012), p. 54.

26 Frank Hurley, 'Diary Entries, 5 and 7 February 1918,' *The Diaries of Frank Hurley*, ed. Robert Dixon and Christopher Lee (London and New York: Anthem Press, 2011), p. 94.

27 Dixon, *Photography, Early Cinema and Colonial Modernity*, p. 54. Eitan Bar-Yosef argues that crusader analogies were more the preserve of the privileged classes than the masses, and – without perhaps the same sort of romantic imagination that Hurley clearly had – ordinary British soldiers had a vernacular (Protestant) biblical culture that viewed Palestine in relationship to home. For more on this, Eitan Bar-Yosef, *The Holy Land in English Culture 1799–1917: Palestine and the Question of Orientalism* (Oxford: Oxford University Press, 2005).

modern crusade in which the British peoples reclaim the Bible Lands from the Turk and make good Richard the Lionheart's failure in the twelfth century'.[28]

Underwritten by the Australian government, the official photograph exhibition, which also featured a number of Hurley's dramatic photomontages supposedly depicting Australians going into battle, subsequently toured a number of British provincial towns. (The largest picture, titled 'The Raid', but which was subsequently known as 'An episode after the battle of Zonnebeke' or sometimes 'Over the Top', was made of a combination of twelve negatives, and measured about 69 metres by 49 metres, and depicted soldiers heading into action against an exciting – and 'real' – backdrop of explosions and new military technology.[29]) These spectacular images of daring and the exotic aimed to show to the British public the value of the Australian contribution to the war. Images of thrilling bravery and the Middle Eastern exotic knit the Australian forces into a narrative not just of the Great War, but into a long-established series of tropes about the romance of empire. In this story, as constructed in Hurley's photographs (and later in Gullett's history) the Australian mounted troops become the elite vanguard of empire, embedded in a long history of imperial warfare.

Even more so than Australia's shows, Canadian official war photograph exhibitions actively manipulated audience desire for an 'authentic' connection to the 'reality' of war in order to create national propaganda within an imperial context. While Britain and Australia both displayed war photographs enthusiastically, Canadian efforts at creating and promoting war photograph exhibitions were particularly intense. Like those of Australia, Canadian exhibitions were designed and promoted in such a way as to emphasise the importance of Canada's contribution to the war and of Canada's significance within the empire. However, at this time, Canadian nationalism had special features differentiating it from Australia's. In this context (and at this time) it was a kind of imperial nationalism not only for its own sake, but also as a way of defining Canada as *not* the United States. Three different Canadian exhibitions toured numerous British towns and cities in 1917 and 1918, depicting war scenes and acts of Canadian valour for large crowds. Canada also sent photographs to the United States for exhibition.

The first series of photographs, featuring 'greatly enlarged prints depicting the Battle of the Somme and the taking of Courcelette', was shown at the Grafton Galleries in London at the end of 1916, and was then exhibited successively in numerous British provincial towns through 1917 and 1918.[30] Its Canadian promoters saw the exhibition as a success 'from the standpoint of records and propaganda' which it was 'impossible to

---

28 Dixon, *Photography, Early Cinema and Colonial Modernity*, p. 54. For more on this, see Christopher Lee, '"War is not a Christian Mission": Racial Invasion and Religious Crusade,' in H.S. Gullett's *'Official History of the Australian Imperial Force in Sinai and Palestine,' Journal of the Association for the Study of Australian Literature* 7 (2008): pp. 85–96. For Gullett's work itself see H.S. Gullett, *The A.I.F. in Sinai and Palestine, 1914–1918* (Sydney: Angus & Robertson, 1923).

29 Hurley, 'Diary Entry, 25 May 1918,' p. 104.

30 Report, Canadian War Records to Robert Borden, 1915–1918, Origin of Records, RG 9 III-D-1, vol. 4746, Folder 175, Folder 5, LAC. See also War Trophies, Memoranda 1–4, RG 37 D 366 Folder. 1A, Public Archives and National Library. 'In December 1916, an exhibition of a selection of Canadian Official Photographs was arranged at the Grafton Galleries. A large number of photographs enlarged to a great size were exhibited. The public were charged admission and all profits were handed over to the Canadian War Memorial Fund. The sum realized from this exhibition, which was a great success, was nearly £2,700.' For further records, see 'Photographs', Exhibition Correspondence, RG 9 III-D-1, vol. 4729, Folder 131 File 4; and 'Photographs', Sales 1st Exhibition, Department of National Defence, RG 9 III-D-1, vol. 4731, Folder 136 File 8, .

exaggerate'.[31] The Canadian War Records Office, which underwrote the exhibition, saw it as part of a multifaceted project of promoting Canadian influence in Britain. This project also included staffing a photographic dark room in London through which all Canadian negatives passed, the production of 'magic-lantern slides' and the supply of 'all recent scenes of Canadian activity at the front or in England' to the illustrated press.[32] Both high attendance at the exhibition and the compilation of a photographic record of Canadians at war (which the Records Office estimated at 2,300 negatives in late 1917) served in their eyes to promote and solidify Canada's national identity and stature within the empire.

Hundreds of thousands of people saw a replica of this first Canadian official war photograph exhibition when it made a tour of a number of Canadian cities and also visited the United States.[33] In Boston, where it was shown between 30 March and 13 April 1918, 55,000 people – or on average four to five thousand people each day – paid admittance to see the photographs.[34] In each American city the exhibition visited, a flurry of publicity and a series of related events accompanied the show. Newspaper reports describing the exhibition focussed heavily on viewer's ability to access the reality of war. For example, the *New York Mail*'s headline proclaimed that the Canadian Official Exhibition's 'Pictures Show Grim Canadians in Actual War', and the *Evening World* declared that the Canadian 'Camera Man Faces Death for Picture of Fierce Battle'.[35] The most famous image in these exhibitions, and the most described by journalists, was the image that the Canadian official photographer Ivor Castle had apparently risked his life to get (or, in the *Evening World*'s purple prose, 'exposed himself to death on the parapet of shell-torn trenches in his effort to picture the story of a battle'). It was titled 'Over the Top' (see Figure 11.2). The *New York Times* reported men resembling 'college football players going down the field after a kickoff', and the image was, the *Evening World*'s reviewer believed,

> without question the most forceful picture of the kind ever shown in the United States. It shows a squad of men leaping over the parapet of a trench at Courcelette during the battle of the Somme in September, 1916. Capt. Castle was not ten feet away, half buried in a shell hole, when he snapped it. The men, Canadians, semi-silhouetted against a sombre sky, led by a smiling young officer, are gripping their guns with bayonets fixed. Some are laughing, while others, in realization of the grim feat they have to perform, are seen with teeth clenched and jaws squared. It is brimful of action and the men are life size. One minute after the picture was taken a German machine gun found the squad and sprayed bullets on them. They were all killed.[36]

---

31 'Report', Canadian War Records to Robert Borden, 1915–1918, RG 9 III-D-1, vol. 4746, Folder 175 Folder 5, Origin of Records, LAC.

32 Ibid.

33 Ibid. In the United States, it travelled to Washington, Philadelphia, Boston, New York and Baltimore.

34 'First Day Record,' *Current Affairs*, 8 April 1918, from Boston exhibition clipping book, Boston exhibition part 2, RG 9 III-D-1, vol. 4632, LAC. RG 9 III-D-1, vol. 4732, Department of National Defence, Folder 138, File 9, LAC; Canadian War Photos, Boston Exhibition March 30th to April 13 Inclusive, Attendance 55,000, RG 9 III-D-1, vol. 4732, Department of National Defence, Folder 138, File 9, LAC.

35 *New York Mail*, 10 May 1918; *New York Evening Post*, 10 May 1918; *New York Evening World*, 10 May 1918, from clipping book in RG 9 III-D-1, vol. 4732, Folder 138, File 10, LAC.

36 *New York Times*, 10 May 1918; *New York Evening World*, 10 May 1918, in clipping book, RG 9 III-D-1, vol. 4732, Folder 138, File 10, LAC.

Figure 11.2   Ivor Castle, 'Over the Top'

Source: Canadian War Museum

The impression of immediacy and reality emphasised by the Canadian exhibition's promoters and widely reported in the news media was, however, an illusion. 'Over the Top' was a forgery, actually taken behind the lines during a training exercise. A breech cover visible on the rifle of the foremost soldier in the image was edited out in contemporary publications of the photograph.[37]

Bristol-born Ivor Castle started his appointment as an official Canadian photographer in August 1916. Prior to this, Castle had been a press photographer for some time, and had photographed the Balkan Wars of 1912 and 1913, as well as the bombardment of Liège and Antwerp in 1914. At the time of his appointment, he was the manager of the photographic department of Lord Rothermere's *Daily Mirror*, the first newspaper in the world to become entirely illustrated by photographs.[38] In a 1917 article for the Canadian War Records Office publication *Canada in Khaki*, Castle claimed:

---

37   'Photography During the First World War,' Imperial War Museum, accessed 13 December 2011, http://www.iwm.org.uk/collections/item/object/205194696. For more on Ivor Castle's 'Over the Top' as a forgery, see Michael J. Carlebach, *American Photojournalism Comes of Age* (Washington, DC: Smithsonian Institution Press, 1997), p. 91; as well as Peter Robertson, 'Canadian Photojournalism During the First World War,' *History of Photography* 2 (1978): pp. 42–5.

38   Robertson, 'Canadian Photojournalism During the First World War,' p. 42.

> Taking photographs of men going over the parapet under such circumstances is a disagreeable business, and you miss many opportunities when the shells are dropping around ... Taking photographs of the men going over the parapet is quite exciting. Nothing, of course, can be arranged. You sit or crouch in the first-line trench while the enemy do a little strafing, and if you are lucky you get your pictures.[39]

In reality, Castle's image of men 'going over the parapet' was not taken when 'shells were dropping all around' while the enemy were doing 'a little strafing'. The image was staged. William Rider-Rider, also a Canadian official photographer, recalled in an interview in the early 1970s that 'these alleged battle pictures were "made", or rather pieced together', from photographs of 'shell bursts taken at a British trench-mortar school outside St. Pol', and photographs 'taken at rehearsal attacks of men going over the top with canvas breech covers on rifles'.[40] Ivor Castle's assistant later told William Rider-Rider that 'the soldier thumbing his nose' in the photograph' 'was not thumbing his nose at the Germans, as has sometimes been surmised, but was rather thumbing his nose at Castle, who was waiting in front of the trench' to take the photograph.[41] As the image had strongly impacted audiences in Britain, Canada and the United States during the exhibition's two-year tour, some Canadian troops were certainly aware of the claims made about it. In the same 1972 interview, Rider-Rider also recalled that he has 'a lot to live down' when he visited particular Canadian units, with soldiers asking him 'Want to take us going over the top?' and 'Another faker?'[42]

Although a twenty-first century sensibility might dwell on the knowledge of the falsity of this image, and in the discovery of official propagandist's manipulation of civilian audiences during the First World War, the *actual* truth of the image was not really what was crucial: the public's *belief* in the truth of these images was key. Fake or not, large numbers of people were searching for a connection to the war and for a sense of the reality of the front. It was the belief that they might come into contact with this reality which brought people to the official Canadian war photograph exhibition and inspired the heavy emphasis on 'reality' and the 'actual' in newspaper reviews of the exhibition. For example, the Ottawa *Journal* reported in June 1918 that '[t]here is a relentless verity about them that eats up the thousands of miles between Canada and the firing line, and brings a man to see the brunt that the fellows ... are bearing.'[43] Many people wanted to believe that Ivor Castle's 'Over the Top' really *did* show the tragic courage and bravado of young Canadians bravely going over the top immediately prior to their deaths. Similarly, they wanted to believe that, as advertised, 200 Canadian mothers really *had* spotted their sons in another official photograph, or that recently in Canada Major Boehm really *had* found the 'three little daughters' of a laughing soldier apparently photographed two days before his death at the exhibition 'standing before their father's laughing face and crying piteously'.[44] It was

---

39 Captain Ivor Castle, 'With a Camera on the Somme,' *Canada in Khaki I.*, London (1917): p. 68, in Robertson, 'Canadian Photojournalism During the First World War.' p. 43.
40 Robertson, 'Canadian Photojournalism During the First World War,' p. 43.
41 Ibid.
42 Ibid., citing Interview of William Rider-Rider by Peter Robertson, 18–19 May 1971, Sound Recordings Accession 1972-27, William Rider-Rider Collection, Public Archives of Canada (PAC).
43 *Journal* (Ottawa), 16 June 1918, p. 18.
44 'War Photographs Aid Soldier Fund. Scenes of Battle of Somme, Ypres and Arras Stir New Yorkers. Views of No Man's Land. 200 Canadian Soldiers Shown in One Picture Were Recognized

by tapping into this need that the exhibition was able to promote the aims of its official sponsors in both raising morale through giving audiences the impression of a connection to or stake in the war and by raising awareness of Canada's military contributions to the war.

Canada's second photography exhibition was even more effective in engendering a sense of connection to and investment in the war and creating an impression of Canada's importance in successfully prosecuting it.[45] This exhibition primarily depicted the Canadian victory at Vimy Ridge in April 1917 and was mounted initially at the Grafton Galleries in London from July to September 1917. It was again heavily attended and financially successful. London newspapers reported that attendance records were being 'created daily' by crowds 'anxious to get a photographic impression of the grim realities of war', and the exhibition's organisers reported to the Canadian government that queues of visitors waiting to be admitted to the exhibition 'frequently extended from the doors to Bond St. fifty yards away'.[46] A replica of the exhibition was exhibited in Paris and then sent to tour Canada.[47] It featured what was billed as 'the largest photograph in the world' apparently taken on No Man's Land on Easter Monday, 1917, when 'four Canadian Divisions were sent over the parapet in line', and was purported to depict the attack on Thelus Village, which was the second Canadian objective in the fighting at Vimy Ridge. It was 'taken in profile from the flank, and the clouds of smoke represented bursts of German shells above our men. In the distance they would see a tank at work, while in the foreground were a number of casualties'.[48]

Two themes are evident in the way this exhibition was promoted: spectacle and empire. The Canadian government used the photograph exhibition as a means of publicising its contribution to the imperial war effort as well as supporting its claims to a significant role in the British Empire, all the while claiming to be doing no such thing. Thus, in declaring the second exhibition of Canadian war pictures open in London in July 1917, the Canadian General Turner stated that 'Canada, in taking part in the world-war, desired thanks from nobody. They were doing their little bit as members of the British Empire, and they hoped to be long spared to be part and parcel of it.'[49]

---

by Families,' *New York Sun*, 10 May 1918; 'Pictures Show Grim Canadians in Actual War,' *New York Mail*, 10 May 1918, from clipping book in RG 9 III-D-1, vol. 4732, Folder 138, File 10, LAC.

45   War Trophies, Memoranda 14–16 Duplicates, RG 37 D 370, Public Archives and National Library, LAC. Together, the First, Second, Third and Fourth Canadian War Photograph Exhibitions were shown in *at least* the following British locations: Aberdeen, Bristol, Brighton (1st and 2nd), Bournemouth, Birmingham (1st and 2nd), Belfast, Dublin, Edinburgh, Eastbourne, Folkestone (1st and 2nd), Glasgow (1st and 2nd), Guildford, Hull, Huddersfield, Hastings, Harrogate, Leeds (1st and 2nd), Liverpool (1st and 2nd), Grafton Galleries, London – 2nd, 3rd, and 4th, Manchester, Newport, Maidstone (2nd), Oldham, Plymouth, Paris, Southend-on-Sea, South Shields, Sunderland, Warrington, Weston-Super-Mare.

46   'Grafton Gallery Crush: Huge Crowds View Wonderful Firing-Line Pictures,' *Sunday Pictorial*, 22 July 1917, in Photographs – General, RG 9 III-D-1, vol. 4728, Folder 128, File 1, LAC; Reports, Origin of Records, 1915–1918, RG 9 III-D-1 vol. 4746, Folder 175 Folder 5. 21, LAC.

47   LAC RG 9 III-D-1 Vol. 4746 Folder 175 Folder 5. Reports. Origin of Records. 1915 to 1918, 21. See also Memorandum. 'Canadian War Memorials Fund. History and Objects,' General correspondence and memoranda war cinematograph committee, 27 August–31 October 1917, BBK/E/2/9, Beaverbrook Papers, Parliamentary Archives, London, UK.

48   'Grafton Gallery Crush,' *Sunday Pictorial*, 22 July 1917, in Photographs – General, RG 9 III-D-1, vol. 4728, Folder, 128 File 1, LAC; 'Vimy Ridge Pictures: The Second Canadian Exhibition,' *The Times*, 17 July 1917, p. 9.

49   'Vimy Ridge Pictures,' *The Times*, 17 July 1917, p. 9.

The centrepiece of the exhibition, Ivor Castle's huge image 'The Taking of Vimy Ridge', emphasised Canada's heroic contribution to the imperial war effort. This 'largest photograph in the world' was enlarged to 36 metres high by 66 metres long and described in the exhibition catalogue as 'an impression, nay, indeed a reality, of the splendid horror snatched by the photographer, in a fraction of a second, from the clutching of Death'.[50] It was in fact a composite of two photographs, with explosions and heroically fallen Canadian bodies deliberately added to the scene.[51] It was one notable exception to the embargo on photographic depictions of Allied dead. Generally, official photographers worked under implicit as well as explicit rules: for British and Dominion official photographers, 'the *quid pro quo* for access being adherence to the policy that images of British dead were unacceptable.'[52] Images of dead Britons were, of course, considered bad for morale. This implicit rule was clearly well understood throughout the empire – Beaverbrook instructed his official Canadian cameramen to 'cover up the Canadians before you photograph them ... but don't bother about the German dead'.[53] However, the inclusion of Canadian dead in 'The Taking of Vimy Ridge' was no statement of the futility of war. Rather, it was an attempt to make the photograph fit conventions of traditional battle painting, and thus conform to audience expectations about the necessity of heroic sacrifice in the course of securing a glorious victory.

'The Taking of Vimy Ridge' was a composite, made from two photographs, with explosions added in the sky, and provided 'an expectant public with an image that accorded with what they anticipated in any depiction of such a significant battle'.[54] The Canadian dead did not appear in the foreground of the original image. In composition, it resembled traditional battle paintings, such as the first painting commissioned by Lord Beaverbrook's Canadian War Memorials official war art scheme, Richard Jack's *The Second Battle of Ypres* (1915).[55] It also conformed to conventions about the representation of battle as exciting long propagated by popular illustrations. Apparent photographic 'realism', as John Taylor observes of wartime photography published in the popular press, 'could never exist in a pure form'. It was tied into convention, and it was conventional to see men cheerful before a battle, or to describe them (in the words of the *Daily Express*) as bravely 'smashing, hacking, and hewing' their way through the enemy. For years, illustrators had pictured

---

50 Exhibition catalogue cited in Robertson, 'Canadian Photojournalism during the First World War,' p. 44.

51 Laura Brandon, 'Words and Pictures: Writing Atrocity into Canada's First World War Official Photographs,' *The Journal of Canadian Art History/Annales d'Histoire de l'Art Canadien* 31 (2011): pp. 122–3, 115.

52 Nicholas J. Saunders, 'Matter and Memory in the Landscapes of Conflict: The Western Front 1914–1919,' *Contested Landscapes: Movement, Exile and Place*, ed. Barbara Bender and Margot Winer (Oxford and New York: Berg, 2001), p. 40. This correlation was of course imperfect – as, for example, Geoffrey Malins' film *Battle of the Somme* did show some dead British; however, none of Malins' or others' subsequent war films display British corpses.

53 Jeffrey A. Keshen, *Propaganda and Censorship During Canada's Great War* (Edmonton: University of Alberta Press, 1996), p. 36; citing W. Watkins to Manley-Sims, 14 July 1916, MD vol. 4772, File CIF-40, LAC.

54 Laura Brandon, 'Words and Pictures,' p. 115.

55 Although due to its medium, it also in other ways resembled the horizontal line achieved when filming action against a landscape in early film. For further discussion of the Richard Jack painting, see Jennifer Wellington, 'Art Exhibitions,' chap. 3 in *Exhibiting the Great War: Museums and Memory in Britain, Canada, and Australia, 1914–1943* (Cambridge: Cambridge University Press, forthcoming).

soldiering as exciting, not only in conservative history paintings of the Royal Academy destined for regimental mess-halls, but in popular prints, and in drawings and engravings for the press.[56]

War *could* be depicted as having a human cost, but it was framed within a narrative of heroic sacrifice with a clear, laudable goal. In this case, the dead made a noble sacrifice in the course of the Canadian victory at Vimy Ridge in April 1917, an event that was later depicted as a national coming of age. Official prohibitions remained on images of the dead outside of this narrative or, in other words, on the taking of 'gruesome' photographs – images of the dead that lay troublingly outside of the official narrative of military glory.[57] In a sense, this image may be viewed as a symbol of the entire British and Dominion project of exhibiting war photographs during the conflict: nothing was ever quite as it seemed, and images apparently depicting the reality and horror of war in fact buttressed claims that the war was a worthwhile and noble (if tragic) endeavour in which the Dominions had played a significant role.

Britain and its Dominions of Canada and Australia all staged exhibitions depicting the Great War during the war itself, with the aim of remobilising the weary populace to continue fighting the ongoing war. The Australian and Canadian photograph exhibitions discussed in this essay were part of this project of cultural mobilisation. They used the public's desire to connect with the experience of war, and to have a sense of the 'reality' of it, to create exhibitions depicting the apparently lifelike glory and bravery of Dominion troops. This created a sense of connection to the experiences of those at the front and encouraged popular commitment to contributing to victory. Canada and Australia also both focussed heavily on exhibiting their deeds to the British public as a way of emphasising their importance to the imperial war effort. Each Dominion asserted, in a series of exhibitions (and in the creation of unique national collections of war photographs as well as other war-related items), that their distinctive national character was a crucial part of the fabric of the empire. Further, in proclaiming both their distinctiveness, and the significant nature of their contributions to the prosecution of the war, Canadian and Australian war exhibitions contributed to establishing the post-war narrative claiming that the war had, indeed, been the crucible of the nation.

---

56 John Taylor, *War Photography: Realism in the British Press* (London: Routledge, 1991), pp. 44–5. He continues: 'When it came to picturing a modern war, the papers were prisoners of their own previous successes. As early as 1890 a journalist, in his article on illustration in books and newspapers, had said "our artistic skill has led us into temptation, and by degrees engendered a habit of making pictures when we ought to be recording facts. We have thus, through our own cleverness, created a fashion and a demand from the public for something which is often elaborately untrue"', citing the *Daily Express*, 7 July 1916; and H. Blackburn, 'The Illustration of Books and Newspapers,' *Nineteenth Century*, February 1890, pp. 213–24; cited in Lucy Salmon, *The Newspaper and the Historian* (New York: Oxford University Press, 1923), p. 377.

57 'In 1917 the official photographers were forbidden to photograph "gruesome" scenes.' John Taylor, *War Photography: Realism in the British Press* (London: Routledge, 1991), p. 44; citing, letter from M17A to Press Bureau, 5 December 1917, PRO HO 139/42.

Chapter 12
A tribute to the British Empire
Lowell Thomas's *With Allenby in Palestine and Lawrence in Arabia*

Justin Fantauzzo

Introduction

On 9 March 1919, Lowell Thomas gave his first performance of *With Allenby in Palestine* – later renamed *With Allenby in Palestine and Lawrence in Arabia* – at the Century Theater in New York, a mile north of the Theater District in Midtown Manhattan. Packing the front row was a who's who of New York's banking families. Jacob Schiff, Otto Kahn, Nathan Straus, Paul and Felix Warburg, as well as a Rothschild, were seated with their wives. After seeing the show, Schiff, a passionate Zionist, and the Warburgs were convinced that Americans needed to see and hear Thomas's tale of the war in the Holy Land. Once the season at the Century ended they encouraged Thomas to move his travelogue to Madison Square Garden, bought large sections of seating for Thomas to give away to working class New Yorkers, and even chartered buses to transport people from The Bronx.[1] Six years later, after a sold-out season in London and a worldwide tour of the rest of England, Scotland, Wales, Canada, Australia, New Zealand, Ireland, Burma, British Malaya, Ceylon and India, Thomas's travelogue had been delivered over 4,000 times. Total ticket sales exceeded 4 million, or roughly 1 per cent of the population of the British Empire.[2]

With Allenby in Palestine and Lawrence in Arabia's attendance numbers dwarf the readership of any of the well-known authors of disillusionment or otherwise. Nonetheless, historians of the First World War have focussed relentlessly on post-war writings by ex-servicemen and non-combatants. Even Michael Paris and Brian Bond, so keen to demonstrate that British and Anglo-Imperial society did not reject the war as a futile slaughter, have bypassed Thomas's travelogue and, in fact, inter-war theatre altogether.[3] Where theatre and stage productions have been discussed, Thomas's name has been noticeably absent.[4]

---

1 Lowell Thomas Remembers the Allenby and Lawrence Show, Lowell Thomas Papers (LTP) 1.25.2.6.505.7, Marist College, Poughkeepsie, New York.

2 Miscellaneous Program, 1925, LTP 1.25.2.5.503.18; Angus Maddison, *The World Economy: A Millennial Perspective* (Paris: Organisation for Economic Cooperation and Development, 2006), p. 98.

3 Michael Paris, *Warrior Nation: Images of War in British Popular Culture, 1850–2000* (London: Reaktion, 2000); Brian Bond, *The Unquiet Western Front: Britain's Role in Literature and History* (Cambridge: Cambridge University Press, 2002).

4 L.J. Collins, *Theatre at War, 1914–1918* (Basingstoke: Palgrave Macmillan, 1998); Heinz Kosok, *The Theatre of War: The First World War in British and Irish Drama* (Basingstoke: Palgrave Macmillan, 2007).

Indeed, Thomas's travelogue has been left exclusively to those writing about T. E. Lawrence. The first, surely, was Graham Dawson in his well-known study of masculinity and hero-making in nineteenth and twentieth-century Britain, *Soldier Heroes*.[5] Dawson argued that the 'originating moment of the Lawrence legend' was Thomas's travelogue, and went on to suggest that Lawrence's carefully manicured public profile, aided by Thomas himself, was that of an imperialist fantasy.[6] Joel C. Hodson has also looked at Lowell Thomas and his travelogue as the catalyst for Lawrence's rise to stardom. While Dawson was primarily concerned with Lawrence and his celebrity as a *British* imperial hero, Hodson, in contrast, focussed on Lawrence's worth as a particularly *American* hero.[7]

This chapter makes two interconnected arguments. First, it suggests that the meaning of the First World War was far from resolved (or uniform) in the years after the Armistice. Tales of triumph, such as Thomas's travelogue, were remarkably popular. They were even preferred to despairing and increasingly unwanted stories of the Western Front. The war's 'sideshows', such as the campaign in Sinai and Palestine, were very much a part of Britain's emerging cultural memory of the conflict. And as much as 'Lawrence of Arabia' spellbound British, Dominion and Colonial audiences, Allenby and the exploits of 'local' troops were just as important in creating a mass, popular audience for the travelogue. Second, it argues that Thomas's travelogue can be seen as a contested site of memory.[8] It was a space where a different side of the war was fought over just as passionately as the struggle to define the meaning of the Western Front.[9] As will be seen, English, Australian, Indian and Irish audiences all found a different meaning in the show and, by extension, what the war in Sinai and Palestine meant, ranging from a heroic episode in the annals of Anglo-Imperial warfare to a stark and unwanted reminder of Britain's continued colonial presence.

Humble beginnings

Before the success of *With Allenby in Palestine and Lawrence in Arabia* in New York, Thomas had been contracted by the National Parks Service of the United States to produce a lecture series on the American wilderness. Following America's declaration of war against Germany in April 1917, Thomas suspended the project. He began planning a tour of the war's main fronts with the intention of creating a war travelogue for presentation in America.[10] To finance his expedition overseas he formed 'Thomas Travelogues Incorporated' in July 1917. Through the sale of private shares to investors, primarily industrialists and lawyers from Chicago, Thomas raised $52,000 across fifty-two shares.[11] After securing advertising

---

5 Graham Dawson, *Soldier Heroes: British Adventure, Empire and the Imagining of Masculinities* (London: Routledge, 1994), chap. 6–8.
6 Ibid., pp. 167, 170.
7 Joel C. Hodson, *Lawrence of Arabia and American Culture: The Making of a Transatlantic Legend* (Westport, CT: Greenwood Press, 1995), chap. 1–3; Joel C. Hodson, 'Lowell Thomas, T.E. Lawrence and the Creation of a Legend,' *American History* 35 (2000): pp. 46–54.
8 See Pierre Nora, *Les Lieux de la Mémoire* (Paris: Gallimard, 1984); and Jay Winter, *Sites of Memory, Sites of Mourning* (Cambridge: Cambridge University Press, 1995).
9 See Janet Watson, *Fighting Different Wars: Experience, Memory, and the First World War in Britain* (Cambridge: Cambridge University Press, 2004).
10 Thomas to Robert Stirling Yard, 6 June 1917, LTP 1.25.2.1.499.35.
11 Preferred Stockholders, LTP 1.25.24.1.502.15.

space from nineteen American newspapers in exchange for wartime despatches from Europe as an official correspondent, Thomas further enlisted the help of Edgar A. Bancroft, an investor in Thomas Travelogues Incorporated and a lawyer at the US Department of the Interior. Lobbying President Woodrow Wilson, Bancroft emphasised the massive propaganda potential of Thomas's travelogue lectures in 'stimulating and sustaining patriotic devotion of our people at a time when such work may be most vital'.[12] Thomas's travelogues were scheduled for exhibition towards the end of 1918.

Thomas, accompanied by his wife, Frances, a talented cameraman, Harry Chase, and Louis B. Plan, a publicity expert for the New York City Administration, sailed for France in August 1917. Dismayed by the condition of warfare on the Western Front, he lobbied the British War Office for permission to travel to and film the Egyptian Expeditionary Force's (EEF) war in the Middle East. Thomas and Chase finally arrived in Palestine days before the capture of Jericho in February 1918. They spent most of their time divided between the Australian Light Horse, the Royal Flying Corps and the 60th (London) Division. After a chance meeting with T. E. Lawrence in Cairo, Thomas spent the rest of the war filming and photographing the Arab Revolt and Lawrence's drive towards Damascus. After eighteen months abroad, Thomas returned to the United States in February 1919. His work, however, failed to excite a war-weary American audience. Only Thomas's footage of the German November Revolution found a buyer in the British newsreel and documentary producer, Pathé News.

With mounting debt and a stockpile of photographs and films, Thomas turned to Fred B. Taintor, a personal friend and managing editor of New York's *The Globe*. Taintor was a shrewd businessman. He recognised the chance to increase the newspaper's public profile and turn a small profit, and he offered to support Thomas's opening season. Thomas accepted Taintor's proposal and set to work by compiling his extensive photograph and film collection from the war into six individual travelogues, including the 'Italian Front', the 'Balkan Front', the 'American Expeditionary Force in France', 'Sinai and Palestine', the 'Arab Revolt' and the 'German Revolution'.

Following the show's run in New York, mentioned earlier, Thomas toured the rest of the American Midwest. Importantly, the popularity of Thomas's New York performances led him to concentrate all of his efforts on the shows about Sinai and Palestine and the Arab Revolt when he brought his show to Britain. The travelogues, with their origin in wartime propaganda and the need to promote the war to the American public, also represented an exercise in Anglo-American relations. Indeed, thrilling the American public with war stories from Europe told by an American was what originally motivated Woodrow Wilson's endorsement.[13] The stage was set for an even bigger spectacle in London.

'America's tribute to British valour'

Percy Burton, an English stage manager who had worked as an agent for Barnum and Bailey, and Sarah Bernhardt sat quietly and watched Thomas's final performance in New York on the Arab Revolt. He was left 'flabbergasted that he, an Englishman, should be ... hearing an American tell a British story about a fabulous British hero of whom he had never

---

12   Edgar A. Bancroft to Woodrow Wilson, 18 July 1917, LTP 1.25.2.1.499.4.
13   Thomas to Woodrow Wilson, 20 August 1917, LTP 1.25.2.1.500.23.

even heard!'[14] Burton met with Thomas after the show and later sent him a provisional contract outlining the arrangements for a tour of London.[15] Thomas agreed to split both the expenses and profits with Burton, but he had two requests: that he appear at one of London's larger theatres, the Opera House at Covent Garden if possible, and that his arrival be approved by the British government.[16]

Initial negotiations between Burton and Sir William Jury, Head of the Cinematograph Department of the Ministry of Information, were unproductive.[17] While much of Burton's discussion with Jury focussed on the financial profitability of Thomas's travelogue, of which Jury saw little prospect, the larger talking point concerned the politics of commemoration in post-war Britain. Burton, writing to Thomas, lamented that Jury was 'anxious to avoid seeming to – or indeed wanting to make anything at all out of the war'.[18] Jury's response reflected official concerns about wartime profiteering, the nature of government intervention, the relationship between violence, as represented by the war, and the British state, and the debate within British society about the ownership of the war's memorialisation.[19] It may also be that Jury had legitimate fears about projecting a martial image of Britain warring on the colonial periphery it now governed. Unrest in Ireland and nationalist revolt in Egypt were ongoing, while the infamous Amritsar massacre in India, perpetrated in April, remained a black mark on British colonial rule. Jury would, however, eventually allow Thomas to make use of a number of official war films. He also put Thomas and Burton into contact with members of the newly formed English-Speaking Union. But the show would not receive an official endorsement or financial support from the Cinematograph Department.[20]

Fortunately, Thomas and Burton were able to secure the support of the English-Speaking Union, which was eager to promote a show that was 'pro-British in sentiment'.[21] He also met with a director at the *Times* in an attempt to 'enlist their sympathetic aid in an editorial way, so as to cut down the advertising expenses'.[22] Having already cancelled a coast-to-coast tour of the United States in anticipation of his journey to London, Thomas made one final and crucial amendment to the contract between himself, Burton and a third investor, William Cunningham: their agreement would last only for one year and strictly for Thomas's performances in London.[23]

---

14 'How I Discovered Lowell Thomas,' LTP 1.25.2.7.505.11.
15 Percy Burton to Lowell Thomas, 22 April 1919, LTP 1.25.2.1.499.11.
16 Thomas to Percy Burton, 30 April 1919, LTP 1.25.2.1.499.11.
17 Richard Abel, ed., *Encyclopedia of Early Cinema* (Abingdon: Routledge, 2005), pp. 350–1.
18 Percy Burton to Lowell Thomas, 6 June 1919, LTP 1.25.2.1.499.11.
19 Neil Rollings, 'Whitehall and the Control of Prices and Profits in a Major War, 1919–1939,' *The Historical Journal* 44, no. 2 (2001): pp. 517–40; Jon Lawrence, 'Forging a Peaceable Kingdom: War, Violence, and Fear of Brutalization in Post-First World War Britain,' *The Journal of Modern History* 75, no. 3 (2003): pp. 557–89; Alison Light, *Forever England: Femininity, Literature and Conservatism Between the Wars* (London: Routledge, 1991).
20 Percy Burton to Thomas, Western Union Telegram, 14 July 1919, LTP 1.25.2.1.499.11.
21 Percy Burton to Donald Baylis, 11 July 1919, LTP 1.25.2.1.499.11.
22 Percy Burton to Thomas, 14 July 1919, LTP 1.25.2.1.499.11.
23 Percy Burton to Thomas, 14 August 1919, LTP 1.25.2.1.499.11.

The show

The travelogue opened on 14 August 1919 at the Royal Opera House in Covent Garden, London. Like the best creative minds, Thomas's script came together at the last second. On the journey across the Atlantic from New York to England, he re-organised and merged his separate scripts for Allenby's war in Palestine and Lawrence's revolt in Arabia into a single, two-part, two-hour travelogue. *With Allenby in Palestine and Lawrence in Arabia* was a marvel of artistic production, technical skill and immersive entertainment. To enhance the feeling that the audience really was on an eastern journey, the Opera House's stage was decorated in a moonlit Nile scene. Silhouetted pyramids from the set of Handel's oratio, *Joseph and His Brethren*, were fixed to a cloth backdrop. The show began with the orchestra – in London, the Royal Welsh Guards Band – playing Middle Eastern–inspired music. As the 'atmosphere music' set the mood, Thomas gave a spoken prologue; the first of its kind in live theatre.[24]

Although no script remains from the inaugural 1919 season at the Opera House and Royal Albert Hall, one script from the 1921 tour of England, Scotland and Wales has survived, and likely resembled the pattern and content of the original tour. Without question, Thomas's travelogue was a feast for the eyes. Around 285 photographic slides and 31 films were used in the production. Thomas's American cameraman, Harry A. Chase, took the preponderance of photographs and slides during the war, while supplemental photographs and films were borrowed from the National Geographic Society in the United States and the War Office in London.

Despite the travelogue's undertones of war, to borrow Edmund Blunden's expression, the show was presented and marketed as a 'magic carpet ride' to the Middle East. Thomas's spoken prologue was careful to clear up any uncertainty about the show's content. *With Allenby in Palestine and Lawrence in Arabia*, he told the audience, was 'not in any sense an historical account of the liberation of the Holy Land and the war in the Land of the Arabian Nights', rather, it was a 'privilege to accompany you tonight on a short trip to Palestine and Arabia'. With a map of the eastern Mediterranean projected on screen and arrows pointing to the location of each city he named, the travelogue started with British soldiers sailing from England, navigating the southern coasts of France, Italy and Malta, before arriving in Egypt. Peppering Thomas's narration were nods to Biblical history: 'the road over which the Children of Israel journeyed'/'the Land of Goshen'/'the ancient home of the enemies of the Israelites – the Philistines'.[25] The novelty of aerial photography and film enhanced the travelogue's visual appeal. For the first time, audiences were treated to overhead tours of the Great Pyramid of Cheops, the Sphinx, the Suez Canal, the undulating desert plains of Sinai and the holy places of Jerusalem and Arabia.

Even though the objective of Thomas's travelogue was to enchant audiences with unseen images of the Middle East and Christian-Islamic holy sites, *With Allenby in Palestine and Lawrence in Arabia* was, in fact, a passable account of the campaign against the Ottomans. Photographic slides and Thomas's narration explained the logistical difficulties of warring in Sinai, paying particular attention to the two failed Ottoman raids on the Canal, the construction of the military base at Kantara, the extension of the railway through Sinai

---

24 Lowell Thomas Remembers, LTP 1.25.2.6.505.7.
25 The Lowell Thomas Travelogues 'With Allenby in Palestine and Lawrence in Arabia,' LTP 1.25.2.2.

and into southern Palestine and the colossal efforts of the Camel Transport Corps. The campaign's military accomplishments were also presented. Films of the captures of Gaza, Mughar Hill, Nebi Samwil, and of the Imperial Camel Corps racing across the desert would have impressed Thomas's audience with the spectacle of the EEF defeating both the geography and the Ottomans. The travelogue ended with film of British and Dominion soldiers entering Aleppo and a passionate appeal by Thomas on behalf of the campaign's historical importance:

> With the fall of Aleppo, Allenby's men had cut off all of Mesopotamia, all of Syria, all of Palestine and all of Arabia. They had smashed the backbone of the Ottoman Empire. In the last six weeks of this great drive Allenby's cavalry advanced over 500 miles – farther than from Paris to Berlin! They had captured over one hundred thousand Turks, and 500 cannons! The great world war on the Western Front was of such vital importance to all of us that it overshadowed what was going on in the Near East, but I believe that historians of the future will agree that this Palestine Campaign was one of the most beautifully executed of all the campaigns in history, and that Field Marshal Lord Allenby, the man who led his last Crusade which freed the Holy Land, will go down in history as one of the greatest cavalry leaders the world has ever known.[26]

Following subsequent performances in London at the Royal Albert Hall, Queen's Hall and the Philharmonic Hall, Thomas accepted an invitation from the Australian government to perform in summer 1920.[27] Before leaving he hired Dale Carnegy, a lecturer on public speaking and later the author of *How to Win Friends and Influence People*, to manage an extensive tour of Britain's smaller towns and cities.[28]

Reception

Who saw *With Allenby in Palestine and Lawrence in Arabia* and what did the travelogue mean? Although Thomas's travelogue often played at opera houses and upper-class establishments, prices were carefully controlled in order to appeal to the working and middle classes. Percy Burton lobbied the Covent Garden Opera House's manager, Sir Thomas Beecham, to dismantle a portion of the expensive box seating to make room for more affordable seats.[29] These tickets could be purchased for as low as one shilling. Because of the reduced prices lengthy queues often wrapped around the venue.[30] Remarkably, for the London season, train schedules in the countryside were adjusted to bring in people from The Midlands.[31] Thomas's travelogue turned out to be so popular that for the first time in its history Covent Garden Opera House postponed its autumn opera season.[32] Outside of London, Thomas's travelogue played to sold-out audiences in Liverpool, Bristol, Edinburgh,

---

26 Ibid.
27 Lowell Thomas to G.J. Hogben, 14 April 1920, LTP 1.25.2.1.499.31.
28 Carnegy would later change his surname to Carnegie.
29 Percy Burton to Thomas, 14 July 1919, LTP 1.25.2.1.499.1.
30 *The Times*, 1 September 1919; Lowell Thomas Remembers, LTP 1.25.2.6.505.7.
31 Lowell Thomas Remembers the Allenby and Lawrence Show, LTP 1.25.2.6.505.7.
32 Dale Carnegy to Unknown, 1920, LTP 1.25.2.1.499.13.

Glasgow, Adelaide and Melbourne.[33] Special rates were also available to ex-servicemen and schoolchildren. In Glasgow, for example, the entire 52nd (Lowland) Division, veterans of the First, Second, and Third Battles of Gaza as well as the advance towards and capture of Jerusalem, filled St Andrew's Hall.[34]

Britain's movers and shakers, including the travelogue's two stars, Allenby and Lawrence, also attended the show. David Lloyd George, Winston Churchill and nearly all MPs attended performances in 1919. The British, Spanish and Norwegian royal families saw shows in 1919 and 1920.[35] Lawrence attended at least once at the behest of fellow Oxford University archaeologist, David Hogarth. In Lawrence's estimation, Hogarth considered his attendance something of a novelty, 'as a sauce to render the dish more piquant'.[36] When Allenby arrived at the Opera House for Thomas's performance on 9 October 1919, the London Metropolitan Police was needed to control a crowd upward of 20,000 people who were desperate to catch a glimpse of one of the show's heroes.[37]

Financially, the show did very well. Gate receipts from the travelogue's London season have been lost, but the *Evening News* and *Evening Mail* reported that early shows were drawing nearly £300 per night.[38] If that number held up over the show's two-month run at the Opera House, it may have grossed around £20,000. The travelogue's success continued as the show grossed over £12,000 from its season at the Royal Albert Hall between 27 October 1919 and 6 December 1919. A single Manchester performance in 1920 made £2,200, even though a tram strike restricted public transport to the Free Trade Hall.[39] Burdened with the high cost of travel in the underdeveloped parts of Burma, Malaya and India, the travelogue still managed to earn around $14,000.[40]

Both press and private reviews throughout the British Empire were overwhelmingly positive. Reviewing *With Allenby in Palestine and Lawrence in Arabia* in Bombay at the Willingdon Sports Club in December 1921, the *Times of India* wrote that Thomas's travelogue had given birth to an innovative and exhilarating form of entertainment:

> His success has been far greater even than was the success of his illustrious fellow-countrymen. This has no doubt been due in a great measure to the fact that Mr. Lowell Thomas has created an entirely new form of entertainment which is a unique combination both of the motion picture screen and the speaking stage. Both picture and story synchronize as though it were done by magic.[41]

Not only was the show heralded as a ground-breaking form of popular entertainment, Thomas's travelogue also pulled at the heartstrings of an empire fascinated by the land that gave birth to the three Abrahamic faiths.[42] *Lloyd's Sunday News* struggled to 'express the

---

33 Ibid.; *The Advertiser* (Adelaide), 28 December 1920, p. 6.
34 Lowell Thomas Remembers, LTP 1.25.2.6.505.7.
35 Dale Carnegy to Unknown, 1920, LTP 1.25.2.1.499.13.
36 T.E. Lawrence to Lowell Thomas, 7 December 1919, LTP 1.25.3.1.514.1
37 Lowell Thomas Remembers, LTP 1.25.2.6.505.7.
38 *Evening News* and *Evening Mail*, 21 August 1919, p. 1.
39 Dale Carnegy to Unknown, 1920, LTP 1.25.2.1.499.13.
40 Thomas to Calvin Fentress, 22 February 1922, LTP 1.25.2.1.499.24.
41 *Times of India*, 8 December 1921, p. 8.
42 Eitan Bar-Yosef, *The Holy Land in England Culture, 1799–1917: Palestine and the Question of Orientalism* (Oxford: Clarendon Press, 2005); for the best survey of the role of Palestine and the Holy Land in Georgian, Victorian and Edwardian England.

mystic charm of it all'.[43] The *Manchester Guardian* admired Thomas's travelogue as a story that 'holds all the pageantry and none of the bitterness of the old wars of the Crusaders'.[44] Christchurch's *Sun* wrote that '[t]here is no more fascinating and romantic story than the modern Crusade, in which soldiers from New Zealand played such an important part.'[45]

Just as Thomas's travelogue had moved American Jews and Zionists like Schiff, the Warburgs, and Straus, so too were English and Australian Jews moved by scenes of the Holy Land. In England, the journal of the English Zionist Federation, *Zionist Review*, wrote '[n]o Zionist should lose the opportunity of hearing and seeing "*With Allenby in Palestine and Lawrence in Arabia*."' 'He will not only see the holy places and historic scenes', the reviewer approved, 'but he will also see something of the life of the Jewish colonists, their pleasant homes, and their achievements'. Furthermore, Thomas's audience would 'hear of the part played by the Jewish boys from England and America in the great campaign, and learn in what esteem Neil Primrose, who insisted on his Jewish origin, was held by his fellow cavalrymen'.[46] The *Australian Jewish Herald* encouraged Australian Jews to go and see the 'rose-red city of Petra', which laid close to the burial place of Aaron, Moses' brother, at Mount Hor.[47] 'Each picture', the *Herald* continued, 'disclosed the beauties of the great fertile country, now happily under British rule' and 'appealed strongly to the sympathies of the Zionist, who saw through them the vast potentialities of Eretz Israel, the land of his inheritance'.[48] Similarly, Sydney's *Hebrew Standard* wrote that the 'soul stirring campaign by which the Holy Land has been wrested forever from the stifling government of the Turk' should resonate strongly with Australian Jews.[49]

What made Thomas's travelogue all the more spectacular was that audiences were supposedly hearing of the campaign for the first time. Even though the capture of Jerusalem in December 1917 was front-page news in the British and Dominion press, and W. T. Massey, the official war correspondent in Palestine, had published the first two volumes of his three-volume unofficial history in 1918 and 1919, a number of reviewers were certain that Thomas's travelogue was the first time the public had heard of the war effort in the Middle East.[50] 'During the war', explained the *Times*, 'the London public heard comparatively little about the "sideshow," and it naturally appreciates the opportunity of hearing a connected story of the Palestine triumph told by a dispassionate outsider who was in the campaign but not of it.'[51] The *Observer* commended Thomas for introducing the public to 'the stirring and romantic incidents of the victorious war in the East'.[52] Even the left wing *Nation*, an open critic of militarism, made a 'well-merited exception' in its praise

---

43   *Lloyd Sunday News*, 24 August 1919, p. 6.
44   *Manchester Guardian*, 13 April 1920, p. 16.
45   *Sun (Christchurch)*, 27 September 1920, p. 10.
46   *Zionist's Review*, n.d., c. 1920, typescript copy, LTP 1.25.2.4.1.502.30. Primrose, a Liberal MP and Parliamentary Secretary to the Treasury, was killed at the Third Battle of Gaza in November 1917.
47   *Australian Jewish Herald*, 10 December 1920, p. 17.
48   *Australian Jewish Herald*, 26 November 1920, p. 14.
49   *Hebrew Standard of Australasia*, 7 August 1920, p. 15.
50   For press coverage of Jerusalem's capture, see Justin Fantauzzo, 'The Finest Feats of the War? The Captures of Baghdad and Jerusalem during the First World War and Public Opinion throughout the British Empire,' *War in History*, forthcoming 2016.
51   *The Times*, 6 December 1919, p. 12.
52   *Observer*, 17 August 1919, p. 5.

of the travelogue, suggesting that the campaign should be commemorated each year on the anniversary of the Ottoman Empire's surrender.[53]

Private reviews said much the same. Sir Sidney Low, Lecturer of Imperial and Colonial History at King's College, London, and a wartime journalist on the Western Front and in Italy, expressed his 'gratitude which I think all Englishman must feel for the service you are rendering us in bringing this masterly record of a great British enterprise'.[54] After seeing Thomas's travelogue at the Philharmonic Hall in London, George Adam Smith, Principal of the University of Aberdeen, and author of the renowned *Atlas of the Historical Geography of the Holy Land*, was so moved that he offered to lobby Scotland's high society to finance a season in Scotland.[55] Thomas even received a request to have the travelogue transcribed into braille.[56] In Madras, India, an anonymous Anglo-Indian university student could barely contain his excitement in a letter he wrote directly to Thomas:

> It was an enchanting experience to be caught up in the clouds and to be able to look at cities, deserts and rivers beneath us; to descend whenever necessary, and see closer the beauties in colour, of the Holy Land and Arabia, places which many of us will never have the opportunity to visit; to be with great General Allenby and young Captain Lawrence during that critical time in the war.[57]

In Australia, Sydney's *World's News* commented that Thomas's travelogue had cleared the malaise hanging over the campaign for an Australian public that 'heard far too little' about it.[58] Perth's *West Australian* singled out Thomas for bringing to life 'the hardships experienced by our troops in the desert' and the war deeds of the Light Horse, which, 'in these regions was regarded as belonging to Australia'.[59] The *Advertiser* in Adelaide wrote that the audience expressed a sort of bewildered 'admiration on the part played by the Australians in driving the Crescent from the Holy Land'.[60] The *Glen Innes Examiner* in New South Wales was proud to hear 'how wonderfully the boys behaved in the Holy Land'.[61]

As much as audiences and reviewers wanted to hear about Lawrence's escapades in Arabia, as both Dawson and Hodson have written, they were just as keen to hear stories about Allenby and Palestine, and of their menfolk in action. At times, especially during the travelogue's tour of Britain, the travelogue relied upon the show's original star, Allenby. At the Athenaeum in Bury St Edmonds, the travelogue was delivered under the title 'With Field-Marshal Lord Allenby in Palestine and Arabia'.[62] In Hartlepool, the show was advertised only as 'With Allenby in Palestine'.[63] Dale Carnegy's tour of Montreal included both shows but did not mention Lawrence by name: 'Gen. Allenby's British Campaign in

---

53 *Nation*, 20 September 1919, p. 726.
54 Sir Sidney Low to Thomas, 10 November 1919, LTP 1.25.2.1.499.40
55 George Adam Smith to Thomas, 31 December 1919, LTP 1.25.2.1.500.12.
56 Mary Walker to Thomas, 31 October 1919, LTP 1.25.2.1.500.34.
57 A College Student to Thomas, 19 November 1921, LTP 1.25.2.1.500.34.
58 *World's News* (Sydney), 4 September 1920, p. 5.
59 *West Australian* (Perth), 9 August 1920, p. 6.
60 *Advertiser* (Adelaide), 20 December 1920, p. 8.
61 *Glen Innes Examiner*, 19 August 1920, p. 8.
62 *Bury Free Press*, 26 November 1921, p. 6.
63 *Northern Daily Mail*, 17 March 1921, p. 1.

THE HOLY LAND (And The Land Of The Arabian Nights)'.[64] Wellington's *Evening Post* was relieved to find that the New Zealanders, who 'had not received a worthy interpretation' of their contribution to the war effort in the Middle East, but had 'played an important role in all the long campaigns which led to the reconquest of the Holy Land from the Turks', finally given their due by Thomas's travelogue.[65] 'Mr. Thomas', it wrote, 'pays the highest tribute to the services of the Australian and New Zealand cavalry, which contributed so much to the victory'.[66] It repeated that theme throughout the week:

> The Palestine campaign was sometimes called a "stunt" and sometimes it was merely described as a "show" in comparison to the Western Front. Mr. Lowell Thomas showed last night at the Opera House that it was a wonderful campaign. The importance from an engineering no less than a military point of view has yet to be fully grasped.[67]

Adelaide's *Daily Herald* praised Thomas's travelogue as a story of 'our sons in the Holy Land'. Had Thomas not brought his show to Australia, 'the brilliant story of the Palestine and Arabian campaigns probably would never have been heard.'[68]

Indeed, all signs point towards a declining enthusiasm for stories of the Western Front. The cinema trade journal *Bioscope* lauded Thomas's travelogue as a production 'superior to the pictures of the Western Front', where the near ubiquitous 'background of ruined buildings and dilapidated trees' became 'melancholy and monotonous'.[69] Thomas's travelogue was also more popular than contemporary productions on the Western Front, such as Henry Beckles Willson's lecture series at the Central Hall in Westminster, on Ypres.[70]

Contested site of memory

While Thomas's travelogue grabbed hold of a centuries-long fascination with the Holy Land and, increasingly, a longing to hear about the war outside the Western Front, for others the show offered undeniable evidence that men of the Anglo-Imperial world possessed an intrinsic capability to lead and govern. Lady Muir Mackenzie's review in the *Daily Mail* positioned Allenby and Lawrence as products of a divine providence; men, it seemed, who had been pre-destined, if not biologically contracted, for greatness. Allenby, 'the superman', personified the British spirit of 'steadfastness, loyalty, and joyous bravery'. Alongside Allenby stood Lawrence, 'a typical example' of the 'many plain young Englishmen' who 'rule over remote States with a justice that has become the ideal of the world'. In Lawrence, in particular, Muir Mackenzie saw unquestionable proof of Britain's special purpose. 'There are thousands of possible Colonel Lawrences in England', she wrote, 'So ought we not to cherish every babe born in this land, try to provide a fair home to receive him, and during his schools days suggest to him that he is a light-bearer – a chosen

---

64 *Montreal Star*, 7 February 1920, NP.
65 *Evening Post* (Wellington), 16 October 1920, p. 6.
66 *Evening Post* (Wellington), 19 October 1920, p. 3.
67 *Evening Post* (Wellington), 23 October 1920, p. 9.
68 *Daily Herald* (Adelaide), 16 December 1920, p. 7.
69 *Bioscope*, 25 September 1919, p. 5.
70 *The Times*, 5 January 1920, p. 10.

child of Destiny?'[71] Likewise, an anonymous reviewer in *Bioscope* found that Thomas's travelogue was 'conclusive evidence that the Englishman seeks not to destroy, but to construct'. Thomas's travelogue left no doubt that the soldier would be able to assimilate back into civilian society and into positions of leadership. 'Tommy may be a man of valour to-day', the reviewer lectured, 'but to-morrow he is transformed into the policeman, the agriculturalist, and the sanitary reformer'. And there were, furthermore, two paths that one could take to achieve prominence. Both Allenby and Lawrence were 'men equally endowed with tenacity of purpose', but they 'achieved success by different methods'. Allenby did it the old-fashioned way by ascending the ranks and winning victory on the battlefield. Lawrence did it the modern way; an intellectual who had used his faculty for foreign languages and knowledge of tribal politics to fight a guerrilla war against conventional Ottoman forces.[72] In short, the British Empire had produced and would continue to produce war heroes in all shapes and sizes.

Yet in the years after Thomas's travelogue had come to London, a comprehensive tour of England, Scotland, Wales and Ireland struck a different chord with audiences. Not all wanted or were comfortable rehashing the war's gory (and upsetting) details, no matter the field of battle. In the *Bath Chronicle*, its reviewer assured would-be theatre-goers not to be deceived by the travelogue's title. 'You will see none of the things we are all trying to forget', the *Chronicle* promised. Instead, Thomas's travelogue became more about seeing the exotic sights of the Middle East from the comfort of a cushioned seat and less about the war. 'There is hardly a citizen of this city', its reviewer continued, 'who would not give a fortnight's wages if he could only trek across the unexplored deserts of the land of the Arabian Nights, fly over the Nile, the Pyramids, see the Suez Canal and do a sort of Cook's Tour of Palestine'. For the price of an 'afternoon tea', Thomas gave Britons a chance to see the land of the Pharaohs and the Bible and to come away 'with all the wealth of a seasoned globe-trotter'.[73]

The *Devon and Exeter Gazette* took a similar stance. 'Anyone who attends this travelogue with the idea of seeing men charging in the face of machine-guns and being mowed down is sure to be disappointed,' it warned. 'It is more like a tale of the Arabian Nights. It is gorgeous, spectacular, and full of the romance and adventure of the land where a man can have four veiled wives at one time.' The *Gazette* was most impressed by Thomas's seemingly unadulterated access to Islamic life in the Middle East. One of the best parts of the travelogue, its reviewer argued, was the chance to see Mecca, a place that 'none but Moslems shall ever visit' and a 'city that only 13 Christian adventurers have ever seen and lived to tell the tale'.[74] The *Green Room*, an Australian stage trade journal, wrote that 'practically nothing is known by the public about the campaigns in the Holy Land and in Arabia.' Australian ignorance was so widespread that, according to the *Green Room*, 'the average person does not know that there was a campaign in Arabia, and if asked where Arabia is he might say next door to Zanzibar.' 'Some of the greatest events that have taken place in the world since the dawn of the Christian era', it continued,

> occurred in Palestine during 1916 and 1918. Allenby's campaign was waged over a land fairly soaked with atmosphere. There were veiled women, camels, palms, deserts and

---

71 *Daily Mail*, 16 September 1919, p. 4.
72 *Bioscope*, 25 September 1919, p. 5.
73 *Bath Chronicle*, 8 January 1921, p. 3.
74 *Devon and Exeter Gazette*, 28 May 1921, p. 6.

places memory-laden by the earliest records of man. These pictures show vast hordes of cavalry charging over the Judean hills and by places where Abraham, David and Solomon lived and where the Prince of Peace walked and taught. These films show unending caravans of camels carrying cannon, water, bully beef and Tommy Atkins over the same roads that caravans used in the days of the Queen of Sheba, when they were bringing sandalwood and myrrh up to Nineveh and Babylon.[75]

And like the reviews from Bath and Devon in 1921, Irish newspapers in 1922 highlighted Thomas's show as 'sight-seeing in the East'. 'The war picture has passed,' wrote Dublin's Nationalist *Freemans Journal*. 'The nations thirst for peace. Nobody wants the perpetuation of scenes of war terror and the humiliation of defeated peoples.' Making matters worse was the fact that Palestine was 'no longer the land Allenby "liberated" three years ago'. Growing Zionist influence and clashes between Arabs and Jews had fundamentally changed the political landscape. Clearly disenchanted with the war's unfulfilled promises, the *Journal*'s reviewer concluded that 'these pictures claim attention as illustrations of travel mainly, though there are shown the movement of troops.'[76]

Although reviews of Thomas's travelogue were generally positive, whether audiences were captivated by the war or exoticism of the Middle East, not all approved of the show. Ghulam Hassan Khan, an Indian Muslim from Kohala, temporarily residing in Regents Park while he worked at the nearby mosque, accused Thomas of misrepresenting the war as a clash between Christianity and Islam. Khan reminded Thomas that the war was a political, not religious, conflict. All British Muslims, he emphasised repeatedly, had supported the war and had 'gathered for the help of France and Belgium' to 'smash the Germans'. Khan ended his letter by threatening to write directly to Prime Minister Lloyd George.[77] Like Khan, other Indian Muslims gave Thomas a cold reception. On Thomas's tour of India, Gandhists stormed the Opera House in Bombay in protest against British rule. The problem was so serious that the Bombay Police was forced to scatter undercover agents throughout the crowd to apprehend protestors. 'They hissed everything that I said about Allenby, Emir Feisal and King Hussein', Thomas wrote to Dale Carnegy in 1921, 'and nearly raised the roof with applause everytime I mentioned the Turks and when I threw that picture of Djemal Pasha on the screen'. 'They considered it too pro-British,' Thomas later recalled.[78]

The travelogue's reception in Ireland wasn't much better. On the heels of the Irish War of Independence and the Anglo-Irish Treaty, Fionán Lynch, the incoming Sinn Féin Minister of Education in the newly formed Irish Free State, tried to block the travelogue from opening in Dublin. Lynch not only objected to Dublin schoolchildren taking the day off to see Thomas's matinee performance on 6 February 1922, he also considered the travelogue as an unwelcome story of Englishness and a distasteful paean to the British Army.[79] Although Lynch was a pre-war teacher in Dublin, and this might partially explain his disapproval of an off-day for Dublin's youth, he was also ferociously anti-British. Lynch was a founding member of the Irish Volunteers, an active member in the Irish Republic Brotherhood, and had fought during the Easter Rising. Lowell Thomas Travelogues'

---

75 *The Green Room* (Sydney), 1 September 1920, p. 9.
76 *Freeman's Journal*, 7 February 1922, p. 8.
77 Ghulam Hassan Khan to Lowell Thomas, 19 August 1919, LTP 1.25.2.1.499.37.
78 Lowell Thomas Remembers, LTP 1.25.2.1.499.13.
79 *Freemans Journal*, 30 January 1922, p. 5.

acting manager, Albert E. Davies, fired back at Lynch in the Nationalist *Freemans Journal*. Davies stressed that the show was not 'an English story, any more than it is an Irish or an Australian one, and it comes to us from America'. It was neither prepared nor financed by the British Government, he argued, but instead by Thomas, an American, it celebrated the achievements of the 10th (Irish) Division, Lawrence 'of the Lawrence family of Galway' and, in a subtle nod to Irish Catholics, the liberation of the Holy Land.[80]

Concerns even arose in Australia and England. Henry Clay, a well-known vaudeville performer in Sydney, wrote to the local *Bulletin* crying foul over Thomas's supposedly scant treatment of the Anzacs. Clay wrongly charged that Thomas had referred to the Australians only twice and, as a result, that the travelogue had downplayed the efforts of Australians in the Middle East. Writing to the *Bulletin*'s editor, Thomas made clear the fact that the show was never intended to be a tribute to Australians alone. It was an 'American tribute to British valour', Thomas responded:

> and when I say "British" I intend that all who hear me should understand that I include the Australian Light Horse, the cavalrymen from New Zealand and Tasmania, the Ghurkas, Scotch Lowlanders and shopkeepers from London who fought so desperately around Jerusalem, the Welsh Fusiliers, the Irish Division, the Hongkong [sic] Singapore Battery, the one hundred thousand men of the Egyptian Labor Corps, the Yeomanry, the men from the British West Indies, the aviators from England, Canada, South Africa and Australia, as well as all the other representatives of the seventeen nationalities who fought with the Anzacs in Palestine.[81]

In England, the opposite criticism was made: Thomas had focussed too much on the Anzacs. Philip Chetwode, the wartime General Officer Commanding of XX Corps in Palestine, wrote to Thomas the day after the travelogue debuted in London. Too much of the travelogue featured photographs and films of Australians and New Zealanders, he complained, even though 'Jerusalem was taken as you said by London + Welsh troops and a London audience wd appreciate any pictures of their marching or doing anything else in Palestine.'[82]

But the biggest challenge to Thomas's travelogue came from the War Office Cinematograph Committee, the Imperial War Museum (IWM) and the film studio British Instructional Films (BIF). Following Thomas's return to Britain from the Dominions and Colonies in June 1923, Harry Bruce Woolfe, head of BIF, sought legal action to prevent Thomas from exhibiting his travelogue outside the British Isles. BIF and the War Office had been preparing their own film version of the campaign, *Armageddon*, and had scheduled its release for British Film Week in November 1923. Woolfe cited Thomas's agreement with the War Office Cinematograph Committee in January 1920, which restricted the use of official war films to Great Britain and Ireland. The contract, he claimed, was incontrovertible proof that Thomas's worldwide tour had violated the terms of the agreement.[83] And in exhibiting his photographs and films across the British Empire and beyond, Thomas had 'skimmed

---

80 *Freemans Journal*, 8 February 1922, p. 6.
81 Thomas to the Editor of *The Bulletin*, 30 June 1920, LTP 1.25.2.1.499.9.
82 Philip Chetwode to Thomas, 15 August 1919, LTP 1.25.2.1.499.16.
83 Harry Bruce Woolfe to Edward Foxen Cooper, 11 June 1923, TS 27/192, The National Archives (TNA), London.

the market', Woolfe argued, and killed demand in London and American theatres for what would become *Armageddon*.[84]

A formal inquest by the Treasury Solicitor's Office followed and a letter was sent to Thomas demanding an explanation for his overseas tour. Initially, Thomas ignored the request. Charles ffoulkes, Secretary of the Imperial War Museum, followed with a thinly veiled threat of legal action.[85] Thomas eventually gave way and wrote back, almost certainly after seeking legal advice, and claimed that he understood the clause of 'exclusive rights of public exhibition' to be a way of protecting Thomas's travelogue from domestic competition. Moreover, he pointed out that the overwhelming majority of the films used in the travelogue were recorded by himself and his crew when they toured Egypt and Palestine in 1918. Not only were the films Thomas's private property, he also paid the Cinematograph Committee a fee of £4,500 before he left England for Australia.[86] What Thomas's coy answer did not reveal was that Carnegy had raised concerns about performing the travelogue in converted motion picture cinemas nearly three years earlier.[87] Still, it seems completely believable that Thomas's interpretation of 'exclusive rights' pertained only to Britain and Ireland. In correspondence with Carnegy shortly before departing for Australia, Thomas considered his payment to the Cinematograph Committee as a fee for a 'free hand in the British Isles'.[88] Thomas's correspondence with the Cinematograph Committee, the War Museum, BIF, and the Solicitor's Office ended with him issuing an ultimatum: the Treasury could sue Thomas, if they liked, for breach of contract, or Thomas could create a 'new and finer production' on the campaign and split the revenues with the Committee.[89] His aggressive tactic succeeded. The Committee backed off from its threat of legal sanction and allowed Thomas to continue delivering the lecture in the United States. Canada, however, remained off-limits, although Carnegy had already toured Ontario and Quebec in 1920. In exchange, Thomas, who likely raised the possibility of a new and improved travelogue as negotiating leverage, agreed not to pursue a cinematic version of his lecture series.[90]

The legal dispute between Thomas, the War Office, BIF, the IWM and the Treasury is important for a number of reasons. First, Thomas's suspicion that the War Office was driven by commercial motivation was likely correct. In his lengthy letter refuting the War Office's claims of exclusive rights, Thomas had accused both BIF and the IWM of piggybacking on the success of his travelogue.[91] Correspondence between Woolfe and the Treasury revealed as much, as the main discussion points were on Thomas's 'damage' to American and Dominion markets.[92] Thus, it seems that the War Office was at least somewhat concerned with making a profit.

Furthermore, the War Office's support for BIF demonstrates an active interventionist policy on behalf of the British government. Working in tandem with the Treasury, the War Office was willing to support British film companies and producers in an effort to keep

---

84 Harry Bruce Woolfe to Edward Foxen Cooper, 20 June 1923, TS 27/192, TNA.
85 Charles ffoulkes to Thomas, TS 27/192, TNA.
86 Thomas to J. Moverley Sharp, April 1920, LTP 1.25.2.1.499.11.
87 Thomas to Carnegy, 20 May 1920, LTP 1.25.2.1.499.13.
88 Thomas to Carnegy, 24 April 1921, LTP 1.25.2.1.499.13.
89 Thomas to ffoulkes, 22 September 1923, TS 27/192, TNA.
90 A.W. Brown to Charles ffoulkes, 2 October 1923, LTP 1.25.2.1.499.1; Thomas to ffoulkes, 23 October 1923, LTP 1.25.1.499.11.
91 Thomas to ffoulkes, 22 September 1923, TS 27/192, TNA.
92 Charles ffoulke to G.S. King, 20 July 1923, TS 27/192, TNA.

content and creative control of the war in British hands. In reference to Thomas, Woolfe's correspondence with Edward Foxen Cooper, in charge of the IWM's growing film archive, made clear the national tension brewing underneath the surface of the controversy:

> We feel sure that the Trustees of the Imperial War Museum had no idea, any more than we had ourselves, that an American who had been treated with every respect and given every facility and help by the British authorities would so flagrantly break his contract, and advertise the fact. But on his own admission he has done so and caused the Trustees and ourselves very heavy loss.[93]

The fact that the War Office was so concerned with maintaining creative control over the campaign in Sinai and Palestine suggests that the war in the Middle East remained an important part of Britain's official post-war narrative, at least until the mid-1920s.

Conclusion

With Allenby in Palestine and Lawrence in Arabia was an inter-war phenomenon. At once, it made an emotional appeal to the British Empire's Christian and Muslim peoples and to those interested in the war in Sinai, Palestine and Arabia. Importantly, it brought the story of Allenby and the EEF's victories – not just Lawrence's exploits in Arabia – onto the world stage. As such, it became a major part of imperial memorial culture. From England to India, millions saw Thomas's travelogue. As late as 1935, Thomas was still performing the travelogue, albeit infrequently, in the United States, and in encore performances across the British Empire, after he delivered separate travelogues on India and Afghanistan.[94]

Yet as popular as the show was, in the more politically sensitive corners of the British Empire (and its former parts), and even in England and Australia, the travelogue courted minor controversy. Whether Indian Muslims, Irish Nationalists, British ex-servicemen or the titans of British memory-making and films, *With Allenby in Palestine and Lawrence in Arabia*'s representation of the war mattered. And, thus, the 'sideshow' in Palestine, not just the war on the Western Front, mattered.

---

93 Harry Bruce Woolfe to Edward Foxen Cooper, 20 June 1923, TS 27/291, TNA.
94 *Traffic Messenger*, 12 November 1935, LTP 1.25.2.5.3.504.9.

Chapter 13
An architecture of imperial ambivalence
The Patcham Chattri

Tim Barringer

High above the seaside town of Brighton, on a remote and windswept eminence of the Sussex Downs above the hamlet of Patcham, stands the Chattri (see Figure 13.1).[1] It is a simple white structure fashioned from Sicilian marble, with a domed roof supported by eight slender columns. Such a refined design seems at first sight drastically at odds

Figure 13.1 **The Chattri, Patcham, Sussex**

Source: Tim Barringer

---

1 The Chattri Memorial Group, http://www.chattri.org/; Doctor's Brighton Pavilion, 2012, http://www.sikhmuseum.com/brighton/; Brighton Museums online, 'WW1 and the Royal Pavilion,' accessed 24 August 2016, http://brightonmuseums.org.uk/royalpavilion/history/ww1-and-the-royal-pavilion/; BBC online, 'World War One At Home,' 2015, http://www.bbc.co.uk/programmes/p01s6x3c. This chapter relies on information gleaned from these websites. Although

Figure 13.2 William Bernard Cooke after J.M.W. Turner, *Battle Abbey: The Spot Where Harold Fell*, 1819

Source: Yale Center for British Art, Paul Mellon Collection

with its rustic surroundings, and today cattle and sheep graze undisturbed around its base. Situated in a landscape that is the very epitome of Englishness, the Chattri has come to resemble the picturesque gazebo, ruin or folly, a central trope of English painting and landscape gardening. English Romanticism was preoccupied with the cultural inscription of historical events through a process of association, exemplified by *Battle Abbey: The Spot where Harold Fell* from J.M.W. Turner's engraved series of *Views in Sussex* (1818–20; see Figure 13.2). In a bucolic scene bounded by historical ruins a hunting dog chases a hapless fox across the site where William the Conqueror defeated the last Saxon king in 1066. Erected only miles away from that site, centuries later, the Chattri likewise inflects the meaning of the landscape through a process of historical association. A quiet but insistent signifier of the inescapable presence of India in British history, and of Britain in India's, the Chattri, unveiled in 1921, acknowledges the involvement of Indians in the First World War. It commemorates the Hindu and Sikh soldiers of the Indian Army who died in the hospitals of Brighton as a result of wounds received in the French and Belgian battlefields, and it

---

little has been published on the Chattri in a scholarly context, much research has been conducted and published online. The Brighton Museums Service and the Sikh Museum have also been active in conducting research into the role of Brighton in the First World War.

is located at the spot where they were cremated. This chapter will argue that the hybrid architectural form of this unusual memorial poignantly encapsulates the paradoxes of imperial participation in the Great War, revealing the British Empire's ambivalent attitude to its colonial subjects.

Indians in the trenches

The British Army in India was a vast human resource. In 1914, it ranked as the largest volunteer army in the world, amounting to around 236,000 men. Ranking above the 159,000 Indian officers and men were a mere 2,300 or so British officers who had an absolute monopoly on the middle and higher levels of command. The division was clear and absolute. This vast organisation was conceived and equipped for regional warfare. The British Army in India had never fought a major campaign outside Asia, and resistance amongst the British military elite to the idea of Indian troops engaging in the European theatre of war alongside their British counterparts persisted until August 1914. However, Viscount Hardinge, the Viceroy of India, anxious about nationalist agitation, was adamant that the inclusion of Indian troops in the conflict would encourage loyalty to the empire in the sub-continent.[2] In any case, the desperate shortage of troops for the Western Front forced the hand of the authorities. Orders were given in late August and the first Indian divisions, inaugurating the new India Corps, arrived in Europe in October 1914.

Visual records of these Indian troops are relatively rare. A studio portrait records the features of Lance Corporal Venkatasami, of the 2nd Queen's Own Madras Sappers and Miners. The diminutive figure of a professional soldier stands at ease, though a little stiffly, in front of a painted backdrop in a photographer's studio, the shadow of a smile crossing his face (see Figure 13.3).

He had served for twelve years, the last four of which he was lucky to survive: he fought on the Western Front and also in Mesopotamia and Egypt, where this photograph was taken in February 1918. He wears standard khaki drill tunic and shorts, and on his left sleeve are stripes for good conduct and long service.[3] Before the war, Venkatasami had worked on civilian engineering projects such as the construction of a railway at Secunderabad, forming the infrastructure of British India that was often held up as a benevolent result of empire.[4] The dust on his battered boots stands metonymically for the arid theatre of war in the Middle East.

As a Subedar or 'chief native officer', Venkatasami held a rank equal to that of a lieutenant; however, the racial hierarchy of the army placed him beneath all British officers in status. He was, and would always remain, a subaltern, both in terms of the army's explicit organisational hierarchy and in the more general, Gramscian sense adopted by the historians of the 'Subaltern Studies' group.[5] The photograph captures the duality of his

---

2 See Sir James Willcocks, *With the Indians in France* (London: Constable, 1920), p. 15.
3 See Paul Reed, 'Great War Photos: WW1 Photos Centenary Website, 2014–2018,' accessed 30 July 2015, http://greatwarphotos.com/2012/02/16/great-war-portraits-an-indian-sapper/.
4 Lieutenant-Colonel H.F. Murlan, *Baillie-Ki-Paltan: Being a History of the 2nd Battalion, Madras Pioneers* (1922; Uckfield: Naval and Military Press, 2005), p. 546.
5 See for example Ranajit Guha and Gayatri Chakravorty Spivak, eds, *Selected Subaltern Studies* (New York: Oxford University Press, 1988). On this question, see also Michèle Barrett, 'Recovered History: Subalterns at War: First World War Colonial Forces and the Politics of the Imperial War Graves Commission,' *Interventions* 9, no. 3 (2007): pp. 451–74.

Figure 13.3 Studio Portrait of Lance Corporal Venkatasami

Source: Collection of Paul Reed

position: a loyal member of the army, badged as such by the uniform, he was nonetheless barred from attaining the rank of a commissioned officer because of the colour of his skin. For the cultural theorist Homi Bhabha,

> Skin, the key signifier of culture and racial difference in the stereotype, is the most visible of fetishes, recognised as common knowledge in a range of cultural, political and historical discourses, and plays a public part in the racial drama that is enacted every day in colonial societies.[6]

---

6 Homi Bhabha, 'The Other Question: Difference, Discrimination and the Discourse of Colonialism, 1982,' in *Literature, Politics and Theory: Papers from the Essex Conferences, 1976–84*, ed. F. Barker, P. Hulme, M. Iversen and D. Loxley (London: Routledge, 1985), p. 151.

The Subedar, who had known no life outside the army, was doubtless aware of the regiment's storied history, reaching back to the origins of British India: they had for example fought under the orders of the future Duke of Wellington at the Battle of Seringapatam in 1799, defeating Tipu Sultan. Doubtless, too, Venkatasami's relationship to the British authorities and to the army was as complex as portrayed in Santanu Das's eloquent account of the 'intimate history' of Indians serving in the First World War based on a close reading of their letters. Das reveals that the Indian soldiers were acutely aware of the unthinking racism of the British army.[7] The diary of the Rajput aristocrat Thakur Amar Singh reveals, in Das's analysis, a complex mixture of internalised imperial ideology, traditional concepts of honour and resentment at poor conditions and the continual 'slurs' against Indian soldiers on the part of British officers and men. The Indian officer, Singh was told, 'can *never* replace . . . the natural instincts of the white man'.[8]

The underlying principles of recruitment and organisation of the Indian regiments were derived from colonial ethnography, which had long been codified in publications like *People of India*, compiled by John Forbes Watson in 1868–1875.[9] Allegedly 'warlike' and 'martial races' were preferred, and the soldiers were generally segregated along lines of religion or caste, as they were understood by the British.[10] The Expeditionary Force consisted of six battalions of Nepali Gurkhas – highly regarded by the British – two battalions of Garhwalis from the foothills of the Himalaya, and four battalions of Sikhs. Most of the remaining units were mixed battalions, typically with separate companies identified as Sikhs, Punjabi Muslims, Rajputs or Mahrattas. By the end of 1915, the number of Indian Army soldiers and Gurkhas who had served on the Western Front reached almost 30,000.

A large visual archive records the presence of Indian soldiers in the First World War. Photographs document the re-equipping and re-training of Indian forces for modern trench warfare, the use of gas masks being one (see Figure 13.4). The photographer Ariel Lowe Varges, whose work is marked by a modernist sensibility, was primarily active as a film cameraman, whose extensive sequences of footage from Salonika and the Mesopotamian Campaign were widely disseminated through newsreels in Britain. In this powerfully-composed still photograph, Varges emphasises the disjuncture between the factory-produced technology of the gas mask and the hand-tied turbans: the expressionless, cyborgian faces contrast with the textile and flesh, indicating that this war is forging a new and troubling relationship between man and machine. The Indian figures, already bound up in the complex hybridity of the imperial army uniforms, appear both

---

7 Santanu Das, 'Indians at Home, Mesopotamia and France: Towards an Intimate History,' in *Race, Empire and First World War Writing*, ed. S. Das (Cambridge: Cambridge University Press, 2011), pp. 70–89; see especially pp. 75–7. See also David Omissi, 'Europe Through Indian Eyes: Indian Soldiers Encounter England and France, 1914–1918,' *English Historical Review* 122, no. 496 (2007): pp. 371–96.

8 Das, 'Indians at Home,' p. 77.

9 J. Forbes Watson and John William Kaye, eds, *The People of India: A Series of Photographic Illustrations with Descriptive Letterpress, of the Races and Tribes of Hindustan* (London: India Museum, 1868–1875). See John Falconer, 'A Pure Labour of Love,' in *Colonialist Photography: Imag(in)ing Race and Place*, ed. Eleanor M. Hight and Gary Sampson (London: Routledge, 2002), pp. 51–81.

10 See Gajendra Singh, ed., 'Fulfilling Colonial Fantasies in Pursuit of the Martial Race,' in *The Testimonies of Indian Soldiers and the Two World Wars: Between Self and Sepoy* (London: Bloomsbury Academic, 2014), pp. 13–15.

Figure 13.4 Ariel Lowe Varges, *On the Salonika Front*, photograph, Ministry of Information First World War Official Collection

Source: © Imperial War Museums (Q 56644)

swallowed up by the larger project of empire and marginalised within it – in Bhabha's much-quoted phrase 'not quite/not white'.[11] A further disparity is suggested by the displacement of the row of Indians amidst the recognisably un-Indian landscape. This relationship of figure and ground seems to prefigure the position of the Chattri – an uncanny combination of belonging and displacement, imbrication and alienation that characterises the Indian experience of the Great War.

In an intimate photograph of *Indian Dogras and Highlanders in a Trench With Dugouts*, a Scotsman wearing a tartan kilt sits with members of the 41st (Dogra) Infantry, in a trench at Fauquissart, France (see Figure 13.5).

'Dogra' refers to a cultural and linguistic group from the Eastern Punjab and Kashmir who was highly regarded by the British authorities and to whom colonial anthropology attributed high military prowess. The photograph, taken between July and September 1915, finds a telling formal equivalent of the claustrophobia and the tension of waiting for action that characterised trench warfare. In the rhythmic passage in the centre, rifles and slats in the trench wall seem to mark receding time as well as space, ticking like the

---

11 Homi Bhabha, 'Of Mimicry and Man,' in *The Location of Culture* (London: Routledge, 2012), p. 131.

An architecture of imperial ambivalence 221

Figure 13.5   Charles Hilton DeWitt Girdwood, *Indian Dogras and Highlanders in a Trench With Dugouts* [Fauquissart, France], 1915

Source: British Library: Photo 24/294

seconds, minutes, hours and days that passed between moments of unspeakable bloodshed and terror. The receding sequence of faces, hands and especially the exposed knee of the Highland solider closest to the viewer, remind us of the vulnerability of human flesh in the theatre of industrial warfare. The slight over-exposure of the photograph de-emaphasises racial difference, so often (to echo Bhabha) a fetish in colonial photography, as in colonial societies. To the right of the composition, the natural world attempts to assert itself: tangled roots grow into the trench, but nature itself, blurred and blanched in a burst of Turnerian light at the upper right, seems entirely lost and unattainable from the submerged world of the trenches.

The photographer who made *Indian Dogras and Highlanders in a Trench With Dugouts*, C.H.D. Girdwood was, perhaps, well placed to perceive the ironies and displacements that accompanied the Indian presence on the Western Front. Indeed, the peripatetic life of Charles Hilton DeWitt Girdwood is itself emblematic of empire. Born in Ottawa, Canada, son of a Baptist minister, he moved to the United States and then in the 1890s to London, where he became a significant portrait photographer. He travelled to India to cover the Coronation Durbars of 1903 and 1911 and was in India when war was declared in 1914. He then travelled with the Indian Army expeditionary force to France, where, under official commission from the War Office, he produced a series of photographs of the Indian troops for propaganda use. His work far exceeded the brief, however, and the resulting portfolio of images of the Indian troops (now in the British Library) provides a humane and sympathetic response to conditions of unspeakable suffering and hardship.

By the end of that year, at least 3,000 of the 30,000 Indian soldiers in combat had been killed and 14,000 injured. In other words, more than half the soldiers that came to Europe entered the official record as wounded or killed. Propaganda photographs showed a well-organised and properly equipped medical staff presiding like redeeming angels; in fact, however, chaos and filth were ubiquitous in field hospitals, especially where gangrene and other infections were commonplace and supplies inadequate. Morale suffered, and a particular focus of anger was the practice of returning wounded soldiers to the trenches as quickly as possible. The military censors were sufficiently alarmed by the situation to allow a petition 'From the Indian sick in hospital' to pass to London. It was addressed 'England. The Emperor':

> Your Majesty's order was that a man who had been wounded once should be allowed to return to India; or that if he is recovered he should not be made to serve again. The heart of India is broken because they inflict suffering on the sick. Blessed King what can I say? . . . Any man who comes here wounded is returned thrice and four times to the trenches. Only that man goes to India who has lost an arm or a leg or an eye.[12]

Indian casualties remained extremely high the following year.

The Brighton hospital

From the earliest stages of the war it was clear that the Indian troops required specific medical arrangements, which would acknowledge the dietary and other cultural requirements of the various groups that made up the Indian army. The Sussex resort town of Brighton, conveniently positioned to receive the incoming wounded from ports along the South Coast, became the main destination for wounded Indian soldiers. The Brighton workhouse, a dismal building until recently inhabited by the indigent, was renamed the Kitchener Indian Hospital and swiftly made over for medical use. Two schools were also repurposed as makeshift hospital wards. Most important, the Royal Pavilion, Dome and Corn Exchange, Brighton's exuberant architectural monuments to royal excess from the

---

12 Letter addressed to the King-Emperor from Indian School Hospital, Milford on Sea, 24 April 1915, quoted in Gajendra Singh, *The Testimonies of Indian Soldiers and the Two World Wars: Between Self and Sepoy* (London: Bloomsbury Academic, 2014), p. 87.

Regency era, were converted, providing 774 hospital beds.[13] The *Brighton Gazette* took time in December 1914 to 'wonder at the greatest of British pleasure towns being made the centre of the greatest hospital system in the Kingdom'.[14]

There were indeed rich ironies in this re-use of the Prince Regent's pleasure palace, whose final design by John Nash in 1815–1822 utilised an elaborately Orientalist style much influenced by Thomas and William Daniell's watercolours and aquatints of Indian monuments such as the Taj Mahal. It has become a popular myth – which may have its origins in First World War propaganda – that the Palace was given for the Indian soldiers because the King thought they would feel 'at home' in the building. It is a bizarre notion indeed that regiments recruited from the ranks of Punjabi farmers might feel at ease in an Orientalised pleasure palace because of its use of Mughal architectural details. In any case, the Pavilion had been in the hands of the Brighton Council for decades, after its sale by Queen Victoria in 1850. There seems to have been a deliberate effort to convince the wounded servicemen, quite incorrectly, that the King-Emperor had lived in the palace and vacated it specifically for them. And even the normally sober *Manchester Guardian* recorded on 28 September 1916:

> It was one of the happy ideas of the war – due, it is said, to the suggestion of the king – to house the wounded Indian soldiers in the Brighton Pavilion. That product of the bizarre imagination of King George the Fourth, after the interval of a century, played a really useful part in making our eastern soldiers feel at home. No one who ever visited the pavilion while it was an Indian hospital will forget the strange look of those huge saloons with their faded oriental decorations in gilt, crimson, and looking-glass, full of dark men from all the Indian races recovering from their wounds got on the fields of France.[15]

An extensive campaign of photography, sanctioned by the authorities, documented the care with which the wounded Indians were treated, but often the static figures appear merely bemused and displaced.

In April 1915, however, C.H.D Girdwood was given permission to make a series of photographs at the Indian military hospitals in Bournemouth and Brighton. Later that year at the front, he created images that, while intended perhaps as purely documentary records, offer striking insights into the experience of the wounded Indians in Brighton. One photograph, probably not intended for publication, is captioned 'The Four Worst Cases in the Brighton Hospital' (see Figure 13.6). It records the injuries of two sepoys and two Gurkhas – who appear to be barely more than boys. The poise with which they confront the camera, despite their mutilated bodies, remains haunting. Girdwood's composition, seemingly a mere documentary snapshot, is a masterly formal construction. The concentric circles of the wheelchair and the volumetric spirals of the turbans are echoed by the neat coils of the freshly-mown grass at the upper left. By raising the camera and angling it sharply downward, Girdwood crops the horizon

---

13 Kevin Bacon and David Beevers, *The Royal Pavilion as an Indian Military Hospital, 1914–16* (Brighton: Royal Pavilion, n.d., c. 2014). Much of what follows relies on this excellent pamphlet published by the Royal Pavilion.

14 Bacon and Beevers, *The Royal Pavilion*.

15 *Manchester Guardian*, 28 September 1916, accessed 20 August 2015, http://www.sikhmuseum.com/brighton/index.html.

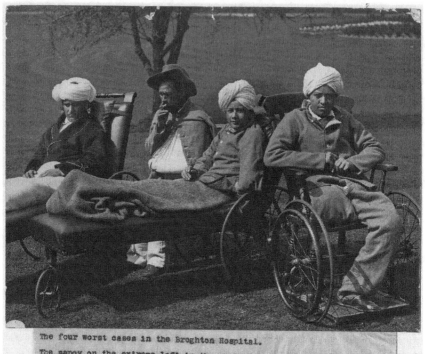

Figure 13.6 C.H.D. Girdwood, 'The Four Worst Cases in the Brighton Hospital', April 1915

Source: British Library: Photo 24/19

and emphasises the horizontality of the figures: none of them, it seems, will ever walk again. Were they to be able to stand, their heads would puncture the upper limits of the photographic frame. A label explains that the smoking sepoy in the centre 'has a fractured arm and elbow, caused by an explosive German bullet'. His dark, shadowed face seems as gnarled and twisted as the scrawny shrub that grows behind him.

There was believed to be great propaganda value in circulating images of the injured troops enjoying the benefits of good medical treatment – a manifestation of imperial benevolence and even-handedness. The Corporation of Brighton published in 1915 *A Short History in English, Gurmukhi and Urdu of the Royal Pavilion and Description of it as A Hospital for Indian Soldiers*, an elaborate tri-lingual propaganda effort which was

An architecture of imperial ambivalence 225

Figure 13.7 'Indian Military Hospital, Royal Pavilion, Brighton', from *A Short History in English, Gurmukhi & Urdu of the Royal Pavilion and Description of it as a Hospital for Indian Soldiers*, 1915

Source: British Library: India Office Records and Private Papers, IOR/L/MIL/17//5/2313

presumably intended for circulation in India as well as amongst the wounded and their families (see Figure 13.7).[16] Gurmukhi was the most frequently used script in the Punjab, accessible to literate members of the large Sikh population; Urdu, the official language of Jammu and Kashmir from 1837, was the dominant language of Muslims in the Indian Empire. The cover illustration played into the Orientalist trope of the Indian soldier 'at home' in the Brighton Pavilion, the shape of Nash's domes echoing that of the sepoy's elaborately-wound turban.

Amongst the features most widely reported was the authorities' scrupulousness in observing – and in the process essentialising and exaggerating – the religious and caste sensitivities of the soldiers, with regard to the preparation of food, bathing and sanitation. There were distinct water supplies for Hindu and Muslim soldiers in each ward, while bathing houses and latrines were segregated. An encampment of so-called untouchables, today referred to as dalits, were positioned outside the building and tasked with cleaning the latrines. Separate kitchens catered, respectively, to Muslims, meat-eating Hindus and

---

16 *A Short History in English Gurmukhi and Urdu of the Royal Pavilion and Description of It as A Hospital for Indian Soldiers* (Brighton: Brighton Corporation, 1915), accessed 24 August 2016, http://www.bl.uk/manuscripts/FullDisplay.aspx?ref=IOR/L/MIL/17/5/2313.

Figure 13.8   C.H.D. Girdwood, 'The Sikh Kitchens'

Source: British Library: Photo 24/(5)

vegetarians. Girdwood provided another artfully composed image, depicting the Sikh kitchen, with chapatties in preparation (see Figure 13.8). All speaks of cleanliness and order in the brilliant sunlight, from the scrubbed white table top to the precise movements of the two cooks, frozen in action. The attentiveness to differences of religion and caste conformed to late Victorian social Darwinist ethnographic beliefs, but it also revealed the deep anxiety of the authorities reaching back to the Mutiny of 1857–1858, whose ostensible cause was to the Army's alleged insensitivity in the use of animal grease – perhaps from the pig, perhaps the cow – for the new cartridges of the period.

Care was taken to maximise the familiarity of the hospital and its inmates to the local community by holding paid open days. For anyone missing the message of civic benevolence, the local artist Charles Phelp provided a rudimentary iconography in which the Mayor, John Otter, a faux-Mughal arch creating a large halo behind his head, benevolently welcomes supplicant wounded sepoys and Ghurka into the Pavilion, theatrically raising the mayoral tricorn hat (see Figure 13.9).

The majority of the soldiers were actually accommodated in the Dome, built in 1805–1808 in loose imitation of Thomas Daniell's aquatint of the Jami Masjid in Delhi, published in 1795. A series of official photographs of the interior pales in comparison with

An architecture of imperial ambivalence 227

Figure 13.9   Charles Phelp, 'Brighton Gives of her best for our Wounded Indian Soldiers – Bravo Otter', *Brighton and Hove Society*, 3 December 1914

Source: Royal Pavilion & Museums, Brighton & Hove

paintings by the local artist Charles Burleigh, who was allowed – perhaps commissioned – to paint the doubly exotic scene. Burleigh's composition is more a display of what David Cannadine calls 'Ornamentalism' than an attempt to evoke an exotic east.[17] The Punjabi soldiers' turbans resonate more closely with the spick and span white bed linen than with the outrageous chinoiserie swags of Nash's interior. The more ambitious painter Douglas Fox-Pitt, utilising a Post-Impressionist style based on clearly differentiated blocks of colour,

---

17   David Cannadine, *Ornamentalism* (New York: Oxford University Press, 2001).

emphasises the seamless transition between Regency Orientalism and the uniforms and turbans of the wounded soldiers, insisting that the troops were in some sense at home (see Figure 13.10). There is a telling echo between the army of India uniforms and the blue formal elements in the dome's décor.

The national and imperial media eagerly covered carefully staged events like the visit of the King and Queen and that of Lord Kitchener visiting the wounded Indian troops. As the King pinned a medal to the chest of an Indian soldier on a wheeled stretcher, in a photograph published in the press, the scene suggested the laying on of hands in medieval times, in which the monarch was credited with Christ-like powers to cure the sick (see Figure 13.11).

That such rhetoric could survive in an era of mustard gas and Howitzer shells – by which many of these Indian bodies were mutilated – is not the least of the ironies of the imperial involvement in the First World War.

Figure 13.10 Douglas Fox-Pitt, *Indian Army Wounded in Hospital in the Dome, Brighton*. c.1919, oil on canvas

Source: © Imperial War Museum (Art.IWM ART 323)

An architecture of imperial ambivalence 229

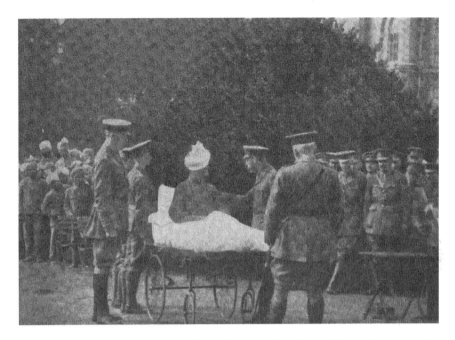

Figure 13.11   Monochrome photograph showing King George V meeting a wounded Indian soldier in the grounds of the Royal Pavilion during its use as a Military Hospital, 1915

Source: Royal Pavilion and Museums, Brighton and Hove, released for re-use under a BY-NC-SA 4.0 Creative Commons licence

With images such as these, the Brighton Hospitals could send a message throughout Britain, but more importantly to India, where Hardinge feared an uprising in 1914, but felt that the population would rally round the imperial cause if Indian troops were seen to be participating. Nor did the usefulness of this imagery cease with the end of the War. In 1921, the Maharaja of Patiala (a princely state in the southern Punjab with a Sikh majority population) visited Brighton and, in a speech, recalled:

> Of the large number of Indian soldiers you entertained, some 2,000 passed through the Pavilion hospital, and the great majority of them, some crippled, some completely restored, survive to tell their friends and neighbours in the towns and villages of Northern India that they were nursed and tended in a Royal palace closely associated with the dynasty of H.M. the King-Emperor. Moreover, they tell of being visited here by his Majesty, and some of them proudly point to Victoria or Military Crosses or other decorations pinned on their breasts by the King-Emperor within the grounds of the Pavilion. Believe me these memories are a great Imperial asset in these days of restlessness.[18]

---

18   *Brighton Herald*, 29 October 1921, accessed 20 August 2015, http://www.sikhmuseum.com/brighton/remembrance/gate/patiala.html.

There were attempts, also, to circulate propaganda images in Germany and German-occupied areas in 1915. The intention was to provide the enemy with a visual and demotic reminder that the population and manpower of the British Empire vastly exceeded that of Great Britain itself. No research has yet been done to establish the effectiveness, if any, of the propaganda campaign in India or Germany.

The actual experience of Indian soldiers in Brighton was by no means a utopian precursor to a multicultural Britain of the future. There was considerable anxiety on the part of the administration of the hospitals about potential sexual relations between the Indian soldiers and British women. The inmates – for they were effectively imprisoned – were not allowed to engage with the people of Brighton unless accompanied by a British officer. Col Sir Bruce Seyton, in command of the Kitchener Hospital in Brighton, surrounded the grounds with barbed wire and threatened a punishment of a dozen lashes for sepoys ignoring the ban.[19] Tensions ran so high that one outraged Indian, Sub-Assistant Surgon Jagu Godbole, went so far as to attempt the murder of the oppressive Col Seyton. Godbole is quoted as saying: 'Notwithstanding the fact that *lakhs* [tens of thousands] of Hindus are dying for the sake of England, they have not been allowed to go about here freely. This very ungratefulness I have been unable to bear.'[20] This was an extreme case, but resentment simmered more widely. Supervised outings were often manipulated for propaganda purposes: a postcard bearing the caption 'From East to West for the Motherland' positions a group of Indian soldiers on an outing to Hove, beneath a formidable sculptural monument to the grandmother of empire by the distinguished sculptor Sir Thomas Brock (see Figure 13.12).

Figure 13.12 **'From East to West for the Motherland', Postcard, 1915**

Source: Collection Royal Pavilion Brighton, released for re-use under a BY-NC-SA 4.0 Creative Commons licence

---

19 Singh, *Testimonies*, p. 85.
20 Letter from Jagu Godbole to unidentified correspondent in India, 19 December 1915, quoted in Singh, *Testimonies*, p. 86.

The iconography of the monument could not have been more appropriate and was surely chosen deliberately: the relief panel beneath the vast figure of Victoria depicts 'Empire' (see Figure 13.13).

The panel is composed around a seated female figure in the centre, with a pair of scales, identifying her as Justice – yet she also resembles the young Queen Victoria. This palimpsestic figure is flanked by emblematic representatives of Canada and Australia to the left and India and Africa on her right. The elegant, turbaned figure of India is Victoria's right-hand man: with long, elegant fingers he points to his heart in a gesture of loyalty. The photographer has consciously positioned one of the wounded soldiers, who obscures the dynamic figures of the settler colonies in the relief, as a living avatar of this allegorical

Figure 13.13   Sir Thomas Brock, 'Empire', bronze relief from pedestal of Queen Victoria Statue, Hove, Sussex, 1897–1901

Source: Creative Commons

Figure 13.14 'At Brighton: Children Paddling With Wounded Indian Soldiers'

Source: [Anon] "How the war has affected children," *The Graphic*, 11 September 1915, 326

figure. Justice – so the photograph, and before it the sculpture, claim – is being done: and Victoria (identified on the granite pedestal as VICTORIA DEI GRA. / BRITANNIAR REGINA /FIDEI DEFENSOR / IND. IMPERATRIX [By grace of God, Queen of Great Britain, defender of the faith, and Empress of India]) guarantees fair play in India as much as in Britain.

In September 1915, the *Graphic* ran an article, undoubtedly managed by propaganda officials, purporting to depict spontaneous encounters between wounded Indian soldiers and local children: a photograph shows them, hands affectionately clasping, in a surprising emblem of cross-racial interaction (see Figure 13.14). An image whose demonstrable artifice contributes to its striking modernity, it silhouettes the frieze of figures against brilliant light. At the fulcrum of the composition is the smile of the central male figure, seen without a turban. This perhaps is what Roland Barthes defines as the punctum, the detail in a photograph that seals its authenticity, an element too indexical, too circumstantial to derive purely from convention or to be determined entirely by the demands or the ideology of a patron. Whatever the propagandistic uses to which it was put, that joyful smile does indeed enshrine – more directly than the Chattri monument – an emotional connection between the wounded Indian soldiers and the city and people of Brighton.

Death and funerary ritual

The hospitals were extremely successful in preserving the lives of their patients. Of 4,306 Indian wounded to arrive at Brighton, there were only 74 deaths, 21 Muslim and 53 Sikh and Hindu. Nonetheless, Sadr ud Din, head of the Muslim faith in England, warned in 1914 of 'the very grave danger of allowing the impression to gain ground in India that England is not showing sufficient respect the memory of her Indian war heroes'.[21] Indeed, propaganda, created with the idea of strengthening the resolve of Germany's Turkish allies, accused the British of not burying fallen Muslim soldiers according to the dictates of their religion. Further propaganda was aimed directly at disenchanted Muslim soldiers with the British forces on the Western Front.[22]

The British authorities did indeed display a degree of sensitivity to the different funerary traditions represented by the major religious groups amongst the Indian forces. The Muslim dead were transported by motor cortège to Horsell Common, near Woking, in Surrey. Responsible for this process was the Assistant Quartermaster of the Royal Pavilion Hospital, Daya Ram Thapar, then a medical student:

> The funeral cortege comprised a motor hearse, a car and a couple of lorries to carry forty or fifty mourners. It was fortunate that we had very few deaths as each one meant a whole day's travelling to London and back. The Imam Sahib insisted on every detail to be correctly carried out and soon I became proficient as an undertaker. On the first occasion it seemed strange that the chief mourner should be a non-muslim, but the Imam Sahib was very kind and considerate and soon initiated me into the procedure.[23]

A hearse was followed by two lorries and as many as fifty mourners. A Muslim burial ground had been built at Horsell Common to the designs of the India Office Surveyor T. Herbert Whinney (see Figure 13.15).[24]

The apparently obscure location can be explained by the fact that the city of Woking already had a connection with Islam: Gottlieb William Leitner, a distinguished Victorian Orientalist who had served as Principal of Government College University in Lahore, had retired to Woking, where he planned to found the 'Oriental Institute'. With designs by W. I. Chambers, and with funding from Begum of Bhopal, he had built in 1889 the Shah Jahan Mosque, an Indo-Saracenic confection.[25] Its intended function was to provide a site for the religious devotions of Muslim students. Although Leitner died before the institute could come into being, the Mosque was something of a success: Queen Victoria's Muslim servants, for example, attended from Windsor.

The larger number of Hindu and Sikh dead were accorded greater attention at both the local and national level. It was decided that cremations should take place according to custom in the open air, but at a remote location so as not to awaken too much curiosity from the local population. A spot was chosen 152 metres above sea level on the Sussex Downs near

---

21 'Statement of Maulvie Sadr-Ud-Din, Mosque,' Woking, 27 August 1915, Woking Muslim Mission, Doctor Brighton's Pavilion website, accessed 20 August 2015, http://www.sikhmuseum.com/brighton/remembrance/muslim/funerals.html.

22 'Muslim Burial Ground,' Historic England website, last modified 2015, http://list.english-heritage.org.uk/resultsingle.aspx?uid=1236560.

23 Daya Ram Thapar, *The Morale Builders: Forty Years with the Military Medical Services of India* (London: Asia Publishing House, 1965). This text, held by Yale University Library, was drawn to my attention by 'Indian Deaths at Brighton,' formerly at http://www.chattri.org/.

24 Horsell Common Preservation Society, accessed 24 August 2016, http://www.horsellcommon.org.uk/musilim_burial_ground.php.

25 *The Building News and Engineering Journal*, 2 August 1889. Chambers' design for the building was celebrated in a large wood engraving printed in the journal.

Figure 13.15 Muslim Burial Ground, Horsell Common, Woking, Surrey, 1917
Source: Historic England Archive

Patcham, a village then beyond the limits of Brighton's suburbs. Three slabs of concrete were laid and fifty-three cremations were held there between 31 December 1914 and 30 December 1915. An anonymous correspondent of the *Times* was invited to attend the cremations – again clearly a move orchestrated by the War Office. He seems to have attended the rites for Mohiya Ram, a member of the Supply and Transport Corps, latterly employed as a storekeeper at the Kitchener Hospital in Brighton. He had died on 13 October 1915.[26] Ram was a Brahmin, and the funeral, attended by enough mourners to fill two ambulances, is described in detail. First, modern technology intervened in the ancient ritual: 'Before the body was put into the big black motor-hearse, a photographer was allowed to come and take a picture of the dead man's features, to be sent to his relatives in India.' He was then taken through the 'intensely English [village of Patcham] with its church and duck pond' to the burning ghat. The contrast could hardly be more pronounced with the most celebrated of ghats, Manikarnika Cremation Ghat in the holy city of Varanasi, then Benares, alive with a mass of people, colours and sounds. Nonetheless, the basic practice was the same. As the *Times* reporter put it:

> The body, under its bright pall and the chrysanthemums, lay outside on the grassy slope; when the preparations had been made the mourners gathered round it. It was sprinkled with

---

26 The identification was made in an anonymous text 'Indian Deaths at Brighton' formerly available on http://www.chattri.org/.

cleansing water: the face was exposed again, and honey and ghee, and minute portions of the eight metals, and other ritual things were passed between the pale lips. Then the mourners gathered round in a semi-circle; and squatting on their haunches with their hands folded and their eyes downcast, chanted their sing-song chants, now shrill, now soft, now a murmur and then a shout . . . At last came the time of the burning . . . When all was ready the body was laid on the pyre . . . crystals of camphor were lighted in a spoon on the end of a long pole; and when they were flaming well were poured on the centre of the fire. A flame leapt up . . . and soon the whole pyre was ablaze. And while it burned the mourners kept tossing upon it little pinches of ghee mixed with grains and fruit, scent, saffron, and spices.[27]

The rhetoric here mixes breathless orientalist rapture with ethnographic precision of detail. The text carefully calibrates the requirements of the British and possible Indian readership. Certainly this vivid text gained a global audience: it was reproduced in its entirety in the *Straits Times* (Singapore) on 18 November 1915 and doubtless in countless other journals across the empire.[28]

The impact of the description rests on the contrast between the English duck pond and the Indian saffron and ghee – an oxymoronic vision of empire, compressing the global and the local in a single picturesque vista. The cremations, which briefly lit up the Sussex skyline during 1914 and 1915, were Indian and British, military and civilian, sacred and secular, public and private – replete with all the ambiguities of India's participation in the war. They ceased suddenly in late 1915 when the Indian Corps was re-deployed to the Mesopotamian Front and the flow of wounded Indian soldiers to Brighton abruptly ended. The last Indian wounded departed from the Pavilion in February 1916, and the facilities were re-deployed for the use of British amputees.

Memorial

As early as August 1915, Lt Das Gupta of the Indian Medical Service had approached the mayor of Brighton, John Otter, asking permission to place a memorial on the site of the cremations.[29] Otter, concerned to provide a lasting monument to Brighton's unique role in relation to the war and the empire, took up the scheme and pursued it to fulfilment despite many formidable obstacles. But the memorial also had national and imperial significance. Sir Walter Lawrence, King's Commissioner with responsibility for the welfare of Indian troops, noted in a memorandum to the India Office of December 1915: 'It would be wise on political and historical grounds to spend a good deal of care and some money on preserving the memory of the Indians who had died in France and in England,' a recommendation endorsed by Austen Chamberlain, the Secretary of State for India. It was agreed that the India Office and the Brighton Corporation would split between them the cost of erecting the memorial, but that Brighton alone would maintain it.

But what kind of memorial? In *Sites of Memory, Sites of Mourning*, Jay Winter sets up a compelling typology in which 'war memorials inhabit three distinctive spaces and periods;

---

27 *The Times*, 16 October 1915.
28 *Straits Times* (Singapore), 18 November 1915, p. 2, accessed 20 August 2015, http://eresources.nlb.gov.sg/newspapers/Digitised/Article/straitstimes19151118-1.2.3.aspx.
29 This narrative relies on http://www.chattri.org/indepthHistory/ih1.aspx?sectionID=h2&mv=0&p=.

first, scattered over the home front before 1918; second, in post-war churches and civic sites in the next decade following the Armistice; and third, in war cemeteries.'[30] The Chattri carries elements of each of these but conforms to none. Completed after the Armistice, it stands as a public monument, but one in a remote location accessible only by foot; not a cemetery, it nonetheless stands as the marker of the place of cremation. Moreover, it is as much an Indian structure as a British one, which 'will be most welcome to the Government of India, and will be deeply appreciated by the relatives of the fallen, and by the people of India generally' as the Secretary of State, Sir Austen Chamberlain put it in August 1915.[31]

Perhaps following India Office advice, John Otter contacted the retired architect Sir Swinton Jacob, whose elaborate official buildings in India established Indo-Saracenic as the house style of the British Raj. Born into an East India Company family in 1841, Jacob was commissioned into the Bombay Artillery in the last stages of the uprising in 1858 – another indirect link between the Chattri and the so-called Mutiny – and became chief engineer of the state of Jaipur in 1867.[32] The Daly College in Indore (1905) gives a sense of the eclectic and highly elaborate architectural style he developed, principally using motifs liberally adapted from Indo-Islamic architecture. These included the onion dome, pointed arches, the minaret and particularly the chhajja – an eave placed on projecting brackets fixed to the wall, seen classically in the elegant tomb of Shalim Chishti in Fatehpur Sikri, built in 1580–1581, and paraphrased in Swinton Jacob's masterpiece, the Albert Hall, now the Government Central Museum (1880–1887), a collection of Industrial arts in the South Kensington vein built for the Maharajah of Jaipur (see Figure 13.16).

Figure 13.16   Swinton Jacob, Tujumul Hoosein, Ram Baksh, Shankar Lal and Chote Lal (architects), Albert Hall Museum, Jaipur, India, completed 1887

Source: Mridula Dwivedi

---

30   J.M. Winter, *Sites of Memory, Sites of Mourning* (Cambridge: Cambridge University Press, 1995), p. 79.
31   Austen Chamberlain to John Otter, 2 August 1915, quoted [Tom Donovan] 'Delay and Frustration,' accessed 24 August 2016, http://www.webcitation.org/6LJwGtaTD.
32   'Sir Swinton Jacob,' *The Times*, 7 December 1917.

Perhaps the most notable feature of Jacob's architecture was his extensive use of the chattri or dome-shaped pavilion. In Indo-Saracenic architecture this element was purely decorative, as in Jacob's spectacular design for St John's College in Agra, where a large, centrally-placed chattri replaces the dome of neo-classical or baroque structures. Perhaps it was Swinton Jacob, then, who suggested the Chattri as an appropriate form for the Patcham memorial, though any idea that it was a traditional Indian style of memorial, as Jacob seems to have believed, is highly questionable. At 75, Jacob had only two years to live, and rather than take on the commission, recommended a young Indian architect undertaking architectural study in England, E. C. Henriques. Little is known about Henriques, who came from Bombay and later became President of the Institute of Architects in 1939–1940. The design was completed by 1917. Henriques created a monument in a powerful and austere style far less ornate than that of Swinton Jacob.

Henriques's chattri is ultimately derived from Mughal architecture, which reached its zenith in the sixteenth and seventeenth centuries, itself a distinctive hybrid architectural form that blended elements from local Hindu traditions, with the forms of the Islamic architecture that had long been established in India under the Delhi sultanates, and added to by craftsmen that the Mughals brought with them from Central Asia. The Chattri shares the lotus finial; the low, rounded dome; the drum; the overhanging chajja; decorated lintels; the slender, elegant pillars; and the octagonal base of its Mughal counterpart. It is important to note that the chattri was not typically a free-standing monument but a decorative element in a larger composition.

Thus, at Fatehpur Sikri, the great red sandstone city built by Akbar in 1571–1585, the skyline of the building is dotted with chattris. Two octagonal chattris rise above the squat, fortified towers flanking the imposing front of the Red Fort in Delhi, begun by Shah Jahan in 1638 (see Figure 13.17); and it was next to a white marble Chattri on the river front of the Delhi fort that the King-Emperor George V, the only reigning British monarch to visit

Figure 13.17 Red Fort, Delhi, begun by Shah Jahan, 1638

Source: Tim Barringer

Figure 13.18 William H. Burke, *King George V and Queen Mary at the Red Fort presenting themselves before the crowd*, **1911**

Source: Alkazi Collection of Photographs

India, greeted his imperial subjects in 1911, wearing the Crown of India – the one and only time it was ever worn (see Figure 13.18).

The chattri is not exclusively associated with Mughal or more generally with Muslim architecture. The Rajput palaces of Rajasthan, such as the Amber Fort, seat of a Hindu royal dynasty, are decorated with numerous chattris, mainly added in the seventeenth century. Intriguingly, the form of the chattri was revived recently in the context of the vast and controversial monumental scheme constructed by Mayawati, the Dalit Chief Minister of Uttar Pradesh 2007–2012.

Chattris were also associated with memorial architecture: the most important Mughal monument in Delhi, Humayun's tomb (begun 1569), bears chattris on its upper parapet, but in red sandstone (see Figure 13.19). The most significant precursor for the use of white marble is of course the Taj Mahal, though the small chattris on its parapet are not close in form to Henriques's design. The Taj does however provide a shared ancestor, linking the austere Patcham Chattri with its exuberant neighbour, the Brighton Pavilion. It is questionable as to whether the Chattri is any more 'authentic' as an 'Indian monument' than the pavilion.

An architecture of imperial ambivalence 239

Figure 13.19 Humayun's Tomb, Delhi, begun 1569
Source: Tim Barringer

Because of the practice of burial rather than cremation, mausolea are far more important in Muslim than in Hindu and Sikh culture, hence, perhaps, the need to appropriate a Mughal form for a monument to the dead. The closest precedent, however, for the memorial use of the individual chattri can be found in one of the Raj's most uncanny and haunted relics, the Nicholson Cemetery in Delhi. Here are found bizarre Christian tombs in the shape of the Taj Mahal and chattris that serve as sepulchral monuments for British soldiers and officials, complete with lotus finial, dome, drum and chhajja, though here with a hexagonal base – an example of the already hybrid Mughal style being shamelessly re-appropriated by the British (see Figure 13.20).

There were, surprisingly, also precedents for the use of the chattri on British soil, though for entirely decorative purposes as seen at Sezincote House in Gloucestershire, designed in

Figure 13.20   British tomb in Nicholson Cemetery, Delhi, n.d., *c*. 1860

Source: Tim Barringer

1805 by Samuel Pepys Cockerell for his brother Charles, of the East India Company. The façade has the familiar arrangement of dome and chattris, which were soon imitated by Nash at the Brighton Pavilion where they took on a Gothicised, fairy-tale look. The Victorian era saw the further appropriation of the form in a new material, cast iron, in one of the more bizarre structures in Britain, the Maharajah's Well, a gift in 1864 from the Maharajah of Benares to the village of Stoke Row in Oxfordshire, in thanks for the activities of the local squire, Edward Reade, while in India. Swinton Jacob himself designed the so-called Jaipur Gate, a decorative structure made in Indian teak, exhibited at the 1886 Colonial and Indian Exhibition and, redundant afterwards, permanently installed in Hove, a suburb of Brighton – where it has withstood the British weather since 1926.

Durbar

My point in delivering this extended typology of the chattri is to emphasise the lack of stable historical meanings for this architectural form. By 1900 the British Raj had made one final appropriation of the chattri that – despite its geographical distance – is of significance for our interpretation of the Patcham monument. From the creation of the title Empress of India in 1877, the celebration of durbars became an ever more significant practice for the Raj. The so-called native princes were summoned to pay feasance to the King-Emperor's

Figure 13.21 Delhi Durbar, with King George V and Queen Mary seated upon the dais, 1911

Source: Public domain

representative.[33] In 1877 Lockwood Kipling created a hybrid Mughal-Gothic pavilion, but in the far grander 1903 Durbar for the coronation of Edward VII – an event that cost many times more than the pageantry in London – the grandiose Lord Curzon, as Viceroy, appeared beneath a chattri. On a more epic scale still, the 1911 Durbar, the only one to be attended in person by the monarch, saw George V seated beneath an elegant iron structure that recalled both the Taj and the Brighton Pavilion (see Figure 13.21).

The King's slight form could hardly be seen from across the vast spaces of the Durbar, particularly because he insisted on riding a horse not an elephant, and was thus not recognised by his subjects, but the chattri was visible from all points, an emblem reaching also echoing the umbrella or parasol – the word chattri also means umbrella – understood in Indian culture as an emblem of royalty reaching back, in fact, to the Buddha himself. Images of the 1911 Delhi Durbar were transmitted by photographic means throughout the empire and, significantly, by the new technology of film.

At the Durbar, George V announced the return of the capital of India from Calcutta to the Mughal capital of Delhi – or rather to a new site nearby that would be called New Delhi. The apotheosis of the Raj's use of the Chattri can be found in the buildings whose early designs by Edwin Lutyens and Herbert Baker pre-date the Great War, but whose construction was largely delayed until the early 1920s.[34] The great central axis of the

---

33 On Durbars see Julie F. Codell, *Power and Resistance: The Delhi Coronation Durbars* (Delhi: Alkazi Collection/Mapin Publishing, 2012).

34 On Lutyens and New Delhi, see Robert Grant Irving, *Indian Summer: Lutyens, Baker and Imperial Delhi* (New Haven: Yale University Press, 1981).

Figure 13.22   Edwin Lutyens, architect, India Gate and Canopy, New Delhi

Source: Creative Commons

British Empire's grandest planned city is flanked by chattris and, like the Mughal palaces it emulated, the architecture of New Delhi is marked out by chattris, some of them extremely similar in form to that in Patcham. In 1913, in a moment of frustration Lutyens noted in a sketch of the Viceroy's house 'chattris are stupid useless things.'[35] He made extensive use of them nonetheless, as he also did of chajjas and jali screens.

The most significant monuments of New Delhi were placed in the massive hexagonal park at the east of end of the ceremonial vista. The first, a triumphal arch, was a classical monument to Indian soldiers lost in the Great War, many times the size of Lutyens's Whitehall Cenotaph. Early designs followed more closely Roman precedents, but the single great arch in pale brick, 42 metres tall, is a structure of distinctive modernity, commemorating, though not by name, the 70,000 Indian soldiers who died in the conflict and, significantly, bearing the names of 13,516 British soldiers who died on the north-western frontier (see Figure 13.22).[36]

---

35 Edwin Lutyens quoted in *Lutyens Letters*, p. 388; see Jane Ridley, 'Edwin Lutyens, New Delhi and the Architecture of Imperialism,' *Managing the Business of Empire: Essays in Honour of David Fieldhouse*, ed. Peter Burroughs and A.J. Stockwell (London: Frank Cass, 1998), pp. 67–83, quoted passage on p. 81.

36 For an excellent discussion of the question of the commemoration of the Indian dead in the First World War, and the question of naming, see Michèle Barratt, 'Subalterns at War'.

An architecture of imperial ambivalence 243

Figure 13.23   C. A. Wiles, Brighton (photographer), *Dedication of the new Indian Chattri by H.R.H. the Prince of Wales on the Downs, Feb.1st 1921*

Source: Creative Commons

The gate was aligned in Lutyens's design with an elegant four-pillared canopy, notably similar to a chattri, its extended height inspired by a no longer extant ancient Hindu structure at Mahabalipuram which had been depicted by William and Thomas Daniell in the 1790s.[37] Crucially, however, this grand chattri in New Delhi was not empty but contained what no Mughal emperor or modern Hindu king ever commissioned: a vast and vainglorious statue of the British king-emperor, 12 metres tall, carved in marble by Charles Sargeant Jagger, who had himself been injured in the First World War (see Figure 13.23).[38]

---

37   'A Pavilion, Belonging to an Hindoo Temple, Acquatint, 1808' from Thomas and William Daniell, *Oriental Scenery*, vol. 5, 'Antiquities of India' (London: London Free-School Press, 1809–10), pl. 21.

38   See Mary Ann Steggles, *Statues of the Raj* (Putney, London: BACSA [British Association for Cemeteries in South Asia], 2000), pp. 26, 100, 162. The statue was commissioned by a group of Indian rulers led by the Maharaja of Kapurthala. It was incomplete at the time of Jagger's death in 1934 and was completed by William Reid Dick.

Ozymandias-like, the statue was removed shortly after Independence and removed to a remote location. No agreement could be reached on a replacement, however, for even Mahatma Gandhi was considered too controversial, leaving a vacant pedestal and returning the chattri to its proper emptiness. The final appropriation of the form of the chattri in the service of the ideology of the British Raj was intended to symbolise the eternal presence of Britain in India. It lasted barely twenty years.

We are far, now, from the Sussex Downs, where to the frustration of the recently knighted ex-mayor of Brighton, Sir John Otter, the struggles of local contractors to extract white Sicilian marble from war-damaged Italy delayed the construction of the Patcham Chattri until 1920. When, finally, Henriques's simple design took physical form, it ostensibly became a site of mourning for the Indian troops, but, in accordance with the architectural history of the chattri as a form, it came to symbolise the British Empire in India as a whole. Treading carefully with regard to sectarian issues, the base of the Chattri is inscribed in such a way as to remember all the Indian dead (including the Muslims buried elsewhere) but also to acknowledge the particular men cremated at this spot:

TO THE MEMORY OF ALL THE INDIAN SOLDIERS WHO GAVE THEIR LIVES IN THE SERVICE OF THEIR KING-EMPEROR THIS MONUMENT ERECTED IN THE SITE WHERE THE HINDUS AND SIKHS WHO DIED IN HOSPITAL IN BRIGHTON PASSED THROUGH FIRE, IS IN GRATEFUL ADMIRATION AND BROTHERLY AFFECTION DEDICATED.

The opening ceremony, held in February 1921, was replete with symbolism (see Figure 13.24).

Figure 13.24   HRH The Prince of Wales unveiling the Indian Chattri on the Downs, Patcham, Feb 1921. Postcard.

Source: Creative Commons

It opened with a 21-gun salute. The charismatic young Prince of Wales (the future Edward VIII, King-Emperor) paid tribute, as the *Daily Mirror* put it, to Indian heroes. The Prince's address noted:

> Our Indian comrades came when our need was highest, free men and voluntary soldiers who were true to their salt – and gave their lives in a quarrel of which it was enough for them to know that the enemy were the foes of their sahibs, the Emperor and their King.

To the Mayor of Brighton, he added: 'India never forgets a kindness and sympathy and from this Chattri a wave of goodwill will pass to India.' Such memorials, he concluded 'strengthen ties between India and our country'.[39] Even if the crowd present on the Downs that cold February day was a local one, perhaps including individuals who had forged personal links with some of the Indian soldiers, it seems the intended appeal of the event was global.

There can be little doubt that the primary audience for this ceremony was not in Brighton, or London, but in India. The political climate in India by 1921 had shifted dramatically from that in 1914. At the beginning of the war, when the King-Emperor George V declared war on Germany in the name of the entire empire, there was a surprising unanimity of support, even from nationalist politicians. In 1921 the events were contrived to emphasise British sensitivities to the religious and cultural traditions of Hindu and Sikh soldiers. Political opposition to the British Raj in India had been contained during the war but by early 1921 the situation was fraught, following repressive actions of the Rowlatt Sedition Committee of 1918 and with the Government of India Act of 1919, widely regarded by Indian opinion as moving insufficiently far in the direction of representative government. The thirteenth of April 1919 had seen the so-called Amritsar Massacre, in the Punjab, in which Brigadier General Reginald Dyer ordered the army to shoot on a peaceful assembly of unarmed civilians, leaving 379 dead and more than 1,000 injured, and resulting in what Thomas and Barbara Metcalfe describe as a 'wrenching loss of faith in Britain's good intentions' amongst the Indian public.[40] It was against this background that the events at Patcham took place. The guests included dignitaries such as the laureate of British imperialism, Rudyard Kipling, an extensive representation of the press corps and a Pathé film crew. It was through this new medium that the symbolic power of the Chattri could be fully exerted.

Such campaigns of imperial propaganda were not enough, ultimately, to sustain the Raj against the unanswerable arguments in favour of independence. But when India was once again requested to support Britain in a world war, in 1939, the sense that Indian soldiers were treated honourably in the Great War may have contributed to the willingness of Indian forces to serve, despite the opposition of the Indian National Congress Party, whose predecessors in 1914 had enthusiastically supported the earlier war effort.

With the combination of local and global that I have emphasised, the *Times* mused about the role of the Chattri as a contribution to the deep history of the Sussex Downs with which I began:

> Not far off is one of those prehistoric camps . . . which succeeding races, Celts, Britons, Romans and Saxons, are supposed to have occupied . . . And now, in the twentieth century,

---

39 *Brighton Herald*, 5 February 1921.
40 F. Thomas and Barbara D. Metcalfe, *A Concise History of Modern India*, 3rd ed. (Cambridge: Cambridge University Press, 2012), p. 169.

come these associations – perhaps the strangest of all – of the cremation of Indian soldiers who fought in Flanders . . . in the Great War, and this temple to proclaim their fame for all time.[41]

The twentieth century, however, was not kind to the Chattri. Already overgrown by 1924, its deteriorating condition was the subject of an endless sequence of complaints to Brighton Council, and it was subject to various campaigns of rehabilitation. In 1932, a group of British veterans gathered there for a service of commemoration, and from 1951 to 1999 the British Legion made an annual Pilgrimage to the site, abandoning the practice eventually because of the difficulty of arranging for tea in the vicinity. Since 2000, however, in a significant development, members of the local Sikh community, led by Davinder Dhillon, have continued and transformed this tradition to remember and honour the Indians who died (see Figure 13.25).

Their pilgrimage effectively identifies the Chattri as a proleptic emblem of the multicultural, post-imperial Britain of the present, and specifically the multiethnic community of contemporary Brighton – even if the historical moment of its creation was one of imperialism, premised on a fundamental ideology of racial hierarchy. In a significant gesture, the community has erected a new monument, less inscrutable than the Chattri,

Figure 13.25 The 2008 memorial service in June at the Chattri, near Brighton, for Indian soldiers who died in World War I

Source: Andrew Hasson / Alamy

---

41 'The Prince's Day at Brighton' (From Our Special Correspondent.) *The Times* (London, England), 2 February 1921, p. 10.

Figure 13.26   The Chattri in 2013 with newly erected tablet bearing the names of those cremated at the site

Source: Tim Barringer

bearing the names of all the individuals cremated, including Mohiya Ram whose funerary rites the *Times* had reported in 1915 (see Figure 13.26).

Such monuments bear the imprint of the communities who create them, perhaps more so than they reflect the subjectivities of the soldiers who died far from home in Brighton a century ago. The placing of this second monument on the site is an act of significant historical revision. Although not conceived in response to the Chattri, it seems to me that this is the underlying message of the Indian-born British sculptor Anish Kapoor in his sculpture *C-Curve* (2007), which was mounted on a plinth on the Downs not far from Patcham during the Brighton Festival of 2009 (see Figure 13.27).

It reflects the landscape around it and in its polished steel surfaces viewers see themselves framed by their physical context. *C-Curve*'s combination of sharp mirroring, inversion and distortion brilliantly reveals the ways in which monuments reflect and magnify the preconceptions not only of those who created them but also of those who view them. In the fragile marble Chattri erected in 1921, then, we can find traces of the hybrid Mughal-Hindu architecture of the sub-continent, of the Indo-Saracenic monuments and the great capital city of the British Empire in India, and we can see the hand of a young Indian architect summoned to the imperial centre to learn his trade. Most visible are the ideologies of the British Raj, anxious to be seen to honour the Indian dead, but nonetheless profoundly

Figure 13.27 Anish Kapoor, *C-Curve*, 2007

Source: Dave Morgan

committed to the hierarchies of class and race that were employed to justify the British presence in India – hierarchies that gave British soldiers names but denied the individual identity of Indian servicemen. But if we strain to listen, still audible (as in the fragments of surviving, heavily censored letters from the trenches) are the voices of those Sikh and Hindu men, mainly listed as 'sepoy' or 'rifleman' – men like Mangal Singh, drummer of the 19th Punjabis, and the humble Kallu of the Mule Corps – whose names are now visible at Patcham where their bodies were committed to the fire a century ago.

Chapter 14
The Great War's impact on imperial Delhi
Commemorating wartime sacrifice
in the colonial built environment

David A. Johnson

In many ways the history of New Delhi is a Great War story. Though the original reason for transferring the capital from Calcutta to Delhi in 1911 pre-dates the war and was done for reasons specific to Britain's colonial rule in India, the city was still in the design stages when Britain became immersed in the war.[1] Edwin Lutyens and Herbert Baker, the renowned architects who designed and built the new capital, had focussed their attention until then on the central forum where the main government structures, Government House and the Secretariats, would rise.[2] Dozens of square kilometres of land had been purchased for the capital and its adjacent military cantonment, but the two architects and the Government of India remained undecided on some of the more important features that would occupy

---

1 Lord Hardinge, Viceroy of India from 1911 to 1916, transferred the capital from Calcutta to Delhi as part of a strategy to reunite the province of Bengal, which Lord Curzon had partitioned at the end of his viceroyalty in 1905. Curzon hoped that partition would break the Indian nationalist movement in Bengal, but the exact opposite occurred. Angry nationalists began a campaign of violence that included assassinations and bombings. The situation became so volatile by the time of Hardinge's arrival in 1911 that he began actively looking for a way to reverse partition. His solution was to link the end of partition to a new and much larger colonial policy: the transfer of the capital to Delhi by royal proclamation. George V announced the transfer at his 1911 imperial durbar (royal assemblage) held at Delhi. Immediately after announcing the transfer, he called for the re-unification of Bengal as a gift to the people of the province for losing the imperial seat at Calcutta. Thus, in the eyes of the public and in point of legislative fact, the transfer became the government's primary colonial policy and all subsequent changes, such as the reversal of partition, became ancillary components of this new direction in British rule.

2 The building of New Delhi has attracted the interest of many scholars. See Anthony King, *Colonial Urban Development: Culture, Social Power and Environment* (London: Routledge & Kegan Paul, 1976); Robert Grant Irving, *Indian Summer: Lutyens, Baker, and Imperial Delhi* (New Haven: Yale University Press, 1981); Thomas Metcalf, *An Imperial Vision: Indian Architecture and Britain's Raj* (Oxford: Oxford University Press, 1989); Jan Morris, *Stones of Empire: The Buildings of the Raj* (Oxford: Oxford University Press, 1983); Sten Nilsson, *European Architecture in India, 1750–1850* (London: Faber & Faber, 1969); Philip Davies, *Splendours of the Raj: British Architecture in India, 1660–1947* (London: Penguin Books, 1987); Stephen Legg, *Spaces of Colonialism: Delhi's Urban Governmentalities* (Oxford: Wiley-Blackwell, 2007); and David A. Johnson, *New Delhi: The Last Imperial City* (London: Palgrave, 2015).

spaces within the city.³ Hence, much of imperial Delhi still was in its formative stages at the beginning of hostilities.

In 1916, one of the most violent and destructive years of the war, the Government of India began thinking about erecting a monument in a central location in the new capital to commemorate Indian soldiers who had died in defence of the king and his empire. Lutyens received the commission to design and build the memorial, and in 1919 he approached the new Viceroy, Lord Chelmsford, with a plan to build a memorial park that would anchor the eastern quadrant of the main government area. Its main features would be a massive war memorial arch and a large memorial statue of George V. Lutyens always had planned to set aside a central space within the main government area to commemorate George V who called the city into being at his 1911 Delhi Durbar, but the Great War and its heavy human costs modified the architect's thinking about this city space. It also provided him with a tremendous opportunity to more fully interpret the meaning and spirit of the British Empire through the built environment. The park was connected to the western quadrant, the central forum that housed the Viceroy's House and the Secretariats, by a large processional avenue called the Kingsway. Thus, at the western-most point of the main avenue stood symbols of imperial power – the Viceroy's House and the Secretariats – while at the eastern end stood symbols of what that power rested upon (selfless sacrifice) and in whose name that power was exercised (the king-emperor). As one travelled east down the Kingsway towards memorial park, the statue of George V stood strong and securely moored directly in the centre of the war memorial's arch. When read together, as they were meant to be, the two large memorials boldly proclaimed that the loyalty of colonial subjects and their willingness to die in defence of the king and his empire had led to Britain's ultimate victory in the Great War (see Figure 14.1).

Lutyens's message had become increasingly important as the war dragged on. The character of modern warfare – total and industrialised – placed tremendous pressure on Britain's resources, forcing it to increasingly draw on the human and material support of its colonies. As is well known, the dominions of Canada, Australia, New Zealand and South Africa eagerly supported the war effort. Perhaps less well known is that nearly half a million Indian soldiers (sepoys) fought under the British flag not only in Africa and Asia but also in Europe. The War Office, in November 1916, sent a memo to the Government of India requesting additional Indian troops.⁴ The Raj responded by raising twelve new Indian Territorial Battalions.⁵ For their part, many Indians avidly jumped at the chance to fight in a 'white man's war' because it suggested their country's elevated status within the empire. Previously, the Indian Army had been used primarily in Africa and Asia. This initial excitement ebbed as the war's horrible destruction and human costs became

---

3   This slowness was typical for large building projects in India. Lord Curzon's announcement to build a Victoria Memorial Hall at Calcutta, for example, had been made in 1901 but actual building did not begin until 1906. Likewise, Hardinge and his architects endlessly deliberated the capital's architectural style, its town plan and its location. In fact, New Delhi rose at a much quicker pace than most colonial building projects in India due to Hardinge's powerful management skills and his need to show progress before the end of his viceroyalty in 1916. While many in India and Britain applauded the transfer, Lord Curzon, his parliamentary allies and Calcutta's European community viciously attacked the decision.

4   Curzon Papers, MSS EUR F111/443A: War Office, 10 Nov 1916: 20/Gen. No./4345 (S.D. 2).

5   Ibid., Minute by E.G. Barrow, Military Secretary, India Office, 2 Jan 1917.

Figure 14.1   The All-India War Memorial and the George V Memorial Statue
Source: Centre of South Asian Studies at Cambridge

obvious.[6] Declining Indian recruitment and growing negative public opinion of the war in India – made worse by heavy sepoy casualties – forced Britain to begin thinking of strategies that would revive Indian support and morale. Working together, Edwin Montagu, the new Secretary of State for India, and Lord Chelmsford agreed in 1917 that India would receive major political advances after the war as a way to honour India's loyalty to its king-emperor. Though tentative political reforms had begun several decades earlier, Montagu and Chelmsford's agreement provided tangible evidence that Britain was serious about changing India's political and administrative status quo, which had been until recently a largely centralised system of government and administration. The Montagu-Chelmsford

---

6   For histories of the sepoy experience in the Great War, see David Omissi, *Indian Voices of the Great War, 1914–1918* (London: Palgrave, 1999); and David Omissi, *The Sepoy and the Raj* (London: Palgrave, 1998); George Morton-Jack, *The Indian Army on the Western Front: India's Expeditionary Force to France and Belgium in the First World War* (Cambridge: Cambridge University Press, 2014); and Santanu Das, ed., *Race, Empire, and First World War Writing* (Cambridge: Cambridge University Press, 2011).

Agreement, as it came to be called, became the foundation for the Government of India Act of 1919, which transferred many political responsibilities to British India's provincial legislatures, which had expanded numbers of elected Indian officials. Other political topics, such as defence and security, remained under the complete control of British colonial officials as 'reserved' subjects. This basic tension between British-controlled reserved subjects and Indian-influenced transferred subjects became the predominate characteristic of all later British-sponsored reforms in India. The Government of India was willing to grant elected Indian officials greater political power in the provinces, but the centre would always remain under British control.

New Delhi became the pre-eminent symbol of this new imperial vision and its political reforms. Though the building project – massive and imposing – was certainly an attempt by the Government of India to symbolise Britain's paramount power in India, it also was an attempt to represent a new colonial strategy in India, one that encouraged Indians to consent to British rule because of the benefits it brought and would continue to bring under the protection of the crown. The building of a memorial park in the heart of Britain's new imperial capital was a perfect way to honour simultaneously George V and Indian soldiers who had died in the war in defence of his empire.

Yet Lutyens's memorial park commemorated more than Indian soldiers and their king-emperor. It memorialised what the British believed was the spirit of British rule. Members of the Indian Civil Service, in particular, saw their work as guided by enlightened reason and an indifference that made no distinction between colonial subjects in their care. Of course, as many scholars have pointed out, they certainly made great distinctions between Indians and themselves. Still, the British believed their rule rested upon essential truths that made progress possible. For Lutyens, these truths were so sublime that only the geometric precision of western classical architecture could express them adequately. The power and beauty of this style was that it reflected universal truths across time and space.[7] A 90-degree angle was the same for an ancient Greek as it was for a twentieth-century architect. Lutyens captured this understanding in his classical design of the All-India War Memorial. Yet these truths could be easily lost or stripped away if not adequately safeguarded by a supreme authority. The George V Memorial Statue, placed next to the war memorial, symbolised just such an authority figure. The Raj was authoritarian by necessity, the British admitted, but it also provided stability and peace that brought India prosperity and civil society. As such, the Raj practised what it considered an enlightened despotism that was grounded in the universal laws of nature.

Interested intellectuals, artists and officials used the Mughal Empire, India's last indigenous empire in South Asia before the rise of the British, as a foil to mark the difference between British and Indian rule. The *Times* took a lead in this regard. During early debates over what architectural style to adopt for New Delhi, the *Times*' editorial staff and numerous contributors to its editorial pages pointed to the different purposes of British and Mughal architecture. British writers and critics readily admitted that the Mughals built magnificent structures, but these edifices were merely places to take emperors or their favourite subjects to their final resting places; they were splendid memorials to the dead but provided little civic good. In contrast, they argued, the British built government buildings and infrastructure including administrative buildings, law courts, museums, post offices,

---

7 James Scott, *Seeing Like a State: How Certain Schemes to Improve the Human Condition Have Failed* (New Haven: Yale University Press, 1999).

railways and railway stations, suspension bridges and canal colonies. Britain's imperial project, in other words, benefitted India by advancing its civil institutions and its various economies. Such stadial thinking where humanity progressed through various stages of development was steeped in enlightened natural laws. The key for colonial officials was to institute in the colonial world those scientific truths that determined civilisational advance.

Lutyens's memorial park worked within this narrative of human progress but also offered a caveat. India was an important member of the British Empire and was slowly evolving into a nation capable of responsibly governing itself, but it still required Britain's help and protection in the foreseeable future. While the Great War tested Britain and India's imperial unity, the park proclaimed that the war's hellish crucible of death, destruction and mutual sacrifice for the king-emperor and the truths he protected reinforced the bond. Great sacrifices were made by both India and Britain, but the eternal truths that gave the empire its strength as well as its progress were worth the cost. Thus, this hallowed park became much more than a site that honoured the sacrifices of Indian soldiers. It was a site of imperial memory, of imperial power and of imperial mourning.

And yet today, a park that once symbolised a strongly unified Britain and India has become a symbol of the impossibility of that union. The George V Memorial Statue has been removed from its central location in the city and moved to an obscure and little visited sculpture park. The All-India War Memorial continues to stand where Lutyens built it, but the independent Indian government has renamed it 'India Gate' to symbolise Indian sacrifices in the making of the *independent* Indian state. Clearly, this imperial space of commemoration and death acted as a site of negotiation that held high stakes for both India and Britain during the colonial period and afterwards.

The creation of memorial park

In 1911, Lutyens won the commission to build the British Pavilion for the British School at Rome. The winning design showcased his imaginative re-working of the western classical tradition for the twentieth century and cemented his profile as a builder of public rather than private structures.[8] His success made him a leading candidate for the architectural member on Lord Hardinge's town planning committee charged with determining a location for the new capital in India and designing its town plan. Reginald Barratt, a painter of landscapes and architectural subjects and a confidante of Hardinge's, advised the viceroy to allow Lutyens to formulate the capital's scheme, to determine and design its general architectural style, to nominate others to assist him and to be 'the moving genius from the outset'.[9] Barratt concluded that 'an exceptional man is best, and Lutyens is a very exceptional man.'[10] The statement has been borne out over time. While Baker was an architect of great political sensitivity and an especially deep thinker about the ways in which architecture could be used to reflect the state, it was Lutyens' two contributions – the Viceroy's House and the

---

8 Hugh Peter, *Lutyens in Italy: The Building of the British School at Rome* (Rome: British School at Rome, 1992). Lutyens already was popular with Britain's wealthy elite who commissioned him to build large estates and accompanying gardens and grounds.

9 Reginald Barratt to Valentine Chirol, Hardinge Official Correspondence, 4 February 1912, Nehru Memorial Museum, New Delhi, India.

10 Ibid.

All-India War Memorial – that have become New Delhi's iconic structures. Indeed, such was the influence of Lutyens' genius and personality that New Delhi is often referred to as 'Lutyens' Delhi' by local residents, guidebooks and travel brochures.[11]

Lutyens, however, was more than a designer and builder of great buildings. He also was one of Britain's foremost war memorial designers and served on a special committee created by the Imperial War Graves Commission to study the problem of how best to commemorate those killed in the Great War. British popular opinion favoured graves and memorials with Christian symbolism, but Lutyens's committee, which included Herbert Baker and Reginald Blomfield, argued that graves and memorials should be more universal, less tied to any one religion and reflective of the diversity of the men who fought and died fighting for the king. Lutyens believed a 'stone of remembrance' would suffice. But if the commemorative purpose required a larger memorial, then it should be designed in the western classical tradition. The universal truths captured in the simplicity of its geometry made this architecture ideally suited to commemorate the broad spectrum of religions, cultures and classes that made up the British armies. This belief was well reflected in his designs for perhaps Britain's three most important war memorials: the Cenotaph in London, Thiepval Memorial to the Missing of the Somme in France and the All-India War Memorial in New Delhi.

By early 1921, Lutyens's plans and drawings for the New Delhi memorial were far enough along for the Government of India to have the Duke of Connaught, the king's brother, lay the memorial's foundation stone. The *Times* declared that his visit was a bold statement of a new era in British India. He laid not only the war memorial's foundation stone but also the foundation stone for a new government structure, the Council House. The *Times* concluded, '[India] has never until now witnessed such a courageous and spacious attempt [the Council House] to unite the immemorial spirit of the East with the principles of popular representation derived from the West.'[12] The Council House, a round colonnaded structure designed and built by Herbert Baker, was added to the main government area in response to the recent passage of Indian political reforms contained in the Government of India Act of 1919 described earlier. Baker's new structure housed a Chamber of Princes for the princely states, a Council of State and the Central Legislative Assembly whose membership was increasingly becoming popularly elected. The *Times* connected the 1919 act's political reforms with the All-India War Memorial's commemoration of Indian wartime sacrifice:

> Not only will it commemorate the fifty thousand [Indian] dead who gave lives for the British Raj, but it should remind future generations that the true birthplace of Indian constitutional freedom were the battlefields of the greatest of all wars for human liberty.[13]

Constitutional reform became linked to India's loyalty and willingness to die not simply for the British Empire but for its ideals. Thus, the memorial and its city were not simply

---

11   The land around Delhi has seen multiple cities, the remains of which can still be seen today. Two of these cities are alive and thriving and distinguished from each other by the terms 'new' and 'old'. Old Delhi refers to the city of Shah Jahanabad built by the Mughal Emperor Shahjahan. New Delhi refers to the imperial city built by the Raj in the first half of the twentieth century. It is now the official capital of independent India.

12   'The New Era in India,' *Times*, 8 February 1921, p. 11.

13   'India in the War,' *Times*, 15 February 1921, p. 11.

symbols of colonial coercion, powerful emblems of British dominance, but monuments that modelled a British paternalism that rewarded Indians for good behaviour.

The All-India War Memorial was so central to the British Raj's new vision of itself that it ended New Delhi's official inauguration in 1931 with its long awaited unveiling. Major-General Fabian Ware of the Imperial War Graves Commission, who gave the opening address, claimed: 'On the day of testing ... India was found standing freely shoulder to shoulder with other nations of the Empire on the side of right and freedom.'[14] Lord Irwin, the then Viceroy of India, used his speech to link Indian political advance to continued British rule:

> [We] are here to recall the four unforgettable years during which nations and peoples and races ... became one in a common impulse of loyalty to the throne and one in the defence unto death of the rights they had won under the protection of that sovereign.[15]

Irwin's speech underscored the tenuousness of the rights and benefits that Indians had gained under British rule in the last several decades and hinted that Indian political advance could be easily reversed without Britain's continued guidance and imperial protection. What better way to indicate Britain's enlightened paternalism than the quintessential symbol of the British Empire, George V, the king-emperor.

Lutyens turned to Charles Sargeant Jagger, one of Britain's most popular and promising sculptors, to design the George V Memorial Statue for New Delhi's memorial park.[16] Jagger was a promising sculptor with deep working class roots, which, according to Ann Compton, shaped his artistic sensibilities.[17] His father, Enoch, apprenticed him to Mappin & Webb as a metal engraver at the age of 14. After finishing his apprenticeship in 1905, he began teaching at Sheffield Technical School of Art. Major awards for further fine arts studies followed. In 1907, he won a scholarship to study at the Royal College of Art under the guidance of Professor Edouard Lanteri, one of the era's more influential sculptors. In July 1914, he won the prestigious Prix de Rome in Sculpture offered by the British School at Rome (BSR). However, like so many other men driven by a sense of patriotism, he instead enlisted in the armed forces in August 1914. Commissioned as a second lieutenant in the Artist's Rifles, his first military action was at Gallipoli where he was shot through the shoulder. He again was wounded, shot through the lung, while serving in France. The horrors of the war, the loss of friends, the high command's seeming incompetence and the inability of civilians to understand the experiences of soldiers made him 'anti-institutional', according to Compton.[18] Yet, as she also notes, his affiliation with the Artist's Rifles

---

14 Transcript of speech by Major-General Fabian Ware, *Lahore Tribune*, 14 February 1931.
15 Transcript of speech by Lord Irwin, *Lahore Tribune*, 14 February 1931.
16 Lutyens also asked Jagger to sculpt the reliefs on the base of New Delhi's Jaipur Column, which sat in the Viceroy's Courtyard in front of the Viceroy's House, as well as statues of Lord Hardinge, Lord Reading and large elephants that flanked the entrance to the Viceroy's Court. The two knew of each other through their affiliation with the BSR and had worked together on a project exhibited at the 1924 British Empire Exhibition at Wembley. For the exhibit, Lutyens created a scale model of a 1920s mansion that included actual works of art, two of which, tiny busts of Earl Haig and Earl Beatty, were sculpted by Jagger.
17 Ann Compton, *Charles Sargeant Jagger: War and Peace Sculpture* (London: Imperial War Museum, 1985). Jagger was born in 1885 near Sheffield where his father worked at a local colliery.
18 Ibid., p. 21.

brought him into contact with an older generation of influential artists who saw a younger generation of artists as fighting a war they could not. In particular, he caught the attention of George Frampton, one of England's most famous sculptors and a professor at the BSR. Through Frampton's recommendations, Jagger received his earliest post-war commissions. For Frampton, artists who had first-hand knowledge of the human cost of the war had special insights into the design of war memorials.[19] Some of Jagger's most important pieces included the Royal Artillery Memorial at Hyde Park Corner, *No Man's Land* at the Victoria and Albert Museum, and the Great Western Railway War Memorial at Paddington Station.

The commission to design and build the George V Memorial Statue challenged Jagger for several reasons. First, he was most comfortable using his sculptures and reliefs to enhance larger memorials or buildings. Sitting within alcoves of larger structures, his sculptures added to a larger architectural context.[20] The George V statue would be free-standing, though located under a large stone canopy, and visible from all directions. Secondly, and far more difficult, Lutyens's commission asked him to move away from the artistic sensibilities and strategies that had helped him infuse tremendous energy into his work. In the past, his working class background had guided his hand in creating an object filled with strenuous labour.[21] His male figures were powerfully-built, often in the act of doing something physical on the battlefield or at work. Even his Great Western Railway War Memorial at Paddington Station – which depicts a soldier reading a letter – is filled with a sense of vigour. The viewer does not see but rather feels a statue of a man reading a letter. But, of course, George V could not be presented as a figure straining at anything. He simply needed to be present, albeit regal and supremely powerful. The British Empire endured not because of the monarch's physical labour but because his very presence rested on and was made possible by abstract principles and values that led to good government. Jagger was forced to exchange 'grim reality' and 'strenuous action' with 'abstraction and decoration'.[22] Just how difficult the transition was for Jagger is suggested by the length of time it took for him to create a design acceptable to Lutyens.

Lutyens tightly controlled the design and aesthetics of the buildings and the areas within the new capital that fell within his purview.[23] In regard to the George V Memorial Statue, he sent Jagger back to the drawing board on three separate occasions. Jagger's first clay model, done in 1932, had the king-emperor sitting in a howdah (a sedan) on the back of an Asian elephant holding the fruits of empire in his trunk. Reliefs of animals and humans covered the base of the statue and signified the king's dominion over both. The ambitious model reflected India's hierarchy quite well, but Lutyens rejected the design since viewers' eyes were drawn to the elephant and the howdah rather than the king.[24] The second model, completed in 1933, had the king sitting on a throne, but Lutyens rejected this design as well. Jagger's third attempt, which had the king standing in ceremonial robes, was accepted in 1934. Unfortunately it is hard to say what Jagger's sculptural sensibility would have

---

19   Ibid., p. 22.
20   Ibid., p. 9.
21   Ibid., p. 67.
22   Ibid., p. 90.
23   Lutyens and Hardinge famously argued over New Delhi's architectural designs with the latter calling the other a 'Philistine' at one point. Hardinge's relationship with Herbert Baker was far better. Lutyens tended to follow his aesthetic inclinations regardless of political context whereas Herbert Baker tried to meet the wishes of his clients.
24   Compton, *Charles Sargeant Jagger*, p. 90.

engendered on the George V Statue because he died before actually sculpting the statue. The commission was passed to William Reid Dick, who supervised the final carving. Once carved and shipped to India, the statue was placed in 1936 under a large canopy previously designed and built by Edwin Lutyens near the All-India War Memorial. The statue's base represented Britain's imperial strength with its firm block-like form, which mirrored the solidity of the war memorial arch's columns. Together, the two large objects commemorated the meaning of the British Empire and the great pillars upon which it rested: regal authority and sacrifice, both of which made India's progress possible.

The problem with this colonial narrative, shared by most British officials, was that an increasing number of Indians had grown sceptical of it. As Stephen Legg and others have shown, New Delhi symbolised political changes that outwardly seemed like liberal advances for India but were actually exclusionary and divisive.[25] An important intent of British sponsored political reform was to drive a wedge between radical and moderate Indian nationalists by giving the latter greater governing responsibilities with promises of further advances in the future. The reforms also stemmed from and helped shape what Uday Mehta has called a 'liberal strategy of exclusion' that privileged western culture and society while denigrating India's.[26] Colonial officials could argue that Britain was one of the great birthplaces of representative, responsible government by pointing to the 1215 signing of the Magna Carta, the 1688 Glorious Revolution and the nineteenth century's three great reform bills as examples of its slow and incredibly cautious exploration of popularly elected government. India's political past, on the other hand, had been characterised by autocratic governments based on the absolute will of the emperor. Thus, as Thomas Metcalf long ago argued, a politics of difference emerged whereby British officials saw themselves as tutors of responsible government to Indians who lacked deep western political traditions.[27] India might have its independence someday, but only when the British deemed that it had learnt its lessons well enough to responsibly govern itself. For many Indian nationalists who had been fighting for independence since the beginning of the twentieth century, freedom from colonial rule became a prize that seemed incredibly close at hand but purposely kept just out of reach by the British government. By the late 1930s, many of them had grown deeply incredulous of British talk about political reform. This scepticism would shape the debates about the All-India War Memorial and the George V Memorial Statue after independence in 1947.

Memorial park after independence

Britain's long rule in India left a lasting legacy on India's built environment. Large infrastructural projects such as railways modernised Indian transport and left indelible traces across the Indian landscape, and massive canal colonies were built by the British to increase

---

25 Legg, *Spaces of Colonialism*; and Johnson, *New Delhi*. Both examine in detail Britain's use of the new capital as a colonial strategy that relied on the promise of political reform to better subjugate Indians.

26 Uday Mehta, *Liberalism and Empire: A Study in Nineteenth Century Liberal Thought* (Chicago: University of Chicago Press, 1999); and 'Liberal Strategies of Exclusion,' in *Tensions of Empire: Colonial Cultures in a Bourgeois World*, ed. Frederick Cooper and Ann Laura Stoler (Berkeley: University of California Press, 1997).

27 Thomas R. Metcalf, *Ideologies of the Raj: The New Cambridge History of India, vol. 3, part 4* (Cambridge: Cambridge University Press, 1994).

India's agricultural output. After independence, India was quite happy to take control of these infrastructural improvements because they were important components of the Indian economy. But other colonial built environments, such as New Delhi's memorial park and its two major objects, the George V Memorial Statue and the All-India War Memorial, posed significant challenges. Sites such as these had little economic value and, worse, were persistent reminders of a colonial past that many nationalists wanted to erase. Some felt that sites of colonial memory had no place in India's new capital. Lala Onkar Nath spoke for many when he claimed that all such colonial relics 'should be moved to some museum . . . [since] they reminded the Indian people of their bitter past'.[28] Political change had come to India, but the capital's built environment did not reflect this change of government or India's long struggle to achieve it. It was a national travesty, in Nath's opinion, that the statue of the king-emperor, the ultimate symbol of the British Empire, should continue to reside in independent India's capital. Likewise, the All-India War Memorial was designed to remind Indians of their colonial dependence on Britain. The only solution, for Nath, was to replace imperial statues, memorials and monuments with ones of Gandhi, Nehru and other heroes of the Indian independence movement. This important step would allow India to break those colonial ties that symbolically linked the two countries thus giving average Indians a chance to *feel* the change of government in the new capital's built environment.

Though many sympathised with this nationalist opinion, other Indian leaders cautioned slowness in the handling of treasured British statues and memorials. Jawaharlal Nehru, in particular, moved with great deliberation on the handling of these colonial objects. As independent India's first prime minister, he understood the need to remain on cordial relations with India's most important trade partner. A second and perhaps more difficult consideration had to be faced as well. If removed, what would replace these colonial objects and how could they be made free of colonialism's taint? People like Lala Onkar Nath were asking for the impossible, for the city wherein these objects sat was one giant statement of British rule. Other less radical solutions had to be found.

In the end, the independent Indian government chose a strategy that simultaneously embraced and transformed the original colonial meanings of New Delhi's many colonial spaces. One of the quickest and easiest ways for changing New Delhi's built environment without disrupting British-Indian relations was simply to give Indian names to objects.[29] The Kingsway, for example, was Indianised to *Rajpath*, though it still is the main ceremonial avenue for the independent Indian government just as it was for the British. The Viceroy's House was renamed *Rashtrapati Bhavan* and repurposed as the President of India's residence. The Council House briefly described earlier was renamed *Sansad Bhavan*. It now houses India's Parliament consisting of the *Lok Sabha* (the elected house of the people) and the *Rajya Sabha* (the council of states). As such, *Sansad Bhavan* now represents the fulfilment of British promises of responsible and representative government in India.

The All-India War Memorial was renamed as well, becoming India Gate, but as a memorial to imperial sacrifice it required a much more nuanced reinterpretation. The independent Indian government needed to address the war memorial's powerful colonial meaning as a site that conjoined political reform and colonial sacrifice. As seen earlier, the memorial represented a particular colonial vision that simultaneously empowered and

---

28 'Statues of Viceroys to Remain in New Delhi,' *Statesmen*, 21 April 1950.
29 'Future of Memorials, etc.,' Dominions Office, 142/255, vol. I, The National Archives of Britain.

disempowered Indians. It symbolised, to a certain extent, a colonial rule that paid greater attention to the political demands of Indian subjects but only in as much as it secured British security in the region. British-sponsored colonial reform came from and was intended to increase British power; to strengthen rather than weaken Britain's hold over India, not through mere coercion but by the consent of Indian colonial subjects. Indeed, Robert Grant Irving long ago showed that New Delhi symbolised Britain's unification of an incredibly diverse sub-continent and that the very *notion* of India as a political unit was made possible by the supreme authority of the British Raj.[30]

India symbolically broke these colonial bounds by renaming the All-India War Memorial India Gate and by inscribing it with subtly changed meaning. This did not entail erasing the memorial's original meaning as a symbol of sacrifice and reform. Indeed, the Indian government built on this original meaning but did so in a way that celebrated the independent Indian state. As India Gate, the memorial came to symbolise a gateway between what India had been to what it had become. From a symbol of Britain and India's colonial unity, made stronger by wartime sacrifice, the memorial became a symbol of a new type of unity. Even as India rejected the memorial's overt colonial significance, it embraced the memorial's deeper meaning as a symbol of universal truth. For these truths – unchanging, found in nature and spanning eternity – provided the foundation upon which to build a secular state in India. By claiming these truths as their own, Indians rejected the notion that Britain had a privileged relationship to enlightened ideals, a view that many colonial officials took for granted during the colonial period. So Indians had indeed made sacrifices for the same greater truths that Lutyens inscribed into his memorial, but these were veracities that all humanity could recognise, experience and use to national benefit. Thus, the memorial continued to represent not simply those who had died, but the meaning and purpose of that sacrifice, while at the same time stressing that the motivation for such sacrifice had changed from imperial to national loyalties.

The transition from an imperial to a national memorial took several decades after independence and was realised at last when the Indian government erected a black marble cenotaph underneath India Gate's arch in the early 1970s. This new object sits on a foundation with eternal flames located at each corner. A rifle pointing downward with a helmet on top sits in the middle of the cenotaph. The words 'immortal warrior' are written in Hindi script on the cenotaph's sides. *Amar Jawan Jyoti*, 'flame of the immortal warrior', as it is called, represents India's version of the tomb of the Unknown Soldier. As such it expands the memorial's original colonial meaning from a memorial to imperial soldiers who died in the Great War to a memorial of collective sacrifice in defence of Indian national sovereignty. This meaning is highlighted during the annual Republic Day ceremonies when high officials lay wreaths on *Amar Jawan Jyoti* in honour of all Indian soldiers who have died defending India. In the process, Republic Day, India's national holiday, is firmly joined to a memorial of collective sacrifice for the nation. In this way, the 13,617 Indian soldiers whose names were inscribed on Lutyens's original memorial are not elided from post-independent Indian history. Rather, they become historical agents within a much broader story of and about India's long struggle for self-representation of which independence from Britain was just one important step.

The All-India War Memorial's abstract meaning allowed it to be reinterpreted by the independent Indian government and to be incorporated into India's new national narrative.

---

30   Irving, *Indian Summer*.

The George V Memorial Statue, on the other hand, was too singular in meaning for such reinterpretation. After several decades of debate in India, the statue along with others was moved in the mid-1960s to Coronation Memorial Park, a little visited and neglected sculpture park located to the north of what had been the civil lines (Delhi's European neighbourhood) during the colonial era. The large canopy that sat next to the All-India War Memorial and housed George V remains empty to this day. Here, amongst pools of standing water caused by the high water table and statues of British viceroys and other great personages of the Raj, the George V statue now stands (see Figure 14.2). The plinths the statues sit on are relatively drab and without any decoration. Most of the statues look the worse for wear, some purposely damaged and others simply succumbing to the ravages of

Figure 14.2   George V Memorial Statue (in its new home at Coronation Memorial Park)

Source: David A. Johnson

Delhi's extreme climate. Periodically, the *chowkidar* (guard), who lives in a *godown* within the park, burns off the grass surrounding the statues.

Coronation Memorial Park's drab and unkempt look conceals the area's rich colonial history. Indeed, few places in India saw such grand imperial spectacles as the area designated for the park. The British Raj staged its three largest and most important all-India imperial durbars (royal assemblages) on these very grounds. Here, Victoria, Edward VII and George V were crowned Empress and Emperors of India in 1877, 1903, and 1911, respectively. These events were much more than opportunities to place imperial crowns on British monarchs or their representatives. As Bernard Cohn has shown, long before the arrival of the British and their rise to sub-continental dominance Indian durbars had been used for ages as a form of high-ritual that cemented imperial relations by having the emperor receive homage from his loyal subjects and to bestow gifts on them in return.[31] Thus, durbars tangibly reflected power relations within the imperial state – whether Mauryan, Mughal or British – by reaffirming the emperor as the ultimate gift-giver, the fount from which good things come to those who are loyal subjects.

The three durbars were massive and costly affairs consisting of state entrances, usually but not always on elephants, tremendous pomp and circumstance, massive shows of military might, Indian princely obeisance and munificence by the newly crowned. The durbars became increasingly grander from the first to the last with George V's surpassing the previous two in size and pageantry and by the physical presence of the monarch himself. For the first time in the history of Britain's Indian Empire, a reigning British monarch travelled to India to personally receive homage from his loyal Indian subjects and to bestow gifts on them in return.[32] Forty square kilometres were set aside to house 233 camps that contained nearly 200 ruling chiefs, representatives of provincial governments, nearly 80,000 troops, special guests and sightseers. Infrastructure was built to handle the massive influx of people, which approximately doubled Delhi's normal population of 250,000. Enough tents were raised to cover 16 square kilometres in canvas. Ninety-six kilometres of new roads were built, 42 kilometres of broad gauge and 14 kilometres of narrow gauge railway were laid, twenty-four new railway stations were erected, and 80 kilometres of new water mains were set with 48 kilometres of pipeline for distribution in the camps. Markets, butchers, dairies, parks, gardens, polo, football and review grounds were arranged, and enough electricity to light the towns of Brighton and Portsmouth was directed into the area. The actual durbar site and amphitheatre where the ceremony took place had enough seating for 4,000 special guests, 70,000 people on a raised semi-circular mound, and space for 35,000 marshalled troops. Today, only a memorial obelisk to the last and greatest of the durbars marks the grand spectacles that took place in the area. Here, at these very grounds, the independent Indian government built Coronation Memorial Park.

India's treatment of the George V Memorial Statue clearly contrasted with its handling of the All-India War Memorial. The latter, for all its deep colonial meanings, its importance to the Raj's identity and its massive size, was abstract enough to be incorporated into a

---

31 Bernard Cohn, 'Representing Authority in Victorian India,' in *The Invention of Tradition*, ed. Eric Hobsbawm and Terence Ranger (Cambridge: Cambridge University Press, 1983), pp. 165–210.

32 Charles Hardinge, *My Indian Years: 1910–1916: The Reminiscences of Lord Hardinge of Penshurst* (London: John Murray, 1948), p. 18. Sir John Hewitt, the Lt Governor of the United Provinces, chaired the durbar committee, which also included four Ruling Chiefs to serve as Other Members. Colonel Maxwell, Hardinge's Military Secretary, was appointed to the committee as well to serve as Hardinge's direct representative.

new Indian national narrative. The war memorial's post-colonial reinterpretation completed what Britain began when it decided to erect a monument to Indians who had died in the Great War. After independence and as India re-worked the memorial's meaning, it embraced certain elements inscribed by the memorial's British designers, rejected others, and, in the end, re-imagined the memorial as a symbol of national renewal. The memorial continued to reflect abstract universal truths, ideals that the Indian state now theoretically rested upon, but it was stripped of its colonial constraints. A memorial that was created to promote a strategy to achieve continued colonial rule in India became a memorial that symbolised not just India's independence but also its rebirth.

The George V Memorial Statue, in contrast, could never be renamed or made part of a new national narrative that independent India could embrace. The George V Memorial Statue is simply a statue of George V. But it *was* given new meaning by changing its environs. The solution elegantly dealt with the problem of not only this specific statue but also all the unwanted statuary that once sat in conspicuous public spaces throughout New Delhi. Statues of various viceroys, for example, had stood in front of the Council House. When objects of colonial memory like these could not be re-codified or given new meaning, they were removed from the public eye and returned to a specifically colonial space. This compartmentalisation of those parts of a colonial past that could not be utilised by the new Indian government represented a kind of post-colonial sanitisation of New Delhi; where movable unwanted relics were thrown like so much colonial dross. Indeed, a site that once held the greatest of all colonial spectacles, the imperial durbar, has become what one travel agency has called the 'junkyard of history'.[33]

Conclusion

Created by war and refashioned after Indian independence, the George V Memorial Statue and the All-India War Memorial are fascinating examples of the tremendous difficulty post-colonial nations face when addressing their colonial past. Independent India's reinterpretation of the war memorial was a remarkably nuanced re-reading of the memorial's history as a Great War monument to Indian sacrifice for the British Empire, but it took almost three decades to craft. The creation of a sculpture park for unwanted colonial statuary at the most imperial of all Delhi spaces was fittingly ironic, but it took the Indian government many years to put the idea into effect. Some of this had to do with the Indian government's desire not to unnecessarily damage relations with Britain. It also had to do with the high degree of effort required by any post-colonial nation to transform colonial spaces into national ones.

How India dealt with both sites also points to the plasticity of meaning inscribed in physical objects. The colonial past cannot be erased in India, especially at New Delhi where it is so embedded in the built environment, but it can be adapted to the needs of the independent Indian state. The names of those Indian soldiers carved into the All-India War Memorial are still on India Gate, for example, but their meaning has been re-worked into a new narrative about love of nation rather than empire. Likewise, the George V statue changed in meaning when it was moved to Coronation Memorial Park. The statue

---

33 Tourist Place, Delhi, The Capital City of India, 5 July 2011, accessed, 1 June 2015, http://shrikantpriyadarshi.blogspot.com/2011/07/capital-city-of-india-new-delhi-capital.html.

represented the imperial unity of Britain and India under the paternal protection of the king-emperor when standing next to the All-India War Memorial. In its new location at Coronation Memorial Park, isolated and little visited, it symbolises the impossibility of that union. Is India committing some kind of violence to history when it alters colonial memories for national benefit? Not really. History has never been about the search for objective truth, as Peter Novick long ago showed; it is about interpretation.[34] In a way, India's re-writing of the histories of the All-India War Memorial and the George V Memorial Statue are no less cogent than their original colonial meanings. It is doubtful that the majority of Indian soldiers who sacrificed themselves in the Great War did so merely out of love and loyalty to George V. Similarly, the rise of Hindu nationalism as a powerful political force in the national life of India today makes one sceptical about the future of India's avowed secular pluralism. Objects have social lives that change in meaning when contexts change.[35]

---

34 Peter Novick, *That Noble Dream: The 'Objectivity Question' and the American Historical Profession* (Cambridge: Cambridge University Press, 1989).

35 See Arjun Appadurai, ed., *The Social Life of Things: Commodities in Cultural Perspective* (Cambridge: Cambridge University Press, 1988).

Chapter 15
Sounds from the trenches
Australian composers and the Great War

Andrew Harrison

A number of years ago, I was seeking to return to the 'art music' enclave after some time spent writing theatrical music and scoring a number of short films. The aesthetic voice in my head, coaxing me back in the direction of 'serious' music composition, had been growing steadily louder. Eventually I arrived at the point where I was ready to re-embark upon a long creative journey that I knew would provide nourishment and fulfilment, as well as frustration and angst. Getting to this moment of clarity had been no mean feat; I needed to convince myself that I had something to compose for – a reason to create. I found this impetus through my connection to the First World War. The prospect of giving voice to the narrative of my forebears through music was most exciting. I had been in dialogue with pianist Zubin Kanga, who was looking for new Australian piano works. He commissioned a composition that allowed me to reflect upon the war experiences of my great-great uncle.[1] I also began a quest to see what other Australian composers had engaged with the Great War in their own compositions. My findings left me surprised; there was little music to uncover. Despite the acknowledged importance of the First World War upon the development of Australian society and identity, few Australian art music composers have written works that grapple with our wartime past.[2]

Yet the spectre of the Great War looms large within Australia's cultural narrative and has been a focal point for a number of seminal Australian artists. Arthur Streeton's wartime images capture the ravaged towns and villages of northern France and Sidney Nolan's mid-1950s Gallipoli-inspired paintings draw the observer into the contradiction between the soldier as warrior-hero and the internal mental anguish of men gripped by fear. Frank Hurley's vivid war photographs speak of the overwhelming brutality of the military industrial-complex and man's struggles to survive against the odds. Henry Lawson's book of war poetry, *My Army, O My Army*, published in 1915, is filled with caricatures of Australian military bravery and larrikinism, tempered with melancholic realism. Alan Seymour's controversial play *One day of the year*, written in 1958, intimates that the legend of Anzac was fast becoming an irrelevant and alcohol-infused farce. Peter Weir's film *Gallipoli*, released in 1982, tells the tragic story of young Australian men, with so much

---

1 The process of commissioning is quite nuanced and symbiotic. The genesis of musical compositions sometimes starts with a composer, who will then begin discussions with an ensemble or musician. On other occasions, it will be an artistic director, ensemble or performer who will seek out a composer to write a new work.

2 This year – 2015 – is the centenary of the Anzac landings at Gallipoli. Over the last six months there has been a large output of new works by prominent Australian composers to celebrate this anniversary. My focus, however, will be on works composed before this particular period; I have examined music written before 2014 (the centenary of the beginning of the Great War) only.

to live for, being mercilessly cut down in their prime. There is, however, no single iconic Australian art music composition dealing with the Great War that can be added to this list of cultural signifiers, although with the benefit of a centenary's hindsight, an attempt is being made to create one for Frederick Septimus Kelly.

So why – until 2015 and the centenary of the Gallipoli landings – was there such a paucity of Australian classical music dealing with the Great War? The reasons for this lack of compositional engagement with the war are not easily discernable. Perhaps the dark shadow of a horrific and 'pointless' war, which cast itself across so many Australian families, left too many psychological scars on composers, and they chose to forget rather than remember. Was it possible that with the construction of state-funded war monuments, the war had been sufficiently memorialised at an official level, and the national cultural discourse had moved on? Did the visibility of irrevocably damaged returned servicemen – and the hardships endured by their families – bring an aspect of 'shame' upon Australian society, which the broader community, including the arts, wished to ignore?[3] Or was it simply that there weren't enough Australian composers with adequate skills to construct a sophisticated musical language that could honour those who served and perished, and those who continued to suffer? Whilst a deeper understanding of these propositions is ongoing, I will address some of these points throughout the chapter, particularly within the discussion of Helen Gifford's *Choral Scenes*.

What can be examined, nonetheless, are the works – and the motivations – of a number of Australian composers, both contemporary to the war and more recent, who have used the Great War as a point of reference for their artistic output. More often than not, they were inspired – perhaps even compelled – to write music about the war through a personal connection to the battlefields. My examination of music written by Frederick Septimus Kelly and Helen Gifford, amongst others, will focus on these connections. A final brief discussion of the development of my own compositional procedures, in light of my family's affiliation to the First World War, will also reiterate this. I have specifically concentrated on art music. I'm aware of research into Australian popular music of the war and compositions for ensembles such as brass bands; however, these works are outside the scope of this investigation.

On 23 April 1915, two days before the Anzac landings at Gallipoli, the English poet Rupert Brooke succumbed to septicemia brought on by an infected mosquito bite, and died aboard a French hospital ship moored in the Aegean Sea. Brooke and a group of friends, including Australian composer Frederick Septimus Kelly, volunteered for the Royal Naval Reserve at the outbreak of the war. Brooke's body was buried in an olive grove on the island of Skyros. Kelly – affectionately known as 'Cleg' to his friends – stayed behind with some others close to Brooke and built a funeral cairn over his grave. Kelly felt Brooke's death heavily. He later noted in his diary: 'For the whole day I was oppressed with the sense of loss . . . [before] the sense of tragedy gave place to a sense of passionless beauty.'[4] Kelly began composing a homage to his literary friend – *Elegy for String Orchestra; In Memoriam Rupert Brooke* – two months later in Alexandria, whilst recuperating from wounds sustained at Gallipoli. The piece was completed on 27 June 1915. The depth of

---

3   Helen Gifford mentions 'shame' when discussing her composition, and this will be explored later in the chapter.

4   Frederick Septimus Kelly, *Race against Time: The Diaries of F.S. Kelly*, ed. Thérèse Radic (Canberra: National Library of Australia, 2004), p. 382.

Kelly's musical eulogy was immediately recognised as 'no mere expression of personal grief or loss, but, a symbol, rather, of the continuity of life'.[5] More recently it has been described as 'a haunting memorial to both Brooke and to the losses sustained in the Dardanelles Campaign'.[6]

The power of the work lies in its simple beauty. Kelly begins the piece with a short unadorned melody in the Dorian mode, referencing the Greek resting place of the deceased Brooke. It is built entirely around stepwise motion, save for two consecutive leaps: a minor third and a perfect fourth (see Figure 15.1).

Within this motive Kelly lays out much of his compositional material for the piece and provides a blueprint for its intended affect. Looking back upon Kelly's diary entry, the 'passionless beauty' that he refers to is implied in the stepwise movement that is heard in many of the short phrases prescribed to the strings, often in rhythmic unison. By contrast, Kelly emphasises his grief – his 'sense of loss' – through the expansion of the initial leap of a fourth to a perfect fifth. Beginning at bar 30 and continuing through to bar 50, this short gesture begins with an ascending fifth, evoking a cry of despair before returning to the tranquillity – and futility – of stepwise motion and a descending minor third (see Figure 15.2).

Kelly also introduces a new accompaniment figure to underpin the aforementioned melodic figure. Beginning at bar 31, oscillating quaver triplets – moving either by step or small leaps – are heard *pianissimo* in the first and second violins and cellos, providing a shimmering backdrop for the melody (see Figure 15.3).

Figure 15.1   F. S. Kelly, *Elegy for String Orchestra*, bars 1–5

Source: Public domain

Figure 15.2   F. S. Kelly, *Elegy for String Orchestra*, bars 30–35

Source: Public domain

---

5   John Buchan, ed., *Balliol College War Memorial Book 1914–1919*, vol. 1 (Oxford: Balliol College, 1924).

6   Frederick Septimus Kelly, *Music from the Great War*, ed. Bruce Steele and Richard Divall, 1st ed. (Melbourne: Marshall-Hall Trust, 2005), introductory notes.

Figure 15.3 F. S. Kelly, *Elegy for String Orchestra*, bars 31–33

Source: Public domain

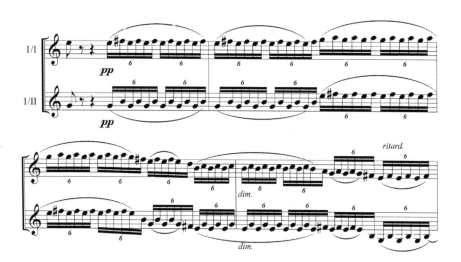

Figure 15.4 F. S. Kelly, *Elegy for String Orchestra*, bars 39–42

Source: Public domain

At bar 39, the background role of these triplets switches momentarily to foreground material in the first violins, when the rhythmic values of the triplet figures are halved from quavers to semiquavers (see Figure 15.4).

This variation brings about a lighter texture whilst simultaneously amplifying the intensity of rhythmic material. The oscillating semiquaver triplets, mostly rising and falling in stepwise increments, evoke the rustling of the wind through an olive tree that 'bends itself over [Brooke's] grave as though sheltering it from the sun and rain'.[7]

Kelly's musical memorial to Brooke portrays the integrity of their friendship and the impact of the poet's death upon the composer. It is the antithesis, however, of what many people might associate with 'war music'. There is no trace of nationalism or triumphalism and no use of dissonance or rhythmic turmoil, and the overall dynamic is soft. The American musicologist Glenn Watkins has identified this trait amongst other art music of the period. He argues that, when considering much of the music written during the First World War, the question that often comes to mind is, 'Where is the war?'[8] Examining Kelly's *Elegy* within the context of Watkins's question could, therefore, imply an apparent absence of the war from his work.

Eric Saylor's study of English 'pastoral music' by Elgar and Vaughan Williams, however, counters this argument. It allows Kelly's *Elegy* to be aligned with a broader musical movement that he was surely influenced by. Saylor maintains that pastoral music contemporaneous to the war modified 'its conventional signifiers in ways that were relevant to contemporary culture ... and therefore exemplif[ied] ... pastoralism's engagement with modernity'.[9] Kelly's use of modal harmony, a narrow dynamic palette and lyrical melodic gestures in the *Elegy* indicate that, whilst he was not seeking to align himself with modernist composers of Europe, such as Igor Stravinsky, he was still hoping to achieve a contemporary work that would 'evoke the unsettling stillness war leaves in its wake – the barren fields [and] the silent dead'.[10] The Australian violinist Chris Latham reinforces this point, describing Kelly's compositional process of writing in a pastoral style as 'a survival mechanism, a way of being home'.[11] (Latham is referring here to Kelly's connection to England, not Australia.)

Frederick Septimus Kelly remained at Gallipoli until the conclusion of the campaign, winning the Distinguished Service Cross for bravery and earning a promotion to the rank of Lieutenant. He was transferred to France in May 1916, commanding B Company of the Hood Battalion, and killed on November 13th, during the final days of the Somme, leading an attack on a machine gun post at Beaucourt-sur-Ancre. He composed other music whilst on active service; indeed, he left behind quite a number of unfinished chamber and orchestral pieces, including a Sonata in F minor that received its first publication in 2005.[12] These works reflect no overt commentary on Kelly's war involvement and are 'essentially conformist'[13] in style.

Kelly's achievements on the battlefield deserve all the recognition they receive. He was by all accounts an excellent soldier, keeping up the morale of his troops during the Battle

---

7   Kelly, *Race against Time*, p. 382.

8   Glenn Watkins, *Proof Through the Night: Music and the Great War* (Berkeley: University of California Press, 2002), p. 7.

9   Eric Saylor, '"It's Not Lambkins Frisking at All": English Pastoral Music and the Great War,' *The Musical Quarterly* 91, no. 1–2 (20 March 2008): p. 45, accessed 2 October 2013, http://mq.oxfordjournals.org.

10 Ibid., p. 50.

11 Chris Latham, 'Chris Latham and the Trumpeter Who "Stopped Gunfire",' interviewed by Andrew Ford, *The Music Show*, ABC Radio National, 25 April 2015.

12 Kelly, *Music from the Great War*, p. 26.

13 Rhian Davies, 'Kelly, Frederick Septimus,' *Grove Music Online*, accessed 19 March 2015, *Oxford Music Online*, http://www.oxfordmusiconline.com/.

of the Somme by singing folk songs and sea shanties. He was also mentioned twice in despatches. In addition, Kelly's athletic prowess was something to behold; an exceptional oarsmen and sculler, he had won a gold medal in rowing with the English eights at the Olympic Games of 1908.[14]

Kelly's importance within Australia's early musical history, however, is a moot point,[15] and needs to be considered with caution and without sentiment. Can Australia claim him as its great wartime composer in the manner that England reveres Elgar or Vaughan Williams? The answer is probably not. His diaries reinforce the fact that, as an adult, he became firmly ensconced within British society, and although fond of Australia, considered himself to be a British-Australian. Unlike the more famous Percy Grainger – who 'saw himself as an Australian ... [and] an outsider',[16] and whose musical vision was 'analogous to [the] national landscape and true to [its] Asian-Pacific location'[17] – Kelly did not write music that was 'overtly Australian'.[18] More important, Kelly drew upon his family's extensive wealth to personally pay to have his music published by the German music publishing house, Schott. This was something that a composer of lesser means could not have achieved (publication was generally offered on the basis of the merits of the music). We can only speculate, therefore, as to whether Kelly's music would have been deemed worthy of publication without the opportunities provided by his family background. This is the fundamental point, regardless of where Kelly's allegiances lay in terms of Australia – his country of birth – or his adopted spiritual home, England. Kelly's scores reveal that he was still in the process of finding his own mature musical voice and that his tragic early death in 1916 prevented this from occurring. Again, all that is left are questions. Frederick Septimus Kelly's rightful position within our cultural narrative is that of 'a puzzle that needs solving',[19] rather than an iconic composer waiting to be chaperoned to the front of the cultural narrative queue.

The three decades following the Armistice saw the creation of a small number of art music compositions that dealt with the war. Henry Tate's solo piano piece *The Australian*,

---

14 See Andrew Collins and John Cecil, 'Composing Music in the Gallipoli Trenches: Frederick Septimus Kelly,' *ABC Great Southern*, accessed 7 June 2015, http://www.abc.net.au/local/audio/2014/04/04/3978640.htm.; and Harold Hartley, rev. Rhian Davies, 'Kelly, Frederick Septimus (1881–1916),' in *Oxford Dictionary of National Biography*, ed. H.C.G. Matthew and Brian Harrison (Oxford: Oxford University Press, 2004), accessed 25 April 2015, http://www.oxforddnb.com.virtual.anu.edu.au/view/article/34265?docPos=1.

15 *Gallipoli – A Tribute* by various artists, produced by the Ian Potter Foundation, the Ian Potter Cultural Trust and Monash University and with the support of the State Government of Victoria, 2015, compact disc. Tony Abbott, the Australian Prime Minister, recently mentioned Kelly's 'legacy of musical compositions' and his 'invaluable contribution to Australian history' in his liner notes for *Gallipoli – A Tribute*, released to celebrate the centenary of the Gallipoli landings. Conversely, composer and musicologist Larry Sitsky has stated that Kelly's work has 'turned out to be somewhat of an embarrassment in musical circles ... he comes across as a well-meaning amateur when one views the scores dispassionately'.

16 Kelly, *Race against Time*, p. 11.

17 Malcolm Gillies and David Pear, 'Grainger, Percy,' *Grove Music Online*, accessed 25 April 2015, *Oxford Music Online*, http://www.oxfordmusiconline.com/.

18 Thérèse Radic, 'Editing the Diaries of F.S. Kelly: Unique Insights into an Expatriate's Musical Career,' *Context: Journal of Music Research* no. 19 (Spring 2000): p. 25, accessed 2 April 2015, http://search.informit.com.au/documentSummary;dn=171752450081118;res=IELHSS>ISSN: 1038-4006.

19 Ibid., p. 28.

written in 1929, examined a number of perspectives on the war in various movements with titles such as 'The Mother', 'Youth's Unrest', 'Surge and Spindrift'. Tate ended the work with a choir hidden offstage, singing an a cappella chorale titled 'Gallipoli Threnody'.[20] The Anzac Fellowship of Women – founded by Dr Mary Booth in Sydney on Anzac Day, 1921 – played an important role in cultivating an engagement between composers and the Great War. Embedded within the group's original constitution (which included duties such as caring for returned soldiers and their families and building relationships between women who worked as part of the war effort) was a pledge to 'foster the spirit and traditions of Anzac Day'.[21] This initial recognition of the cultural value of memorialising the Great War was further consolidated a decade later. In 1931 the executive of the organisation 'called together a number of men and women in the arts of music and the drama and in education'.[22] The Anzac Festival Committee was subsequently formed to 'emphasise the value of the Arts in helping to foster the Anzac tradition'.[23] With an ironically prescient warning to present-day Australia, the Fellowship realised that 'Anzac Day, being now a public holiday, would probably become an ordinary sports day unless something constructive was done to maintain its commemorative character.'[24]

The inaugural Anzac Eve Festival was held at the Conservatorium in Sydney the following year. A competition was run as part of the festival, which included a prize for the best musical setting – for voice or voices – of an original poem about Anzac history. Alfred Hill composed the art song *Anzac Day* for the occasion, setting the text of Dora Wilcox's poem to music. The composition competition ran until 1941 and then was reinstated from 1950–1957. Despite its fairly limited outreach – it was predominantly popular within Sydney and across New South Wales – the Anzac Eve Festival competition became an important opportunity for musical reflection on the Great War. Its association with two prominent female composers – Miriam Hyde and Dulcie Holland[25] – throughout its time, also highlights the significant role that woman have played in the creative commemoration of the war. From 1934 until the middle of the 1950s, Hyde and Holland were the only composers of art music inspired by the First World War,[26] save for Roy Agnew's *Anzac Symphony* that remained incomplete at the time of his death in 1944. Hyde also composed

---

20 Henry Tate, 'The Australian: Cycle for Piano Solo,' unpublished manuscript, 1929, ms2324/1, Canberra, National Library of Australia.
21 Bridget Brooklyn, 'The 1920s: A Good Decade for Women in Politics,' in *Seizing the Initiative: Australian Women Leaders in Politics, Workplaces and Communities*, ed. Rosemary Francis, Patricia Grimshaw, and Ann Standish (Melbourne: eScholarship Research Centre, The University of Melbourne, 2012), p. 162.
22 *Anzac Eve Festival Concert Program*, ed. Anzac Festival Committee (Sydney, Australia: Anzac Fellowship of Women, 1935).
23 'Anzac Fellowship of Women,' *Trove*, National Library of Australia, 2008, accessed 18 November 2013, http://nla.gov.au/nla.party-468893.
24 'Anzac Fellowship,' *Trove*, 2008.
25 Dulcie Holland won the 'Anzac Song Prize' in 1937 with her composition entitled *ANZAC Day*, in 1954 with *Welcome To Her Majesty*, and again in 1956 (the title of this last work is currently unknown). Miriam Hyde won the prize in 1951 with *ANZAC Threnody*, in 1952 with *Dawn Service* and lastly in 1955 with her composition *The Illawarra Flame*.
26 Both composers felt the impact of war upon their own lives. In 1939, Dulcie Holland was forced to cut short her studies at the Royal College of Music in London and return home to Australia following the outbreak of the Second World War. Later in the war, Miriam Hyde's husband, Marcus Edwards, became a German prisoner of war after the fall of Crete in 1941.

Heroic Elegy for orchestra in 1935, in addition to her Anzac Eve Festival compositions. *Heroic Elegy*, dedicated to a friend's husband who had served in the war and subsequently died in an unrelated accident, received a negative review in the *Sydney Morning Herald*, following its premiere performance.[27]

Martin Mather's large-scale work *ANZAC Requiem*, composed in 1967 and premiered in 1976, was the next orchestral piece to deal with the war in an extended fashion, and the first since Hyde's *Heroic Elegy*. Following bravely in the footsteps of Britten's 1961 monumental *War Requiem*, Mather's composition was inspired by 'the notion that a new image for Anzacs had been long overdue in the arts'.[28] His work suffered the unfortunate fate of being composed at the height of the Vietnam conflict, at a time when the Anzac tradition was perceived as being at odds with a modernising Australia. In Australian classical music, composers such as Peter Sculthorpe, Larry Sitsky and Richard Meale were defining a new set of aesthetics and creating a fresh sonic landscape and accordingly reviews of Mather's work in *The Age* and *The Australian* newspapers criticised him for being anachronistic.[29] His late-Romantic compositional language, it was felt, utilised 'a musical idiom that died with World War 1'.[30] How could he 'approach the dislocation of war in the comfortably secure idiom of a past era'?[31] And whilst Ralph Middenway's review in *The Australian* acknowledged that the *ANZAC Requiem* displayed some compositional technique – albeit antiquated – he suggested that the texture of the work was 'so full that the detail was lost'[32] and could be improved by 'cutting out many notes on many pages'.[33]

Following an absence from the musical landscape in the 1970s, the First World War returned as a creative theme in Vincent Plush's 1984 composition *Gallipoli Sunrise*.[34] After seeing Peter Weir's film *Gallipoli* numerous times whilst residing in the United States, Plush became aware of how the film's portrayal of Australian soldiers as larrikins changed when they were about to land at Anzac Cove: 'Like the twist of a knife in the stomach, the mood of the film changed in a split-second.'[35] Exploring the national sentiment surrounding Anzac Day – 'baptized in blood, Australia became a nation that day . . . or so our social

---

27 *Sydney Morning Herald*, 31 October 1940, p. 9. Neville Cardus, in his review in the *Sydney Morning Herald* on Thursday 31 October 1940, stated that 'frankly, Miss Hyde's composition disappointed me. It sounded obviously conventional . . . the work was clearly written in a mood of sincere feeling and good intention. Alas, sincerity and good intention are not enough in the practice of the arts.'

28 'Martin Mather: Represented Artist,' *Australian Music Centre*, accessed 9 November 2013, http://www.australianmusiccentre.com.au/artist/mather-martin.

29 See Warren Bourne, 'Mather's Requiem 60 Years Too Late,' *Adelaide Advertiser*, 12 November 1976, p. 28; and Ralph Middenway, 'Requiem Swamped by Sound,' *The Australian*, 16 November 1976, p. 10.

30 Bourne, 'Mather's Requiem,' p. 28.

31 Ibid.

32 Middenway, 'Requiem,' p. 10.

33 Ibid.

34 The war also served as a backdrop for Ralph Middenway's singspiel *Barossa*, set in South Australia's Barossa Valley in November 1918. This work, with libretto written by Andrew Taylor, was commissioned in 1988 by the South Australian College of Advanced Education to celebrate Australia's bicentenary. It had several performances at the Scott Theatre in Adelaide in October of that year.

35 Vincent Plush, *Gallipoli Sunrise for Solo Tenor Trombone and Seven Other Instruments (5 Tenors, 2 Basses)* (Grosvenor Place, NSW: reproduced and distributed by Australian Music Centre, 1984), performance notes.

historians would have it'[36] – Plush embeds two Australian folk songs, *Waltzing Matilda* and *The Road To Gundagai* within the texture of the work.

The late 1990s saw the arrival of two large-scale works inspired by the Great War. In 1998 the Australian Ballet commissioned Graham Koehne to compose *1914*, based upon David Malouf's novel *Fly Away Peter*. Koehne's approach to the music was to make it 'lyrical and accessible',[37] stating that 'in many ways, the music is quite traditional'.[38] Following on from this point, the writing is evocative of a film score through its lush orchestration and melodic hooks.

Composed one year later in 1999, Helen Gifford's *Choral Scenes: the Western Front, World War 1* – commissioned by the Astra Chamber Music Society – takes a starkly different approach to Koehne's sentimentality and Mather's Romanticism. Gifford utilises a tightly controlled compositional vocabulary to underscore with pathos and poignancy the various war texts heard in the work. Written for speakers, choir and ten instrumentalists, it is arguably the finest example – up to the Anzac centenary – of an extended Australian work that deals with the First World War.

Helen Gifford's personal connection to the Great War comes through her father, John. John Gifford was a soldier in the 14th Battalion, joining up just before the beginning of the Gallipoli campaign in April 1915. After surviving the war, Gifford and his brother returned to Melbourne and started a successful shoe and boot factory in Abbotsford. In 1923 he became the secretary of the 14th Battalion Association, remaining in this position until his death in 1958. Gifford said that her father 'felt so guilty coming back; [he] had survived and the others hadn't'.[39] He determined to look after other returned soldiers from the 14th Battalion – 'those that were hard up [and] couldn't get work'[40] – assisting them financially during the Depression and beyond. Gifford's father was, in essence, cognisant that his former comrades could become marginalised within Australian society.

Gifford considered composing *Choral Scenes* for some time; however, she states that she couldn't have written it 'when the old boys [her father and his friends] were alive . . . it would have been too personal for them'.[41] She also contends that composers born between the wars – she was born in 1935 – were reluctant to write music about the Great War because 'they felt they couldn't speak with their own voice'[42] about it. Tied into this creative resistance was the fact that it was women who were left to deal with the aftermath of the war and its impact upon families. Her mother and aunt, like so many others, deliberately chose to forget the war: 'They were the powerful generation in their prime in the mid-century [and] they didn't want to hear about it.'[43]

Gifford talks of the 'shame' that overshadowed many families after the war and the desire of many people to simply get on with their lives: 'Men were told not talk about it [because] they wouldn't have known how to lie about it.'[44] This conscious act of forgetting and ignoring was driven by concerns that 'even for the able-bodied, civilian life after years

---

36 Ibid.
37 Helen Gifford, interviewed by Andrew Harrison, 23 July 2015.
38 Gifford, 'Interview'.
39 Ibid.
40 Ibid.
41 Ibid.
42 Ibid.
43 Ibid.
44 Ibid.

away from home presented difficult social and psychological adjustments.'[45] Research into post-war life within Australian families has demonstrated the ongoing hardship endured by many households. Family members were often left to look after permanently disabled veterans, 'yet their work was largely absent in official discussions of war disability and not widely reported in the public domain'.[46] Furthermore, families of soldiers who died after returning from the war were often left out of the broader memorialisation process. Marina Larsson describes how 'the grief of the post-war bereaved was disenfranchised within Australia's national public commemorative traditions of war'.[47] There was a general sense that the war, and *ergo* its survivors and those who died upon returning home, was not something to memorialise. This attitude – save for the ongoing cultural efforts of the Anzac Fellowship of Women – appears to have encroached upon the art music world.

Gifford's background as a theatre composer strengthens the dramatic tension she develops throughout the piece. Her use of a minimal, almost barren, texture, punctuated by stark dissonant gestures and *subito* dynamic changes, achieves a powerful emotional affect, displaying 'Gifford's skills in text setting and her profound connection with the Great War'.[48]

The scoring of Charles Vildrac's *Reléve*, the twelfth movement of her work, reveals the composer's astute understanding of text-music interplay. The poem describes the anxiety and anticipation of soldiers waiting to be relieved of their duty in the trenches and their joy as they finally arrive safely beyond the terror of the front line, back to some semblance of normality. The piece begins with a solitary ominous D-flat on the tuba, calling the men to arms. A rich six-note harmonic response from the choir immediately recontextualises this note as the root of a chord, invoking a momentary sense of calm. The tuba breaks this respite by sounding another single melancholy note – an E-flat – triggering the beginning of the poem[49] and reinforcing the reality of the troops. The composer further intensifies this tension by transitioning from the tuba to solo cello with a descending tritone interval (see Figure 15.5).

As the narrator describes the drastic measures the soldiers must undertake to flee the trenches,[50] the cello returns to the opening tuba's note – C-sharp/D-flat – this time as a series

---

45 Stephen Garton, 'Demobilization and Empire: Empire Nationalism and Soldier Citizenship in Australia after the First World War–in Dominion Context,' *Journal of Contemporary History* 50, no. 1 (2015): p. 130, accessed 20 June 2015, http://jch.sagepub.com.virtual.anu.edu.au/content/50/1/124.full.pdf+html.

46 Marina Larsson, '"The Part We Do Not See": Disabled Australian Soldiers and Family Caregiving after World War 1,' *Anzac Legacies: Australians and the Aftermath of War*, ed. Martin Crotty and Marina Larsson (North Melbourne, Australia: Australian Scholarly Publishing, 2010), p. 41.

47 Marina Larsson, 'A Disenfranchised Grief: Post-War Death and Memorialisation in Australia after the First World War,' *Australian Historical Studies* 40, no. 1 (2009): p. 80, accessed 27 May 2015, http://www.tandfonline.com.virtual.anu.edu.au/doi/pdf/10.1080/10314610802663035.

48 Rosalind Appleby, *Women of Note: The Rise of Australian Women Composers* (Fremantle: Fremantle Press, 2012), p. 62.

49 *'A notre place/ On a pose/ Des soldats frais/Pour amorcer/La mort d'en face'*. [In our place/ Fresh troops have come/Sent up the line/As bait for death/Met face to face]. Translation by Christopher Middleton, supplied by composer in score.

50 *'Il a fallu toute la nuit pour s'evader. Toute la nuit et ses ténèbres/Pour traverser, suant, glacé/Le bois martyr et son bourbier/Cinglé d'obus'*. [We needed all night to make our escape/All night and its darkness/Sweating, frozen, to cross/The martyr forest and its swamp/That shrapnel scourged.] Translation by Christopher Middleton, supplied by composer in score.

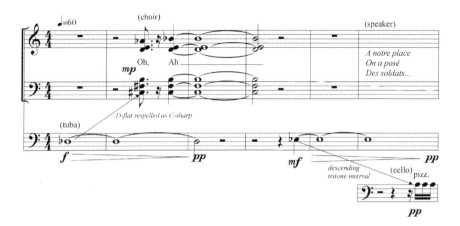

Figure 15.5 Helen Gifford, *Choral Scenes – the Western Front, World War 1*, bars 340–345, 1999

Source: Australian Music Centre

of percussive repeated semiquavers. This recurring rhythm fuels the sense of the soldier's urgency further, spurring them on to take their chance. Gifford conveys the soldier's sense of dread – 'each man picking his moment, trusting to nerve and instinct and his star'[51] – by gradually slowing down the pulse of the cello's repeating C-sharp.

Once the men have made it away from the firing line, the instrumentation changes markedly to reflect their happiness. With this next stanza,[52] a flute plays a rapid phrase, almost imitating bird-song. In contrast to the rhythmic monotony of the cello's C-sharp, the flute's phrase bursts forth, quasi-improvised. A clarinet soon joins the flute, and together they enter into a humorous dialogue that imitates the textual description of men happily meeting together and lighting their pipes on the road after reaching safety (see Figure 15.6).

These compositional techniques demonstrate the composer's affinity with the text and her ability to set the spoken word to music. As a complete work, *Choral Scenes* is a fine example of Gifford's compositional style, creating theatrical and musical drama using 'delicate textures [and] tensions . . . through percussive and vocal counter-effects'.[53]

Gifford has also composed a second smaller work for solo piano titled *Menin Gate*. This piece was inspired by the painting *Menin Gate at Midnight* by Will Longstaff and

---

51   Helen Gifford, *Choral Scenes: The Western Front, World War 1, for Speakers, Chorus and Instruments* (Sydney: The Australian Music Centre, 1999), p. 6.

52   *'Mais passé le dernier barrage/Mais hors du jeu/sur la route solide/Mais aussitôt le ralliement Aux/lueurs des pipes premières/Dites, les copains, les heureuz gagnants'*. [But beyond the last entanglement/Out of it all, on the firm road/Met together, with no delays/In the glow of the first pipes lit/Then, mates, O lucky winners]. Translation by Christopher Middleton, supplied by composer in score.

53   Thérèse Radic, 'Gifford, Helen,' *Grove Music Online*, accessed 19 March 2015, *Oxford Music Online*, http://www.oxfordmusiconline.com/public/.

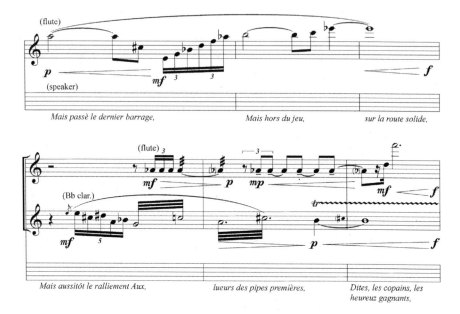

Figure 15.6 Helen Gifford, *Choral Scenes*, bars 362–367, 1999

Source: Australian Music Centre

premiered in 2005.[54] A number of other small pieces were composed during the first decade of the twenty-first century, including Monique Carole-Smith's *War Song* for voice and piano, Grant Sheridan's first string quartet titled *ANZAC* and Graham Koehne's piece for brass ensemble *Albany Harbour (The Voyage)*, inspired by the first soldiers who departed Albany Harbour in 1915, bound for the Middle East.

Finally, I will briefly discuss my own examination of the war from an artistic perspective. In 2011 I was commissioned by Australian pianist Zubin Kanga to write a piano piece that reflected my family's connection to the Great War. The title of the piece, '*The Drumfire Was Incessant, and Continued All Night With Unabated Fury*',[55] is a quote from British historian Newton Wanliss's harrowing account of the Battle of Pozières.[56] The battle occurred between July and August 1916 as part of the Somme Offensive. The composition focusses on the days leading up to 9 August 1916, when my great-great uncle Private Leslie Robins, an infantryman in the 14th Battalion, was shot and wounded.

In the early stages of writing the piece, whilst conducting preliminary research into the Battle of Pozières, I was struck by the disparity between the British High Command's notion of formulating a 'plan' for the battle, and the actuality of what occurred once soldiers

---

54   Gifford's connection to Longstaff's painting was formed from an early age as a print of the work was on display in the family home.

55   Andrew Harrison, '*The Drumfire Was Incessant, and Continued All Night With Unabated Fury' for Solo Piano* (Sydney: The Australian Music Centre, 2012).

56   Newton Wanliss, *The History of the Fourteenth Battalion, A.I.F.* (London: Naval and Military Press & Imperial War Museum, 1929; repr., 2010).

'went over the top' into no-man's land. This dichotomous concept – exerting control over an inherently fluid and dynamic situation – I found to be most intriguing. It fitted in well with my aesthetic explorations of the role of improvisation (a dynamic process) within a larger notated context (a controlled environment). I decided that this dichotomy would play a fundamental role within the piece.

The composition is made up of three distinct parts; the main notated section, and two structured improvisations 'Counterattack 1' and 'Counterattack 2'. The work begins with a sombre march, reminding us of the fear that filled many soldiers as they made their way towards the firing line. The march is abruptly subsumed by a torrential rhythmic onslaught, symbolising the artillery bombardment that both the Allied and German soldiers endured throughout the Battle of Pozières. The bombardment is brought to a jarring halt as 'Counterattack 1' gets under way. After a brief period of introspective respite following 'Counterattack 1', the bombardment returns, building to a crescendo before giving way to 'Counterattack 2'. In the aftermath of 'Counterattack 2' the melancholia of the opening march returns, serving as a poignant reminder of those that fell during the battle.

The 'Counterattack' sections seek to capture some of the pandemonium and chaos of hand-to-hand combat. Once the soldiers went 'over the top', any concept of working to a plan was eradicated, as the reality of close-range fighting became apparent. Structured improvisation is employed in each of the 'Counterattacks', leaving the overall shape of the section to the pianist's discretion. Each 'Counterattack' section is cued in with the blow of a whistle from a designated person seated in the audience. The entry point of each 'Counterattack' is variable, adding an element of unpredictability to each performance. In other words, in theory, the pianist is never quite sure of when they will move to the structured improvisation. The following excerpt from 'Counterattack 1' exemplifies the flexible notation approach used within the structured improvisations (see Figure 15.7).

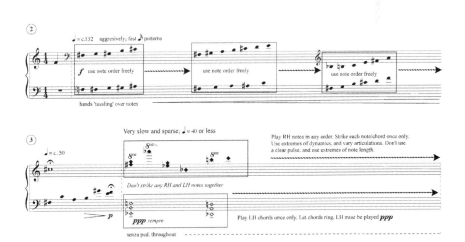

Figure 15.7   Andrew Harrison, *The Drumfire Was Incessant, and Continued All Night With Unabated Fury, Counterattack 1*: sections 2 and 3, 2012

Source: Australian Music Centre

The centennial year of the Anzac landings is seeing numerous works commissioned and premiered across Australia, commemorating the significance of the event within our cultural and historical narrative. In a sense, however, the 'ink is not dry on the page'. This means the official line drawn by the centenary (often funded by the government) not only marks a new phase in the musical commemoration of the Great War, but also – as here – is a break in the historical understanding of this response. The current attempt to realise the sounds from the trenches will provide future scholars with rich material for analysis and comparison.

Chapter 16
'Brutalised' veterans and tragic anti-heroes
Masculinity, crime and post-war trauma in *Boardwalk Empire* and *Peaky Blinders*

Evan Smith

One of the enduring tropes from the end of the First World War is the notion of the 'damaged' man returning from the front, unable to re-enter civil society and drawn to the worlds of organised crime, violence and political extremism. The attraction of the alienated demobilised soldier to the criminal underworld or to political violence was something feared by many across the Western world and has continued to shape how we see the returned soldier in the socio-economic and political chaos that plagued the inter-war period. The mechanised brutality of the war had upended the social order across the globe and in the economic and political vacuum that emerged at the end of the war, these 'damaged' men (supposedly) stepped forward to stake a claim.

Two contemporary depictions of these 'damaged' men and their entrance into the world of organised crime can be seen in the recent television dramas *Peaky Blinders* and *Boardwalk Empire*.[1] Starting in the immediate years after the First World War, both series chart the rise (and fall) of criminal gangs on both sides of the Atlantic. *Peaky Blinders* revolves around the Shelby family, led by three brothers Thomas, Arthur and John, and their crew, the Peaky Blinders, who run a gambling racket out of Birmingham and, as the series progresses, expanding across the south of England and to London. Both Thomas and Arthur had been stationed in France during the War, with Aunt Polly taking over the family business and looking after several of the younger Shelby children. Many of the Shelbys' associates also served on the Western Front, including Ada Shelby's husband, Freddie, who was a decorated soldier, but now a communist agitator.

Boardwalk Empire is set in the initial years of Prohibition after the First World War and revolves around the criminal empire built in Atlantic City, New Jersey, by Enoch 'Nucky' Thompson. As the Treasurer of Atlantic City, Thompson uses his public office to run a bootlegging business, with assistance from his brother, Eli, who also happens to be Sheriff, and his right-hand man, Jimmy Darmody. This business allows Thompson to be the unofficial ruler of Atlantic City but is connected to organised crime groups in New York, Chicago and Philadelphia. Darmody had served in France during the War and upon his return, turned to working for Thompson rather than resuming his studies Princeton

---

1 See Natalie Zemon Davis, '"Any Resemblance to Persons Living or Dead": Film and the Challenge of Authenticity,' *Historical Journal of Film, Radio and Television* 8, no. 3 (1988): pp. 270–4. It is recognised that there is a difference between historical 'fact' and how historical episodes are depicted by film and television, even though both shows have strived to attain a look of 'authenticity' for the period.

University. He also enlists another returned (and injured) soldier, Richard Harrow, to help enforce Thompson's rule over the City and the local bootlegging network.

Emma Hanna has written:

> If the memory of the First World War is an amalgamation of the stories that have been told about it, then television programmes are building blocks in Britain's national memory of 1914–18.[2]

Set against the great social, economic and political upheaval at the end of the war (Prohibition in the United States, the 'Red Scare' and the Anglo-Irish War in Britain), both series depict a generation of men, many returning from action in the War, viewing crime as a means to obtain social mobility and seeking to re-build the family unit after being ripped apart by the war. This chapter will explore televisual portrayals of crime and violence being used by men to reassert their masculinity and patriarchal dominance in the post-war era.

The dreams of 'damaged' men

In both series, those who went to war are haunted by their experiences and suffer from recurring dreams and memories of the war. In *Boardwalk Empire*, Jimmy Darmody recounts his memories of a German soldier who lay dying on the barbed wire fence, while he was unable to help him. In one scene, he tells a gangland rival about this German:

> There was a soldier a German. Him and his men tried to attack our position in the Argonne Forest. It was night time. And while he was trying to climb through some barbed wire, I shot him twice, once in the stomach, once in the neck. He slumped over the barbed wire. And no matter what he did to try and wriggle free, it just got worse for him.
>
> I left him there like that for days, listening to him moaning, crying, "mutti, mutti, mutti!" That's German for "mama, mama!" That's what he kept saying.
>
> The curious thing is that despite the fact that his situation was utterly hopeless, he didn't want to die. I offered to kill him several times, but he just kept fighting, like some miracle would befall him and get him out of his predicament. We hold on so desperately to life. Some people feel, certainly in that soldier's situation, that being alive is much much worse.

This memory that haunts Jimmy reinforces the idea that the war was futile and only succeeded into turning young men into murderers. Jimmy had given up his studies at Princeton to join the war effort, possibly to escape the Ivy League world that surrounded him, but returned to the United States as a changed man. For Jimmy, like the German soldier, being alive is much worse than death.

Joining Nucky Thompson as his driver and enforcer, Darmody is ambitious but also cynical about how much time he has on earth while being involved in the world of organised crime. After hijacking a delivery of bootlegged alcohol for Thompson, Jimmy is castigated by Nucky for his foolhardiness and his cynicism. Jimmy replies:

> The war, Nucky, the shit I did over there. You live in a trench months on end, the killing, the smell of death . . . I'm nothing but a murderer . . .

---

2 Emma Hanna, *The Great War on the Small Screen: Representing the First World War in Contemporary Britain* (Edinburgh: Edinburgh University Press, 2009), p. 4.

You know how many times I went over the top? They called me a hero but the truth was I didn't fucking care anymore.

The weariness of living causes Darmody to take risks to further his position within the criminal empire created by Thompson and embraces his self-image as a 'murderer', undertaking several hits for Thompson. However this ambition and world-weariness also brings Jimmy into a plot to kill Thompson and take over his business. Although Jimmy eventually returns to Nucky and kills several people to wreck a criminal case against Thompson, Nucky does not forget Jimmy's betrayal and kills him at the end of the second season. In this final confrontation, Jimmy shrugs off the inevitability of his death and says to Nucky:

I died in the trenches, years back. I thought you knew that?

As Jimmy lies dying, he dreams of going over the top of the trenches one final time, back to where he had metaphorically 'died' before.

Jimmy Darmody is not the only 'damaged' soldier returning from the War in *Boardwalk Empire*. In the first season, Darmody recruits Richard Harrow to help him in Chicago, and then both return to Atlantic City to work for Thompson. Harrow was severely injured in the war and lost half of his face to a sniper bullet. Due to medical advances, Harrow survived the War and wears a mask to hide his disfigurement. After the war, he returned to live with his sister in Wisconsin, but found the reality of life after war too unbearable. As Katherine Feo has argued, these facial masks were promoted by the manufacturers as objects that did more than cover a man's injuries, but also returned them to a pre-war existence.[3] Harrow discovers that despite his ability to hide his disfigurement, he could not hide from his past and moves to Chicago. Jimmy meets Richard in a hospital and convinces him to join Darmody's criminal network. Once part of the criminal world that Darmody and Thompson inhabit, Harrow convinces himself that the only place in the world for a 'damaged killer' is within this world, killing for hire.

Like Darmody, Harrow dreams of the war and of life before it. One of his recurring dreams is that his face is whole and he is back with his family and girlfriend in Wisconsin. He usually wakes when his injuries are revealed and those close to him recoil in horror. His yearning for his previous life and his life as a hitman for Thompson leads Harrow to attempt suicide in the second season, but he changes his mind and returns to Atlantic City. In season three, he meets a group of veterans and becomes involved with a young woman, Julia Sargosky, whose brother died in the war. This relationship gives Richard a reason to live and by the end of the fourth season, he has accumulated enough money by working for Thompson to retire to Wisconsin with Julia and his sister. However in his final job for Thompson, he is fatally wounded. Like Darmody's death scene, we see Harrow dream of making it to Wisconsin and meeting up with his family. We are unsure whether this is a dream or not until we see his face intact and realise that it is his final dream.

In *Peaky Blinders*, both Thomas and Arthur Shelby, the leading figures in the Peaky Blinders gang, suffer from their memories of the war. In the first season, we see Thomas's recurring dream of tunnelling in the First World War. Between 1915 and 1917, the Allies dug numerous tunnels on the Western Front in attempts to break up the German-Austrian

---

3   Katherine Feo, 'Invisibility: Memory, Masks and Masculinities in the Great War,' *Journal of Design History* 20, no. 1 (2007): p. 25.

trenches, using large explosive charges to destroy enemy lines. P. M. Varley writes, 'These blasts, delivered without warning and coordinated with an infantry attack, could have a devastating effect.'[4] The work of the tunnellers was highly secret and with less than 1 per cent of soldiers employed in this line of work.[5] The work was also quite dangerous, although the number of deaths does not compare greatly with the amount of soldiers killed aboveground.[6] Thomas had led his company of tunnellers in France and in the second season, when he negotiates with the War Secretary, Winston Churchill (incorrectly depicted in the series as Home Secretary), he is held in high regard for his bravery and leadership.

In the series, we see that in his dreams, Shelby is troubled by a mission that when tunnelling a hole, a group of German tunnellers break through from the other side of the wall. In the ensuing chaos, one of the men from Thomas's company is shot and Thomas himself is injured, while he also kills the German soldier at very close quarters. The show suggests that this death, in such close proximity, greatly troubled Thomas and made him the violent man that he is when returning to Birmingham. In the first episode, we see Thomas smoking opium from a clay pipe, and it is suggested that he uses this to ease the stress of his recurring nightmares.

Arthur Shelby also suffers for the trauma of the war and this is played out the second season of *Peaky Blinders*. While Arthur is seen as volatile and troubled in the first season, his behaviour becomes more erratic and more violent in the second. Part of this can be attributed to his continued mental health problems stemming from his wartime experience, but also it can be attributed to his use of cocaine – a habit which he acquires while working in London. Arthur tries to deal with his anger through boxing, but this leads to an incident where he kills a teenage boy in the ring. One of the younger Shelby brothers tells Thomas:

> Arthur, he's blown a few times lately. Six, seven. It's like he's not there in the head. He can't even hear 'stop'. Even his own name. And then he cries.

When confronted by Thomas in the aftermath, Arthur is remorseful and describes the feeling:

> It's like a fucking boat, Tommy. Full of heavy cargo, like coal or iron. Sometimes it slips to one end. And the boat tips. I can feel it slipping. And I can feel the boat tipping. But there ain't nothing I can do about it. It's like me fuckin' head's just like this fuckin' black fucking barge! And it just fucking drifts. In and out, in and out.

Thomas seems very unsympathetic to Arthur's situation, although he also suffered from post-war trauma, saying:

> Well, we're home a long time now, Arthur. We're home a long time. I thought you were all right . . .

---

[4] P.M. Varley, 'British Tunnelling Machines in the First World War,' *Transactions of the Newcomen Society* 65, no. 1 (1993): p. 1.

[5] Peter Barton, Peter Doyle and Johan Vandewalle, *Beneath Flanders Fields: The Tunnellers' War 1914–1918* (Montreal and Kingston, CA: McGill-Queen's University Press, 2004), p. 11.

[6] Nigel Cave and Phillip Robinson, *The Underground War: Vimy Ridge to Arras, vol. 1* (Barnsley: Pen & Sword Books, 2011), p. 12.

I've had enough. Just fuck off! I'm supposed to treat you like a fucking kid again, eh? Keep you away from guns and fucking rope, is that it? You think I haven't got enough on! ...

The war is done! Shut the door on it. Shut the door on it like I did, eh?

Jessica Meyer has critiqued the show for this, arguing that Thomas 'should know that the war is never truly over for some men' and that war trauma can't easily be overcome.[7]

As well as the Shelby brothers, another one of the Peaky Blinders gang, Danny 'Whizz-Bang' Owen, suffers from 'shellshock' and probably does so to the worst degree. Danny first appears in the show by coming into the pub while having a psychotic episode. It takes several men to calm him down, while Thomas reassures him:

You're not an artillery shell, Danny, you're a man. You're not a whizz-bang, you're a human being. You're alright. You're alright.

However Danny continues to suffer from these episodes and kills a man in public during one, an Italian man with possible criminal ties. To avoid retaliation, Thomas orchestrates the faking of Danny's death and sends him to London. However Danny's freedom is short-lived; he is killed at the end of the first season in gang warfare. Before his death is faked, Danny asks Thomas not bury him in any mud, referring to his experience as a tunneller in the war, and when he does die, Thomas sees that he is buried at the top of a hill, away from the mud.

As Jay Winter has written 'shellshock' was used to describe 'the damage the war had caused to many of the men in uniform, whether or not they were physically disabled'.[8] Apart from Richard Harrow, most of those depicted in the two series are mentally, not physically, 'damaged' by the war and could be described as suffering from 'shellshock' or some other form of trauma. As depicted in the two shows, the war irrevocably changed those who went to fight and made them confront the barbarism of humankind – what Clive Emsley has described as the 'brutalised veteran'.[9] Upon their return, these men found it difficult to fit into 'normal' society and found use for their violent pasts within the criminal underworld.

Crime as social mobility

At the heart of both series is the question of whether crime can bring social mobility, particularly for those who have returned from the war and those outside civil society. The end of the First World War presented new opportunities for criminal activity in both the

---

[7] Jessica Meyer, 'We Need to Talk About Arthur Shelby,' *Arms and the Medical Man* [blog], 17 December 2014, accessed 13 January 2016, https://armsandthemedicalman.wordpress.com/2014/12/17/we-need-to-talk-about-arthur-shelby/.

[8] Jay Winter, 'Shell-Shock and the Cultural History of the Great War,' *Journal of Contemporary History* 35, no. 1 (2000): p. 9.

[9] See: Clive Emsley, 'A Legacy of Conflict? The "Brutalised Veteran" and Violence in Europe after the Great War,' in *Problems of Crime and Violence in Europe, 1780–2000: Essays in Criminal Justice*, ed. Efi Avdela, Shani D'Cruze, and Judith Rowbotham (Lampeter and New York: Edwin Mellen Press, 2010), pp. 43–64.

United States and Britain. In 1920, the United States government passed the eighteenth amendment that prohibited the production, distribution and sale of alcohol nationwide, and introduced the era of Prohibition until 1933, when the ban was lifted by the twenty-first amendment. As Howard Abadinsky wrote:

> The "Great Experiment" was a catalyst for organized crime, especially violent forms, to blossom into an important force in American society. Prohibition led to the mobilization of criminal elements in an unprecedented manner, and the ensuing competitive violence turned the power structure upside down.[10]

In Britain, organised crime networks expanded around the world of horse racing and bookmaking, which were described as the 'racecourse wars'.[11] Although criminal enterprises around the bookmaking industry had existed in the pre-war era, Heather Shore states, 'in the post-war period it seems to have increasingly organized.'[12] These 'racecourse wars', Shore explained,

> involved mainly metropolitan criminals in affrays and fights on the streets of London and on the racecourses of South-East England. The core objective of the racecourse gangs was in securing the control of the protection business, which basically took the form of offering 'protection' to bookmakers and intimidating their rivals, and then taking a share of the earnings from the pitch. Bookmakers on the most profitable pitches who did not comply were threatened with violence until they moved off or submitted to the gangs' demands.[13]

As Abadinsky states, the illegal production and distribution of alcohol in the Prohibition era greatly expanded those involved in criminal activity because of the variety of vocations needed to ensure that the illegally produced liquor reached the customer. As this industry was so lucrative, all of those involved needed protection, particularly as there was no possibility of appealing to law enforcement officials to help protect these illegal activities. Abadinsky wrote, '[p]hysical protection from the unparalleled surge of violence that accompanied Prohibition was essential for anyone seeking his fortune in the alcohol business.'[14] In *Boardwalk Empire*, we see the massive criminal network needed to operate Nucky Thompson's bootlegging business and while Nucky is already one of the most powerful figures in Atlantic City (if not the East Coast of the United States), almost everyone else involved in the business sees it as a way to make a considerable amount of money and climb the social hierarchy.

For example, in the first season, we see Al Capone as a mere bodyguard and driver to Johnny Torio, who is a major organised crime figure in Chicago. In his discussions with Jimmy Darmody, we learn of Capone's ambition and his yearning to reach the upper

---

10 Howard Abadinsky, 'History of Organized Crime in the United States,' in *Encyclopedia of Criminology and Criminal Justice*, ed. Gerben Bruinsma and David Weisburd (New York: Springer, 2014), p. 2, 204.

11 Heather Shore, 'Criminality and Englishness in the Aftermath: The Racecourse Wars of the 1920s,' *Twentieth Century British History* 22, no. 4 (2011): pp. 474–97.

12 Ibid., p. 475.

13 Ibid., p. 474.

14 Abadinsky, 'History of Organized Crime in the United States,' p. 2, 204.

echelons of criminal world (and wider civil society). By the fifth and final season, set in 1932, Capone is at the top of the criminal underworld and is a terrifying and powerful man.

Another character who uses the bootlegging industry to better his position in life is Albert 'Chalky' White, an African American who, in the first season, runs one of Thompson's distilleries outside of Atlantic City. As part of Thompson's burgeoning enterprise, Chalky rises through the ranks and by the fourth season, runs Thompson's nightclub on the City's boardwalk, having run a 'honky-tonk' bar previously. However, by tying his fortunes to that of Thompson means that Chalky is caught in the firing line as Thompson's enemies seek to destroy Nucky and take over his business. Robert M. Lombardo has shown that this interaction between African Americans and 'white' organised crime gangs (principally the Italian and Irish migrant gangs) occurred in reality, although criminal figures like Chalky were more likely to exist in Harlem or the south-side of Chicago than Atlantic City.[15]

In *Peaky Blinders*, it is Thomas Shelby who sees crime as the path to social mobility and in the end, legitimacy. In both seasons, Thomas pushes the Shelby gang to take on their rivals in the bookmaking business, first Billy Kimber and then Charles Sabini, to increase their share of the industry. His family is initially sceptical of this, particularly after the Peaky Blinders had already taken over Billy Kimber's business in the Midlands. In the first episode of the second season, Thomas proposes challenging the bookmakers and the gangs that 'protect' them in London. John objects to this:

> I see all the books. Legal and off track. Sort of stuff you don't see. And in the past year the Shelby Company Limited has been making £150 a day. Right? A fucking day. Sometimes more. So what I want to know is why are we changing things? . . . Look what's happened already. We haven't even set foot in London yet and they've already blown up our fucking pub.

Thomas attempts to sway the family towards expansion, holding out the prospect that once the Peaky Blinders dominate the bookmaking industry and the associated protection racket, they can transform their illegal operations into a legitimate business. At the same meeting, he pleads:

> We've nothing to fear from the proposed business expansion so long as we stick together. And after the first few weeks, nine tenths of what we do in London will be legal. The other tenth is in good hands.

However things don't go smoothly for the Shelby gang. Although they take the business from Sabini, intervening factors means that Thomas is almost killed at the end of the second season.

Like Thomas Shelby, Nucky Thompson is driven by the attempts to transform his bootlegging empire into a legitimate business. Thompson and, for a time, his brother, occupied positions of power within Atlantic City, and are economic and political kingmakers; but while extremely wealthy and powerful, Thompson is plagued by feelings of illegitimacy. For Thompson, his continued involvement in the bootlegging business brings him into contact with the criminal elements of society, which he detests. He opines that he has to deal

---

15 See: Robert M. Lombardo, 'The Black Mafia: African-American Organized Crime in Chicago, 1890–1960,' *Crime, Law & Social Change* 38, no. 1 (July 2002): pp. 33–65.

with the lower ranking criminals of his organisation and be embroiled in deals with other gangsters, such as Arnold Rothstein and 'Lucky' Luciano. Throughout the series, Thompson claims he is merely a 'business man', while others retorted that he was still a 'gangster', no matter how high he tried to climb. He calls other people, such as King Solomon 'gangsters', while describing himself to Joseph Kennedy, a prospective business partner in 1932, as 'an advocate for repeal [of Prohibition]'.

In the final season, Nucky campaigns for an end to Prohibition (which had brought him enormous wealth over the previous decade) in the belief that this would bring him legitimacy and confirm his role at the high end of society. However even as he campaigns for this, he finds that many businessmen are unwilling to associate with him because of his criminal associations. Kennedy reminds Nucky that he had never broken the law, unlike Thompson, although Thompson dismisses that as a 'technicality'.

In the final episodes of the series, Nucky loses all his business holdings to New York gangsters Lucky Luciano and Meyer Lansky and is finally shot dead by Jimmy Darmody's teenage son, Tommy. Thompson's eventual decline follows one of the most popular tropes in gangster films since the late 1920s – the rise and fall of the mobster. Historians of the gangster-crime film genre have argued that since the days of *Little Caesar* and the original *Scarface*, gangster films, more or less, correspond to the 'rise and fall' motif[16] and reinforce the narrative that while crime can draw the ambitious out of the lower class and seems to offer a chance at the 'American Dream', the same criminal behaviour will also bring them down in the end. In his famous essay, film critic Robert Warshow described the gangster as a 'tragic hero' and that 'irrational brutality' and 'rational enterprise' become inter-mixed for the gangster.[17] The rise and fall trope, which Nucky Thompson embodies, is explained by Warshow:

> Since we do not see the rational and routine aspect of the gangster's behaviour, the practice of brutality – the quality of unmixed criminality – becomes the totality of his career. At the same time, we are always conscious of the whole meaning of this career is a drive for success: the typical gangster film presents a steady upward progress followed by a very precipitate fall. Thus brutality itself becomes at once the means to success and the content of success . . .[18]

Thompson's strive for financial and political success is accompanied by a legacy of violence carried out by himself and his associates and this eventually undermines his bid to enter the legitimate business world as Prohibition comes to an end.

The nexus between organised crime and political violence

Along with the dawning of a new era in organised crime, the post-war period ushered in an upsurge of political violence across the globe, including Britain and the United States. In both countries, the shockwaves of the Bolshevik Revolution of 1917 reverberated intensely,

---

16 Jonathan Munby, *Public Enemies, Public Heroes: Screening the Gangster from Little Caesar to Touch of Evil* (Chicago: University of Chicago Press, 2009), p. 56.
17 Robert Warshow, 'The Gangster as Tragic Hero,' in *The Oxford Book of Essays*, ed. John Gross (Oxford: Oxford University Press, 2008), p. 584.
18 Ibid., p. 584.

leading to communistic revolts and strikes, as well as anti-communist repression, in many British and American cities, colloquially known as the 'Red Scare'.[19] These strikes and revolts involved many soldiers who had come back from the war and did not want to return to the pre-war era after four years of brutal warfare. This caused the authorities to be concerned about potential communists, socialists and trade unionists keeping hold of firearms that had been issued during the war, with the Firearms Act 1920 implemented to help prevent any form of armed revolt in Britain.

This can be seen in *Peaky Blinders*. Freddie Thorne had been part of Thomas Shelby's tunnelling company in France and had now returned to Birmingham as a communist agitator amongst the workers at the local factory. In his speech trying to get consensus for a strike, Freddie made connections between their experiences on the battlefield and poor conditions experienced in the workplace. Thorne pronounces:

> Comrades we're here today to take a vote on strike action . . . But before we have a show of hands for that let's have a show of hands from all those who fought in France, all those who stood side-by-side with your comrades and watched your comrades fall. Raise your hands . . .
>
> The blood shed on Flanders fields, the sweat of your brows! Who reaps the rewards? . . . Do they stand among us? . . . Or do they sit at home, comfortable, with a full belly while you scrape to find enough to put shoes on your children's feet! . . . And what is the reward they offer you for your sacrifices made? A fucking cut in your wages! That is your reward! Raise a hand, all those who want to strike!

As much as the British were worried about a communist revolution, they were also very concerned about Irish Republican activists and the potential for political violence on the streets of 'mainland' Britain.[20] Between January 1919 and July 1921, the Irish War of Independence raged, with several attacks on British politicians, troops and installations in London, Liverpool and Glasgow during the war. *Peaky Blinders* is set during this war and the 'threat' of the Irish Republican Army (IRA) is ever present.

One of the major plot lines in the first season of *Peaky Blinders* is that the Shelby gang has stolen a shipment of machine guns and is seeking to sell them (or use them for its own ambitious plans, as mentioned earlier). Representatives of the IRA in Birmingham threaten Thomas to hand the guns over to them, but he is reluctant to do so, but uses this threat as a bargaining chip in his dealings with CI Chester Campbell. A former Loyalist police inspector in Belfast with a reputation for taking on the IRA, Campbell has been sent by Winston Churchill to find the stolen machine guns. With rumours around the criminal underworld of Campbell's arrival in town, there is debate over whether Campbell will target the Irish or the communists. Campbell, however, declares that he will target both:

> If it is IRA Fenians, I will find them and find the guns. If it is Communists, I will find them and find the guns. If it is common criminals, I will find them and find the guns. To me there is no distinction between any of the above.

---

19 Regin Schmidt, *Red Scare: FBI and the Origins of Anticommunism in the United States, 1919–1943* (Copenhagen: Museum Tusculanum Press, 2000); Sharman Kadish, 'Jewish Bolshevism and the "Red Scare" in Britain,' *Jewish History* 34, no. 4 (1987): pp. 13–19.

20 See: Gerard Noonan, *The IRA in Britain 1919–1923: 'In the Heart of Enemy Lines'* (Liverpool: Liverpool University Press, 2014).

This reflects the British concerns that both communists and Irish Republicans could potentially get hold of dangerous weaponry in the aftermath of the war and introduced the Firearms Act in 1920 to crack down on their access to arms.[21]

In *Boardwalk Empire*, the spectre of communism and the 'Red Scare' is conspicuously absent, but Irish Republicanism does feature. For Nucky Thompson and his brother, Eli, they cynically tap into the divisions between Anglo and Irish American society to gain favour with those in the Irish American community in Atlantic City. This involves obtaining money and votes from the community when needed. Thompson also makes overtures to the IRA in Ireland to obtain whiskey in exchange for weapons and uses a shared Irish heritage to try to convince the IRA leadership to accept this deal. Both series show that the IRA is very concerned with obtaining the necessary weaponry to fight the British, although in *Boardwalk Empire*, the IRA commander that Thompson deals with is reluctant to deal with a bootlegger. However, some of the more 'realistic' sections of the IRA kill those standing in the way of the deal with Thompson and are able to reach an agreement.

Although the threat of Bolshevism and the 'Red Scare' is not mentioned in *Boardwalk Empire*, another political 'scare' by white America in the post-war period is depicted – the anti-black riots and lynchings that swept across the United States in conjunction with the 'Red Scare' in 1919–1920.[22] In the first and second season, the Ku Klux Klan (KKK) is shown at different times opposing the involvement of 'Chalky' White in the bootlegging business. In the first instance, the KKK lynches one of White's associates as a warning, while in the second instance, the KKK uses a machine gun to shoot up White's distillery. Thompson finds the KKK an impediment to his business and acknowledging Chalky's loyalty to him, helps Chalky take revenge on the KKK, by arresting the local leader and handing him over to Chalky. In the second season, Jimmy Darmody hands over to Chalky the three KKK members involved in shooting up his distillery, in return for his setting up a meeting between Darmody and Thompson.

In the last two seasons, the Pan-Africanist organisation of Marcus Garvey, the Universal Negro Improvement Association (UNIA), is featured heavily as Dr Valentin Narcisse emerges as a rival to Chalky, selling heroin out of an establishment in Harlem. In the series, the UNIA acts like an organised crime group in Harlem, offering protection to African Americans who cannot go elsewhere. In this regard, the UNIA acted as Robert M. Lombardo described, controlling criminal activities in their community and working alongside the Italian American mafia where necessary.[23] Before his death, Narcisse holds considerable territory negotiated with Thompson, Rothstein and the other gangs in New York.

In both series, the authorities (the Special Branch in *Peaky Blinders* and the fledgling FBI in *Boardwalk Empire*) are more concerned with the political threats than the criminal activities of Shelby and Thompson. However individual agents, namely CI Chester Campbell in *Peaky Blinders* and Agent Jim Tolliver in *Boardwalk Empire*, press that the focus should be on Tommy Shelby and Nucky Thompson, rather than the IRA or the UNIA. In the end, these become personal vendettas that are blown apart by the changing political situation in both Britain and the US during the inter-war period.

---

21   Heather Shore, 'Rogues of the Racecourse,' *Media History* 20, no. 4 (2014): p. 356.
22   David F. Krugler, *1919–the Year of Racial Violence* (Cambridge: Cambridge University Press, 2014).
23   Lombardo, 'The Black Mafia,' p. 59.

Conclusion

Both *Boardwalk Empire* and *Peaky Blinders* are loosely based on historical criminal figures that existed in the era following the First World War and depict the rise (and fall) of these criminal gangs in an era of great socio-economic and political upheaval. Both series portray the returned soldier as a 'damaged' man, who has been 'brutalised' by warfare, and ready to turn to criminal enterprise (and violence) to better their social position – unrestricted by the norms of pre-war society. In *Boardwalk Empire*, both Jimmy Darmody and Richard Harrow choose to become stand-over men for Nucky Thompson because they no longer feared death and believed that their morality had been extinguished by the war. In *Peaky Blinders*, Thomas Shelby is driven by his ambition more than an existential crisis, but uses the war as an argument for the need to enjoy life in the present – those who served sacrificed their sanity for King and Country, and on returning, believed they were owed more than the lower class existence offered to most demobilised soldiers after the war. Although Heather Shore has shown that, in the case of the UK, most of those involved in violent and organised crime in the 1920s around the bookmaking business had a criminal record prior to 1914,[24] both television shows indulge in the myth that the war was a decisive moment that irreversibly changed all of those who served. From this perspective, we see the characters of *Boardwalk Empire* and *Peaky Blinders* as 'brutalised veterans' who we may have some sympathy for and we watch them on their rise (and fall) as tragic anti-heroes, attempting to use violence and criminal behaviour to further their social standing, only to succumb to violent world they inhabited.

---

24 Shore, 'Criminality and Englishness in the Aftermath,' p. 490.

Chapter 17
The politics of forgetting the Cypriot Mule Corps

Andrekos Varnava

In summer 1916, the British Salonica Army and the Cypriot colonial government established the Cypriot Mule Corps in order to provide vital logistical support in carrying supplies and wounded at the Macedonian front. Composed of Christian (Eastern Orthodox and smaller numbers of Maronites, Catholics and Armenians) and Muslim Cypriots, after the Armistice service continued in Constantinople. Although sometimes referred to as the 'Macedonian' Mule Corps, it was almost exclusively Cypriot in composition, with a staggering enlistment of about 12,000 Cypriots, meaning that about 25 per cent of the male population ages 18–35 served at one time or another. My recently published article explored the push and pull factors that resulted in so many men being enlisted,[1] while my forthcoming monograph will explore in depth all facets of the story.[2] This chapter explores the subsequent absence of the story from Cypriot national consciousness.

Growing up in Australia I could not avoid the Anzac legend and the enormous pride Australians feel over the contribution of their ancestors to both world wars. It is also impossible to fail to make the connection that these contributions, especially at Gallipoli, are increasingly important to Australian national identity in new and evolving ways.[3] As an Australian of Cypriot heritage the place of the Great War in the Australian national script piqued my curiosity for the Great War, yet it made me feel excluded because there was little information on the Cypriot contribution. The two world wars pre-dated my father's arrival to Australia in 1952, and although he was too young to have served in the Cypriot Regiment he lived through the war and experienced its limited impact on the island, even being one of the first to the scene of a shot-down enemy aeroplane. The Cypriot contribution in the Second World War is obvious because of the Cypriot Regiment, even if there has been little scholarly work on it.[4] But for the Great War there is nothing. In 2004, as a PhD candidate, I came across a reference in *A Chronology of Cyprus* by Governor Storrs to Cypriots serving

---

   1   Andrekos Varnava, 'Recruitment and Volunteerism for the Cypriot Mule Corps, 1916–1919,' *Itinerario* 38, no. 3 (2014): pp. 79–101.
   2   Andrekos Varnava, *Serving the British Empire: The Cypriot Mule Corps, Imperial Identity and Silenced Memory* (Manchester: Manchester University Press, 2016).
   3   See Michael Walsh and Andrekos Varnava, *Australia and the Great War: Identity, Memory and Mythology* (Melbourne: Melbourne University Press, 2016).
   4   See Jan Asmussen, '"Dark Skinned Cypriots will not be Accepted!" Cypriots in the British Army, 1939–1945,' *Britain in Cyprus: Colonialism and Post-Colonialism 1878–2006*, ed. Hubert Faustmann and Nicos Peristianis (Mannheim: Bibliopolis, 2006), pp. 167–85; Anastasia Yiangou, *Cyprus in World War II* (London: I.B. Tauris, 2010); her effort is unsatisfying. See my review, *The Cyprus Review* 24, no. 2 (2012): pp. 147–50. It is pleasing to see Marios Shamas tackling this subject for his PhD at King's College.

as muleteers in the Great War.[5] I asked my father if he knew anything about it. To my surprise my father revealed that his grandfather, his namesake, Varnavas Michael Varnava, had 'gone to the war with the mules'.

I feel great pride that my great-grandfather served in the Great War and had therefore contributed to the coalition that defeated the Central Powers. Yet I did not then nor now feel any more included in the Australian commemorations as an ancestor of someone who had served in the Great War. My desire to feel included in the story of the Allied victory in the Great War and to research and write the Cypriot story is not felt by Cypriots back in 'my old country' since there is a clear lack of awareness of the Cypriot contribution and a failure to remember and memorialise it. Upon the revelation that my great-grandfather had served I immediately realised – since I had never heard anything of the Cypriot contribution in the Great War from Cypriots in Australia or from Cypriots when I had visited Cyprus in 2000, 2001 and 2002, and lived there between September 2006 and January 2009 – that it had been excluded from Cypriot national consciousness.

Indeed since there was no Cypriot national script, with a common Cypriot history, the memory of the Cypriot Mule Corps was not a desirable point on the script of the 'Greek' or 'Turkish' communities in Cyprus. The Cypriot Mule Corps would have been hard to explain within the context of the struggles for *enosis* (union with Greece desired mostly by right-wing Greek Cypriot political elites and masses) and *taksim* (partition of the island between Greece and Turkey mostly favoured by right-wing Turkish Cypriot political elites and masses) and the violence that gripped the island in the 1950s, 1960s and 1970s, which saw Cypriots endure a violent war to unite the island to Greece (1955–1959), followed by a civil war (1963–1964) that resulted in the collapse of the Republic created in 1960, and finally the coup and Turkish military intervention in 1974, that partitioned the island. The Christian and Muslim Cypriot peasant and labouring classes, which formed the bulk of the Cypriot Mule Corps, lacked the political voice and organisation to express their problems during the inter-war years, and so they perhaps recalled their role and experiences in the Cypriot Mule Corps to family, but there was no possibility of using their involvement in the Great War for their political, social or economic advantage, and therefore there was no public discourse or consciousness on its existence. This is self-evident given the lack of interest in the Cypriot Mule Corps by the political elites of the island, both during and after the Great War, which corresponded also with their lack of interest in the social and economic problems of the peasantry and labouring classes.

On the other hand, there are commemorations and a memorial for the Cypriot Regiment. Consisting of about 30,000 Cypriots, it was founded on 12 April 1940, served in France, Greece, Crete, North Africa (Operation Compass), the Middle East, Italy and in France again after the Normandy landings. It included infantry, mechanical, transport and pack transport companies, with the latter being once again important, and indeed Cypriot muleteers were the first colonial forces sent to the Western Front.[6] There are two fundamental reasons why the Cypriot Regiment is commemorated and remembered in Cypriot national consciousness, although it was also an example of Cypriot integration given its Christian and Muslim composition: 1) the nationalist elites and bourgeoisie, and after Nazi Germany's attack on the Soviet Union, the Cypriot Communists (represented

---

5   Ronald Storrs, *A Chronology of Cyprus* (Nicosia: Government Printing Office, 1930), p. 35.
6   'Cyprus and the War,' 14 September 1945, Special Operations Executive, (HS) HS3/120, National Archives of the UK (NAUK),

by AKEL, or the Progressive Party of the Working People) actively supported enlistment for their own respective political ends, including, for the nationalists, *enosis*; and 2) in the aftermath of the war, the peasant and labouring classes became integrated into the established political and ideological structures – they made political choices and these were limited to supporting the nationalists, who wanted '*enosis* and only *enosis*', the communists, who now also supported *enosis*, or for Turkish Cypriot leaders who cultivated Turkish nationalism, opposition to *enosis* and preference for the *status quo* and later for *taksim*. The few voices from the Cypriot Orthodox Christian community that supported the British were marginalised and in many cases compelled to emigrate.[7] The co-option of the peasantry and labouring classes into the existing limited political structures of the island meant the sidelining of the social issues that they had and that these problems would only be solved, in the minds of the 'Greek' Cypriot leaders, in the life after *enosis*. It also meant that the discourse on the motivations to enlist in the Cypriot Regiment revolved around *enosis*, claiming that the Cypriots fought for the British during the Second World War expecting to be rewarded with *enosis*.[8]

The lack of a Cypriot public consciousness and official commemoration of the Cypriot contribution to the Great War is also reflected in the British failure to acknowledge the Cypriot contribution and to include the Cypriots in the commemorative events and memorials in the UK. There are no memorials in Britain that commemorate the service of Cypriots in the British armed forces in either of the world wars.

This neglect on the part of both the British and the Cypriots is arguably best reflected in the significant discrepancy in the number of Cypriot Mule Corps deaths recorded by the Commonwealth War Graves Commission (CWGC) and the number I found, mostly arrived at through the official honour roll.[9] The CWGC has only a portion of the dead in their cemeteries and many were buried at the front and graves were lost, destroyed or forgotten. According to the CWGC only about 40 Cypriot muleteers died in the Great War,[10] but the honour roll and other documents showed 177. The discrepancy indicates the failure of the CWGC to properly investigate the number of Cypriot muleteer deaths and therefore reflects their lack of interest, as well as that of Cypriots, until now.

This chapter therefore contributes to the historiography of memory and war, shifting the focus away from the settler/former settler colonies and from remembering the Great War to forgetting it. A compelling conceptual contrast can be made between the Cypriot case of 'forgetting' versus the typical focus of so many scholars, such as Winter, on remembering and memorialising. Memory and the Great War have been significantly studied, from Winter[11] to

---

7   This had started as far back as 1934 when Antonios Triantafyllides, a leading lawyer and member of the Advisory Council, was assassinated. See Colonial Office, (CO) CO67/251/7, NAUK; CO67/253/10, NAUK; CO67/253/11, NAUK; CO67/254/3, NAUK; CO67/255/12, NAUK; and Foreign and Commonwealth Office (FCO) FCO141/2497, NAUK. In the early 1950s, people who preferred British to Greek rule left, including the Aristovoulos family, who migrated to Australia. Interview with Mr and Mrs Aristovoulos, December 2010.

8   Asmussen, 'Dark Skinned Cypriots'; Yiangou, *Cyprus in World War II*.

9   War Office (WO) WO405/1, NAUK; and WO329/2357, NAUK.

10   See *The War Dead of the British Commonwealth and Empire: The Register of the Names of Those Who Fell in the 1939–1945 War and Are Buried in Cemeteries in Syria, Turkey and Cyprus* (Maidenhead: Commonwealth War Graves Commission, 1959).

11   Jay Winter, *Sites of Memory, Sites of Mourning: The Great War in European Cultural History* (Cambridge: Cambridge University Press, 1995); Winter, *Remembering War*.

accounts on individual nations and regions,[12] with Australia featuring prominently.[13] These studies focus on how the war has been remembered and commemorated. With the case of the Cypriots, however, it is about forgetting, both consciously and unconsciously, and the exclusion of this extraordinary contribution to the Great War from national consciousness. The erasure of the Cypriot Mule corps from Cypriot national narratives is striking for the stark contrast it presents to the more well-known cases of the impact of the Great War on other former colonial territories. In particular, scholarship has argued for the centrality of the experience of the Anzacs to national narratives of Australia and New Zealand and of the *tirailleurs senegalais* to the anti-colonial nationalist narratives of the successors to colonial French West Africa. In the West Indies and in West African anti-colonial nationalists harnessed the memory of the unrecognised heroism and sacrifices of those men who served, precisely to argue for their worthiness of political independence.[14]

Cypriot Elites on the Cypriot Mule Corps

One of the main reasons for the Cypriots 'forgetting' the Cypriot Mule Corps was the failure of Cypriot political elites to exploit the corps both during and after the Great War for their own political ends: for Greek Cypriot elites to show Greek Cypriot loyalty to the British and that they were deserving of *enosis* or other political concessions and for the Turkish Cypriot elites to show their loyalty and support for the *status quo*.

During the Great War, unlike Indian, Jamaican and Egyptian political elites,[15] Greek Cypriot political elites did not attempt to exploit the British need for Cypriot muleteers for their own political ends. Instead of highlighting that the peasantry and labouring classes were loyal to the British and thus deserving of *enosis*, they ignored this opportunity and played no part in recruitment efforts. The local Greek language newspapers, which were mostly controlled by the Greek Cypriot nationalist elites, rarely mentioned the mule corps during the war. When the mule corps was mentioned it was restricted to basic information such as how many muleteers left for Salonica, with the exception of the call for men to volunteer in *Eleutheria* newspaper by Evagoras Savvides, the director of the recruiting station at Kalo Chorko near Lefka.[16]

There are many reasons to explain why the Greek Cypriot nationalist elites failed to exploit the loyalty of the Cypriot peasant and labouring classes for their political ends during

---

12   Paul Fussell, *The Great War and Modern Memory* (London: Oxford University Press, 1975); Angela Gaffney, *Aftermath: Remembering the Great War in Wales* (Cardiff: University of Wales Press, 2000); George Robb, *British Culture and the First World War* (London: Palgrave, 2002); Ray Westlake, *Remembering the Great War in Gloucestershire & Hertfordshire* (Studley, Warwickshire: Brewin Books, 2002).

13   Alistair Thomson, *Anzac Memories: Living With the Legend* (Oxford: Oxford University Press, 1994) (revised 2013); Simon Miles, *Anzac Memorial, Adelaide, South Australia: Remembering the Sacrifice of Those Who Fought in the Great War, 1914–1918* (Adelaide: Workskil Inc, 1995).

14   Myron J. Echenberg, *Colonial Conscripts: The Tirailleurs Sénégalais in French West Africa, 1857–1960* (London: J. Curry, 1991); Smith, *Jamaican Volunteers in the First World War*.

15   See David Lockwood, *The Indian Bourgeoisie* (London: I.B. Tauris, 2012), pp. 30–51; Smith, *Jamaican Volunteers in the First World War*; M.W. Daly and Carl F. Petry, *The Cambridge History of Egypt* (New York: Cambridge University Press, 1998), p. 246.

16   *Eleutheria*, 9/26 (December 1916): p. 3.

the Great War. The fact that the nationalist political elites were not involved in recruitment efforts was one reason. Another reason was that after the British offer to cede Cyprus to Greece in October 1915 failed[17] and the war ended, they expected the offer to be repeated or taken up with more vigour by the Greek government, neither of which happened.[18] A third reason was that most of the Greek Cypriot elites supported King Constantine over Venizelos in the 'great schism' and therefore held pro-German sympathies. Although not actively working for the enemy they did not help the British either, unless it lined their own pockets.[19] The fact that the mule corps would not have lined their pockets, except those few (if any) who bred mules, must also have been a turn-off, since fewer peasants would have borrowed from these usurers.

It is a similar story for the Muslim Cypriot elites during the war. Cypriot Muslim loyalty was more complicated. As regards the status of Cyprus the majority would have preferred the *status quo* and feared *enosis*, yet believed that the British would handle their interests appropriately, despite the offer of 1915.[20] For this reason there was no need to constantly refer to their loyalty and when they did, reference to the mule corps was not considered necessary. The vast majority of Muslims had remained loyal during the Great War despite the Ottoman Empire being on the side of the Central Powers. The British believed that they were exceptionally loyal, which was an exaggeration given the efforts of some Turkish Cypriots to break-out Ottoman prisoners of war at the camp at Karaolos, Famagusta, as well as the Turkish Cypriots who stole a vessel and at Adana revealed much of the military activity on the island to the enemy.[21]

During the inter-war years much had changed, but not as regards using the significant service of Cypriots in the mule corps for social, economic and political advantage. Although the economy and prospects for society in general, for peasants, labourers, the growing middle and upper classes, was mostly bleak, especially when the Great Depression hit by 1930, there was no reference to the loyalty and hard work of the Cypriot muleteers. This differs from Jamaica and India, where the political elites constantly advocated for a better deal for those who had served. Soon after the war ended the Jamaican government paid small sums to each veteran, gave them access to credit of up to £25 from the Agricultural Bank to buy land, stock or seed, then in 1924 introduced a scheme that gave 5 acres to veterans for farming if they had £10 in savings, and in 1933, with the onset of the Great Depression, the government introduced a land settlement scheme to stem the flow of peasants and unskilled labourers to urban areas. Meanwhile, veterans groups were active.[22] The inter-war experiences of the Jamaican peasantry and unskilled labourers were comparable to that of the Cypriots, except that the Cypriot government did not respond

---

17 See the last chapter in Andrekos Varnava, *British Imperialism in Cyprus, 1878–1915: The Inconsequential Possession* (Manchester: Manchester University Press, 2009).

18 George Georghallides, *A Political and Administrative History of Cyprus* (Nicosia: Cyprus Research Centre, 1979).

19 See Andrekos Varnava, 'British Military Intelligence in Cyprus during the Great War,' *War in History* 19, no. 3 (July 2012): pp. 353–78.

20 Altay Nevzat, *Nationalism Amongst the Turks of Cyprus: The First Wave* (Oulo, Finland: Oulu University Press, 2005), pp. 218–55.

21 See Varnava, 'British Military Intelligence in Cyprus'; For the stolen vessel see State Archives, Nicosia, Secretariat Archives (SA1) SA1/806/1917.

22 Smith, *Jamaican Volunteers in the First World War*, pp. 156–7.

in the same way: there were no significant veteran groups active, and the government referred Cypriots to the British Legion for welfare.

The Cypriot elites, from both communities, continued to ignore the opportunity to exploit the Cypriot contribution. The Cypriot Muslim elites fought a rear-guard defence against the *enosis* agitation of their Cypriot Orthodox co-inhabitants. They steadfastly opposed *enosis* and preferred the *status quo*,[23] although several also called for the 'return' of the island to Turkey, which succeeded the Ottoman Empire.[24] Several Cypriot Muslims led in trying to prevent conflict between the two communities.[25] The Greek Cypriot political elites, thoroughly obsessed with *enosis*, had only increased their demands for it after the war. Their deputation to London in 1919 and 1920, led by Archbishop Kyrrillos III and members of the Legislative Council, including the firebrand Greek national Dr Zannettos, demanded *enosis*.[26] Opposition to it from other educated elites, especially merchants and civil servants, was damned, for example by the Bishop of Kyrenia, Makarios, in a sermon on 29 February 1920, and therefore not allowed to express itself.[27] When Whitehall rejected *enosis* the 'professional politicians and leading clerics', as Malcolm Stevenson, the high commissioner, characterised them, protested by organising petitions in various towns and villages, mostly signed by the local teacher and cleric and by few civil servants, merchants and members of the peasant and labouring classes.[28] Stevenson claimed, not without foundation, that:

> Your Lordship's announcement (rejecting *enosis*), which has caused much satisfaction to the Moslem Community has been received with apathy by the mass of the Greek Christian Community which evinces little interest in the activities of its political leaders regarding the union of Cyprus with Greece. The meetings, which were of most orderly character, were poorly attended and little or no enthusiasm was displayed regarding union with Greece except on the part of the professional orators whose speeches were of the usual bombastic nature.[29]

Of these petitions only two protested at their denial of 'liberty' by referring to how they deserved it because they had contributed in the victorious British coalition. These petitions were from two of the villages that had been the largest contributors to the Cypriot Mule Corps, Lapithos and Karavas, in Kyrenia.[30]

---

23 Stevenson to Milner, 6 August 1920, including letter by Musa Irfan Bey, member of Executive and Legislative Councils, 4 August 1920, CO67/198/40907, NAUK; Stevenson to Milner, confidential, 12 December 1920, including message from Chief Cadi of Cyprus, 10 December 1920, CO67/199/63298, NAUK.

24 Stevenson to Devonshire, confidential, 24 December 1922, including enclosures, CO67/208/1092, NAUK.

25 Stevenson to Churchill, confidential, 25 April 1921, CO67/202/22445, NAUK.

26 Stevenson to Milner, 15 April 1920, CO67/197/21724, NAUK. See also the pamphlet published by the Cyprus Deputation in 'The Cyprus Cause: Official Correspondence,' CO67/201/30005, NAUK No mention of the Cypriot contribution in the war is made. See also correspondence and other documents in this file.

27 Stevenson to Milner, 15 April 1920, CO67/197/21724, NAUK.

28 Stevenson to Milner, confidential. 6 November 1920, CO67/199/56234, NAUK.

29 Ibid.

30 Stevenson to Milner, confidential, 25 November 1920, CO67/199/59863, NAUK; with relevant enclosures.

The orderly meetings may not have initially appeared threatening to Stevenson, but they soon took a nasty turn when the Greek Cypriot members of the Legislative Council resigned.[31] Initially Stevenson believed that 'the mischievous activities of the political leaders have led to no disorder whatever and do not appear to be likely to do so,'[32] yet he recommended, as a precaution, that martial law continue until the Provisional Powers Law (1919), and the Provisional Powers (Amendment) Law (1920) came into force upon peace with the Ottoman Empire.[33] Indeed, initially the Greek Cypriot agitators, led by Kyrillos III, complained, asking that the new Colonial Secretary, Winston Churchill (who had visited the island as colonial undersecretary in 1907),[34] visit to ascertain the people's wishes.[35] But when this was rejected, the Greek Cypriot agitators became increasingly desperate, especially when a moderate faction emerged that accepted cooperation with the British.[36]

On 6 and 7 April 1921, during the 100-year anniversary of the Greek War of Independence, a rare celebration in Cyprus before 1900,[37] disturbances occurred in Nicosia. The police put the disturbance down with difficulty, but Stevenson warned that intercommunal clashes might eventuate, and so he re-enlisted ninety ex-policemen and asked Egypt to send two platoons of British troops.[38] The troops from Egypt could not be sent, despite Stevenson's pleas and those of the Colonial Office. Fiddes explained to Sir Herbert Creedy, the private secretary to the War Secretary: 'You will appreciate the importance just now of preventing anything like a serious shindy in the island.'[39] Despite this setback the Cypriot government successfully cracked down on the most extremist agitators, especially those who were not of Cypriot heritage, exiling several Greek nationals.[40] Not only did this response further split the nationalists, cause Muslim ill-feeling and preparedness to defend and avenge their co-religionists, but it further showed how divorced these so-called representatives of the people were from the rural and labouring classes. As Stevenson revealed to Churchill on 25 April:

> There are also signs from the villages that the people are chafing at the agitation for Union with Greece. Several instances have just been reported to me in which the Village Councils

---

31 Stevenson to Milner, 14 December 1920, CO67/199/63192, 386, NAUK; Stevenson to Milner, confidential, 14 December 1920, CO67/199/63301, NAUK.
32 Stevenson to Milner, confidential, 14 December 1920, CO67/199/63301, NAUK.
33 Stevenson to Milner, secret, 14 December 1920, CO67/199/63302, NAUK. Martial Law was eventually lifted on 1 September 1921, despite the disturbances that had occurred. See CO67/204/46764, NAUK.
34 Varnava, *British Imperialism in Cyprus*, pp. 183–6.
35 See CO67/202/15566, NAUK.
36 See CO67/202/15567, NAUK; and CO67/203/24636, NAUK.
37 Varnava, *British Imperialism in Cyprus*, p. 167.
38 See CO67/202/17380, NAUK; and CO67/20543, NAUK.
39 See CO67/202/20073, NAUK. Also on 4 May 1921 the Battleship *Ajax* visited Famagusta, in apparent response to Stevenson's pleas for assistance, but in something out of a comic-tragedy, nobody expected the ship, even Stevenson. See CO67/205/31214, NAUK; includes report from commanding officer of the *Ajax*. See also CO67/205/27114, NAUK, CO67/205/22860, NAUK, CO67/205/21978, NAUK; and CO67/205/24117, NAUK.
40 For the deportation and exiling of Nikolaos Katalanos, see CO67/202/22444, NAUK; CO67/203/32629, NAUK; and CO67/203/30260, NAUK. For the deportation and exiling of Philios Zannetos: see Fenn to Churchill, secret, enclosures and minutes, 16 September 1922, CO67/208/48068, NAUK.

have refused to sign resolutions for the Union of Cyprus with Greece which they had been directed by the agitators to pass.[41]

These communities, who had sent their husbands, sons and brothers to serve in the Cypriot Mule Corps, where not interested in *enosis*, but for a better today and tomorrow for themselves and their families. Yet even when the threat of violence subsided, the Greek Cypriot members of the Legislative Council continued to ignore the real problems facing society. They refused to return to their seats, instead forming the so-called 'Political Organisation' which led a Greek Cypriot nationalist boycott of the upcoming elections, in a move the Colonial Office believed was modelled on the successful Maltese strategy.[42] But after summer 1922 the Cypriot government believed that the Political Organisation was 'moribund', that there was widespread dissatisfaction with it and by the end of the year Archbishop Kyrillos III had started lobbying the Cypriot government for self-government rather than *enosis*.[43] Stevenson smashed the idea in his letter to the Duke of Devonshire, the new Colonial Secretary, a Unionist in the new Conservative government:

> While I would naturally be disposed to consider in a liberal spirit the just desires of a subject people for greater responsibility, I fear that I cannot from my knowledge of the Cypriot or of his history honestly advocate under present conditions, the grant to the inhabitants of the Island of self-government or of any extended constitutional powers incapable of being balanced by precisely equivalent safeguards. The villager is ignorant, casual, credulous, and improvident; the townsman is half-educated, cunning, conceited, and selfish. The former is content to be ruled; the latter is happy to be protected at the expense, danger, and responsibility of anyone but himself. The average standard of intelligence and education of the Cypriot is low, while those who possess these advantaged in any degree turn them almost invariably to unworthy uses. While possessed of many good qualities, not the least of which is an attractive childlike simplicity of thought and expression, he is at heart Oriental. The Island is in truth immature even yet for the advanced constitutional system which was grafted on the country shortly after the British Occupation in 1878, and any question of granting it a further measure of political liberty is one which, in my opinion, must be approached with the greatest care and deliberation.[44]

The elites of both communities, especially the Greek Cypriot, continued to focus on obtaining power in the island and determining its political status, failing to understand

---

41   Stevenson to Churchill, confidential, 25 April 1921, CO67/202/22445, NAUK. The British also questioned the petitions which were sent in June, which took months to prepare, came from most villages with a majority Greek Cypriot population, and only had the signatures of leading individuals, the priest, teacher, school councils and sometimes the mayor. The British also had information that duress was used and that the vast majority of the populations in the towns and villages were unaware that such a petition had been sent in their name. See CO67/203/33691, NAUK.

42   Stevenson to Churchill, confidential, 25 October 1921, CO67/204/55086, NAUK; and see also minutes from this file. Also see, CO67/204/62275, NAUK; and CO67/204/978, NAUK; For more on the 'political organisation' see Stevenson to Churchill, confidential, 23 March 1922, CO67/207/16623, NAUK; including articles of the political organisation.

43   See CO67/208/54911, NAUK; and CO67/208/1091, NAUK.

44   Stevenson to Devonshire, confidential, 24 December 1922, CO67/208/1091, NAUK; also see enclosures.

the possible political capital in referring to the Cypriot Mule Corps and the issues facing veterans. Meanwhile, the British also missed an opportunity to memorialise the mule corps and understand the needs of the veterans and broader peasant and rural labouring classes. The battle to win the hearts and minds of the Cypriot peasantry and labouring classes had not yet begun and in the process of ignoring them, the mule corps was also being silenced.

During and after the 1931 events, which resulted in the burning of Government House in Nicosia and the subsequent British repression that impacted on all communities and classes,[45] nothing was said about the Cypriot contribution in the Great War to show Cypriot loyalty. The Cypriot Mule Corps had all but been erased from memory, yet as the decade progressed there were signs of mass politicisation across the island that brought together classes and different religious groups, not behind the banner of *enosis*, but behind constitutional reform.[46]

Earlier, smaller, more ideologically based movements had united some peasants, labourers and the more socially and politically conscious educated people, but these also failed to refer to the Cypriot Mule Corps. The British took peasant support for granted. In the 1925 legislature elections there was a massive defeat for the nationalists, and for the first time more than 10 per cent of the Greek Cypriot population voted.[47] The Communist Party of Cyprus (CPC), formed in 1926, had direct links to the Cypriot Mule Corps yet failed to use this politically. In the spirit of the 'United Front' for workers and peasants and recognising the Christian-Muslim particulars in the island, it wanted to unite all Christians and Muslims against British rule and therefore advocated Cypriot independence and strongly criticised *enosis*. Its unofficial leader during the repressive early to mid-1930s, Christos Savvides, had served in the Cypriot Mule Corps,[48] and yet he did not draw attention to it. Service in the Cypriot Mule Corps indicated a loyalty to a regime for which he was agitating against. Interestingly, he did not attempt to use the Cypriot Mule Corps in a negative way either given the British failure to look after veterans. Savvides was probably not the only Cypriot communist to have served in the Cypriot Mule Corps. Additionally in the 1920s there formed the Agrarian Party, which had much greater success than the CPC in forging Christian and Muslim membership, but did not survive after the events of 1931.[49] It too failed to use the Cypriot Mule Corps and support veteran issues, although many of its members would have served. The movement that developed from the mid-1930s and climaxed in the unsuccessful delegation visiting London in 1937 to ask for constitutional reforms was far more numerous in support and broader ideologically. As Rappas argued, the movement failed not because it lacked legitimacy, but because it had legitimacy, as the first mass movement and one which included people from all socio-economic and ethno-religious groups, with the exception of the nationalists who had been sidelined. That the British succeeded through their harsh measures to create this movement and yet failed to embrace it was the tragedy.[50] That the Cypriots behind it continued to ignore the

---

45 See George Georghallides, *Cyprus and the Governorship of Sir Ronald Storrs: The Causes of the 1931 Crisis* (Nicosia: Cyprus Research Centre, 1985); and Alexis Rappas, *Cyprus in the Thirties: British Colonial Rule and the Roots of the Cyprus Conflict* (London: I.B. Tauris, 2014).
46 Rappas, *Cyprus in the Thirties*, pp. 88–122.
47 Yiannos Katsourides, *The History of the Communist Party in Cyprus: Colonialism, Class and the Cypriot Left* (London: I.B. Tauris, 2014), pp. 54–6.
48 Ibid., pp. 138–9.
49 Ibid., pp. 75–82.
50 Rappas, *Cyprus in the Thirties*.

contribution of the Cypriot Mule Corp in the Great War and the issues that the veterans faced was a political failure that can only be attributed to immaturity and the intentional silencing of the Cypriot Mule Corps.

Ultimately, their hearts and minds were still to be won and if the Cypriot government had focussed on commemorating the Cypriot Mule Corps they may have shown that the 'Greek'-Christian and 'Turkish'-Muslim divide in Cyprus was a nationalist manifestation and that the peasants, as the British repeatedly argued during the inter-war years, were in fact loyal. The British failed to win peasant and labourer 'hearts and minds' and after the Second World War pushed them into the anti-colonial movements that developed during the 1930s, either the nationalists or the communists.

Failure of Cypriot colonial government to commemorate the Great War

The erasure of the Cypriot Mule Corps from Cypriot national consciousness meant that no memorial was erected, not even one that acknowledged those who lost their lives serving. Did the Cypriot people not care? Was it the fault of the anti-colonial political movements? Or was this the fault of the British authorities?

It is certainly not merely the fault of the British, yet it is interesting that the British contributed to the silence. After the Great War the Cypriot government did little to acknowledge let alone commemorate the Cypriot muleteers who served in the British army beyond their duty to distribute medals in autumn 1921 and send medals to those unable to attend the ceremonies.[51]

Those ex-muleteers who fell on hard times, whether peasants or not, were encouraged by the government or by civil servants involved with the British Legion to take up their problems with the branch, or with other agencies, such as the Red Cross. In this way the Cypriot government handballed the problems of ex-muleteers to the private sphere, which included, in large part, members of the government and the civil service as active members.[52]

The Cyprus conflict, 1955–1974

The Cyprus conflict does not begin in 1955 nor does it end in 1974, but it is during these nineteen years when mass political violence was used, on and off, that saw both communities militarised against each other. After the Second World War the British authorities failed to build upon a second loyal contribution from both Christian and Muslim Cypriots. Instead they allowed the Greek Cypriot nationalist elites to use the Second World War contribution for political leverage on *enosis* and gave fuel to the fire by returning to the island some of the most extreme nationalists interested in '*enosis* and only *enosis*'.[53] For this reason the British initiative to reintroduce a constitution, with a legislative council, was doomed.[54]

---

51 Army Council to CO, 5 October 1920, CO67/201/49076, NAUK; See SA1/1380/1921; DCNi to CSC, 15 September 1921, SA1/1453/1920/3.

52 See numerous files in SA1/978/1916/2 relating to the British Legion.

53 See Yiangou, *Cyprus in World War II*, pp. 147–51. Bishop of Kyrenia, Makarios, was one example, becoming Archbishop in 1946.

54 See Rolandos Katsiaounis, *Η Διασκεπτική, 1946–1948: Με Ανασκόπηση της Περιόδου, 1878–1945* [*The Consultative Assembly, 1946–48: With a Survey of the Period, 1878–1945*] (Nicosia: Cyprus Research Centre, 2000).

The rejection of a constitution, in preference to *'enosis* and only *enosis'*, alongside the island's increasingly important role for British military policy in the Middle East, help explain the recourse to violence.[55]

As part of these preparations for the use of violence the Greek Cypriot nationalist elites needed to convert the peasantry and labouring classes into *enosis* faithful and the youth into active, even violent, tools against the British and anyone opposed to EOKA (National Organisation of Cypriot Fighters).[56] After a long planning stage, starting in 1951,[57] civil disobedience and violence were adopted in April 1955. This civil disobedience did not resemble that implemented in India, since it did not revolve around a protest against damaging and exploitative British policies,[58] but took a more petty form, such as when schoolchildren were ordered to break the commemorative mugs given to them to mark the coronation of Queen Elizabeth II.[59] Some veteran muleteers also destroyed their medals, but it is unclear if this was an order or a personal choice. Many opposed doing so, highlighting the more general opposition to EOKA methods, and the medals served to protect them and their families from British searches.[60]

Cypriotism, yet still no Cypriot Mule Corps

Independence in 1960, hastened by violence which resembled a civil war in the island between its two communities and the British administration in the middle, did not forge a common history. Indeed, neither side wanted a common national history of shared memories. This was also enshrined in the constitution, which allowed for separate Communal Chambers that gave the Greek and Turkish communities separate powers to deal with the cultural needs of their respective communities independently of the 'other'. This was reflected in the 'research' of 'national historians', such as Constantine Spyridakis, the Minister of Education in the first decade of the Republic of Cyprus and the opponents of a university in Cyprus and Makarios' new policy of independence (the policy of the 'feasible', rather than the 'desirable' – *enosis*) after 1967 because both would alienate Cyprus from its 'Greek motherland'.[61] The Greek Cypriot position was that they were the majority and so they should determine the status of the island, namely *enosis*. The Turkish

---

55   Andrekos Varnava and Christalla Yakinthou, 'Cyprus: Political Modernity and Structures of Democracy in a Divided Island,' *The Oxford Handbook of Local and Regional Democracy in Europe*, ed. John Loughlin, Frank Hendriks, and Anders Lidström (Oxford: Oxford University Press, 2011), pp. 455–77.

56   For a primary source see, George Grivas, *The Memoirs of General Grivas*, ed. Charles Foley (London: Longmans, 1964); For secondary sources see Nancy Crawshaw, *The Cyprus Revolt* (London: George Allen & Unwin, 1978); and David French, *Fighting EOKA: The British Counter-Insurgency Campaign on Cyprus, 1955–1959* (Oxford: Oxford University Press, 2015).

57   Grivas, *Memoirs*, pp. 13–32.

58   Lockwood, *The Indian Bourgeoisie*, pp. 133–42, 165–7.

59   I have been told this by many Cypriots growing up at the time. Also, see Chris Sutton, 'Gauge, Battleground, Weapon: Celebrations in Cold War Cyprus, 1945–1955,' *ex plus ultra* 3 (April 2012).

60   Europeana website entries and web pages for Panay Polycarpou and Michael Michaelides, both from Palaiohori; and Demetris Christodoulou, Lapathos, Famagusta.

61   Constantine Spyridakis, *A Brief History of Cyprus*, Publications Dept. Greek Communal Chamber (Nicosia: 1963, 2nd ed., 1964); See Kyriacos C. Markides, *The Rise and Fall of the Cyprus Republic* (London: Yale University Press, 1977), pp. 98–9.

Cypriot view was that both groups had lived peacefully under Ottoman and most of British rule, but that since *enosis* had become violent the two sides could not co-exist, and partition was desirable and inevitable.

After the 1974 war that partitioned the island both sides altered their official propaganda. The Greek Cypriot political establishment now argued that relations before 1974 were peaceful and neighbourly. This has been referred to in Cypriot historiography as 'peaceful co-existence' and 'Cypriotism', although there was no serious attempt to develop a Cypriot national consciousness.[62] Rather the aim was to downplay Greek Cypriot responsibility or to blame foreign powers for the violence of the 1950s, 1960s and 1970s by showing that Greeks and Turks in Cyprus had lived peacefully before 1974. One of the chief architects of this politically motivated revisionist history was Costas Kyrris, the director of the Cyprus Research Centre, in the Ministry of Education. In his *Peaceful Coexistence in Cyprus* he offered various examples throughout the centuries of Greek and Turkish 'peaceful co-existence' in the island.[63] Kyrris, a thorough researcher, still failed to mention the Cypriot Mule Corps. On the other hand, the Turkish Cypriot official writers continued with the opposite extreme, focussing on what had divided rather than what had united Cypriots.[64]

It was left to a British officer serving in Cyprus in the 1970s to take an interest in the Cypriot Mule Corps. Major J.P.B. Condon, Royal Irish Rangers (formed 1968), while on service in Cyprus as part of the United Nations Force in Cyprus (UNFICYP), produced a short report on the Cypriot Mule Corps, which is contained in various UK archives.[65] He readily admitted it was incomplete and would one day return to it, but he did not.

Europeana 1914–1918

'Europeana 1914–1918' was the first attempt since Condon to record the stories of Cypriot Mule Corp members, even if these were from second-hand accounts and contained several problems. The most common error was the statement that the men served in the Greek army, which serves to show the Greek nationalist orientation of those relaying the stories, as they assumed their relatives had served in the Greek and not the British army, and those conducting and transcribing the interviews who did not correct this.[66] Many of the accounts also focus on how some of the men followed their service in the British armed forces with service in the Greek army. This is celebrated in much greater tones in the accounts. But this must be questioned in light of the archival evidence. Few Cypriots served in the Greek army and the Greek authorities used coercion and even kidnapping to compel Cypriots to serve

---

62 See Yiannis Papadakis, Nicos Peristianis, and Gisela Welz, eds, *Divided Cyprus: Modernity, History, and an Island in Conflict* (Bloomington: University of Indiana, 2006).

63 Costas Kyrris, 'Symbiotic Elements in the History of the Two Communities of Cyprus,' *Kypriakos Logos* 8 (1976), pp. 243–82; Costas Kyrris, *Peaceful Co-Existence in Cyprus Under British Rule (1878–1959) and after Independence* (Nicosia: PIO, 1977).

64 See A.C. Gazioglu, *The Turks of Cyprus: A Province of the Ottoman Empire 1571–1878* (London: Rustem, 1990); A.C. Gazioglu and M.A. Demirer, *Cyprus: The Island of Sustained Crisis* (Nicosia: CYREP, 1998).

65 Aside from at the National Archives, UK, it is also at the Imperial War Museum and the Shropshire Archives.

66 Europeana web page entries for Apostolos Argyrou, Damianos Ioannis and Costis tiw Haritous, all from Palaihori, and Demetris Christodoulou, Lapathos.

against their will, including former members of the Cypriot Mule Corps. In 1920 the Greek government, informed by the nationalist Greek Cypriot elites, claimed that there were 4,000 Cypriots in Cyprus willing to enlist in the Greek Army and that they would be willing to send warships to collect them. The British government was utterly bemused since there were no Cypriots thronging to enlist and rejected the idea as a breach of British neutrality, which it was since Cypriots held British Cypriot nationality.[67] If it were not enough that the Greek government and their own political elites were trying to volunteer the peasant and labouring classes into the Greek army, Greek consular representatives in Egypt and Greek military personnel in Greece started kidnapping, even providing false identification papers to, British Cypriot nationals. This included at least four men who had served as muleteers, Victor Vernardakis, 4650, Limassol; S. G. Hatzakos, 8273, Pano Akourdalia, Paphos; Triphonas Irakli, Kilani, Limassol; and Nearchos Christodoulides.[68]

Conclusion

Despite the monumental contribution of Cypriot men in the Cypriot Mule Corps various issues and developments came together to result in this service being silenced. From nationalists creating separate scripts of the 'Greek' and 'Turkish' communities in Cyprus, excluding any common Christian-Muslim past, to simply not wanting to associate with the imperialist's war, the memory of the service of the men in the Cypriot Mule Corps was reduced to a personalised family affair at best, at worst it was not discussed at all. The British failure to commemorate the service of the Cypriots, possibly linked to their unwillingness to compensate widows and incapacitated muleteers, contributed to its silencing.

---

67 See Stevenson to Milner, telegram, 29 June 1920, CO67/198/32080, NAUK; Stevenson to Milner, telegram, 4 July 1920, CO67/198/32699, NAUK; FO to CO, 7 July 1920, CO67/200/33415, NAUK; FO to CO, 10 July 1920, including cable, very urgent, Granville to FO, 7 July 1920 (received 9 July 1920), CO67/200/33991, NAUK; minute, n.d., CO67/200/33991, NAUK; CO to FO, 14 July 1920, CO67/200/33991, NAUK; Granville to FO, cable, 10 July 1920 (received 11 July 1920) CO67/200/34783, NAUK; Cyprus Deputation to Colonial Secretary, 17 July 1920, CO67/201/35475, NAUK; CO to Cyprus Deputation, 27 July 1920, CO67/201/35475, NAUK..

68 See the relevant files in CO67/205/43709, NAUK; CO67/204/62276,NAUK; CO67/205/45201, NAUK; CO67/205/47192, NAUK; CO67/205/52622, NAUK; CO67/205/57437, NAUK; CO67/205/57871, NAUK; and CO67/205/59599, NAUK. There are two men on the honour roll with the name Nearchos Christodoulou, 9963, Evrihou, Nicosia; and 12728, Kritou Marottou, Paphos.

Index

Abdullah, Emir of Transjordan 146–7
Adana 295
Adelaide 205, 207–8
Africa/African 7, 11–12, 15, 22, 24–6, 28–9, 31–7, 62, 89–90, 105, 111, 122, 129, 137–8, 165, 175, 211, 231, 250, 285, 288, 292, 294
Aitken, Sir Max 187
Aitken, William Maxwell 167
Albany Harbour 276
Aleppo 204
Alexandria 266
Algeria/Algerian 74, 137
Allenby, Sir Edmund 130, 135
Amery, Leopold 27
Amman 146–7
Amritsar Massacre 146, 202, 245
Anglo-Irish Treaty 179, 210
Anglo-Ndebele War 1893 30
Antarctic 190
ANZAC 211, 129, 265–6, 271–8, 291, 294
Arab/Arabs 137, 141, 143–4, 147–9, 157, 161–2, 201, 210
Arab Legion 148
Ashwell, Lena 68, 70
Asia/Asian 6, 11, 23, 25–6, 32, 36, 62, 118, 217, 237, 250, 252, 256, 270
Asmara 31
Asquith, Herbert 52, 164
Assyria/Assyrian 151
Astra Chamber Music Society 273
Athens 72
Atkins, Tommy 68, 210
Atlantic City 279, 281, 284–5, 288
Austerlitz 122, 126
Australia/Australian 1, 3, 5, 7, 11, 12, 15, 18–21, 28, 31–2, 35, 58, 60–1, 84, 86, 90, 96, 118–25, 127, 141, 185–6, 188–92, 198–201, 204, 206–9, 211–13, 231, 250, 265–6, 269–74, 276, 278, 291–2, 294

Baker, Herbert 20, 31, 241, 249, 253–4
Bancroft, Edgar A. 201
Bean, Charles 188–9
Beatty, David 122, 124, 126
Beaverbrook, Lord 56, 167–8, 187, 189, 197
Beethoven, Ludwig van 76

Beirut 147
Belfast 18, 174, 176, 179–83, 287
Belgium 10, 16, 53, 73, 77, 79, 91–2, 95, 135, 187, 210
Bell, Gertrude 155, 160
Bengal/Bengali 26, 132, 142, 165, 249
Berlin, Isaiah 118
Bernhardt, Sarah 201
Bible/Biblical 191–2, 203, 209
Blake, William 3, 132
Blomfield, Reginald 254
Boardwalk Empire (TV show) 279–81, 284, 288–9
Bombay 73, 75, 205, 210, 236–7
Bonaparte, Napoleon 50
Bonar Law, Andrew 89, 162
Bone, Muirhead 167
Booth, Dr. Mary 271
Borden, Robert 122
Borneo 11, 31
Botha, Louis 122
Brighton (UK) 20, 215–16, 222–5, 229–30, 232, 234–5, 238, 240–1, 244–7, 261
British Empire Exhibition, Glasgow 1938 29
British Museum 138, 151
British School at Rome 19, 253, 255
Brooke, Rupert 21, 266–7, 269
Brooke-Popham, Robert 157
Brown, Oliver 158
Buchan, John 56, 167, 178
Buchanan, Zetton 160
Burleigh, Charles 227
Burma 25, 30–1, 197, 205
Burton, Decimus 17
Burton, Percy 201, 204

Cairo 138, 146–7, 201
Calcutta 73, 241, 249
Canada 3, 7, 10, 18, 31–2, 34–5, 55, 84, 86, 90, 135–6, 185–90, 192–9, 211–12, 222, 231, 250
Canberra 14, 31, 35
Caribbean/West Indies 10, 13, 17, 22, 25–7, 34, 129, 211, 294
Carline, Sydney 18, 151, 153–5, 158, 161
Carnegy, Dale 204, 207, 210, 212
Carruthers Gould, Sir Francis 48

Carson, Edward 176
Carter, Howard 147
Central Powers 1, 44, 61, 292, 295
Ceylon/Sri Lanka 11, 25, 31–2, 199
Chamberlain, Sir Austen 235–6
Chase, Harry 201, 203
Cheesman, Edith 161–2
Chetwode, Philip 211
Chicago 200, 279, 281, 284–5
China/Chinese 5, 11, 13, 17, 37, 62, 74, 122, 124, 130, 134, 136
Chishti, Shalim 236
Chopin, Frédéric 80
Christchurch 206
Churchill, Sir Winston 110, 119, 122, 124, 147, 176, 205, 282, 287, 297
Clay, Henry 211
Cockerell, Sameul Pepys 204
Colmo, Eugenio 45
Colonial and Indian Exhibition 1886 240
Communist Party of Cyprus 299
Condon, J. P. B. 302
Conor, William 18, 168, 179, 180–3
Constantine I, King of Greece 295
Cooper, Edward Foxen 213
Copt/Coptic 141
Coupland, Sir Reginald 34
Creedy, Sir Herbert 297
Crete 292
Cromwell, Oliver 96
Cunningham, William 202
Curzon, Lord 122, 241
Cypriot Mule Corps (WWI) 21, 291–4, 296, 298–300, 302, 303
Cypriot Regiment (WWII) 291–3
Cyprus/Cypriots 1, 3, 8, 13, 21, 291–303

Damascus 143, 146–7, 153, 201
Dancey, George Henry 59
Daniell, Thomas 223, 226, 243
Daniell, William 223, 243
Deakin, Alfred 60
Derby, Lord 63
Devonshire, Duke of 298
Din, Sadr un 232
Djemal Pasha 210
Dodgson, Campbell 138
Dogras 131, 220–1
Doughty, Sir Arthur 187–8
Doyle, Arthur Conan 166
Druze 147
Dublin 18, 168–9, 171, 176, 179, 210

Dugdale, Thomas 17, 142–3, 149
Dundee 26
Dunedin 29
Dyson, Will 58, 60

Easter Rising 22, 169, 176, 210
Edinburgh 178, 204
Edward VIII 31, 245
Egan, Eleanor Franklin 152
Egypt/Egyptian 17, 31, 73, 129–30, 137–40, 145, 146–7, 149, 151, 153, 201–3, 211–12, 217, 294, 297, 303
Egyptian Camel Transport Corps (ECTC) 139–40
Egyptian Expeditionary Force (EEF) 129, 137, 201
Egyptian Labour Corps (ELC) 138–9
Elgar, Edward 15, 77
Empire Marketing Board 29, 31
EOKA (Ethniki Organosis Kyprion Agoniston) 301
Eritrea 31
Evans-Pritchard, E. E. 32
Ewart, William 182

Faivre, Jules-Abel 48
Famagusta 295
Faruq, King 146
Feisal, Sherif 141, 143, 146–7, 210
Ferriman, Frederick 86
Ffoulkes, Charles 188, 212
Fisher, Andrew 58
Flagg, James Montgomery 56
Fontaine, Charles 61
Fox-Pitt, Douglas 227
France/French 11, 15, 18, 22, 30, 32, 37, 49, 61, 68–9, 72–3, 79, 129–36, 153, 167, 170–1, 174, 183, 187, 189–90, 201, 203, 210, 222–3, 235, 254–5, 265, 269, 279, 282, 287, 292
Friez, Otto 48

Gallipoli 19, 16, 70, 73, 81–2, 94–6, 98, 101, 123, 129, 255, 265–6, 269, 271–3, 291
Gandhi, Mahatma 37, 244, 258
Garvey, Marcus 288
Garwhalis 131
Gaza 139, 153, 204–5
George, IV, King 223
George, V, King 20, 237, 241, 245, 250, 252
German South West Africa/Namibia 35
Germany/Germans/German Empire 15, 41–2, 46, 55, 62, 64, 87, 92, 95, 97, 103–5, 109, 111–16, 135, 166–7, 200, 230, 233, 245, 292

Gifford, Helen 21, 266, 273
Girdwood, Charles Hilton DeWitt 221–3, 226
Glasgow 26, 29, 175, 205, 287
Godbole, Jagu 230
Goupil Gallery 159–60
Graves, Robert 26, 147, 254–5, 293
Gray, Cecil 77
Great Depression 14, 28, 295
Gullett, Henry 191–2
Gurkha/Gurkhas 73, 131, 219, 223

Haifa 135, 147
Haig, Sir Douglas 170, 174
Hailey, Lord 33, 38
Harcourt, Lord 188
Hardinge, Lord 217, 229, 253
Harmsworth, Alfred 46
Haselden, William K. 48
Haward, Lawrence 159
Hearst, William Randolph 46, 55
Hecht, George, J. 61
Hejaz 148
Helena Victoria, Princess 69
Henriques, E. C. 237, 244
Henry, Paul 180
Hindu 20, 216, 225, 230, 232–3, 237–9, 243–5, 247–8, 263
Hitler, Adolf 61
Hoare, Sir Samuel 156
Hogarth, David 205
Holland, Dulcie 271
Holland, Frank 46
Holst, Gustav 15, 71, 72
Hopps, H. R. 60
Hughes, William Morris 122–6
Hurley, Frank 18, 21, 190–2, 265
Hussein, Ali ibn 148, 210
Hyde, Miriam 271

Imperial War Museum 143, 151, 168, 174, 179, 189, 212–13
India/Indian 1, 3, 7, 10–12, 15, 17, 19–20, 22, 24–6, 28, 31–4, 37, 62, 72–6, 79, 86, 97, 122, 129–38, 141–4, 146, 149, 154, 156, 199–200, 202, 205, 207, 210, 213, 216–17, 219–25, 228–38, 240–2, 244–63, 294–5, 301
Ireland/Irish 1, 10, 18–19, 22, 26, 106, 163–6, 168–9, 174, 176, 179, 182–3, 199–202, 209–12, 288
Irish Republican Army 287
Irwin, Lord 255
Israel, Eretz 206

Italy/Italians 31, 203, 207, 244, 292

Jack, Richard 197
Jacob, Sir Swinton 236
Jagger, Charles Sargeant 16, 19–24, 44, 243, 255–6
Japan 79, 120–2, 124
Jats 131
Jellicoe, Lord 16
Jodhpur Lancers 132, 134–5, 147
Johannesburg 29
John Bull (journal) 46, 78
Johnston, Lyell 66
Jones, Adrian 15, 19, 22
Jury, Sir William 202

Kanga, Zubin 265, 276
Kashmir 131, 220, 225
Keating, Sean 169
Kelly, Frederick Septimus 21, 266–7, 269–70
Kennington, Eric 17, 131–6, 138, 147, 148, 149, 167
Kenya 27, 34–5, 103
Kenyatta, Jomo 34
Khan, Ghulam Hassan 210
Kilkenny 179
Kipling, Lockwood 210, 241
Kipling, Rudyard 132, 245
Kitchener, Lord 79, 228
Koehne, Graham 21, 273, 276
Konody, P. G. 162
Ku Klux Klan 21, 288
Kuper, Hilda 32
Kyrenia 296
Kyrillos III, Archbishop of Cyprus 297–8

Lane, Hugh 169, 179
Lanteri, Edouard 255
Lauder, Harry 64
Lavery, John 18, 168, 174
Lawrence, Sir Walter 235
Lawrence, T. E. 143, 146, 200–1
League of Nations 28, 35, 111, 122, 146
Leandre, Charles-Lucien 48
Lebanon 17, 146
Lee, Arthur 132
Leech, John 46
Leitner, Gottlieb William 233
Lewis, Percy Wyndham 17, 136
Leys, Norman 34
Lhote, Andre 180
Limassol 303

Limpus, Lady 70
Lincoln, Abraham 96
Lindsay, Norman 60
Liverpool 26, 66, 92, 94, 96, 174, 204, 287
Liverpool, Lord 92
Livingstone 31
Lloyd George, David 55, 122, 123, 166, 205
Lloyd, Marie 64
London 4, 7, 14–17, 22, 29–30, 35, 45–6, 51–2, 55, 58, 60–1, 65–6, 68, 70–1, 79, 111, 131, 134, 136, 139, 141, 143, 145–8, 151, 158–60, 164, 166–9, 171, 174–7, 179, 182, 185, 188–90, 192–3, 196, 199, 201–7, 209, 211–12, 222, 233, 241, 245, 254, 279, 282–5, 287, 296, 299
Low, David 60
Low, Sir Sidney 207
Ludendorff, Erich 61
Lugard, Frederick 33
Lusaka 14, 31
Lutyens, Edwin 20, 176, 241, 249, 257
Lynch, Fionan 210

McBey, James 17, 135, 137, 142, 143, 145
MacCarthy, Maud 72
MacKenzie, Lady Muir 208
McKinley, Alex 60
MacKinney, Herbert Wood 62
MacMunn, Sir George 131
McNair, J. B. 175
Madras 207, 217
Magna Carta 257
Makarios, Bishop of Kyrenia 296
Malaya/Malaysia 11, 26–7, 32, 199, 205
Malcolm, Ian 188
Malinowski, Bronislaw 32
Malouf, David 273
Malta 21, 66, 69, 70, 203
Manchester 26, 151, 159–60, 162, 171, 205–6, 223
Maori/Maoris 12, 97–8, 100–1
Massey, William 92, 122, 206
Masterman, Charles F. G. 166
Mather, Marian 21, 272–3
Matisse, Henri 137
Mauryan 261
Mawson, Sir Douglas 190
Mead, Margaret 32
Mediterranean 13, 26, 67, 158, 203
Meighen, Robert 122
Melbourne 58, 60, 120, 205, 273
Melville, Arthur 158

Mesopotamia/Iraq 3, 11, 17–18, 72–4, 129, 146, 151–9, 161–2, 204, 217, 219, 235
Milner, Alfred 122
Miura, Tamaki 65
Montreal 207
More, James Allen 87
Morocco/Moroccan 137–8, 149, 175
Mott, Helen 76
Mughal Empire/Mughals 237, 252
Mussorgsky, Modest Petrovich 65

Nairobi 59
Nash, John 20, 168, 223
Nash, Paul 19, 130, 168, 170, 225, 227, 240
Nath, Lala Onkar 258
National Volunteers 166
Nehru, Jawaharlal 258
Nelson, Lord (Horatio) 16, 95
Nepal 5, 73, 131
Netherlands 51–2
Nevinson, C. R. W. 19
Newbolt, Henry 166
New Guinea 35
New York 55, 58, 193, 199–201, 203, 279, 286, 288
New Zealand/New Zealanders 3–5, 7, 11–12, 16, 20, 28–9, 31–2, 35, 60, 81–4, 86–99, 101, 120–2, 129, 141, 199, 206, 208, 211, 250, 294
Nicosia 297, 299
Nolan, Sidney 20, 265
North Africa 137–8, 275, 292
Northcliffe, Lord 46, 52
Nova Scotia 188
Nowakowski, Bogdan 50
Nowodworski, Henryk 50
Nuttall, James Charles 60
Nyasaland/Malawi 35–6

Olympic Games 270
Orpen, William 18, 168–71, 174, 176, 179, 182–3
Ottawa 35, 136, 195, 222
Otter, John 226, 235–6, 244
Ottoman Empire/Ottomans/Ottoman Sultan 60, 129, 139–40, 155, 204, 207, 295–7

Pacific 11, 26, 28, 32, 121–2, 125, 270
Palestine 11, 17, 19, 25, 73, 76, 129–30, 134–5, 138–9, 141–3, 146, 151, 153–4, 190–1, 200–1, 203–4, 206–13
Paphos 303
Paris Peace Conference 122, 146

Partridge, Bernard 46, 48, 60
Pathans 131
Peaky Blinders (TV show) 279, 281–3, 285, 287–9
Pearson, Lionel 22–3
Penang 122
Perham, Margery 33, 38
Perth (Australia) 207
Petra 206
Phelp, Charles 226
Philharmonic Hall 204, 207
Phillips, Sir Percival 157
Plunkett, Joseph 169
Plush, Vincent 21, 272–3
Poland 50, 113
Pretoria 35
Primrose, Neil 206
Prokofiev, Sergei 65
Puck (journal) 55
Pulitzer, Joseph 46
Pulteney, Sir William 132
Punch: or the London Charivari 45–6, 48, 60, 62

Rachmaninoff, Sergei 65
Radcliffe-Brown, A. R. 32
Raemaekers, Louis 15, 45, 50–3, 55–6, 58, 60–2
Rajputs 131, 219
Ram, Mohiya 234, 247
Reade, Edward 240
Red Cross 68, 188, 300
Redmond, John 176
Reid, Stuart 17, 143
Rhodesia 26, 27, 30, 31, 32, 35, 79
Richard I (the Lionheart) 192
Richards, Audrey 32
Rider-Rider, William 195
Robinson, Boardman 55
Roosevelt, Theodore 15, 55, 62
Rothenstein, William 17, 131–2, 134–5, 146, 149
Rothermere, Lord 194
Royal Academy 151, 153, 174, 176, 198
Royal Air Force 67, 141, 144, 148, 153
Royal Albert Hall 19, 203, 204, 205
Royal Australian Air Force 141
Royal Naval Reserve 266
Royal Opera House 19, 203
Russell, Lord John 17
Russia 15, 37, 42, 50, 62, 64–5, 79, 122

Saint George 50
Saint Helena (island) 48
Salisbury/Harare 35, 103

Salonica 17, 72, 291, 294
Sambourne, Linley 60
Samoa 32, 35
Saud, Ibn 148
Scotland/Scottish 29, 135, 158, 167, 175, 178, 199, 203, 207, 209
Senegal/Senegalese 74
Serbia 16, 79
Seyton, Sir Bruce 230
Shackleton, Sir Ernest 190
Shalaan, Nawaf 147
Sicily/Sicilian 215, 244
Sikeini, Saad El 148
Sikhs 131, 219, 244
Sinai Peninsula 17, 19, 138–9, 146, 191, 200–1, 203, 213
Singapore 1, 3, 14, 16, 22, 27, 29, 32, 38, 118–26, 211, 235
Singh, Pratab 132
Sinn Fein 169, 210
Skyros 266
slavery/slaves/slave traders 10, 24
Smith, George Adam 207
Smuts, Jan 37, 122
Soldier's Entertainment Fund (SEF) 66
South Africa 7, 11–12, 15, 22, 28, 31–2, 34–6, 62, 89–90, 122, 129, 165, 211, 250
South America 27, 31, 62
Spencer, Stanley 22–3, 168
Spyridakis, Constatine 301
Standford, Charles Villiers 77
Stead, W. T. 46
Stern, Herbert 15
Stevenson, Malcolm 296–8
Storrs, Sir Ronald 147, 291
Strauss, Richard 15, 64
Stravinsky, Igor Fyodorovich 65, 269
Streeton, Arthur 20, 265
Suez Canal 97, 146, 203, 209
Sullivan, E. J. 48
Swaziland 32
Switzerland 55
Sydney 45, 120, 123, 151, 206–7, 211, 271–2
Syria 17, 141, 143, 146, 151, 204

Taintor, Fred, B. 201
Taj Mahal 20, 223, 238–9
Tayi, Auda abu 148
Tchaikovsky, Pyotr Ilyich 79
Tennant, J. E. 157
Tenniel, John 46
Thapar, Daya Ram 233

Thomas, Lowell 199–200, 205, 208, 210
Tilley, Vesta 64
Tolstoy, Leo 17, 118
Townshend, Sir Charles 154
Transjordan 146–7
Treaty of San Remo (1920) 146
Treaty of Versailles (1919) 109, 111
Tromans, Nicholas 152
Turner, J. M. W. 216

Ulster Volunteer Force 164
UNFICYP (United Nations Force in Cyprus) 302
United States of America 15, 28, 30–1, 46, 55–6, 58, 61, 88, 121–4, 166, 171, 190, 192–3, 195, 200–3, 212–13, 222, 272, 280, 284, 286, 288
Universal Negro Improvement Association 288

Varges, Ariel Lowes 219
Vaughan-Williams, Ralph 66
Venizelos, Eleftherios 295
Victoria, Queen 106, 175, 223, 231, 233
Victoria League 88
Vildrac, Charles 274

Wagner, Richard 15, 64–5
Walford-Davies, Henry 66

Walker, Jack 48
Ware, Fabian 255
WeiHeiWei 37
Weir, Peter 21, 265, 272
Wellington 15–19, 29, 35, 56, 88–90, 120, 166, 208
Wellington, Duke of 10, 16–17, 219
Wembley Exhibition 1924–1925 14, 28
Whinney, T. Herbert 233
Wilhelm II, Kaiser 19, 41–2, 44–6, 48, 50, 52–3, 56, 58, 60–2, 106
William I (the Conqueror) 216
Williams, Elgar 269–70
Williams, Vaughan 66, 269–70
Wilson, Woodrow 55, 122, 201
Wood, Frederick Derwent 18
Wood, Sir Henry 64
Woolfe, Harry Bruce 211–13

Yeats, William Butler 180
Young Men's Christian Association (YMCA) 15, 63

Zambezi 31
Zambia 26, 32, 35
Zannettos, Philios 296
Zionist/Zionism 199, 206, 210